CULTURAL POLITICS

Comics: ideology, power
and the critics

CULTURAL POLITICS

Further titles in preparation

Comics: ideology, power and the critics

Martin Barker

MANCHESTER UNIVERSITY PRESS
Manchester and New York

distributed in the USA and Canada by ST. MARTIN'S PRESS

Published by Manchester University Press
Oxford Road, Manchester M13 9PL, UK
and Room 400, 175 Fifth Avenue, New York, NY 10010, USA

Distributed exclusively in the USA and Canada
by St. Martin's Press, Inc., 175 Fifth Avenue, New York, NY 10010, USA

Reprinted in 1990

British Library cataloguing in publication data
Barker, Martin
    Comics: ideology, power and the critics. – (Cultural politics).
    1. Comics – Critical Studies
    I. Title II. Series
    741.5

Library of Congress cataloging in publication data
Barker, Martin.
    Comics: ideology, power and the critics / Martin Barker.
        p.   cm. – (Cultural politics)
    Includes index.
    ISBN 0-7190-2589-3 (pbk.)
    1. Comic books, strips, etc.–United States–History and criticism.
    2. Ideology. 3. United States–Popular culture.
    I. Title. II. Series
    PN6725.B35   1989
    741.5'09–dc19   88-35612

ISBN 0 7190 2589 3 paperback

Typeset in Joanna
by Koinonia Limited, Manchester
Printed in Great Britain
by Billings & Sons Ltd., Worcester

Contents

Figures and tables

Nothing is simpler than to maintain that a certain type of thinking is feudal, bourgeois or proletarian, liberal, socialistic, or conservative, as long as there is no analytic method for demonstrating it, and no criteria have been adduced which will provide a control over the demonstration.

Karl Mannheim

Analysing concepts of ideology and mentalities is a bit like trying to nail jelly to the ceiling.

Craig Littler

Acknowledgements

This book has been a long time in the making. Some eleven years ago, two parallel processes began which finally led to it. Its final shape owes a great deal to those two processes, and to the people who accompanied me, willing or unwilling, through them.

About eleven years ago, I was supervising a student's project on *Superman*. She wanted to consider his significance in the light of Jung's psychological theory. I became uneasy at such an apparently arbitrary way of looking. Why Jung? Why not a hundred other approaches? Looking beyond, I discovered just how little had been written on comics that could help me or my student. Chasing down that little – odd articles, occasional pamphlets – I became engrossed. Initially, I confess, it was simply the ephemera. Never having done this kind of research before, I loved the grubby feel of the old pamphlets. But through them, I learnt about the horror comics campaign of the 1950s (about which I later wrote in my *A Haunt of Fears*). I began to formulate questions which puzzled me. As I evolved a strategy for handling these, the comics themselves began to fascinate me. I was, at this stage, ridiculously ignorant about the comics – and my first acknowledgement has to be to all those comic fans, who have patiently told me about the history, the artists, the publishers. They have tolerated my naive questions, and my sometimes arrogant claims. I hope that I am now beginning to make my repayment.

But from this same source, and connecting with a lot of my teaching, there grew a more general unease with the ways in which media researchers make claims about effects. There seemed to be connections between the way people gazed at the media and the effects they claimed to locate. For each way of looking, a matching effect. And that didn't feel right. Now, media research is undertaken in a whole series of ways: psychological (including both physiological and social kinds), sociological, literary, linguistic, popular-cultural, journalistic. If I was to research these, I had to learn how. Starting as a philosopher, I have had to train myself to understand the language and procedures of each of these – and here again, in various fields, I have been helped by friendly colleagues, even some whom I was openly criticising.

Quite early on, it became clear to me what my strategy would have to be. I wanted to review all the main kinds of claims about media-effects, but in a way that would enable me to look back at the original materials about which the claims were being made. And comics, it turned out, almost uniquely gave me that opportunity. But it meant I had to find those discussed comics. Getting hold of them became an obsession all its own. I have spent a lot of money on buying rare copies of *Tales From The Crypt*, *Uncle Scrooge*, *Action*, *Jackie*, and *Nasty Tales*. Acknowledgements here must start with my family, who somehow held on to their belief in my sanity when I would come home from yet another Comic Mart, excitedly clutching a new expensive comic. Many dealers, collectors, and artists have helped me find the things I needed. Only twice, for all my naivety, did I get ripped off (and that one shop and one dealer shall remain nameless – and unvisited in future). Among the remainder, I acquired many new friends.

Inevitably my work has brought me in touch with the comic publishers. In the past, many researchers have treated them shabbily. More than almost any other medium, comics have been lambasted with little hesitation, and with even less knowledge. So it is not surprising that I was met with initial suspicion. But in the end, received a great deal of help. I am not uncritical, by any means, of the comics I have been studying. But I hope the publishers who opened their memories and their archives to me will feel that I have been fair and scrupulous.

The aim of this book is to reconsider claims about media-effects, by looking closely at the theories advanced by others, and their methods of investigation and analysis. Writing it, I have been aware of a tendency in myself to be very harsh in judgements; and, though I have tried, I am pretty sure that I have not wholly excised this tendency. I found myself walking a line between being pettily obsessive, pulling out for display every little bit I didn't agree with; and on the other side, being casual and dismissive with arguments that I disagree with. May I apologise to all those whom I criticise in this book, if I come across as hostile? It is not my intention.

I do not want to make many personal acknowledgements, but a very few are necessary. Thanks to my father, Fred Barker, for drawing out the diagrams for the book so carefully and comprehensibly. And thanks to my son, Garrick Barker, for drawing the illustrative figures for Chapter 1. I wish I had either of your skills.

I have had very perceptive comments and advice on the draft of this book from David Buckingham from the University of London, and John Banks of Manchester University Press. To both, my genuine thanks – without their efforts, the book would have been much more marred by my tendency to go on for ever.

I am extremely lucky to work in a small unit which I find extraordinarily stimulating. To an extent I would not like to measure, the good ideas in this book are dependent on years of joint work, discussions and arguments with Anne Beezer and Jean Grimshaw. Contrary to the normal disclaimers, I know some of the bad ideas also come from there.

Thanks to Fleetway Publications for kind permission to reproduce the following strips:
Ivor Lott and Tony Broke from Buster, 12 August 1978.
Individual covers and frames from Action, 1976.
Hell's Highway, from Action, 23 October 1976.
Dredger and Breed, from Action, 20 March 1976.
Scream Inn, from Shiver & Shake, 2 March 1974, 7 July 1973, and 4 August 1973.
(Particular thanks to Mike Fowler, archivist at Fleetway, for his unstinting help in searching out original materials.)

Thanks to D C Thomson for kind permission to reproduce the following strips:
  'Yesterday', from *Jackie*, 8 January 1966.
  'Take Me Away From All This', from *Jackie*, 9 January 1971.
  'Where Have All The Flowers Gone?', from *Jackie*, 15 March 1975.
  'I Didn't Stop To Think', from *Jackie*, 13 January 1979.
  Cherry and the Chimps, from *Tracy*, 14 August 1982.
  Nothing Ever Goes Right, from *Judy*, 13 June 1981.
(Particular thanks to Harrison Watson of D C Thomson for his help in arranging this permission.)

Thinking about ideology and comics

This book is about two things. It is about the idea of 'ideology', and about the ways 'ideology' may influence us. Ideology is one of those big concepts, which sets off large arguments. My scope is seemingly narrower. I am interested in the way theories of ideology talk about persuasive forms of communication in our society. And one of the main forms of these is the mass media. This book is about the arguments that have gone on, for such a long time now, over the mass media. How might they be influencing us? How can we know?

Secondly, it is about comics. Because it is adults who study the mass media, comics have been usually either neglected, or dismissed. Once we passed into adulthood, we (of course?) left comics behind. Now only when we are 'worried about our children' do we look at the comics they are reading. I'd like to change that. I'd hope that readers of this book will join in with me in two ways: facing some very important issues about how people may be influenced, persuaded, even shaped into kinds of human being by the mass media; but at the same time enjoying with me the subtlety, the complex construction and the sheer delights of the art of strip-storytelling. Two topics, then, and of course closely related. Why 'ideology', first?

Thinking about ideology

Books on ideology have mainly been of two kinds. First, there have been the grand theories. To mention the word calls up the ghosts of a whole tradition: Karl Marx, Max Weber, George Lukács, Karl Mannheim, Lucien Goldmann, Antonio Gramsci, Louis Althusser . . . These are the people who have formulated general ideas about the role of ideology in society, and about its connections with other elements of the social structure. I am not directly debating these general ideas in this book. My interest begins with the vast gap between these studies, and attempts to study ideology empirically. Having read any of these general books on ideology, I always want to ask: yes, but how do I go on from what you say, to investigate ideology in the mass media? For example, I follow all the debates over the 'ideology of Thatcherism' of recent years.[1] They have a direct political relevance, and I have contributed to them myself. A lot of it is very sophisticated stuff, with subtle expositions of Gramsci on 'hegemony'. Yet I'm left wanting to ask: do I now know how to study Thatcher's speeches? Or isn't that what I should be studying? Perhaps that isn't 'where the ideology is'? The same is true repeatedly. If we opt for any one of the main positions on the function of 'ideology', do we then know how to study, say, advertisements, or TV soap operas, or forms of educational practice, or legal discourse, or the novel – or comics? Even more importantly, do we know how to study these in *ways which would enable us to test our theory of ideology?*

Often it even seems that the general theory renders the empirical work unnecessary. If all ideologies work to 'reproduce the status quo', as my students often insist on saying in essays, what is the point of empirical investigations, which will probably only reveal *differences*? Or, as three of us put it:

> All too often what we have found is the juxtaposition of 'grand theory' and appar-ently detailed empirical description, with little mediation between the two. This is unfortunate . . . by forcing incommensurate objects into unwieldy and overrigid theoretical frameworks, it can make close observation seem to be a redundant exercise. If all women's magazines are to be explained by their effect of 'construct-ing women in imaginary relations with the real relations of production and repro-duction', then there seems little point in examining them in their particularity. Their differences are in danger of becoming lost from view.[2]

At the same time, a lot of empirical studies of ideology-in-particular-materials are just as troublesome. Colin Sumner makes my point perfectly: '(W)hatever temporary overproduction of general theory there may be pales into insignifi-cance compared to the persistent overproduction of untheorised data . . .'[3] This is true enough, as I shall try to show, if we only take those books which *know* that they are studies of ideology. But so many don't even realise that is what they are doing. Consider, for instance, all those (literally) thousands of studies of how cinema, or television, or comics, or videos 'affect children'. You will hardly find one acknowledgement that these are investigations of ideolo-gical effect. Still less do the authors realise they are themselves using a particular theory of ideology.

Probably the most common claims about media influence are those about 'sex' and 'violence'. Hardly a week goes by without claims that children and young people are being corrupted by television, or video, or video-games, or whatever. These researchers regularly cloak themselves in the banner of neut-rality. Pause then on one book by two psychologists, who make a particular virtue out of their own scientificity: Eysenck and Nias reviewing the state of the evidence on television, sex and violence, and concluding that there is now clear evidence that television can give rise to higher levels of sexual and violent crimes.[4] They are cautious, and concerned to be scientific. They distance them-selves from those, for example, who argue by anecdote (though they are not above rehearsing a few, in sufficient detail to be disturbing but without our having the chance to assess them as evidence).[5] In their conclusions, they care-fully insist that the issue of controlling television should not become part of a generalised puritanical politics. The bulk of their book is a review of the research, to discover where a 'balance of evidence' should lead us.

And yet. My objection is not simply that I disagree with their confidence in laboratory studies, nor just that they are too dismissive of counter-evidence (though both are true). My challenge is that they have already decided the issue by the way they decide to ask questions. Their 'scientific' theory is already political. It commits them to assumptions which not only precede their evidence, but shape it. The key is to be found in the way they describe their problem:

> The media – TV, films, plays, pornographic magazines, even advertising – have come under increased criticism because of the suspicion that their more and more overt portrayal of scenes of violence and sex may be responsible for changes in our civilisation which to many people are undesirable – an increase in violence, in vandalism, in pre- and extramarital sex, in perversions, in rape and in the sexual exploitation of minors. If these complaints are justified to any reasonable extent – and of course no one has suggested that all the changes that have happened in the last thirty years or so can be laid at the door of the media – then clearly society will have to think seriously what possible controls ought to be instituted in order to restrain these influences from tearing our society to pieces. (p. 9)

There is a general theory in this. It tells us about the forces that 'move' human society – and thus already, how the media might have effects. This theory instructs them on what to look for in the media. It also limits what kinds of theory and evidence could possibly be relevant to deciding television's responsibility for all that 'violence'. In fact, Eysenck and Nias can only conceive of three kinds: Pavlovian conditioning, those which talk of modelling and imitation, and theories which refer to identification and the like (see their p. 44). But what is important is that all three theories share one assumption: that 'violence' can be an independent factor within a television programme, a film, or whatever. Now suppose I wanted to ask if 'violence' could mean different things in a cartoon, say, as opposed to a police series, a documentary, or a soap opera; or if the way it is filmed might make a difference? I can't. The only questions of scientific interest are the amount of violence, and the amount of effect that violence has. And this is because Eysenck and Nias are wedded to a general model of human beings, that we are beneath the surface wild uncivilised beings, over which has been built a precarious veneer. 'Violence' is like a sandpaper, rubbing away at that veneer. The more sandpaper, the thinner the veneer. This is the model that gives sense to saying that 'violence' is a separable unit. Therefore at bottom of their approach is an argument which their evidence cannot test, because the evidence does not mean anything in its absence. Eysenck and Nias illustrate my point that inevitably any discussion of mass media influence must involve ideas about ideology. It is just that some people don't want to admit it.

So just what does a theory of ideology have to say about the mass media? It has to explain how ideas, images, attitudes, forms and contents of the media can exist within media 'texts', and can also reproduce themselves in us. Thus it is a theory about the *power* of the media to affect us. Of course there will be important arguments about the kind of influence. Is it the relatively superficial capacity to insert particular beliefs ('Guinness is good for you!')? Is it a tendency to give us preferred ways of understanding the world? Is it the wholesale con-struction of personality, 'subjectivity', that is involved? These are particular arguments within the domain. But *any* theory of ideology, applied to the media, must commit itself on how the processes are supposed to take place. It must answer certain questions, even if only implicitly: (1) What is it about human beings that makes them prone to being influenced by certain kinds of message from the media, and in what aspect of their minds are they affected? (2) What forms of communication, or what relations of communication are judged cap-able of having that power? (3) What 'mechanisms' are there which work to enable the messages to be transmitted, powerfully?

This book is about attempts to answer these questions. The trouble is that, with so many competing ideas about how this should be done, it is hard to know where to start. There have been important studies of all different kinds of media-materials: the news, soap operas, advertisements, police series, etc, etc. We seem stuck in a situation where direct comparison of theories of ideol-ogy is ruled out because different approaches rarely talk about the same object. Imagine that situation in chemistry. Suppose that there are competing theories of the way pollution affects plants, which are never able to confront each other. One talks about processes of chemical signalling, another talks of direct take-up of destructive elements, a third says it results from destructive resonances, while a fourth describes it as the triggering of self-destructive genetic tendencies. Not only that, but each insists on studying only those plants that will best exemplify its own theory, using methods that can only verify their own assump-tions – and there are mechanisms in each theory for 'discarding' or counting as unimportant any problematic pieces of evidence. How could we know if the theories are mutually compatible, or mutually exclusive? How could we judge between them? Allowing for a little tongue-in-cheek exaggeration, this is basically the situation in theorisations of ideology. And that is one major reason this book is all and only about comics.

Thinking about comics

There are in fact several reasons, apart from purely autobiographical ones, why I am writing about comics. I have been bothered for a long time that it is nigh on impossible to see the original materials being analysed in most critical studies. Too many critics expect us to take their descriptions on faith. Often they tell us their conclusions with only fragmentary quotations. When studying pieces of popular culture, very often they do not bother to note their sources. No dates, no edition numbers. It doesn't seem to matter, since their description surely must be accepted. This is not a matter to be taken lightly. The way critics look at their materials is already conditioned by their theories of ideology and influence. If we want to question those theories, it is vitally important to be able to re-view those original materials.

The advantage of comics, in this respect, was several-fold. It is possible (with difficulty) to track down the originals being discussed. It has cost me much labour, hours and days spent in the British Museum and the British Newspaper Library to trace unreferenced materials; months and years looking through dealers' piles, to find obscure issues. Still, it could be done; and I have tried in every case to do so. Comics also have the delightful advantage of being usually quite short; and they stay still when you look at them. It means I can get to their complexities that much quicker, and not feel overwhelmed by detail. Also, they can be reprinted. I wanted this to be like a work-book. That is why I have tried where possible to reprint examples. You, as readers, can follow my analysis, and decide for yourselves how convincing it is. Where I could, I have used examples which other critics have discussed, so that you can compare approaches.[6] Where I couldn't, I have tried to devise ways of retelling them that retain their flavour and character.

Second, I realised early on in my own research that there were real dangers in talking about a medium of which one is pretty ignorant. Just studying comics, I discovered how painfully ignorant I was of their history. I also realised, as I began to understand that history, how many of the critics who have made 'devastating' attacks on them, themselves betray gross ignorance. No one would dare to be so careless in making claims about, say, the novels of Dickens, or the films of Fellini. It seems that with popular culture or mass culture – and comics more than most other kinds – critics can get away with character assass-ination based on ignorance, and hardly anyone will mind. Staying within the one medium reduced the risks of me repeating the worst of those errors.

The third advantage was a big one. It happens that just about all the main-theories of ideology had been tried out on comics. And even while I was researching the book, one important gap was neatly filled in by a new publica-tion. Claims about influence come in many shapes and sizes: ranging from psychologically-oriented 'effects' theories (of the kind beloved of 'common-sense' and heated journalism), to highly sophisticated theories based on forms of literary analysis, neo-Freudian theory, and Marxism. In the briefish history of comics as a mass medium, at one time or another, on various kinds of comics, each kind has been exemplified. I have simply turned this accident to my advantage.

There is one other reason for studying comics, and of no small importance.

In the course of studying them, I became absorbed. I think it was Albert Einstein who remarked that good science requires an intellectual love of the object being studied; and I believe this. If something fascinates a researcher, s/he is more likely to take the patience necessary to unravel all its complexities. Imagine a chemist who has become convinced that a particular compound is making people ill who ingest it. What would we expect her to do about it? Surely the larger she thought its impact, the greater her wish to investigate its structure, its interactions, possible countervailing chemicals, and so on. The fact that the compound was her 'enemy', in the sense that she wanted to counteract its effects, would not reduce her wish to study it carefully. It would increase it. Sadly, with comics especially, the opposite is true. Those who criticise them, show least interest in understanding them. And the greater the impact they attribute to them, the less the care they seem to show.

What is a comic?

Exactly. What is one? One tradition tries to understand the comic in terms of a lineage stretching back to the Bayeux tapestry, even to the Lascaux cave paintings.[7] This approach focuses on one aspect of comics, that they are made up of sequences of pictures. They tell stories using the convention of pictures following each other. This is not unimportant. Readers have to learn the skills of understanding the relation between separate pictures. Each one is a 'still frame' out of a moving sequence; and that one is 'later' than this one. Umberto Eco reports an interesting piece of research in this respect. An Italian researcher showed a comic story in which a man was being shot by firing squad. The frames showed him standing blindfolded, then the guns being fired, then the man dead on the ground. She found that people tended to fill in an extra frame of the man falling. In other words, in making sense of the causal connections, they imagined in the necessary frame, and attributed it to the comic.[8]

But modern mass-produced comics are defined by much more than this one feature. All the following seem to me importantly part of their nature:

1. they appear at regular intervals;
2. they have recurring characters, with relatively predictable ranges of behaviour;
3. characters appear within distinct genres among other characters of the same kind, involved in similar kinds of actions and events;
4. comics have accumulated a great number of conventions, which allow still frames to represent an enormous range of things. Among these: speech, movement, relationships, emotions, cause and effect, reader-involvement, and the fictional nature of the comic itself and its characters.

As a tiny example, compare these two representations of a football match (Fig. 1). The comparison is striking. Of course, Spot-The-Ball competitions

Fig 1 Goal! The difference between a photograph and a comic frame. Photograph courtesy of Bob Lowrey and the Bristol *Evening Post*. Frame from *Roy of the Rovers*, © IPC Magazines 1978.

depend on the fact that such real photographs are quite confusing. The picture of a goal being scored seems odd. The onlookers look singularly uninterested. That is because it takes time for the crowd to register the goal (and a great one it was, too – I was there!) and leap for joy. The comic frame has no such problem. It condenses time within its still image; and we learn to read so many elements in sequence, recognising and being guided by the conventions of comic strip art. At the same time, a good deal of information about the status of the players, and their relations with one another, can be conveyed in the single image. The evolution of all these conventions has enabled even individual frames to become rich in meaning. (In the course of the book, I shall have much more to say about the nature and the meaning of comic conventions. Here, I invite my readers to count how many conventions they can see at work in this single frame – begin your analysing and enjoying together here.)

But as well as these internal characteristics that define what a comic is, something else is involved in their definition. It is hard to state without sounding tautological: *a comic is what has been produced under the definition of a 'comic'*. There has been a historical process whereby public arguments about comics, and what is acceptable under that name, have become in their turn powerful determinants of what is produced. To explain this fully would involve much more than I can cover here. Let the following almost-notes do for now.

There are different national traditions of 'comics'. The bulk of my examples are of British comics, and I will therefore focus here. Modern comics, with that name, began in the 1880s. They appeared towards the end of the campaigns against the Penny Dreadfuls (on which see Chapter 5), the 'street literature' of the Victorian era. Alfred Harmsworth, the newspaper publisher, wanted to bring out some children's publications which would counteract the attractions of the Dreadfuls. He also wanted to find a way to use the spare space on his printing presses. At a halfpenny a time, his *Comic Cuts* did both – and publicly declared their purpose. They were to be non-serious, 'harmless' but attractive material for youngsters. At the same time, the Religious Tract Society were looking for ways of doing the same for slightly older children. Their solution was the *Boy's Own Paper*, and later the *Girl's Own Paper*. Their purposes were well captured in a recent recollective book on the BOP. Talking of George Hutchison, its first editor, Jack Cox writes: 'Hutchison undertook the enormous task of working out a compromise between the kind of paper boys would read, the kind of paper parents and teachers would approve, and the kind of paper the Society as responsible Christian publishers wanted to produce.'[9] His solution was 'adventure + sport', a combination that proved well-matched to imperialism.

From the beginning, then, comics were produced within a climate in which they were counterposed to everything dangerous. They were guaranteed to be non-serious literature, specially suited to children. It is no surprise that during World War 1, the name given by soldiers to the reports on enemy positions and movements brought in by pilots was 'comic cuts'. Unreliable, silly things – not to be taken seriously. For more than half a century, this definition determined virtually everything about comics. The titles from the period capture well this deliberate innocence: *Funny Wonder, Happy Days, Merry and Bright, Butterfly* and *Jolly Comic* . . . It survived without serious challenge until the 1950s and the great horror comic scare – and then among the headlines of the time were many denouncing 'these so-called comics'. It was not just that they were not funny; they refused to be non-serious, and harmless. Of course there was nothing wrong with producing witty, naive, and innocent fun for children. The problem was that nothing else was permitted. The definition of a comic had become a constraining force, requiring publishers to abide by it. Some were very willing – Rev. Marcus Morris who began the *Eagle, Girl, Swift* and *Robin* once again set out to produce a 'safe' set of comics – and once again, his products were taken as a model for other publishers to follow.[10] (Ironically, the Scottish publisher D C Thomson partly isolated itself from these constraints precisely by virtue of being such a Victorian paternalist publisher. It set its own standards, and did not allow English upstarts to tell it what to do.) The next chapter tells the story of a further stage, when IPC in the 1970s sought to change the automatic assumptions about stories and readers, with *Action*. Once again, as we will see, the binding force of the definition blocked them.

This was not only a question of being inoffensive. On each occasion when the definition of a 'comic' came under threat, one of the first responses was to reinforce the gender separation of readers. The Penny Dreadfuls were widely read by both girls and boys (as the Victorian critics noted to their dismay). One of the first acts of the new comic producers was to enforce a clear distinction. The horror comics, likewise, were popular with both sexes. *Eagle* and *Girl* ended that. *Action* had a significant female readership – its withdrawal coincided with a massive new production of romance comics for girls. A syndrome of ideas has persistently constrained the history of the production of comics in Britain. It has changed over time, and its power to control has been subject to many other factors. Even so, we cannot answer the question 'What is a comic?' by formal qualities alone. A comic is what has been produced under that controlling definition. Any history of British comics worth its salt (and the notes above make no claim to that title) has to be built around this fact.

Beginning analysis

What are 'conventions' in comics? 'Convention' originally meant (and still sometimes means) a coming together; over time it has accrued the extra meaning of an 'agreed way' of coming together. To understand comics, we need to understand both parts of this definition: the agreement, and the coming together.[11] The best way to explore this is to look briefly at the humblest of comic conventions: the speech balloon (Fig. 2).

Fig 2 Speech balloons and their conventions.

How does a speech balloon work? In one sense, it is obvious. A set of words are accredited to a represented character by a tail running from the balloon – or by a set of small bubbles if it is 'thought'. So, we read the words, see the direction of the tail, and thus recognise who is supposed to have said (or thought) them. Good enough. Now compare 1 to 3. What is the difference? Of course we know immediately – the second shows loudness, shouting; the third suggesting whispering. Yet there is a puzzle with the third. Who would whisper 'Help!'?

The puzzle comes from how the size of the balloon relates to the size of the word. It is as if, in fact, we don't *read* the words at all. We hear them.[12] We might put it that in the comic form, there is an interaction between the pictureness and the verbalness of the speech-balloon, to produce the meaning of sound. 'We 'hear with our eyes'. This is possible because the balloon is more than just a convenient container for the words, more than just a way of fitting them onto the page. The balloon itself conditions the meaning, by showing us the kind of force the words are to have. So, look at 4.[13] What is going on? The emptiness of the thought-balloon is itself a significant fact. That is because the balloon itself conveys meaning, otherwise we could not understand this joke.

Take it a stage further. What about that other speech balloon, coming in from the frame at the side? The natural thing is to take this to be the 'voice of the reader' or the artist, or some such. How do we manage this interpretation? It is only possible because the frame is not simply the boundary of the picture. The way the frame is used also establishes our relation to the world being presented. The point I am making is that, when analysed, this simplest and humblest of comic conventions, when analysed, turns out to be involved in much more than simple transmission of meanings. It also conditions that meaning, and establishes our relationship to that meaning. Conventions in comic strips condense social relationships; they help to determine the kind of reader we become. They make reading a social relationship between us and the text.

This can't yet be totally clear. Hopefully, the rest of the book will make it clearer.

How should we study comics, then? It would make no sense to try to pre-empt here all that is to follow. I only want to spotlight right from the start one fundamental aspect of comics. They tell stories. All different kinds of stories, of course; but still, all stories. The great majority of them are fictional, but not all. A very large proportion are of very predictable kinds. They are what a number of analysts have called 'formulaic'. That is, they repeat the same situation in different forms; they follow a typical set of stages; and end in predictable fashion. Now the aim of this study is to answer questions about possible influence. How can we find out what are the 'messages' in a story, and how they might be received? How might we be persuaded into views, attitudes, reactions which we might not otherwise have had?

Consider a strip from *Buster* (Fig. 3). How should we understand this? What should we say about any messages it might be offering to its readers? The problem is to know how we may locate 'messages' within a story. Should we take particular actions, and say that they are being offered as exemplars? Or particular things said? Should we focus on how things 'turn out' in the end? Do we need to look to see 'whose side' the strip is on, and how would we know? Being playful, I could suggest there are so many ways we could take this story:

1. We could interpret it as showing stereotyped images of wealthy and poor

Fig 3 From *Buster*, 12 August 1978. © IPC Magazines 1978.

– but then 'whose side is it on'? Or would it be the sheer fact of stereotyping that we should comment on?

2. We could take it as representing class conflict, and teaching the working class not to trust their rulers. Look, after all, at the way Ivor makes off with Tony's deposit.

3. On the other hand, at the end, Tony is such a 'good boy', only taking back what was his. Perhaps it is teaching that only the working class really have any morals – a sort of 'honourable poor' story.

4. On the other hand, it could be read as a Marxist fable on the capitalist system. It takes no action by Tony – Ivor self-destructs his bank.

5. On the other hand, we all know that the story was back next week, and guess who still had all the wealth!

All these are possible 'readings' of the story. I am not seriously proposing any of these. My serious point is that in the face of such a multiplicity of possible 'meanings', we need a theory and a method to advise us on how to look at such a story. And I want to propose that all these suffer from the sheer fact that they try to abstract bits from the whole narrative. They are all arbitrary interpretations, and that the reason for the confusion of possible 'meanings' comes just from that. I hope to show that a methodical, checkable account can be given of just this kind of comic strip, and that that account has interesting consequences. Crudely, it matters. But for that, we need not only a theory, but one that is sensitive to the significance of these being stories. The problem is, how do we tell a good theory and method from a bad one?

As far as *Ivor Lott and Tony Broke* is concerned, you may feel that it really doesn't matter. Anyone who spends time finding deep meanings in something as 'harmless' as that must be either daft or an academic. Well, perhaps.[14] But it does matter in a host of other cases, for there have been bitter complaints about various kinds of comics – and the 'readings' of those are every bit as problematic as the ones I have constructed above. The history of comics is a history of controversies. And every controversy has involved claims about the meanings, messages and potential influence of some comics.

Being controversial

The history of controversies over comics really begins with George Orwell's essay on the boys' weeklies of his time. In an essay much-cited but less understood, Orwell accused *Gem* and *Magnet* of perpetuating a pre-World-War-1 set of social attitudes.[15] His essay is, to me, a model of a certain kind of left-wing elitism: expressing deep concern about the vulnerability of working class people to the influence of popular culture, but with little understanding of the forms of that culture. I do not deal with this essay directly in this book, for two reasons. I have not been able to track down the particular issues of *Gem* and

Magnet to which he refers (it would be too kind to say that he analyses them). And anyway, his approach is better exemplified in others (see Owen Edwards, discussed in Chapter 5, for a straight attempt to update his approach; and Connie Alderson, who shares his literary-critical ideas, discussed in Chapter 7).

Orwell was very English in both approach and choice of objects to criticise. He has much less to say about the American comics which he touches on. But not long after his essay, the most important controversy of all time over comics was to begin – the 1950s crusades against the American crime and horror comics. This was a truly international fever. In America, it was led by the crusading Dr Fredric Wertham. The campaign took the form of local pressure from parents' groups, religious groups and the like, plus the public forum of the Senate Hearings under Senator Kefauver into possible links between the comics and juvenile deliquency. Although it did not lead to actual laws banning them (with exceptions in one or two states), the head of pressure forced many publishers out of business, and enforced a destructive system of self-censorship.[16]

In Britain, the campaign succeeded in getting an Act of Parliament passed making publication or distribution of 'horror comics' illegal. The British campaign was most peculiar, as I tried to show in my study of it, drawing on a largely hidden presence of the British Communist Party; yet ending up focusing on those comics which were most hostile to anti-communism and McCarthyism.[17] In many other countries, also, these American comics threw up shockwaves of anger, and demands for censorship. Ireland, Canada, Australia, New Zealand, Denmark, Norway, Germany, Italy and Holland at least all had their versions of anti-crime and horror comics campaigns. In most cases, little research has been done on them.[18] This was surely the low tide for comics. There have been no comparable cases, since then, of a group of comics energising such an international hostility. But the remarkable thing about that campaign is how, under its umbrella, so many diffuse points of view and kinds of theory and politics could be united.

This book is not a 'compleat historie of complaintes against comickes'. I have been tempted by that idea. But it would have lost my primary purpose, to use comics as a case-study of the ways critics have investigated the mass media for possible 'influences'. But as a result, one huge gap in its coverage is the Superhero comics. This may seem odd, given the importance of these (just in terms of sales and marketing) in the last thirty years. But although from time to time people have raised arguments about these comics, there has been little around which I could focus such an argument.[19] To deal with the phenomenon of the superheroes would be a whole historical and analytic enterprise in itself. Perhaps one day . . .

The other main kind which I have quietly ignored are the Underground Comix.[20] These deliberately outrageous and determinedly oppositional comics emerged at the end of the 1960s, partly because of cheap reprographic methods, partly in connection with the pop, drug and political movements of that time. Their provocative stances, and graphic illustration of sex for example, led to frequent seizures, court actions and destruction orders. I have not touched on them because I suspect the main approaches of this book would be irrelevant to understanding their history, and the antipathy they aroused. Their attackers hardly bothered to theorise what might be 'harmful' about the Undergrounds. They just damned them as 'offensive', 'disgusting', and 'perverted'.

I have not organised this book chronologically. The case-studies chosen are the ones which can most illumine the issues of influence and ideology. And that has meant, on one occasion, choosing an example simply because rare information about it came to hand. Had I been choosing on merit, I would have had to choose the *Beano* among the juvenile comics. It has pride of place in sales, length of life and contribution to our culture – and in the number of complaints about it. But some marvellous information accidentally came to light about a much more minor comic, *Shiver & Shake*. Though I briefly connect this with the *Beano*, I can't claim to have done it justice. But useful information about readers is so hard to come by, it has to be taken as it comes.

The book is structured as follows: after this introductory chapter, Chapters 2 and 3 look in detail at the case of *Action*, the 1970s boys' comic. *Action* was the subject of a traditional 'effects' controversy, with claims that it was promoting forms of violence and delinquency. I have used these chapters to set an 'agenda of issues' which the rest of the book explores: of how to analyse comics, and of how to look at the concepts and methods deployed by critics.

Chapter 4 uses the case of *Scream Inn*, from *Shiver & Shake*, to broach the issue of methods systematically. There, I try out the ideas of Vladimir Propp on this strip, and return to consider the general theory that underlies those ideas in Chapter 6. The intervening chapter counterposes my approach to more traditional critics, in particular those who fall back on the concept of 'identification' to explain the link of influence between media and audiences. Chapter 5 retraces the history and politics of this concept, and argues for its removal from media analysis.

Chapters 7 and 8 look at the romance comics, and the many critiques of them (predominantly from various kinds of feminist criticism). Taking *Jackie* as my focus, I first examine the literary-critical, stereotyping and semiological accounts of the mass media. Against these, I develop my own account of *Jackie* (with special emphasis on the stories), tracing significant changes since its beginning in 1964. Chapter 9 then attempts to do for the concept of a 'stereotype' what I have already done for 'identification': to discover the politics of its use in its history and shape as a concept.

Chapter 10 deals specifically with recent 'post-structuralist' theory, exemplified in an essay on the pre-adolescent girls' comics *Bunty* and *Tracy*. My reasons for finding this unsatisfactory set more of the ground for my own approach. This is brought to the fore in my review, in Chapter 11, of various kinds of research into comic-readers.

Chapter 12 lays out my approach to ideology, drawing on the work of Valentin Volosinov, the Russian theorist of language of the 1920s. His notion of language as essentially 'dialogical' is explored, and a link made to the ideas of Propp. I try to show how those ideas can bind together the theory and methods which emerge from my critique of other approaches in earlier chapters.

Chapter 13 tries out the now explicitly formulated theory and method, in a reconsideration of one of the most important studies of comics ever undertaken: that by Dorfman and Mattelart of the Disney comics. Finally, a Postscript once more suggests why we should return to celebrate this lovely, misunderstood medium.

Action – a suitable case for the treatment

This is the story of *Action*. *Action* was produced by IPC in 1976, attracted the loyalty of more than 150,000 young readers, was withdrawn after a wave of criticisms in October of the same year, was revised and returned in December, and finally died an ignominious death-by-merger with the comic *Battle* just under a year later. There is much to be learnt from the life and death of *Action*.

Action was born out of an attempt by the publishing giant IPC to turn around the long-running decline in the sales of comics, which had begun in the mid-sixties. By the early 1970s this had reached almost epidemic proportions, and was approaching the point of no financial return. It wasn't the first attempt to turn the tide, nor was it to be the last: 'Everything began with a comic called *Tammy*. That was the beginning of what could be called the 'new-wave comics'. Up till then IPC had been in the doldrums; and this was a girls' comic that tried to imitate *Bunty*; it was very evil and powerful. It never had censorship problems because mental cruelty isn't visual on the page.'[1] Early in the 1970s, two unknowns wrote to IPC offering their services as scriptwriters. They were employed, first, on the boys' comic *Lion* writing a story called *The Can-Do Kids*. It never aroused much enthusiasm, either in the kids who consistently rated it one of the least popular stories, or in IPC – no other editors rushed to offer work to the two writers, Pat Mills and John Wagner. But then the chance arose for them to work on the new girls' comics with which IPC set out to challenge D C Thomson. Here, they had found their forte. Now they produced taut, frightening stories of mental cruelty and loneliness for the new IPC girls' comics: *Tammy*, *Sandy* and several other lesser titles until the great *Misty*.

Now that they were known, the opportunity came for each of them to make his name. Thomson brought out *Warlord* in 1974, a new boys' comic which was an immediate success. This had to call forth a reply from IPC. But there was a problem. The IPC boys' comic department was terribly tradition-bound. At this time John Sanders was the Managing Editor of the comics division of IPC. He took a decision which was to have long-term consequences. In secret, Pat Mills was asked to prepare a new boys' comic. Nominally, it would be within the boys' department; actually it would be directly answerable to Sanders: 'We had to lock our office, write all the stories ourselves. And people would say: 'What are you doing in your office?' Ultimately of course, only I think a few weeks before we went to press, the word got out. And in the boys' comic department they were bloody livid.'[2] Most livid of all was Jack LeGrand, then head of the boys' department. He was annoyed both at the secrecy of the project and at the kind of comic being planned. The resultant split between LeGrand and the 'old brigade', and John Sanders and the 'new boys' was to have many consequences.

The comic was *Battle*. It was a new kind of war comic, even more so than its Thomson rival. What distinguished it, above all else, was its psychological tenseness. No longer were the characters either the calm, confident heroes of the 1950s, typified by Dan Dare of the *Eagle*, or the silly, over-the-top heroes of the 1960s, such as Captain Hurricane of *Valiant*, who every week lost his temper with the Huns, and went bare-fisted to teach them a 'jolly good lesson'. Now the heroes were scrubby, dirty, hard; and they didn't find life all that easy. At this time, one of IPC's main boys' titles was *Valiant*. It was on its last legs, fading fast, with leading character Adam Eterno, the man from the future who solved problems in our time. Sanders took away the editorship of *Valiant* from Sid Bicknell, an old-timer with IPC, and gave it to John Wagner. Overnight, *Valiant* changed. The covers became splash panels, full of vigour and excitement. Inside, *One-Eyed Jack*, an ugly derivative of Dirty Harry, and *Paco* a very wild dog rampaged. (In fact, IPC's policy of planning the deaths of their comics didn't give time for Valiant to achieve turn-around. It died, just as its sales seemed to be reviving.)

Mills brought other things to his creation of *Battle*. The first is a function of his enormous energy, exhausting to anyone who can't quite keep pace with him. This was his wish to be involved in the discussion of every story line. He didn't simply go to standard writers, give them a story brief and leave them to get on with it. He would discuss the minutiae of the stories with them; and out of this would come a subtlety and a seriousness that had often been missing. It also made him impossible as an editor, as he himself has the grace to recognise. 'So they brought up Dave Hunt, a very good editor. John and I wouldn't compromise, and at the end of the day it needs someone to say 'That page is ready'. We gave Dave a good idea, and he made a bloody good comic of it.'[3] The tendency up to this point had been for editors to do more controlling and limiting, than spurring and stretching, their writers. Mills changed this.

The other innovation was research. With rare exceptions comic stories drew on commonsense funds of knowledge in writers and artists. Only in matters of technical detail would comic artists have to be very knowledgeable, because their readers would soon spot the German tank with British guns on it, or the uniform with the wrong flashes. One later story in *Battle* exemplified Mills' new approach: *Charley's War*, a story of the First World War, told from the point of view of a young working-class volunteer; it is unstinting in its picture of the horrors of the war, and it is carefully and accurately detailed in all its portrayals – including, incidentally, giving a pretty full account of the troops' revolts that were the topic of the BBC's recent and controversial 'Monocled Mutineer'. What was so controversial on TV went unnoticed, except by grateful comic readers, in *Battle*. Only twice before had a comic gone so close to presenting an anti-war message. The first time was in the great EC war comics of the 1950s, such as *Frontline Combat*; they were killed off in the purge of comics in 1954-5. The second was the short-lived 1966 Warren comic *Blazing Combat*, killed by reluctant distributors after only four issues.

I am already pointing to one source of tension in these comics. The slogan under which they were all produced was 'realism'. The stories in the 'new-wave comics' were to be 'realistic', John Sanders told me. But 'realism' could mean several different things. Even in the war comics, it could mean either just more acknowledgement of the horrors of war, therefore more direct showing of violence and its consequences; or it could mean the creation of story-forms which are full of the tension and anguish, loneliness and uncertainty; or it could mean, much more politically, facing through the stories some of the moral and political questions generated by war. If that was a problem with the war comics, and one which was never resolved, it would be an enormous problem when the next comic came along: an all-purpose comic, taking its themes from all fields of adventure and conflict – *Action*.

Battle was on the streets, and had proved itself (to the chagrin of the 'old brigade') a real success. In late 1975, Mills was asked to prepare the ground for a wholly new comic. It was to be a mixture: a war story, a spy story, a sports story, and so on. But more, it had to be up-to-date, a comic of its time. Mills had a virtually free hand in its planning, and three months to get a first issue together (a 'ludicrously short time', according to Pat Mills, or a 'surprisingly long run-in' according to its first editor, Geoff Kemp). Original ideas for its title ranged from *Boots* to *Dr Martens*. But the idea that nearly stuck came from one of its new scriptwriters, Steve McManus. He suggested the comic should carry its own dateline in its title, to stress its up-to-the-momentness. In combination with the simple title *Action* which emerged as front-runner, it looked good. *Action '76* would be followed by *Action '77*, always changing, always in touch. But the newsagents didn't like it. At the last minute, under their pressure, the date was dropped. Mills started looking for ideas for stories, for writers capable of handling such stories, and then artists to match. (The first was always a problem, since writing for comics has long been seen a low-status activity; the second in particular was a problem because IPC had come to depend in a large way on foreign artists.)

The strategy for getting the comic up-to-date was ludicrously simple: rip off all the latest film, TV, and other favourites. So, Jaws was gnashing his way through the subconscious of the generation at the time. Easy, then: *Action* would have its own shark story. Then there was *Rollerball*, one of the new wave of science fiction films. Fine, rip that off too. What about *Dirty Harry*? Yup, we can do that, as well. And so on. A cast of characters and a list of story-lines thus emerged, looking as follows at the beginning:

1. *Hookjaw* (based on *Jaws*), a story of a rampaging great white shark;
2. *Dredger* (based on *Dirty Harry* and a dozen other tough spy films). This was the only story done as separate episodes, telling of the counter-espionage exploits of the tough Dredger, and the suave Breed;
3. *The Running Man* (based on the TV *Fugitive* series), of an athlete visiting the USA, only to be subjected to a face change so that he looks like a wanted Mafia man – and has to run both from the police and the Mafia, who want him caught;
4. *BlackJack* (drawing on the living legend of Muhammed Ali), about a black boxer caught between realising he is going blind, and not wanting to let down all the ghetto kids who worship him;
5. *Hellman of Hammer Force* (which borrowed from the popular *Gunnar Asch* novels). This was the first British comic story to look at the Second World War through German eyes.

Three others were not so obviously derivative:

6. *The Coffin Sub*, a poor story, much more traditional than the rest, very unpopular with readers and therefore – by the strange internal logic of IPC – one of the few it has ever reprinted. It told of a submarine captain who blamed himself for the death of a former crew;
7. *Sport's Not For Losers*, a curious story, originally to be called *Smoking's A Drag* about an injured boy who has to get his yob of a brother to become an athlete;
8. *Play Till You Drop*, a reasonable football story, about a player being blackmailed over supposed pictures of his footballer-father taking bribes.

But *Action* was not only in the business of ripping off; it changed the things it 'stole'. Take *Hookjaw* by comparison with *Jaws*. In the film, the great white shark is an anomymous threat that we only see when it rears out of the depths to take a leg, a torso, a whole person. The shark is a devilish, unintelligible danger, lurking, destroying. In the comic, Hookjaw is the hero; we see it clearly, we see it hurt, we think with it, we understand its blind anger when its domain is entered. And when it rises out of the depths, it is to rid the sea of polluting humans, of money-mad oilmen, of island tyrants. It is a kind of primitive behemoth, sorting the world. Of course on the way many innocents lose limbs. But the shark is hardly to blame. It just is; and shark-essence is biting and eating.

This difference runs through all the stories in *Action*. And the differences became more marked as the comic progressed, and early stories were replaced. In their place came new, more *Action*ish stories. They included *Green's Grudge War*, the story of two soldiers who loathe each other but are constantly thrown together in action. The replacement for *Play Till You Drop* was *Look Out For Lefty*, about a very unlikely-looking young scruff who joins his local Football League team – his problems being his own very short temper, and a dad drawn direct from *Steptoe and Son*. After *The Running Man* came a rip-off of *Rollerball*, *Death Game 1999*, about a team of players of a futuristic motorbike game. They are all condemned prisoners only allowed to live because they bring glory to the prison governor by their mean play of the murderous game – but who become a bit too glorious for their own good. Then there was Hell's Highway, a rip-off in quite another sense. This was the story of two American truckers blackmailed by a government agency into doing 'dirty tricks'. On this and the other story he scripted, Jack Adrian told me:

> My own two stories were in fact terribly moral – and there's a touch of self-right-eousness if you like! Even so . . . Hell's Highway was, I believe, the first story in this field that could be called a 'post-Watergate' story. Prior to this, organisations such as the CIA and FBI were invariably shown to be good guys. What I was trying to do was show to a juvenile audience that they were not necessarily so damn fine a body of men as we'd been led to believe. My two heroes were blackmailed/ forced into doing dirty tricks for a shadowy US Government Agency, and they were forever trying to sabotage them and escape from the agency's clutches.
>
> Kids Rule OK was supposed to be about honour, loyalty, comradeship in the face of dreadful circumstances. But before it could elaborate on all that it was sabotaged utterly, then simply cut dead when the paper was taken off the newsstands.[4]

We'll see how far his comment stands up. The latter story was one of the last to start in Action not long before an ill-fated day in September 1976 when, as Adrian indicates, a decision was taken to withdraw the comic. It had become too controversial. This new story was very much part of that controversy. The premise was that the pressures of modern living had reached such a peak that a biological change had taken place. Virtually everyone over the age of 25 suddenly died of heart disease – leaving a world of kids to try to rebuild a society.

Then there were editorial pages, again different from usual. In place of the hearty, jolly atmosphere of most comics at that time, Action had 'MoneyMan' who went round Britain giving away fivers to kids who could produce that week's comic: a very down-market Lobby Ludd. There was Steve (McManus) as 'Action Man' who was paid £10 a throw to undertake daring stunts – stopping short of the Director's secretary's suggestion that he be thrown into the North Sea to be rescued by a Navy helicopter. Wise man, he lived to become editor of 2000AD, soon to become a cult comic in Britain. And alongside these was a column entitled 'Twit Of The Week', to which readers were encouraged to send the names of their favourite 'berks'. Among those to grace its pages were Russell Harty, the Bay City Rollers and Nicholas Parsons (twice!). Action also encouraged kids to write in with their grumbles; like, complaints about adverts for things being 'under a pound' when in fact they are 99p.

This, then, was Action. After a messy first few issues (in which Mills' perfec-tionism interfered too much between writers' and artists' submissions, and the printed product), the design skills of Doug Church began to stamp a style: 'busy', full of movement. At the start, this didn't particularly affect the way stories were laid out on the page. IPC still worked to a pretty rigid number of frames to the page. Towards the end, under the editorship of John Smith (who

Fig 4 Sample covers from *Action* showing the first issue, the powerful 8 May issue, the controversial 18 September issue, and the 'lost' 23 October issue. All © IPC Magazines 1976.

took over in the summer of 1976) this began to change. In a development that presaged the much greater freedom of layout found in 2000AD, he allowed and encouraged artists to 'explode' panels over the page if they were dramatic enough. This reached its climax in the issue dated 23 October 1976, where virtually the whole of the last page of *Death Game 1999* was given over to one panel. It was an enormous drawing by Massimo Belardinelli of a motorbike exploding, blowing up the villain at the height of the final Death Race. What happened to that panel is symbolic.

Hitting the fan

Right from the start, *Action* was controversial. In its first few weeks, there were several newspaper articles, and a number of radio and TV reports and interviews about it – some of them explicitly comparing it with the 1950s 'horror comics'. On the BBC, towards the end of February, both *Today* and *Newsbeat* carried hostile interviews with John Sanders. The *Sun* ran a centrespread on the comic (30 April 1976), entitled 'The Sevenpenny Nightmare', though the tone of this was half-critical, half-admiring. Then in September, this steady trickle of criticism became a deluge. Two bits of the 18 September issue set it off. The cover showed a wild-looking young man with a huge chain looming over a fallen adult, who might be a policeman. Behind him is what look like a marauding pack. But what caused more outrage was a frame in that week's episode of *Look Out For Lefty*. It showed a bottle being thrown on to the pitch at a football match, clunking a player on the head. This frame was featured in a large denunciatory report in the *Daily Mail*.[5]

A flood of complaints hit the publishers. John Smith frequently found himself on the phone direct to an outraged parent. A number of newsagents started refusing to stock the comic, and their national association, whose National Council happened to be meeting then, met IPC to protest vigorously. In the West Midlands, the Consumer Protection department was asked to investigate *Action*. Almost inevitably Questions were asked in the House of Commons. Faced with this barrage, IPC's Board of Directors ordered that the comic should be suspended for 'editorial reconsideration'. The last issue of the first series of *Action* appeared on 16 October 1976. The 23 October issue never made it to the distributors; that Belardinelli splash panel was never to be seen by the public.

All this sounds quite straightforward. Here is a comic that went over-the-top, was brimful of violence, perhaps even directly inciting delinquency. Wasn't it gross irresponsibility to show football hooliganism so graphically when there had been serious trouble recently? As always, there is more to this whole story than meets the eye. It is a feature of such censorious campaigns that they present themselves as simple, wholesome, and moral. It fixes the ground of debate;

and that ground favours the censors. For who but the 'academics', the ivory-towered sophisticates, will want to defend things which are 'excessively violent', when it is so simple to change them? Isn't it commonsense that people are affected by what they read, and even more by what they see? And anyway, 'even if only one child is affected', that is enough reason that this comic must be stopped. I have put that phrase in quotation marks, because I have found it identically within the horror comics campaign of the 1950s, the campaign against *Action* in 1976, and in the campaign against the 'video nasties' of 1983-4. It shows signally how this innocent face favours the censors. For the logic is that such media cannot possibly do any 'good'. They can have no positive function at all, just because they are mass media. It only needs one putative case of harm, therefore, to warrant their suppression. And the critics of such campaigns are thus trapped into having to show how 'good' can be done by things which 'every ordinary person' knows at one glance to be bad.

Which is the reason why we must question that naive face. In the case of *Action*, we need to look closer at several aspects of the affair. How did the comic come to be withdrawn? What changes was it felt necessary to make to the comic? For *Action* did not die. It returned in 'cleaned-up' form on 4 December 1976, and ran for another year.

Several people whom I have interviewed have blamed the closure of *Action* on John Smith: not on anything he purposely did, but on his inexperience. Smith became editor of *Action* after its first editor, Geoff Kemp, decided to leave IPC. Smith had been working on the nursery comics for several years. But in 1975 IPC contracted out their nursery comics and, facing redundancy, he agreed to a move. After an unhappy spell working on *Whizzer and Chips*, he was offered Kemp's job. He came on to a comic already committed to a certain style. In fact, one of the first issues which he edited was the chain-and-bottle 16 September issue. He himself told me that he sought to continue the trend towards 'realism' as he understood it. He recalled, for instance, discussing *Look Out For Lefty* with its writer Tom Tully, suggesting that it had gone a bit dull and needed making 'nastier'. He also recalled the scene where *Hookjaw* finally gets to eat one of the main characters, and a survivor emerges from the sea to confront the arch-villain with the all that remains: the head. The artist had tucked it away at the bottom of the page. Smith had it enlarged, and featured it – thus helping to breach the policy of '36 frames over 5 pages' rule.

But Smith was simply carrying on a policy long laid down for the comic. When John Sanders told me that the problem with *Action* was that the 'old guard' only knew to equate realism with violence, he was surely being a bit disingenuous. Too many people have told me the story how, one day when *Hookjaw* (being centrepage spread) was being coloured in, Sanders leant over the open-plan partition to tell the Art Assistant 'There's not enough going on in there, Colin. It's boring. Put some more blood in. I want to see legs coming off.' There is no question but that the comic was being promoted as a violent comic. And the reason is clear: it was selling like hot cakes. Action had an initial print-run of 425,000, and a starting sale of 250,000. By mid-year, as always happens, it had dipped to somewhere in the region of 160,000. But at the time of its suspension, it was actually rising – a virtually unprecedented feat for any comic during this period. A figure of 180,000 per week is the most reliable for sales at time of withdrawal. It was IPC's best-selling boys' comic and was making a lot of money. But even more important, it was gaining a kind of loyalty and enthusiasm from its readers that had never been seen before. When the complaints were at their height, a reporter from Radio London visited IPC's Kings Reach Tower to interview John Sanders. Sanders defended the comic strongly, and invited the reporter to dip into the bag of mail just then arrived, and read any letters she liked. Two were pulled out; they were typically brimming with enthusiasm for the comic. In fact, Action's mail was legendary with the postroom at IPC, for its quantity. (When the report went out, the letters were not included.)

Smith was encouraged to carry on with Action's style precisely because it was so successful. Smith's own view was that the comic was more than 'realistic'; it was a kind of 'fantasyland', where all the stories are deliberately over-the-top, obviously far more violent and action-full than ordinary life.[6] Even so, faced with the hostility engendered by the 16 September issue, he felt that he had made a mistake, and advised that they should not seek to 'defend the indefensible'. But Sanders chose to defend it. In a much-noted interview with Frank Bough on Nationwide, he argued that Action existed in an environment in which there was an enormous amount of violence within all the media children encountered. On its own, that is not much of an argument. But given that the comic had deliberately followed the course of pinching story-lines from those other media, his argument was stronger. If Action was going to be picked on, when would the critics turn their attention to those other media? . . . unless, of course, the problem with Action lay precisely in those aspects of it which it did not share with its sources. We will see that it was just those new elements that were the 'problem', not the violence which it had in common with other media of the time, including its comic rivals.

Sanders was in fact prepared to ride the storm out, and keep Action going, because he thought it a good comic, with a very healthy circulation. But other forces were amassing. And indeed within a short period of time, IPC was speaking with two quite distinct voices, as noted by Bob Holbrow, columnist in the Retail Newsagent:

> Did Action, IPC's most successful juvenile launching in five years, go too far in its realistic portrayal of violence? If so, will all such offensive material be banned from future issues? Were those IPC executives, who now so contritely express

regret, unaware of those undesirable features until their attention was drawn to them by the Newsagents Federation and other objectors? . . . When an NF working party met IPC Magazines on September 21 and vigorously protested at what they considered excessive violence in this comic for the 9 to 14-year olds, the publishers accpted their complaints, offered no defence and were 'extremely penitent', we are told. So far, so good. But there were no signs of penitence, not even of the mildest variety, in IPC's editorial director of juvenile publications, Mr John Sanders, when on September 17, only four days previously, his replies to criticism were quoted in the *Daily Mail*.[7]

While Sanders (courageously or foolishly, depending on your point of view) defended *Action*, a concatenation of forces was making his position impossible. First, there was the fact of the continuing annoyance within the boys' department at IPC. Spokesperson for this feeling was LeGrand, a man of some influence and with friends on the Board of IPC. Persistently I have been told that LeGrand 'wanted *Action* to fail'. Second, among the protestors to complain about the comic was a strong contingent from the newly re-emergent Christian evangelical movement, some within the Responsible Society (especially in the West Midlands).[8] It was rumoured that on the Board of Reed International, then parent company of IPC, was at least one man with a very strong revivalist Christian bent. He and many other members of Reed's and IPC's Boards, looking at *Action*, declared it to be 'unsuitable for the image of IPC'.[9] But all these influences seem not quite enough. Among the bodies which contacted IPC to express concern, were the two main distributors, John Menzies and W H Smith. Menzies simply referred the matter to IPC for consideration, relying on the fact that IPC were, in their view, 'the most professional organisation with whom we have to deal'.[10] Smiths took a different line. Though it is now impossible to establish this exactly, it is clear that Smiths warned IPC that if something was not done about *Action*, there would be some kind of reprisal. Mr W E S Clarke, W H Smith's manager in this field at the time, told me that his memory was uncertain on the matter, but that it was most likely to have been a warning that Smiths would not 'box out' *Action* to newsagents in future. This would mean that, in any future promotions, they would not carry copies sale-or-return.[11] The problem I have with this is that, as Pat Mills pointed out to me, by this time *Action* would no longer have been issued sale-or-return, so such a threat would have been pretty hollow. Still, let us suppose that was it: this itself would have been damaging enough. But more sinister is the repeated story, now impossible to check, that Smiths warned IPC that if they did not withdraw *Action*, they would not only not carry this comic, they would also refuse to handle all IPC's publications. I can neither confirm nor deny the validity of this rumour. That it was current is without question, and believed by quite a few of those who were working on *Action*. The two most likely possibilities are: that the rumour is true – in which case, given its seriousness, it may have been

Fig 5 The lost page from *Death Game* 1999, which showed the climax of the Death Race, a shattering experience for Chief Warder Kruger. The 'BAROOM' was put in place to meet the likely complaints of the critics. © IPC Magazines 1976.

issued over the head of Mr Clarke, whose responsibility was essentially day-to-day contact with IPC's many departments; or if not true, then the consistency of the rumour within IPC suggests that the hint may have been deliberately dropped to justify what was an unusual and extraordinary act on the part of Reed and IPC.

It is most unusual for a firm like IPC, with a commitment to profit before all else, to withdraw a publication which is thriving when all around it are declining fast. And it is particularly strange for them to withdraw the comic, when an alternative way of dealing with 'the problem' was clearly available. When the rumpus began, Sanders had not only gone public, defending the comic. He had also acted behind-the-scenes to reduce the damage. And this had been communicated to the Board. He called a meeting of all those involved in the editorial control of *Action*, and made clear that it was to be toned down. The 'excessive violence' was to be removed; and from then on, all pages of finished artwork were to be cleared with him . . . which is where we can return for a moment to Belardinelli's symbolic splash-page.

The page was the climax of the *Death Game 1999* story; the game involving a (futuristic) series of clashes between professional teams in which competitors had to risk death on souped-up motorbikes, trying to capture and then fire a giant ball-bearing into a vast series of springs (like a huge pinball table). The highlight was when the leading team had the right to run the 'death race', to win the match. The opposing team could do literally anything to stop them. But on this occasion they had an unexpected ally. Kruger, chief warden at Taggart's prison, had been co-opted to the team, at the Governor's insistence – with the job of sticking an explosive device up Taggart's bike, primed to go off when Taggart fires the vital ball. But someone has scotched this plan. So Kruger decides to eliminate Taggart himself by firing a ball straight at him. But it is Kruger himself who goes up with a giant 'Baroom'. Or at least he did once the artwork had been shown to Sanders. The original panel was 'realistic' alright. It depicted graphically the departure of many bits of Kruger to various parts of the Spinball arena. John Smith knew this was controversial stuff, but equally he knew both that this was the climax and point of the story, and that he had a quite outstanding bit of artwork on his hands. (Belardinelli has gone on to become a cult artist on *2000AD*.) So he took it down to Sanders' office, untouched. Sanders was sitting with Leonard Matthews, former head of Fleetway comics, from the time when they were caution personified. They looked at the artwork, bewildered. Was Smith serious? It had to go. And so Smith arranged, as he had known he would have to, to have the word 'Baroom' overlaid on all Kruger's departing parts – but was sufficiently in love with the artwork that he had it done on cell-overlay rather than damage the original. With this emendation, but with the *story* unaltered, the edition of 23 October headed for the printers.

The edition never came out. Some thirty copies were run off for internal final consideration, as normal. But at that point, the hammer fell. Belardinelli's masterpiece never saw the light of day, even in its amended form. Sanders was away on holiday in Italy when it happened. Passing through the town of Villa Reggio, just after the end of the tourist season (at the beginning of October), he chanced on a shop selling English newspapers. In a copy of the *Daily Telegraph*, he read of *Action's* suspension. In his absence, the decision to suspend 'for editorial reconsideration' was announced, and a new editor – one of the 'Old Guard' – was installed. Sid Bicknell's task was to make *Action* safe again.

Back to adventure

Or, to be more precise, the instruction was given 'to take all this adult, political stuff out of it and turn it back into a boys' adventure comic'.[12] There is a vital clue here to what happened. Here is an opposition between boys' adventure on the one hand, and adult, political stories on the other. This is an opposition with a long history of influence in comics. In *Action's* case, it not only operated within the publisher. We can also see it in a curious letter published in the *Retail Newsagent*:

> I see no point in thrusting violence into the minds of six to ten-year olds, and this is certainly the age group who buy these comics. If children read these now, what they read will be remembered, as in my own case I still remember Robot (Robert) Archie and Dan Dare, from the *Lion* and *Eagle*. Children should not be 'wrapped in cotton wool' but let them have their childhood and find out about our cruel world in their own time.'[13]

Think through the logic of this. It is not here violence per se that is worrying, but too-early introduction to an adult world. Making them 'grow up too fast' will damage them for ever. They must come to it in their own way. But if they tell you that reading *Action* is their way of coming to it, they are wrong. Things like *Action* are not freely chosen by children; they are in one way or another 'forced on them', *whatever the kids themselves may say*. They are certainly not natural to them.

The categorisation 'boys' adventure', then, was put back into motion. How? We can know this precisely because happily I have been able to compare directly the unissued 23 October edition, with the revamped 4 December issue. This tells us exactly what it was felt necessary to delete. *Action* ran eight stories in each edition. In the closure edition were *Dredger*, *Probationer* (a virtually new story about a lad who'd got himself trapped on the wrong side of the law, and was trying to get out), *Hell's Highway*, *Look Out For Lefty*, *Hookjaw*, *Kids Rule OK*, *Death Game 1999*, and *Hellman*. Of these, only two escaped effectively unscathed: *Dredger* and (ironically) *Look Out For Lefty*. The changes in the remainder give remarkable substance to the instruction recalled by Colin Wyatt.

In *Hellman*, the change was small. The story then running showed Hellman on the Russian Front, nearly captured by the Russians. He manages to outwit them, capturing one of their tanks and turning it on them. The uncut version ended with two pictures: one showed a lone German tank in a snow wilderness, while Hellman and his colleague congratulate themselves on their good luck, wishing they could see the faces in the Kremlin tonight. The last frame showed just that, with a moustached figure saying: 'One German tank commander outwits a whole Russian regiment! He must be made an example of . . . I will offer a personal incentive to my men – a million roubles for this man Hellman . . . dead or alive!' The figure was Stalin, unmistakably. The cue underneath for the next edition said: 'The Russians want blood, and Hellman has to fight!' In the revised version, the Stalin frame has just disappeared; the preceding one has been stretched to fill its space. The cue has become: 'Where will Hellman's adventures lead him? See next Saturday!'

Two stories disappeared altogether. When Johnny Johnson announced *Action*'s suspension to the Press, he insisted that there were no plans to drop any particular stories. Two must have proved refractory to the changes required: *Kids Rule OK*, and *Probationer*. In their place came two quite dreadful stories, one called *Roaring Wheels* about a world champion racing driver fighting to hold his title; and the even worse *Double Dynamite*, a boxing story. This latter had the distinction of having been dug out of the back of a filing cabinet. If my information is correct, it was the start of a story that had been rejected as too weak even for one of the tamer comics. When it was decided to resurrect it, they found that they had lost the dialogue and story-line beyond episode one. Jack Adrian was asked to invent a dialogue to go along with the drawings.

This is revealing, of a comic that has lost its character. But far more revealing are the stories amended in a major way. In these we can see how a story can be made acceptable, what changes it back from 'adult, political' fiction into 'boys' adventure'. The stories affected were among the popular stories. First, *Hell's Highway* (Fig. 6). The 23 October edition carried the third and final episode of a story about running Cuban refugees to mount a mini-invasion of Cuba. But the order had been countermanded. Instead both the refugees and the truckers have become 'embarrassments'. This final episode saw the truckers successfully thwart the attempt on their own lives, and then rescue the refugees after dealing in violent fashion with the hired murderers who would have eliminated them. In the revised edition, the story itself does not change, in that they still thwart, and rescue. Two things go. First, there are some reductions in the overt violence of the story. For example, where before a grapnel had three prongs, now it was allowed only one. Where before a machine gun could be seen expelling four empty shell cases, now only one is permitted. And where before, under great stress and within feet of a watery grave in a Floridan

Fig 6 This episode of *Hell's Highway* was to have appeared in the 23 October issue. That was withdrawn, and only a 'cleaned-up' version ever appeared, in the 4 December issue. Readers may like to consider what they would have changed, either to meet their own criteria, or in the light of critics' charges about 'violence'. © IPC Magazines 1976.

WILL STEVE AND DANNY EVER GET OUT OF TROUBLE ?

hurricane, our hero could let out a 'Hellfire', now he exhibits real nonchalance and linguistic reserve; 'Heckfire' he mutters. There were in all thirty-three substantive changes to *Hell's Highway*. Two were rewritten cues at start and finish. Two were alterations to story-guiding information for which I could not work out any reason at all. Six were deletions of foul language like 'Hell' and 'Blast'. Nine were to turn the grapnel into a hook. Three were for other cleansings of visual violence. A further four took out threatening talk between characters, such as 'Hitmen deserve all they get!' and 'I'm gonna blast that rat!'. That leaves six, six whose alteration actually changed the sense of the story. For these were deletions of *every reference to Cuba in the story*. The fact that we no longer have any sense who is doing anything is irrelevant – it is 'adult, political stuff' and therefore must go. And in particular, you *can't possibly* say the following: 'Due to a sudden shift in Government policy, we're now friends with Castro. Those refugees have become, uh . . . redundant'. Out came the Tipp-ex, to make it: 'Due to a sudden shift in policy, those refugees have become, uh . . . redundant'. Whose policy? What refugees? No matter. You can threaten, and you can make people 'redundant'; but you can't mention governments.

Seeing this in *Hell's Highway* helps to make sense of what happened in the other two. At time of closure, Hookjaw was cruising the English channel nibbling the odd holidaymaker. But he was being disturbed by an attempt to raise a sunken bullion ship. In the unissued version, a helicopter is lowering a diver to explore the sunken ship, when Hookjaw appears. He seizes the diver, and drags the helicopter down into the water. On shore, soldiers are guarding the gang of hijackers who had sunk the boat. They are distracted and caught off-guard. The hijackers kill them, take their uniforms, and manage to board another navy vessel unsuspected. The shark is driven off the wreck with depth charges. The episode would have ended with two unresolved issues: what will happen to the hijackers, now aboard the other vessel? And what will Hookjaw do, so close to all those South Coast resorts, angry – and hungry?

Little of this survived the scissors. In the published version, both diver and helicopter escape ('Only the quick reactions of the pilot saved the diver from the snapping jaws'. . .), and a minesweeper arrives to pick up the remaining soldiers. We are casually told that the hijackers are already masquerading as soldiers; but never fear – 'Get your hands up! We have just been in contact with the main army unit. They have found the men you attacked. . . . you must be part of the gang that hijacked the bullion ship.' And when they are lowered into a boat to transfer to another ship, who should come along but Hookjaw – who very discriminatingly eats only the villains. At the end of the episode, instead of remaining an unresolved menace, we see Hookjaw's fin as he leaves the channel. Would you believe that 'Hookjaw had had enough. The waters in the channel were getting colder, and the shark's primitive brain made him head towards warmer waters, leaving the gold to be retrieved'?! In this nonsense, nothing remains of the irresistible leviathan, the monstrous primitive threat who rends all invaders of his ocean. Hookjaw died that day, though he continued to be rolled by the waves for almost another year.

And finally *Death Game 1999*. First to go was the title. Now it was simply *Spinball*. In the unissued episode, the entire story was of the 'death race' needed to win Taggart and his team's pardon and release. The story is punctuated by the chat of a cynical radio commentator. The game 'explodes into life', and Taggart's team use all their skill and tactics, to deadly effect – apparently unaware of the threat of the bomb up Taggart's spout. We see warder Kruger's vicious smile as Taggart gets ready to shoot the 'bomb'. But it doesn't go off. (A fragment surviving in the archive would have explained why two weeks later. Taggart, suspicious, had switched bikes.) So Kruger sweeps into action himself, brushing others aside; he'll kill Taggart directly. But when he lines him up in his sights and fires . . . Belardinelli swung into action. And the prison governor is left cursing, having lost his chief warder; and, if Taggart goes on to win the game, he has to grant his release. Where does all this excitement go, in the revised edition? Nowhere. Now Taggart's team win without the slightest trouble – not one body, not a drop of blood, and Kruger just doesn't feature at all. The governor is still very peeved about it. 'You've won, curse you!', he yells. But the surly-looking government agent Schroeder snarls back: 'You fool! The Government had to show the fans that spinball worked. These men have won their freedom. They deserve it.' Oh yeah!?

In each case, what has been removed is not the 'excessive violence' (if I was quite sure what that meant). It is every cynical reference to authority. Authority is just not allowed to be shown in compromised positions, or behaving unjustly, or doing wrong as a matter of policy. Yet this has all happened under the guise of removing excessive violence. What does this tell us about the nature of *Action* in its original form? To answer that convincingly, we need to delve much more systematically into *Action's* narratives, and to compare them with other comics of the time.

Understanding *Action*

What kind of a comic was *Action*? It certainly was very violent, with (crude measure) a high 'body-count'. But in truth that does not tell us much. A comparison with the other main boys' comics of the time would have revealed virtually as high a level of deaths and injuries. *Battle*, *Warlord*, *Valiant* and *Bullet* all organised their narratives around fighting, and killing. Yet only *Action* came in for systematic abuse. But also, using that word 'violence' tends to stop us asking important questions: what *kinds* of violence? What part do they play in the narrative? How are readers invited to understand and to relate to them?

Action's violence tended to be of very unusual, and shocking, kinds. For example, in one *Dredger* episode, the two agents have been given the job of protecting an important Arab oil negotiator. Somehow he disappears from the locked and impenetrable room which they were guarding. At the end, Dredger uncovers how he was murdered. The shower unit was rigged so that it delivered sulphuric acid – the man had simply been dissolved away down the plug hole, only his gold ring surviving as evidence. In *Blackjack*, Jack Barron the hero is being pressurised to 'take a fall'. As he is about to go into the ring, a box is delivered to him. It contains a finger of his manager. The shocking threat is thrown at him: lose, or your manager will die horribly. These are, of course, among the extreme cases, but they illustrate an important tendency. Violence in *Action* is deliberately shocking, and extraordinary; and that relates to the nature of the stories being told, and their narrative intent.

The narratives in *Action* unfold in predictable patterns. When I interviewed Jack Adrian, he interpreted my question about formulae in a technical way, agreeing me that there was indeed a formula. The opening of any episode dumps the character back in the dilemma he had ended in the week before; he would then have about four frames to get out of that. Then there would be a short developmental piece, as he reconnoitres or is moved to the next 'dangerous location'. A small crisis would be met with, and resolved. Then the scene would be set for a new desperate situation, the 'cliffhanger' to hold the readers for the next issue. This is the simplest sense of 'formula', and not an unimportant one. But in narrative theory, 'formula' has a more specialised meaning. This invites us to look for rules of construction that underlie the form of the story, governing the interactions between characters, and inviting a kind of interest as the story unfolds. In this sense, to look for a formula, is to look for common elements within the stories which govern more than the pace at which stories unfold.

There do indeed seem to be certain elements in common between almost all the stories – and the exceptions themselves are revealing. The most striking common element is the kind of predicament each character finds himself in. For example: Hellman is caught between the demands of fighting and winning as a German tank commander (and thus earning the hostility or the grudging respect of whomever he fights, because he is good at it), and the demands of Herr Kastner, the vicious Gestapo man who is 'attached' to him. He constantly has to negotiate his way between these pressures, in order to survive, and to remain true to himself. Or again: in *The Running Man*, Carter is the victim of the face-change operation so that he can 'take the rap' for Mafia man Vito Scarlatti. He is caught in a desperate dilemma. The police are after him with a 'shoot-to-kill' policy, and the Mafia want him dead, so that the heat will be off the real Scarlatti. He has to keep clear of both groups. Yet he must also seek out the Mafia in order to reestablish his identity. Another case: Green in his *Grudge War* with Bold (both commando recruits) battles constantly to prove his worth when all credit is always given to his rival. Yet he must also co-operate with Bold, because they have been teamed up together. (This had a twist at the end. Green becomes a mass of hate for Bold, incapable of rational judgement about him. But in the 18 September issue, Green dies and in the process saves Bold's life. Thus almost accidentally he vindicates himself. It is hard to think how else it could believably have ended.)

A similar account of predicaments and resulting motives can be given of nine out of the twelve remaining stories. In *Play Till You Drop*, it is between playing football honourably and well, and playing it in a way which will keep the blackmailing journalist off his back. But the more he plays it the latter way, the harder it is for him to get close to exposing the journalist. In *Sport's Not For Losers*, it is the dilemma between a father whose pride he doesn't want to see hurt, and a brother whose grubby bad behaviour makes him a most unsuitable candidate for athlete. In *BlackJack*, the dilemma is between fighting and remaining loyal to his East End fans, and going blind; then there are subsequent dilemmas between 'fighting clean', and promoters' pressures. In *Death Game 1999*, it is the dilemma between surviving the pressures of the prison governor, who wants a successful prison team but not a team of heroes, and surviving the game itself – which Taggart and Co can only do if they develop a real team loyalty and skilled interdependence.

To those who know it, *Look Out For Lefty* might seem not to fit this account. True, he has a problem in that his father keeps embarassing him as he tries to get accepted by his League team. But that is not the same as a 'dilemma', in the sense that the other stories have them. No, Lefty Lampton's dilemma is *himself*. The father is partly by-play (the strip owing a lot to *Steptoe and Son*), and partly shows up the background out of which Lefty's own personal problems flow. For he does have one hell of a bad temper, which constantly threatens

Table 1 Dilemmas in *Action* Stories

Strip	Dilemma 1	Dilemma 2	Resolution
Hellman	Surviving and being successful as a soldier	Surviving honourably, against the Gestapo	None – the story was still running at time of at time of closure.
Black Jack	Going blind through boxing	Boxing on to repay a debt to his fans	Ultimate success.[1]
Play Till You Drop	Being blackmailed over 'dishonour'	Playing football honourably	Ultimate success.[2]
Sport's Not For Losers	Maintaining family honour	Forcing the 'dishonour-able' member of the family to do the right thing	Ultimate success (he returns to sport himself).
The Running Man	Surviving loss of identity by running away from danger	Recovering identity by running towards danger	Ultimate success.
Green's Grudge War	Proving his ability	Overcoming/ cooperating with his rival	Ultimate success (but in death).
Death Game 1999	Surviving/succeeding by developing team spirit	Overcoming dangers resulting from their survival/success	None – the story was still running.
Look Out For Lefty	Succeeding by using his natural skills	Overcoming elements in his own nature	None – the story was still running.
Kids Rule OK	Surviving by re-building society from from their own nature/abilities	Overcoming elements their own/other people's natural/ social/tendencies	None – the story was killed.
Hell's Highway	Surviving/escaping pressures from 'above'	Maintaining their own principles	None – the story was still running.
Probationer	Surviving/escaping pressures from 'above'	Surviving/escaping pressures from 'below'	None – the story was killed.

his chances as a footballer. For example, a fortnight after the notorious 'bottle-throwing' incident, bottles were again thrown – this time, from a hooligan section of the crowd who have been baiting Lefty. One of them misses him by a whisker. In a fury, he is about to return it to its sender when his captain and the referee jump in to restrain him. I am not saying anything as simple as that this negates the 'message' of the first bottle-throwing. No, what this reveals is that the leading characters are not conventional 'heroes'. Of course, we are supposed to be on their side, and to be interested in their fortunes. But they are not embodiments of all things good. They can't be – their dilemmas are far too great, the dangers they face far too daunting for them to be simply moral.

Still, in each case there is a 'moral centre' to each character which guides him on how to face his problems. Table 1 summarises (I think, without distortion) the dilemmas for eleven of *Action*'s stories:

Exceptions that make rules

Consider now the two stories that do not easily fit: *Dredger* and *Hookjaw*. Unlike all the other stories in *Action*, *Dredger* is a series, not a serial. Though each separate episode does pose threats to Dredger, they do not seem to attack his 'being' in the way that other lead-characters are threatened. Is it simply an exception? The key to the story is in the relation between the two agents. Dredger, as his name applies, is the grubby one. He is crude, often cruel, but highly effective. Breed is smooth, not unaccomplished, but no match for Dredger except in the more polished aspects of life. In fact, on the surface, Breed ought to be the hero, Dredger a kind of animal-like sidekick. So how does Dredger become the hero? Certainly Dredger is much more cunning, physically able and alert to danger. But that is not all. Breed, also, continually interprets Breed for us. Consider the closing frames below from a few *Dredger* stories. In each case, we see Breed, in thought, accounting for Dredger's character. He is cold, brutal, animal-like – but then that is what was called for in the situation. He seems to owe loyalty to no one – or almost no one. He acknowledges a debt to former comrades, and is capable of real anger towards a certain kind of vicious person (for example the episode of 14 August 1976, where he met an old enemy, a Russian agent whom he blames for the massacre of civilians). He is no simple patriot – in another episode, he met his Russian counterpart, who is killed by terrorists while they are together protecting a sensitive diplomatic meeting. Though they fought instinctively on meeting, Dredger shows real emotion in burying him with full honour (see Fig. 7). But in all this, Dredger himself never explains or gives any hint as to why he does what he does. He simply is, Dredger. He is an enigma. Breed has to voice the high motives. On board a plane with a diplomat facing terrorists, Breed gives the standard reasons why they must not fail ('if Gadezo is killed, the oil deal will fall through, Dredger.

That's why this job is so important – for Britain's future'), Dredger has no time for such things: 'Spare me the flag-waving, pal – I want some kip.'

Fig 7 Dredger's silence and Breed's role as his 'interpreter'. Frames from *Action*, 14 February and 2 October 1976. The complete story (following pages) is from *Action*, 20 March 1976. All © IPC Magazines 1976.

We might say in fact that Breed's relation to Dredger is as ours to the rest of the characters. They are not like us, but we can and must admire their tenacity. What keeps them going? We can never fully know, because we are not them. Always they are beyond us, as Dredger is beyond Breed. We can thus understand one exceptional episode (27 March 1976), where Breed and Dredger are for once fully allied. The story concerns the gaol breakout of three convicted spies, the Mackay brothers and 'superspy' James Reilly. At the start a rather officious police inspector is trying to organise things, complaining about 'slackers and glamour boys' – whereupon he is introduced to Dredger, the ultimate non-glamour-boy. Dredger proceeds to take over, as they give chase to the villains. The Mackay brothers are shot as they try to escape. But Reilly escapes in a plane, and though Dredger manages to half-clamber aboard as it is taking off, he is forced out and crashes to the tarmac. Inspector: 'For all your great heroics, Dredger, all you've managed to do is sweep up a couple of yobs . . . The big one's got away. You're useless, man, useless!' The final two frames show Dredger and Breed driving off laughing together. The policeman can never know that the whole thing was staged to plant Reilly, a double-agent, into the Russian side; their attempts to recapture him had to look realistic, to avoid suspicion. Just this once, the two agents can be 'in it together' only because there is another figure, the policeman who is there to be the ignorant, inadequate one.

Let us try this account of the story-formula on the other two difficult cases. The first is simply different. *The Coffin Sub* was included because Pat Mills wanted a sea story. It told of Lieutenant Commander Mark Kane, whose first commission had ended in the death of his entire crew except himself. The story proceeds through his self-agonisings in various actions at sea, until the chance

D.I.6. KEPT THIS STORY OUT OF THE PAPERS!
THEY HAD TO KEEP QUIET ABOUT...

42

NEXT ISSUE—DREDGER STARS IN "MOTORWAY MURDER"!

arises again to risk his own life for his crew. This time he does die, but is vindicated in the process. Well, this is a real dilemma, it is lived out, and resolved. How is it different, then, and why might it have been so unpopular? Probably the answer is complicated, a mixture of many factors such as the art-work (a bit arid), the slow pace of the story, etc. But one real difference was that Kane himself was unsure. His was an internal dilemma, a panic about whether he was what he thought he was. The week before its demise, the last frame shows Kane agonising on his bridge about himself and the German submarine commander whom he keeps sparring with: 'Hauser hoped to rattle me with his games. But I'm used to living with ghosts. My dead crew are always with me' (27 March 1976). The Coffin Sub was a sort of compromise between the pre-Action comics and the new kind of narrative embodied in Action.

The other problematic case is Hookjaw, consistently the most popular. In part, I am sure, its popularity is to be explained by the grossness of Hookjaw's predations. His regular dental excursions into human anatomy gave it a real frisson of excitement. Ken Armstrong's already bloody scripts were added to by douches of red paint – Hookjaw hardly left the centre pages, and thus the use of colour. But that is not the whole of the story. Hookjaw is the hero. He is an elemental force, repeatedly threatened by the spin-offs of human greed and malice, and driven by his primitive brain to protect himself, by biting. In this sense, therefore, Hookjaw lives a dilemma – the dilemma of surviving everything that lousy humans – or other creatures – can throw in the way of his nature. When he is most at risk, then his shark-nature most asserts itself. For example (28 February 1976) Hookjaw is nearly captured by a professional shark-hunter, hired by the evil and mad McNally to safeguard his oil-hunting activities. But at the vital moment something arouses the shark. A memory of a past wound, a past brush with humans reawakens the old instincts, and the Great White Shark is alive again. Or when (17 April 1976) Hookjaw has been terribly stunned by a powerful electric shock, and a school of huge hungry barracudas set about him, what happens? 'The teeth of the six-feet-long scavengers ripped into the Great White – the tearing of the needle-sharp teeth caused a stirring in the shark's dulled brain. His jaws reacted automatically. In their attempt to kill the big shark – the barracuda had given him life. The pain of their attack had triggered off his instinct for survival.' This talk of 'instincts' runs through the strip; repeatedly we have 'feeding frenzies', Hookjaw's 'primitive brain' is activated – but most and especially by his 'hatred of humans'. All this dates back to his first encounter. One of those revolting American fishermen, the kind who want to have every 'prize' (in the way British hunters used to need every trophy on their walls), stuck a huge gaffe in the shark's jaw. This became an ever-present reminder of pain from humans – and, of course, gave the shark his unmistakeable identity. (See below, Fig. 8, for this and related frames.)

Hookjaw embodies the same formula of survival and maintenance of 'integrity' under stress. He cannot speak for himself, but the story makes sure we know. When his nature is threatened, it comes out as shark-essence. This is, if you like, the organising motif of the comic's stories. It is the reason why characters cannot change throughout their stories – they can only succeed or fail. It gives some backing to the claim of Jack Adrian that his stories were essentially moral stories. They are, in the sense that the characters' lives are devoted to maintaining their sense of identity. That they use violence results from the overwhelming nature of the threats to their selves. Here again, we have to challenge the argument that the objections to the comic were simply its 'violence'. In fact, were the objections based on body-counts, without question the uproar should have been over Hookjaw whose rate of (messy) consumption of humans was prodigious. But intuitively perhaps, the objectors understood that this story was not the heart of the problem. The problem lay in those stories that came 'close to home'. In some, the sense of threat came not in historically-distanced events like World War II, not in the deeps of various oceans (even if preferably distant deeps), nor in stylised villainous boxing set-ups. Being 'close to home' need not mean closeness of physical time or space, but what we might call 'social closeness'. Kids Rule OK may be science fiction, but it is science fiction of a kind that can comment on today. It doesn't only show gangs at war, more, it shows them up against outrageously unfair residues of authority, and trying to make their own authority in opposition. Look Out For Lefty is not a problem just because of violence (when it was, in fact, one of the least violent stories in the comic), but because its 'hero' is scratching together a makeshift morality. What after all led to the first bottle-throwing? Lefty was being deliberately pushed out of his side by the nasty tactics of a team-mate. No one would believe what was going on, except his girl-friend Angie (tough cookie, this one). In the game, the villain had several times slyly put the boot in on Lefty to try to injure him. Seeing this, and Lefty in trouble, Angie 'intervenes' with her bottle – and thus creates the space for Lefty to go on and prove his worth with his good sinister foot. Though it is unproveable except by the weight of circumstantial evidence, I am confident that the 'problem' of Action was not as simple as 'violence'. It was in fact a political objection.[3]

Action meets its readers

How can we explore *Action*'s relations with its readers? An issue of *Action* had thirty-two pages consisting of: a cover, twenty-six pages of stories, and five pages of varied editorial material. Each section contributes to the whole relaationship.

Covers. Their style mixed the bizarrely cramped, and the outrageously brilliant. They were 'busy', all right, but something else as well. At their best, they were so distinctive, startling and vibrant that on their own they give a sense of newness and unpredictability to the comic. Much of the cover-language is typical comic self-congratulation. 'Exciting, extravagent, explosive!!!', 'Gamble with death!', 'Not for the nervous!'. 'Bold! Bad! When the going gets rough, they send for DREDGER!'. These are of course standard comic superlatives.

Fig 8 How *Action* characters 'survive'. 'Lefty' Lampton (from *Action*, 9 October 1976), fighting for his place in the team, has his own background to contend with as well. Hookjaw (from *Action*, 17 April 1976), faced with a threat, calls on his very 'essence' to survive. A government official (from *Death Game 1999*, *Action*, 18 September 1976) warns what happens to 'heroes' like Taggart. All © IPC Magazines 1976.

But there was another element, a knowingness. 'The paper they can't stop talking about!' – you can almost hear the grin behind that. Why can't 'they' stop talking about it? Because 'WARNING – This comic is not suitable for adults!' *Action* proudly set itself apart from/against other comics. It laughed at its own excesses, in a way that prefigures its successor *2000AD*. '*Action*'s only out once a week – you need six days to recover!' And the address to readers is, to get in there, experience it for yourself. 'Wanna die for $10,000? HOOKJAW's inside!' 'You don't know the meaning of fear until you read . . . *ACTION*'.

These covers are striking for their self-conscious, ironic challenge to readers. We're different, they announced. We're proud of being disliked by all, except you the readers, of course. We won't mollycoddle you. There's almost a promise of direct involvement in the action that is to come. Look at the cover of the lost issue (reproduced above, page 22) for its daring invitation. No messing, get in there.

Once inside, one aspect hinted at on the covers grows in intensity. There is a remarkable cynicism in *Action*, about itself and the world it inhabits. Most comics have tended to shut readers into a world that seems self-sufficient. But *Action* looked outward. It continually noticed the world around it. As we've seen, it had the 'Twit of the Week' column. Alongside this was a fragment of a column, giving fragments of useless but fun information. It was called 'SO WHAT?'. With these, also came a space' for readers to ask for any kind of information, from *Action*'s own Norris McWhirter, Milton Finesilver, but known to readers simply as . . . 'KnowAll'. On another page, Steve McManus as 'Action-Man' was sent to do daring deeds, whilst writing of the editor as 'Old Wooden-Leg'. There was even a column in early editions, called 'Gripes and Groans', in which readers were invited to get off their chests their complaints about how they were treated. This never took off as the editors hoped. But its style is significant.

Then there are the readers' letters. Compare with two other comics: D C Thomson's *Warlord*, and *Bullet*. *Warlord* was the first of the new-wave comics. But it is not new-wave in anything like the sense that *Action* is. Sampling the first ten issues, the pattern of letters is quite clear. Not only were all the stories World War II related, but the letters also are boys recalling their fathers' and uncles' lives in the war – their courage, their problems, their funny happenings; and the kids' relation to it now – like, visiting sites of old battles, finding unexploded shells, or wearing a handed-down army greatcoat. The editor encouraged more letters along these lines. Of the forty-seven letters sampled, none strayed outside these formulae. *Warlord* seems to invite its readers into a self-enclosed tradition, in which deeds of courage and fortitude are endlessly rehearsed, against a background in which there are no moral choices; we know whose side we are on, because of who we are. The letters reflect and participate in this.

Of course, letters are selected, and often for early editions solicited or ghost-written. They are not produced by some 'natural sampling' of readers' responses. That only reinforces my point. They are a part of the self-image of the comic. They present that self-image, and help to encourage the right kind of future response from readers. Now compare with *Bullet*, D C Thomson's attempt to match *Action*. Born in the same month, it was also a multi-theme comic, with a number of stories similar to *Action*. The keynote story was *Fireball*, codename for a superdetective-cum-agent who also fronted the comic's letters page. Again a sample reading of early issues reveals a pattern. Of forty-five letters, seven told 'odd facts' (of legends, of the Bermuda Triangle, etc); sixteen were humorous letters (like the one about the teacher who switched putty for chewing gum . . .); five began 'I would like to tell you about . . . ', telling of things attempted or experienced by readers – these were typically 'exciting events', like visiting a corroboree. Then come two revealing groups. Seven letters were about attempting brave things – like learning karate, getting injured and rescued while rock-climbing – in all of which there is a sense of knowledge being gained, of 'growing up' in a certain way. Finally come twelve letters, specifically comic-related, which treat the comic as holding that special know-

ledge. Consider: 'What a guy Fireball is! Me and my pals would love to be like
him! How is he able to do all the things he does?' Editor: 'Sorry, man. That information
is strictly confidential. Only those who join the Fireball Club allowed into the secret' (Bullet
no. 3). Here is an aura of a special community, which you have to go out of
your way to join. If you join it, you can become more than you already are:
like the ones who started Fireball Football teams, or the one who tried to be
as tough as Fireball but failed ('keep practising', advised the editor). In all senses,
you sought admission to a privileged club – the comic was a world beyond
you, made up of people larger and more successful than you. In a different
way, this had been true too of Warlord. All through, there is this sense of trying
to live up to a tradition others have established.[4]

This simply wasn't true of Action's letters. Letters to Action were addressed to
Steve, the 'ActionMan'. The letters from early editions (forty-six) showed: virtually half saying, simply, this is the greatest comic ever. These included two
from girls, saying it is not for boys only, and one from a boy who loved it but
commented on the level of violence. Twelve told little stories about reading
Action, from not being able to read Hookjaw late at night because the shadows
from the curtains reminded him of a pair of jaws. . . , through suggestions for
the comic, to correcting an error in an early story. The remainder were four
Warlord-style letters, and a few humorous ones.

Action readers were so enthusiastic about their comic. I have mentioned the
IPC postroom's comments on the total volume of mail. But it was more than
sheer enthusiasm. It was also the kind of response letters were given. The
comic was on their side. Contrast: 'The discipline in my uncle's battalion in World
War II was so strict that he was put on a charge for having the handle of his
mug facing the wrong way during a room inspection' (Bullet no. 8). No comment. It's just another letter on the facts and foibles of life in wartime. Now, a
letter from Action no. 11 about a Scottish teacher demonstrating the strap by
turning a stick of chalk to powder: 'Steve says: Gulp!' Tiny, but typical. There
was a relation of banter between comic and reader. This enabled one reader
to write in and get published – (comparing the editor to a sandwich – only 'a
sandwich is only an inch thick'. It also meant that the comic could and would
publish openly condemnatory letters. In the 16 October edition a letter damned
the comic as 'sick perverted garbage. It should be banned'). Action encouraged
way-out responses, welcomed them. Small wonder, as we shall see, that readers
rated it the least patronising comic.

By the end of its first series, the majority of its letters were about things that
happen to readers in connection with their reading of the comic, ranging from
being so engrossed in it that one walked right through wet cement, to battles
over who should read it first, and so on. Action had entered their lives. And
Action readers knew themselves to be different because of reading Action. Unlike
Bullet readers, who sought access to a special superior world, there to gain

secret knowledge, to read *Action* was already to be in it. You read it as it was, and as you were.[5]

Action, then, was sensational, knew and delighted in the fact. It talked direct and invited readers to join in making mock of stupid things in its world. It was cynical, but not just for the sake of being so. There was plenty around it to be cynical about. And here we can begin to fit the stories into the editorial context. For the stories also are not cut off, self-enclosed in their own world. Their characters have no easy heroism; they have struggled up from under, and must go on struggling. If ever their struggling ends, their story ends. They are driven to prove themselves, against an uncaring, unpitying and hostile world. Look back at those frames (Fig. 8, p. 46) in the last chapter. In each case, it is not just that we are on a character's side; we also know what they are up against, what has made them as they are. The world is cruel to them. Their battle is to survive that world, and to make an honourable space for themselves. This is the link between stories, editorial style and content and readers' letters. Why shouldn't they be cynical about a world that pressures them so? The characters are recogniseable, their dilemmas perhaps magnifications of readers' feelings about their own lives. The comic speaks to them in the language of those feelings. In short, *Action* stood at the edge of a very radical politics – and that couldn't be allowed. Unlike its own characters, *Action* was not a survivor. This time, it was the kids who were betrayed. Kids ran the streets of Brixton on the day its withdrawal became known, shouting 'They've taken away our comic!'. They were marking the collapse of an agreement into which they at least had entered wholeheartedly. A school sent in a petition with literally hundreds of names, boys and girls, demanding the return to *their Action* after its awful reappearance in December 1976. They were sticking to their side of the bargain. Cheated and ignored, no doubt another grain of general resentment against the way 'authority' treated them was laid down, another brick on the wall of helplessness.

Action may have stood at the edge of a radicalism – but it couldn't cross over. The limits of its radicalism are revealed by the unpublished ends of the stories. IPC's art archive contained more than a hundred unpublished pages, some of them unlettered. They were mainly from *Hookjaw*, *Death Game 1999*, *Probationer*, and *Kids Rule OK*. The last pages of *Hookjaw* show the battle and the hijackers. This would have gone on at least another seven episodes. I can best give the flavour of the 'lost' pages by looking at the 30 October issue. Recall, *Hookjaw* was in the English Channel, angry and hungry. The beaches are close by, and a small boy wants to go swimming. But an over-large, over-protective Mummy, dozing on her deck-chair, has forbidden him. Disobedient, he sets off. Wearing a rubber ring because he is a poor swimmer, and twitted by the 'hunks' on the beach because of this, he decides he'll prove he's brave by going furthest out. But – as the caption at the top had told us – 'Julian should have listened to his Mummy'. There is a wicked knowingness about this which encapsulates a lot of *Action*'s qualities. Julian (the choice of a 'soft' name is surely not accidental) should have listened – he gets eaten because he didn't. At the same time, he is the object of just a little derision because he is the kind of child who might listen to his Mummy – he almost deserves to get eaten.

Look Out For *Lefty* had been following Lampton's conflict with a gang of hooligan followers of neigbouring Rotherfield FC. These had escaped the police after being arrested (after a Lefty ploy) at the match where the bottle-throwing happened. They had taken their revenge on his Grandad by robbing him, and tarring and feathering him. Lefty set out for revenge, with Angie, on a 'borrowed' motorbike (which he did return afterwards). They find the yobs in their local, and Lefty belts their leader who is boastfully displaying the stolen money. A fight breaks out, the police are called, and in the confusion our two heroes make their getaway, having retrieved the stolen money. This was an operation of what we might call Lefty's 'primitive justice'. He takes the law into his own hands, because that, he feels, is his only chance of recompense.

But the story that reveals most where *Action* was heading, and the limits of its challenge to authority, is *Kids Rule OK*. With the exception of one episode, all the remaining pages are in the archive, to finish the story. The story had opened with the conflicts between two surviving gangs, one of them vicious and murderous. After several deadly encounters, the relatively decent group had got away. At time of withdrawal, they had just encountered some surviving adults – a group of police cadets led by a fascistic Commander, who was going to enforce his style of authority by any means he liked. Several battles take place between them, as the kids try to escape from custody and virtual torture (the police trying to find the whereabouts of a gun cache). Finally escaping, they make their way into central London, where (in a lost episode, for which only a cover survives) they clearly had some fun with the Crown Jewels in the Tower of London. After joining up with a March of Kids to Trafalgar Square calling for peace and reconciliation, they suddenly find themselves confronted by more police. But these are different – they have Dan Dare-type faces, telling us that these are good chaps. And, would you believe it, the story ends with the police getting the two rival gangs to be friends. It ends with them sitting together in a classroom, learning about farming, health and social work so that they can all rebuild a happy England. Hmph.

This ending reveals the limits of *Action* perfectly. Having set up a drama, in which kids' own natures are put on the line, in which 'authority' became the central issue, the comic didn't know what to do with it. Its contract with its readers began the story; a failure of political imagination ended it, in a *Coral Island*-style harmony. It would be fascinating to know how readers would have responded to that ending, compared with the ways they responded to the comic as a whole. Or perhaps it is as well it was never published . . .

Finding out about the readers

During 1986-7, I carried out some research on former readers of *Action*. I wanted to explore how they thought about their comic, and compare their views with *Action*'s critics. A mixture of letters to some a hundred local newspapers, leafletting at comic conventions, personal contacts, and an advertisement in 2000AD produced a large number of names and addresses, to each of which I sent a questionnaire (reproduced as Appendix 1). From these I gathered 135 completed questionnaires, a response rate of about two-thirds (a further five came in too late to be included in the analysis). These were analysed quantitatively and qualitatively.

Researching audiences is notoriously difficult, and I will be the first to admit the difficulties with evidence based on such recollections. My defence is that there was no other way. Still, I do think that some of my evidence gives pointers to important conclusions. Where those conclusions are supported by other kinds of evidence (triangulation), their value is surely increased. In brief, my aim was to discover, first, what readers recalled of the comic and of their reactions to it, their memories of its closure and the events surrounding that, and their retrospective assessment of it. For this last, I developed my own variant of the Semantic Differential Test (SDT), the device first developed by Osgood.[6]

I decided to take seriously the claim that the more committed readers are, the more likely they are to be influenced. I therefore asked my respondents to class themselves as Committed, Regular, or Casual readers of *Action*. I wanted to compare committed readers' responses with the rest. In devising the SDT, I included dimensions that might show significant differences. Many were suggested by other aspects of my research. For example, Pat Mills had commented that *Action* should be seen as a 'girls' comic'. I therefore incorporated a male/female dimension, in order to see if readers agreed with him. (They didn't.) My analysis of the comic had suggested a problematic relationship between an internal *politics*, and external judgements on its *violence*. I designed dimensions that would measure these. I also wanted to see how closely defined or diffuse readers' perception of *Action*'s politics were. I therefore offered three separate dimensions, to test this: Right/Leftwing, Pro/Anti-authority, and Cynical/Non-cynical.

My sample of 135 comprised 47 aged ten or under (at time of *Action*), 63 aged eleven to fourteen, and 22 over fifteen (3 no answers). Of the 135, 13 regarded themselves as Casual, 48 as Regular and 73 as Committed readers. I combined the Regular and Casual categories (henceforth CasReg) for purposes of analysis. This gave comparable sets (61 CasReg to 73 Committed). Committed readers were slightly younger than average (all ten or under = 34.8%, Committed = 38.4%; all over fifteen = 16.3%, Committed = 12.3%).

I was able to check how far my sample was representative of *Action*'s readership, by asking (with no prompting list) readers to recall which stories they had enjoyed. I compared the results with a table of popularity drawn from interviews with publishers, editors, etc (among whom there was only small disagreements). There is a high degree of consistency between them (see Table 2). The first three match exactly, and stand clearly ahead of the rest in both lists. The fit is not so perfect in the next group. First, *Kids Rule OK* was not mentioned by publishers, but for a very good reason. It only managed a very short run, before being killed. There had not been time for it to establish itself. The fact that on the basis of only six episodes it rated sixth place indicates an appeal in it which fits with my analysis of its place in the comic. There was also some division of opinion over the popularity of *The Running Man*, with most interviewees agreeing it came in the second rank. However Pat Mills recalled it as disastrously unpopular. He himself had loved it (particularly liking the artwork), and he had disappointed/annoyed when it 'bombed'. My only explanation of this is that, perhaps, its early unpopularity was because *Action* was still establishing its 'style'; certainly my figures do not suggest a total failure. There was less agreement about the order of popularity in this second group. But there was no basis in my interviews for *Hellman* standing head and shoulders atop this group. It was therefore significant that when I distinguished story-preferences between Committed and CasReg readers, *Hellman* was the only story on which there was a significant difference. Its high proportion is entirely the

Table 2 Popularity of *Action* Stories

Publishers' etc recall of popularity	Readers' list	% of mentions
Hookjaw	Hookjaw	76.3
Death Game 1999	Death Game 1999	63.7
Dredger	Dredger	54.1
Hellman of Hammer Force	Hellman	30.4
Look Out For Lefty	Look Out For Lefty	22.2
	Kids Rule OK	17.0
The Running Man	The Running Man	14.1
Hell's Highway	Hell's Highway	8.9
BlackJack	BlackJack	8.1
Sport's Not For Losers	Sport's Not For Losers	3.7
Green's Grudge War	Green's Grudge War	3.0
The Coffin Sub	The Coffin Sub	2.2
	Probationer	1.5
Play Till You Drop	Play Till You Drop	0.7

result of liking by CasReg readers. In the third group, there are no surprises. *Probationer* is the other example of a story which had so short a run (only three weeks before it was 'killed') that it was not mentioned at all by publishers. Overall, my sample seems representative of the comic's original readership.

Some of the questions produced no positive information. For example, I found nothing distinguishing meaningfully between Private and Shared readers. There was a slight tendency for reading *Action* to be seen as more a shared activity than reading other comics. But that did not correlate with anything else. Again, readership of other specific comics did not seem to make a difference to responses to *Action*.

I asked respondents what other comics they read around the time of Action. I also asked them to compare their ratings of *Action* with one other comic they had read. (Respondents who had only read *Action* were asked to rate that on its own. This built in a check on whether asking respondents to compare two different comics caused artificial widening of responses. Results were encouraging. There was no single direction to the differences in the meaning of *Action* for those who rated it alone compared with those who rated it against another comic.)

The first positive result to note was in response to the question: How different was *Action* from its contemporaries? The unanimity of answers to this is striking. Committed or CasReg, younger or older, no matter what other comics were read (or if no others were read) virtually all respondents said the same. On a scale 1 – 5, all bar five rated *Action* very different from other comics available then. Such unanimity is so strong, it sets a measure for interpreting other results, very few of which approach this extremity, as we shall see.

First, a pen-portrait of how *Action* looked to its readers: overall it was quite well-written and well-drawn. It was very up-to-date, especially when compared with others around it; and was somewhat unrespectable. Not clearly either right- or left-wing, it was determinedly male, rather cynical and not patronising towards its readers. Its stories were violent and fast-moving, a bit unpredictable (again, contrasting with the other comics in this). While the others were pretty unbelievable, *Action* stories were in the middle on this dimension – but they were very exciting. They were a bit pessimistic, not clearly either patriotic or otherwise, but extremely anti-authority. The characters meanwhile are not very moral, are vulnerable, but relatively successful and very strong. They are a little lonely but not really either handsome or ugly. More than anything they are distrustful of authority. Finally our composite reader is undecided whether the characters were like him, but he slightly thinks he would like to be like them.

There are only two dimensions on which readers' perceptions of the differences between *Action* and its contemporaries approaches their certainty that there was a difference. These are that the stories are anti-authority (mean for *Action* = 4.01, mean for other comics = 2.00); and that the characters in the

Table 3 Results of the Semantic Differential Test completed in 1986 by 135 former readers comparing *Action* (shaded) with its contemporaries (solid) expressed in averages.

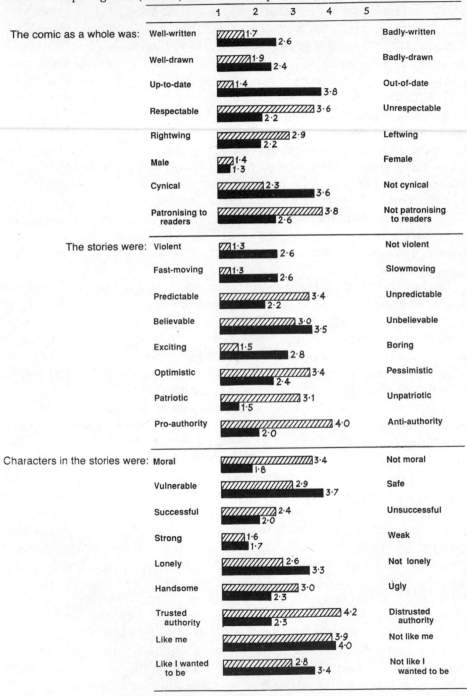

stories distrust authority (mean for *Action* = 4.18, mean for other comics = 2.31). Other comics are rated as less violent, more boring, their characters more handsome and moral, but never so markedly. I want to suggest that these two cases come closest to readers' sense of the special character of *Action*. See Table 3 for full results.

It would be possible to go on reprocessing these data ad infinitum. Given the problems with them (small sample, recall etc.), it would be pointless. Like any other researcher I have pursued those that looked promising. My criteria for doing this were straightforward. I have pursued those data which might relate to other parts of my analysis. Both in designing and interpreting the questionnaire, I tried to tackle areas where controversy reigns. And once the data were in front of me, I reinvestigated any puzzling results. The problem is that this kind of number-crunching tends to homogenise individual responses. I have long been critical of content-analysis as a technique for media-investigations.[7] Content analysis fractures people's responses into elements which can quickly lose their sense. It also tends to flatten differences; each individual response is 'worth' as much as any other. Some individual responses can reveal a situation more fully than others. Because of these problems I have used the quantitative data to raise problems. Where the figures suggest there is something of interest, at that point we have to leave purely quantitative investigation. After that, we have to find ways to discover the patterns of ideas within the data. It is for this reason that I included a number of open-ended questions in my questionnaire. My analysis moves between quantitative and qualitative information.

On being a committed reader

What are the differences between Committed and Casual/Regular readers? There was one striking difference regarding popularity of stories. Not surprisingly Committed readers made many more nominations of popular stories than the others (263 to 149). But still, as proportions of their groups, they are fairly constant. If 60 Committed readers out of 73 mention *Hookjaw* (82.2%), then 42 out of 61 CasReg readers mention it (68.9%). That ratio holds constant with the one exception already mentioned: *Hellman of Hammer Force*. This is mentioned by many more CasReg readers. Intuitively, my guess is that of all the stories in *Action*, this was more like stories in other comics. It was a war story, albeit with the novelty of being told from a German viewpoint. Its morality was much more clean-cut and clear-cut. It was not therefore part of *Action*'s specific contract with its readers, and would not attract those committed to that contract.

Beyond this, the differences were slight. On most dimensions there is far more agreement than disagreement. To both groups, *Action* is well-written, well-drawn, up-to-date, unrespectable, male, and unpredictable; the characters are as non-moral and vulnerable for each. There are some slight differences; to the Committed the comic is a bit more violent, fast-moving, and believable, and considerably more exciting (Committed: 1 = 84.9%, 2 = 11.0% (Sample = 73); CasReg: 1 = 40.0%, 2 = 42.6% (Sample = 61)) – but this is hardly surprising. It is almost part of being committed. The Committed are slightly more likely to see the characters as successful, strong, and handsome but also lonely and distrustful of authority. On two dimensions the Committed readers showed less ability to assign definite meanings: on political slant (Left-/Right-wing) and on whether the characters were like them. In both cases a notably higher proportion nominated category 3.

We learn more if we compare their responses to other comics. Despite the overwhelming emphasis on the difference between *Action* and other comics, the Committed group score higher on the qualities of writing and drawing of the other comics than do CasRegs. This suggests that 'commitment' means not only commitment to *Action*, but to the comic medium as a whole. On a lot of characteristics (Respectability, Politics, Cynicism, Morality, Optimism, Predictability), there is virtual agreement. But there are some interesting divergences. While the Committed group accentuate the differences on certain key elements (they see *Action*'s companions as less violent, more patriotic, more pro-authority, up-to-date, and their characters as stronger, more successful), on others they become less certain – and it is those characteristics one might call 'personal'. On the Vulnerable/Safe, Lonely/Not Lonely, and Handsome/Ugly dimensions, the Committed readers tended to plump for category 3.

There seems little doubt that 'Commitment' does include an element of liking the comic medium in general. Committed readers reported more reading of other comics (Committed = 2.8 average; CasReg = 2.3 average) and a higher proportion of Regular to Occasional reading (Committed = 50/50%, CasReg = 34/66%).[8] If we turn now to the responses to open-ended questions, we will see this does not exhaust the meaning of 'commitment' by any means.

It would be easy to exaggerate differences by selective quotation, especially of unusual responses. However they do have a particular value. At the level of *describing the comic*, Committed and CasReg readers hardly diverge. But as they begin to move beyond description differences emerge. That poses a problem. Individuals move beyond description to a greater or lesser extent. I have therefore drawn word-pictures of the two groups, composed almost entirely of quotations. If challenged, I would simply say that the results seem worth it.

As I say, descriptions do not differ significantly. Where Committed readers called *Action* 'more violent', 'gory', CasRegs spoke of it being 'all blood and gore', and 'more bloodthirsty'. To Committeds, it was 'tense and exciting', 'fast' and 'entertaining'; to CasRegs, it was 'compelling reading', 'dynamic', 'exciting and readable'. Both sides state that buying their copy on a Saturday was the 'highpoint of the week': 'I looked forward to it, and felt it as a real loss when it went' (79, Committed); an integral part of my Saturday' (3 CasReg).[9]

They are equally split on *Action*'s private/shared qualities. A number in both groups talk of their 'gang' playing out *Action* stories (one reporting an attempted game of Spinball, aborted when they learnt how much a golf ball can hurt!). Many tell of playground discussions of the comic. But others on both sides saw *Action* as an escape: 'Escapism from life, and Banff' (67, Committed) and 'I had a difficult home life – found comics an escape' (30, Committed), balanced by 'I didn't have much friends, so I stayed in and read comics' (73, CasReg). Both sides are agreed in calling *Action* more 'uptodate', and more 'adult' than other comics of its time. 'Way ahead of its time' (1, Committed); 'less traditional, more modern' (14, CasReg). Finally both groups agree that these are what made it different from its competitors: 'violence vs bland others', from 49 Committed, sums it up. More diverse in its story-lines – not all war and football; and the violence more realistic – no shootings without blood, no kidding the kids that people can be hurt without pain and mess. But there the overlaps cease. The differences enter when readers evaluate, and when they try to state their relation to the comic, and the kind of reader it appealed to.

Committed readers, first, are virtually unanimous. *Action* was a summation of good qualities. Not only was it exciting, new, uptodate and violent ('the gore!', wrote 12, Committed, summing up all he liked), but it was also *intelligent*. What did this mean? 'More violent, and intelligent story-lines' (13) implying a distinction and relation between them which bear some thinking about. 'Its violence was more true to life' (66); and 'we never talked about any other comic the way we talked about *Action*' (111). It was 'Hill Street Blues as opposed to *Dempsey and Makepeace*' (58). Then in a revealing coupling: 'It seemed to have a high readers' participation, and stick its fingers up' (9). The implications of that would seem to be that *Action* was simultaneously close to its readers, and anti-authority. It talked to them like a mate about a world they didn't trust. It was 'more anti-establishment' (15), 'more grown-up, sarcastic, cynical' (44); 'it preached lawlessness and rebellion but officially sanctioned' (96); and 'Point is, it made you think, that says it all!' (33).

How did it do these things for the Committed readers? First by involving them. Poignantly, 116 recalled: 'It was just better, a friend'. It had a 'down-to-earth style; there seemed to be a certain 'we're one of you' style' (29). The stories also were special. Repeatedly, replies said that in *Action* stories 'the good guy didn't win' (42), 'not like the 'always win' heroes of other comics' (44), 'anti-heroes rather than heroes' (46), 'anti-hero rather than good guy' (64), 'didn't always have a happy ending' (17). And yet: 'characters seemed to have a conscience' (67), 'dealt with the seedier side of things, yet still moral!' (75). So the attraction was 'seeing an 'underdog' rising above the odds to conquer all' (75). *Action* 'had real stories with feelings, real people, morals, fear etc' (37).

To call *Action* 'real' and 'realistic' as so many did may have meant that it coincided with something already felt. But for some, perhaps, it was capable of more than that: 'The idea that the heroes were not always good guys and did not always win helped destroy the black and white image I had learned' (123). Though only one person said this directly, it is astonishing how many others testify in a general way to how important *Action* was for them. It gripped them, and made them think.

The characters in the stories embodied the 'realism' for many Committeds: 'Dredger – man of mystery; Spinball – good characters forced to work for corrupt authority – very original! Lefty was working class – not virginal, but still a good guy' (15); 'probably gratuitous violence but also the tongue-in-cheek political send-up' (81); 'Dredger, a no-nonsense character who hated authority and criminals alike' (40). But *Action* was different in letting its readers see connections outside the comics. Obvious ones, of course, like the links with films and TV: typically, 'it reflected films I was interested in' (26) – on this, the CasRegs agreed. But more, it commented on the world the readers recognised. 'It showed governments could play dirty' (33).

So what sort of reader did they think it was aimed at? One of course who is 'tired of the same old rubbish' (1), who wants variety. Very curiously, Committed readers see the target readership as somewhat older than do the CasRegs. Committeds estimated target-audiences as follows: 10 and under = 8%, 11-13 = 39%, 14-17 = 38%, 18 and over = 15%; CasReg, on the other hand: 10 and under = 9%, 11-13 = 44%, 14-17 = 38%, 18 and over = 9%). This, despite the lower average age of Committed readers. What did this mean? It meant they wanted a 'more adult kind of comic' (75), to 'read stories with alternative solutions, and aspects of life' (17), 'believable adventure stories' (30); they were 'teenagers who wanted a flexible comic, that went beyond stagnation' (8). What kind of a reader, then? Of course a watcher of *Jaws* and *Rollerball* (if they were old enough – some cannily remarked that the comic was a substitute for films they couldn't get into!). But also they are 'people with a good imagination' (24), 'socially aware but with a good imagination' (7); they were the 'slightly rebellious ones' (9), the 'young rebels' (68), 'working class teenage boys' (66) – and perhaps most strikingly, in the explicit judgement of seven respondents, 'members of a post-punk generation' (85), and the 'modern teenager who was enjoying a new freedom' (62).

To the Committed readers, then, *Action* was violent alright. But that was just a part of its style. Of course many Committed readers talk only about this. Their answers stay at the level of description of the comic. But a significant proportion go beyond to discuss the implications of their description. And where they do, a pattern surfaces – and certainly hardly any of their comments conflict with this pattern. *Action* was friendly to them, but cynical to the world. It engaged with a punkish, working class antagonism. But it didn't just engage – it opened

eyes and minds, it made you stop and think . . . This was the power of the
stories, the 'strong narrative' (51). The good artwork, diversity of stories, the
connection with current films were all grist to this mill. 'Art and violence and
futuristic settings' (9) were what made it all so enjoyable.

Casual reading

Not so the CasRegs. In subtle ways the picture changes. The descriptive overlaps
are there. Good artwork, exciting stories, action-packed, violent: these are common denominators. But when they step outside to evaluate, make comparisons,
connections, a gap opens. CasRegs seem to occupy a more middle-class world.
Where Committeds saw authority as that which *Action* opposed, I could find
no clear sign of this with the CasRegs. Instead authority is *parents*: 'It was a comic
you secretly felt your parents wouldn't want you to read' (24); 'seedy realism
your parents wouldn't like' (103). It was a 'guilty pleasure' (19), and a 'morbid
fascination' (98). One dismissed it as 'just part of growing up' (52) – a very adult
judgement on his past self. There was even a sense that maybe *Action* wasn't
attractive in itself. It was because adults wouldn't approve: 'the fact that it was
criticised made it feel 'naughty'' (53).

Any claim by the comic to incorporate a moral is discounted: 'it didn't
moralise' (55), 'didn't take any moral stance whatsoever' (19); 'the writers just
pulled out all the stops' (25). There are two extremes of response to this amorality: either it 'seemed to glorify violence and brutality' (53), 'was quite sick and
gruesome' (57) – 'appealing to violent instincts' (71); or 'its mindless violence
became hilarious' (69). But notice the common denominator: either way *Action*
is pretty mindless. To the Committeds, typically, it was intelligent and imaginative. The CasRegs prevaricated; they 'looked forward to it, a 'proper' boys'
paper' (29), but 'worried about its extreme nature' (15). For certain, though,
there was 'not much thinking involved' (11) (though one or two did think it
'more intelligently written' than other comics, eg, 28).

Who did *Action* appeal to according to the CasRegs? 'Mindless yobs and kick
hunters (like me at the time)' (109), 'a boy who wants excitement mixed with
a good laugh' (114), 'young, imaginative, probably slightly warped' (122),
'screwed-up pubescent, potential football hooligans' (133). These self-mocking
descriptions are one end of a spectrum: the badness of *Action* is virtually dismissed as a 'phase'. At the other end it was something to worry about: 'impressionable boys' (18), 'boys with Airfix soldiers' (50), 'quiet boys with aggressive
fantasy lives' (3): 'I think they wanted people (males) who found mindless
violence exciting and could put themselves into the stories, eg, *Kids Rule OK*' (69).

Either the picture of reader is very bland ('your average schoolkid' (38), 'the
adventure TV generation' (100)); or it stresses vulnerability ('someone who
was impressionable' (56)) and danger ('boys who get a kick out of violence'

(60)). In part, this parallels Ien Ang's findings in a very different context.[10] Ang looked at how audiences talked about the pleasures of watching *Dallas*. She delineates one group who adopt the language of mass culture critics to state their fascinated dislike ('cheap', 'crude', 'shallow'). But the analogy will not work entirely. For Ang's viewers did dislike and criticise *Dallas* but watched it despite. Even ten years on only a small minority of my CasRegs accept the standard criticisms of *Action*. I think their view reflects a *genuine difference in the way they related to the comic at the time.*

For it is not the Committeds who talk of losing themselves in the comic, or whose answers reveal that as a possibility. It is the CasRegs who come closest to this. 'You seem to become involved with the characters' (52); 'you could identify with the heroes' (50). Such remarks are not common, but they are only to be found among the CasRegs. Where the Committeds place *Action* as Punkish, as anti-authority, and as intelligent, provoking thought, CasRegs turn instead to phrases like 'mindless', 'appealing to base instincts', and 'morbid fascination'. As *comic* they can agree; as *social document*, they evaluate it quite divergently.

Agenda for *Action*

There is a suggestive pattern in these responses. *Action's* committed readership located itself in a way that its more casual readership did not. A number of *Action's* committed readers felt befriended by it and used the comic as a way of working out ideas about the world. Others of course simply read the stories as stories, and made no connections outside. The uncommitted who link the comic to outside contexts locate themselves as children, guiltily enjoying something risky. This not only throws light on the quantitative results I cited earlier, but also sits up and begs for two final acts of interpretation. Neither is directly warranted by the questionnaires; on the other hand nothing contradicts them. Let them stand as possibilities which the rest of the book may help to give substance to.

Action invited a commitment which challenged notions of childhood and subordination. As a result the more committed the readers, the more they saw *Action* as more than just a comic, telling unusual stories. They saw it also as a social document. In this they connected its goriness with its anti-authority stance. Or better, the bloodthirstiness takes on the meaning of being anti-authority. This is because the stories take the form of *melodramas of social and political cynicism.*

The more this happens, the more likely readers are to relate to the comic as to a friend. The implication of this is that they have a complicated *social* relationship to it. There is a kind of dialogue between comic and readers in which the comic is seen as having a personality. The implications of this need pondering.

They relate to an argument first put forward by Horton and Wohl who suggested that audiences have a 'parasocial' relation to the mass media, especially ones of a certain kind.[11] If we are to understand the medias' potential for influence, we need a theory that begins from this. This will be quite different from the usually-assumed view that the media work to 'take us over' and make us helpless in the face of their messages.

Apart from this large suggestion, there are some other more local issues which can form an agenda for the rest of this study.

1. We have seen with *Action* a disturbing gap between the language deployed by critics ('violence', 'invasion of childhood') and what is revealed by the comic itself, and its readers ('politics', 'thinking friend'). We need to explore this in several ways. We must look further at the comics and how they offer a set of expectations or a 'contract' to readers. And we must study the sources of critics' conceptualisations to find out how their (mis)readings are brought about.

2. But looking at the comics has not proved easy. Among other things the case of *Action* has suggested that some stories may be more 'typical' than others. This would seem to imply that there are rules governing story-construction. How can we know what these are?

3. With all its limitations, my study of *Action*'s readers has suggested that we may need to distinguish among all readers those who are 'naturally' drawn to a comic. Their relationship to it will be markedly different from other people's.

4. To understand *Action* it has turned out to be necessary to have a particular kind of knowledge of its history: under what circumstances it came to be produced, the requirements and constraints on it, and how readers were able to relate to it. That history was both a history of comics, of publishers and their organisational practices, and of wider social and political processes. To this and other 'agenda items' the rest of the book is devoted.

Ye 'orrible 'aunted 'ouse

Between 10 March 1973 and 1 October 1977, a strip (or a 'set', as the producers often call it) appeared in two IPC comics. First in *Shiver & Shake* (until 5 October 1974), then in *Whoopee!*, *Scream Inn* had a four-and-a-half year run. Only in one respect was this juvenile strip atypical, but this special quality offered me a unique opportunity to study a comic strip's relation to its audience.

Scream Inn's atypicality consisted in this. The Inn, a grotesque Gothic hostelry, held a haunted room in which no one had managed to stay the whole night. A challenge: any creature that did succeed in staying the night would win a million pounds! But just to make sure no one did, the Inn had a set of ghoulish characters, ranging from a Dracula-lookalike Innkeeper to an animated skeleton and a devilish woodworm, who spent their nights scaring away the visitors. Readers of the comic were invited to write in suggesting challengers. By happy accident when I interviewed him in 1982, Bryan Walker, the artist for the set, still had one complete batch of children's proposals, on a form from the comic. 618 of these were there for me to analyse. This serendipity gave me access to a kind of information rarely available about children's relations with a comic. These forms were a product of their *actual*, *live* relations with the comic, not of an artificial recall, brought out by interview or questionnaire that I had to use with *Action* readers. Their very 'uncontrolled' production is what makes them so valuable. You might say that they are thus under the control of the ordinary relations that children will have with a comic of this kind.

I interviewed artist Bryan Walker, the scriptwriter Cliff Brown, and Roy Davies the strip's originator. During *Scream Inn*'s history, several thousand children must have written in, making suggestions, though there is no reason to think that it was the most popular strip in the comic. The idea was for an atmospheric strip, a bit evil (within bounds),[1] involving readers. Bryan Walker had recently been working on a rival D C Thomson comic, drawing a strip called *I Spy*. This also used atmospheric drawing techniques, with large patches of black and grey, rather than the usual spare lines. He was approached to draw *Scream Inn* for IPC; and agreed. The first three issues were scripted by Roy Davies, all the remainder being done by Cliff Brown, a scriptwriter/artist living near Bath. Because Bryan and Cliff lived near each other, they were able to hold frequent script conferences; and a lot of the humour of the stories, they both recalled, resulted from mad sessions in each others' houses, as they faced the challenges the children set them.

The very first set fixed the style and mood. We see (frame (F) 1) the Inn:

'We're only here for the fear'. Up drives a boxing champ and his spiv-like manager in the fog. They decide they will have to stay overnight in the Inn. Then they see the challenge written on a board outside: 'Ye Scream Inn. One million pounds to anybody who can stay all ye night in ye Haunted Bedroom', all in mock-Gothic script. Fearless champ is sent in . . . while the manager thinks perhaps he's not tired. He'll just walk up and down outside for the night. Here (F5) is the bedroom with its four-poster bed with skulls mounted on each corner, and rats scurrying for cover. Our champ quickly converts it into a boxing ring, and challenges the ghosts to come and haunt him. In they come. The skeleton (Boney Part, as he would soon be called), drawn realistically as Bryan Walker proudly pointed out to me; an odd spectral shape like a spilled glue-pot (to be Bertie Bedsheet); a rather moth-eaten devil with tails and horns (Dennis the Devil), a second spectral figure (who became even mouldier as time went on, with a dripping body and drooping eyeballs); and a witch (Cookey). These were joined shortly by one with an axe in his removable head. But all their hauntings come to nothing – you can't scare a boxer. So he challenges them to a fight. Bertie accepts. From the centre of the (bed)ring, Champ throws a mighty right at him. The punch goes right through him and, losing his balance, the champion falls straight through the window on to the head of his manager who was pacing up and down outside, dreaming of ££££££££££s!

The first eight strips were based on editors' and scriptwriters' nominees. Besides the boxer, we had a henpecked husband, a drill sergeant, a firm of dry-rot specialists, the invisible man, a producer of horror films, a male beautician, and a whole team of girl guides. Thereafter it was readers' suggestions. Eventually it was closed by taking the suggestion of Sandra Green of Keighley (are you still out there, Sandra?), that the Innkeeper himself should try to stay the night in the Haunted Room. He did, but at great cost to himself. The other spooks, thinking he was doing them out of a job, went on strike. Carrying placards proclaiming 'We demand a fair day's haunting', and 'National Union of Webmakers', they invade the bedroom and belabour him. Bruised but victorious, he emerges in the morning to tell them he has decided to reform. He will use the £1 million to fund a new project: a sort of 'ghosts for goodness' which will go out into the world and fight baddies. It began in the next issue of Whoopee!, entitled The Spooktacular Seven. But the magic had gone. Perhaps the hearts of the artist and scriptwriter weren't in it.[2] Perhaps the change destroyed the special relation with readers. Anyway, it didn't last long. With its passing, Bertie, Dennis, Cookey, spiders, toads, woodworms and all were finally laid to rest.[3]

The readers respond

What characters appeared to challenge the Inn and its denizens for the £1

Table 4 Readers' responses to *Scream Inn*
(upper figure in each group: number; lower figure: percentage)

Categories of characters	Comic sets	Readers' suggestions	Age 6-7	8-9	10	11	12-13	14-16	No age given
Other characters from the comic	16	220	7	47	61	55	41	6	3
	7.3	35.7	34	30	38	39	36	33	
Strip-related characters	8	22	0	5	8	4	5	0	0
	3.6	3.5	0	3	5	2	5	0	
Other media characters	12	69	3	18	18	14	12	4	0
	5.5	11.2	13	12	11	10	11	22	
Legendary figures	37	29	1	8	5	7	6	1	1
	16.5	4.6	4	5	3	5	4	6	
Real named individuals	3	49	1	15	12	12	6	2	1
	1.4	8	4	10	8	8	5	11	
Personality types	7	3	0	0	1	1	1	0	0
	3.2	0.5	0	0	1	1	1	0	
Activity types	128	95	2	26	21	25	18	2	1
	58.2	15.3	8	17	13	18	16	11	
Animals and other non-humans	8	3	0	1	0	1	1	0	0
	3.6	0.5	0	1	0	1	1	0	
Self and/ or friends	–	78	4	16	23	16	17	2	0
	–	12.6	16	10	15	11	15	11	
No character suggested	–	48	5	18	10	7	6	1	1
	–	7.8	21	12	6	5	5	6	
TOTALS	219	618	23	154	159	142	113	18	9*
	100	100	3.7	29.9	25.7	23	18.3	2.9	1.2

* This includes two whose suggestions were illegible.

million? Analysing 218 out of the 239 editions, I divided them into eight categories:

    a. *Other characters from the comic* – for example, Sweeney Toddler, Ghoulgetters Ltd, or Scared Stiff Sam;

    b. *Strip-related characters* – for example, the Innkeeper's twin, the artist, the editor, the *Whoopee!* office boy, or 'a reader';

    c. *Other media figures* – for example, the Six Million Dollar Man, Dr Doolittle, Kojak, or a comic superhero;

    d. *Legendary figures* – for example, Cinderella, Good King Wenceslas, Sherlock Holmes, or Robin Hood;

    e. *Real named individuals* – for example, Florence Nightingale, or Edward Lear;

    f. *Personality types* – for example, a normal person, an absolutely beautiful female ghost, or a practical joker;

    g. *Activity types* – for example, a plumber, a tax inspector, or a pop star;

    h. *Animals and other non-humans* – for example, a boxing kangaroo, a pet tortoise, a robot, or a man from Outer Space.[4]

Readers' applications generated two other categories, which couldn't occur in the strips themselves:

    i. *Self, or friends;*

    j. *No character suggested.*

These resulted, I think, from the way the application panel appeared in the comic, which read 'I would like . . . . to try to stay the night in the Haunted Room'. Some applicants wrote their own, or friends' names, in the space. Others left it blank. I decided to keep the latter separate, on a suspicion that they might reflect a revealing misunderstanding of the task. So it proved.

Table 4 shows the distribution of these categories within the issues, compared with their distribution within the children's applications which I had. These are broken down by age. As with the statistics for *Action*, I don't want to make exaggerated claims for what can be learnt from these. Still, I want to draw what I can from them, because of the fact that, unusually, they came out of children's living relations with the comic. Bearing in mind all the obvious qualifications, then, none the less what can be gleaned from these statistics?

The figures do show a considerable constancy in percentages across age-groups, even when the samples are getting dangerously small and could be heavily bucked by one or two more or less responses. This consistency is quite remarkable. I double-checked this by looking, under *Activity Types*, at the range of actual nominations. Might the younger children be working with a narrower range of suggestions, more limited lists of possible challengers for the Inn? In fact, there was no noticeable difference betwen the 6-9 year-olds, and the 13-16 year-olds in this respect. A very young reader was as likely to propose an exorcist, a gambler, a gardener or a ghost train owner as one of the oldest. I venture to suggest that this indicates children picking up quickly, and holding on to, a sense of what the *point* of the strip is, and therefore what sorts of character are appropriate. The one exception to this stability is itself revealing; this is in the *No Character Suggested* category. There is a noticeable decline in the number who put nothing as ages increase, suggesting that this was at least partly a function of readers' knowledge of how to complete a form like this.

Given this, though, the stability elsewhere is all the more noticeable. Age was apparently no barrier to more sophisticated responses. Even though (as I shall show later) certain characters, notably the ones I have called 'strip-related', produced much more complex story-lines, this does not affect children's willingness to propose, let us say, the Innkeeper's Auntie.

Perhaps the most striking statistic is the gap between what the comic itself had been offering children, and their own preferred choice. (Bear in mind that this batch was sent in after the strip had been running for three years.) While 58.3% of the sets printed were of Activity Types (your GPO engineers, headmasters, soldiers, scientists and deep sea divers), children's most common choice (35.7%) was for other characters from the comic itself. I am going to argue that this relates closely to the way *Scream Inn* presents itself as inhabiting a distinct 'comic world'.

Note also that seventy eight children, again spread evenly across the ages, suggested themselves or friends (though with an interesting tendency for the younger ones to propose relatives or friends – 'my ugly sister', for instance – more than themselves). Not once had the 'Good Artist' allowed a child to be the challenger (though he did always mention the name of the successful child). The nearest he came was in *Shiver & Shake* (26 May 1973) where a doctor had been nominated by Suzanne Bennett of Birmingham. Suzanne was pictured as accompanying the doctor; but always in silhouette, never as an active agent in the story. The only other significant example was when Clifford D'Souza of York (12 May 1973) suggested a Man from Outer Space. Such a one arrived and settled in, and was much taken with the unparalleled beauty of the spooks – they were lovely! In despair and the grey light of dawn, the Innkeeper sent for Clifford to present the £1 million the Alien was clearly going to win. But when the boy (again in silhouette) appeared in the door, our Man from Beyond fled in terror. The boy was so ugly! With no encouragement, then, from the producers, some children felt easy enough in their relation with the strip that 12% of all ages suggested themselves or their friends as challengers. This raises for thought what sorts of relationship young readers have with a strip like this. Cliff Brown suggested to me that it was simply all a matter of greed. The story was based around the desire to win money, and kids writing in could fantasise about winning a million pounds. That answer has an attractive simplicity, and I don't dismiss it. But there are good reasons to think it is only part. For a start, there is the amount. £1 million is not only a sum beyond the meaningful experience of a child. It is also just the sum that fits childhood mythology and takes meaning from there ('I bet you a million pounds that . . .').

I am going to propose an interpretation of these statistics. But for that to make much sense, we need to look first at the form of the stories themselves.

Vladimir Propp reads Scream Inn

In order to begin deciphering the strips, I want to try out the approach developed by the Russian theorist of folk-tales Vladimir Propp.[5] In Chapter 6, I will discuss Propp's ground-breaking work more generally. Here, I want only to take the method, and see what it might reveal. Propp analysed a group of Russian folk-tales to show that, underneath apparently very different specific contents, a single and repeating form was present. So 'a dragon kidnaps the king's daughter' would for Propp be formally identical with 'a witch steals the merchant's ring'. Each contains four elements: a villain, a loss, a family figure, and a valuable item. Propp defined a set of *functions* for his kind of folk-tales (which he termed 'wondertales'). A 'function' was any component of the tale, considered abstractly, which is necessary for the unfolding of the tale. He claimed to find thirty one, and only that number, which had to occur in strict sequence.

This is not a study of folk-tales, though perhaps there are important analogies between them and comics. But I believe that it is possible, with care, to transfer Propp's method. For comics and folk-tales are certainly alike in two respects. They are both examples of 'formulaic literature'. That is, they embody repeating patterns; and they are not in the main produced by 'named authors' whose particular authorship is stamped on the stories. A method that throws light on folk-tales, then, might just prove useful on our material. Let's try Propp out, and postpone discussion of his theory and the objections that have been voiced against him, until we see what comes out of the trial.

Propp says that first one has to determine the 'initial situation' of a tale. Phrases such as 'Once upon a time . . .' or 'Faraway in the distant kingdom . . .' are typical to folk-tales, followed by an introduction to the characters and their problems. In folk-tales these settings create a no-place, and no-time geography for the tale. That is not quite right for *Scream Inn*. Here the initial situation really is one; it is a built-in challenge. Here is an Inn, with a notice-board outside, promising a prize of £1 million to any guest who can manage to stay the night.

We might then define the initial situation of *Scream Inn* as

(A) *A Challenge: do something absurd to achieve the impossible.* That the challenge is absurd is clear. Here is an Inn in which it is nigh on impossible to stay. If someone tries to be a guest here, they will meet mock-terrible dangers, to stop them doing what Inns are supposed to be for: staying in.

In the layout of the strip, we are not always reminded of the initial situation until the second function is fulfilled: that is

(B) *Arrival of a challenger.* The frame containing the notice of challenge was always there. Bryan Walker had copies of it printed full front, and slanted left or right, for quick pasting on. Sometimes the frame containing it would not occur until well into the set. But wherever it appears, the episode doesn't really begin until the challange has been formally taken up. Like a mediaeval knight blowing the horn outside the giant's palace, you are not a challenger until the rituals are complete.

In fact, the acceptance of challenge went a stage further. You did not properly count as challenging until in situ within the Haunted Room. When, for example, a Man with a Saucepan on His Head came to challenge (in the hope that a man who can't see the ghosts can't be scared by them), he was adjudged to have 'broken the rules'. So the haunters broke them too, by leading him to the local zoo instead of the Haunted Bedroom. He of course fooled himself by thinking the animal noises were made by the ghosts. Morning brought disillusion and disappointment! (9 November 1974)

Function (B) concerns the arrival of a challenger and completion of the rituals. I have already distinguished eight kinds of challenger. In every case, the producers chose characters for their ability to have a particular way of answering the challenge. Cliff Brown explained that the first thing they did, was to look for a 'weak spot' in any proposed character. This involved looking for a way in which that character would inevitably behave, and then finding a flaw in it.

Many found novel ways to be brave. William Shakespeare decided to write a new play with the ghosts as characters (19 March 1977). The Girl Guider trained the ghosts for their First Aid badges by making them take the axe out of Sam's head (28 April 1974). The nervous soldier brought his tank with him, and then hid inside it (14 July 1974). Many more were picked for their apparent fearlessness, or because their way of behaving seemed to negate anything the haunters might throw at them. The Knight in Armour (10 November 1973), Dracula (1 September 1974) and school bully (5 July 1975) were all examples of unfrightenability; while Rip van Winkle (31 January 1976), Sherlock Holmes (8 December 1973) and the Invisible Man (who visited twice – 7 April 1973, and 23 July 1977) would never notice the threats in the first place. Sometimes the challengers turn the tables, and reduce the ghosts to some form of quivering heap. Edward Lear, for example, reduced Bertie, Dennis and Sam to helpless laughter by making up limericks about them (10 September 1977).

Challengers then are marked by their potential ability to disrupt every attempt to get them out. Be it Little Jack Horner who puts his nose in his corner and refuses to come out, or Uri Geller who makes everything fall to pieces, including Boney's skeleton, their manic involvement with their own nature makes them apparently undefeatable.

Function (B) then, provides the *field of possibilities of action*, and thus points to the next one.

(C) *Struggle*. A great deal of most strips is taken up with this third function. It is a manoeuvring over the field of possibilities. Each character has strictly delineated actions. They can do nothing that isn't already 'written into their job description'. It would be inconceivable, for example, that a character should behave multidimensionally. The surgeon (26 May 1973) could not take an interest other than an anatomical one in the situation. The nervous soldier could not take tranquillisers (and not just because IPC would never have allowed such a thing to be shown) in order to calm himself. Only the dry-rot firm (31 March 1973) could interest itself in the nature of the room.

The Struggle, then, will give the appearance that the character is about to win. This is important. For the duration of this function, the haunters must be thwarted. They don't have a chance. A paradoxical case shows this nicely, where the challenger was a coward (16 February 1974). The scene opens with a terrified fat man trying to back away from the Inn, but being propelled forward by a small girl. 'Oh, p-please Sarah Jampel, don't make me stay in that place! Let's go home to B-barcroft Avenue in London!' No mercy. 'Don't argue with me! I suggested that a coward stayed at Scream Inn, and I need a pound – so get in there and try for that million quid, you great jelly!'

Is this an easy one for the haunters? It looks like it. He swoons at merely being asked to sign the visitors' book in red ink. He doesn't like climbing the stairs to the Haunted Room, because there are no bannisters. He won't stay on his own, because he's scared of the dark. This is a bit of a poser for the Innkeeper: 'I'm a bit worried about this one, boys! You'll have to go easy with him or you might literally *scare him to death!*' The ghosts decide their only safe way is to stiffen his backbone a bit before they scare him out. How do you do that with someone who wouldn't say Boo to a goose? Simple. Get a goose. After much cringing and shrinking, he hesitantly whispers 'B-b-b-boo?'. The much-affronted goose lets a hideous SQUAWK! – which terrifies not only the coward, but all the ghosts, right out of the Inn.

Notice what has happened. In order to be a challenger at all, he had to be given a position from which he might win. Therefore the phantoms have to change sides, and help him. Having been on his side, they have to share his fate. 'Come back, you faint-hearted phantoms!', cries a despairing Innkeeper as they flee.

(D) *The challenger defeats him/herself* At the climax of the struggle, a means is found so the challenger loses. Sometimes it might appear superficially that the Innkeeper or one of the others causes the defeat, but this is misleading. Take, for example, the Sergeant-Major episode (27 August 1977). Here the Sergeant-Major is defeated by the spooks' overpolishing of the floor. He has had them on polishing as a punishment for slipshod haunting. They sneakily polish the soles of his boots – well, he did say to polish *everything* . . . Then he orders a parade. Unable to keep his feet, he departs through the window ('Quite a polished performance!' chuckles the Innkeeper). Here the spooks act as *agents* of the challenge to enable the challenger to defeat himself. There's no essential difference between this case, and an earlier Sergeant-Major who lost through teaching them to stamp when coming to attention (24 March 1973). He leaves straight through the woodwormy dry-rotten floor! It is the very character of the challenger that creates defeat. Every defeat is immediately an outcome of the absurd field of possibilities generated by their character. Of course this depends on the virtuosity of the scriptwriter on the particular occasion.

Take the Edward Lear episode as a test case. The spooks have been reduced to helpless laughter, and the Innkeeper alone is maintaining the struggle. His solution is to make up a limerick himself:

> 'An Innkeeper said with a grin,
> That he makes all his guests leave 'Scream Inn'.
> Some leave by the door . . .
> And some through the floor,
> So their chances of winning are thin!'

And therewith he pulls a lever that opens a trapdoor under Lear, who picks himself up outside and leaves muttering 'Let me see now – what rhymes with scheming, sneaky, rotten cheat?' Why didn't the Innkeeper just pull the lever? We immediately realise how the different the strip would then be. There would be no relationship between struggle and defeat. It would seem arbitrary. On this occasion, perhaps, the link between character and method of defeat is a bit mechanical. But the incidental humour of the limericks is so good that it doesn't matter. The important thing is the use of the character's own characteristics to occasion their defeat. The ghosts are merely devious mirrors of the challengers' weaknesses.

(E) *The initial situation is reasserted*. This last function may not be distinguished within the text. But it is still distinct, and must be fulfilled, even if covertly. In the early days, each set had a final frame inviting readers to send in their suggestions, and an end-caption asking 'Who will turn up at *Scream Inn* next week?' Later, it was always clear that defeat did not end the matter. It was also a reopening of the challenge. Hence the last set, where the Innkeeper finally won, had to mark the closure of Inn as a whole.

We have, then, an initial situation and four functions, as follows:
(A) Initial situation: an absurd open challenge;
(B) The arrival of a challenger, and ritual of challenge;
(C) Struggle, with apparent victory to the challenger;
(D) The challenger defeats him or herself;
(E) The initial situation is reasserted.
There are further things to be said about these functions. But as we explore

them, they begin to take us beyond the limits of a Proppian analysis.

1. There is an inherent circularity in the strip-form. Unlike Propp's folk-tales, it is vital to *Scream Inn* that there is no development. In folk-tales there are transitions, passings beyond the initial situation to which there can be no return; almost, a growing up. That is why so many of them end with marriages, with mounting thrones, or winning prizes. The tales tell of tests the hero(ine)s undergo, and then arrive somewhere. In *Scream Inn* we are frozen within a narrative circle. This freezing is achieved by the *situational logic* of the strip. Let me illustrate with two examples:

In *Shiver & Shake* (16 June 1973) the challenger was the editor of the comic himself. The editor was delighted at the idea, stamps and addresses himself, and hands himself to the postman. Arriving at the Inn, strangely, no struggle apparently takes place. The Innkeeper's mob wine and dine him, as an old friend, and send him merrily to bed, where he spends a happy night in contemplation of money leaping a five-bar gate like sheep. No struggle, no hauntings, nothing. Descending in the morning, he triumphantly claims his million. 'Heh, heh, and heh again, sir! That's a good 'un! Better write to the editor – he's the one who pays up, not me! Even more hehs!' Why no struggle? Because the initial challenge was a contradiction-in-terms. The logic of the situation was that he was struggling with himself! Winning would be losing, and losing would be winning.

Let us note, then, two points needing more examination. There is a kind of unity or completeness in these stories in which the parts are mutually dependent. What kind of unity is this? Second, a character like the editor, who is elsewhere a real person, can appear within the comic. But on entering, becomes subject to the logic of the story. We need to ask about the relationship between the real and the fictional character.

2. Look now at the other example of an apparent defeat. In the 17 November 1973 *Shiver & Shake*, Jane Winwood's (Shropshire) suggestion was taken up that a wizard should attempt to stay the night. The two daft wizards, Treacle and Brimstone, turned up from *Wizards Anonymous* in the *Shake* section of the comic (notionally separate from the *Shiver* section which held the Inn). As the wizards levitate him, the Innkeeper scowls and mutters: 'Right! In you go! And if you think a couple of Shakers can put it over on an innful of Shiverers, you've another think coming! Heh, heh, and heh again!' Brave words, indeed, and struggle commences. The wizards are planning what they'll do with the £1 million – they'll return to their own time, back to Merlin's Camelot, by building a time-machine. Haunting begins, but with a quick 'Allagazoom!', the wizards transform the spooks into a motley array of headless toad, pussy cat, billy goat, jelly baby and filleted kipper. It's no contest, the Haunters are utterly routed, and – Shakers or no – the Wizards have won! The Innkeeper sheds terrible tears as he shells out. But as they leave, laden, he hears them planning their

time machine, and a wicked look crosses his face. 'Time machine! *Time machine!* That could be the solution to my problem! Methinks I'll nip over to the *Wizards Anonymous* pages and see what they're up to! *Are you coming with me, readers? Heh, heh!.'* And there the episode ended.

And we have to turn the pages, literally, to the other strip. There the triumphant Treacle and buoyant Brimstone head for the shop to buy the parts for their time machine. But who's this, weeping (crocodile) tears in the corner? The Innkeeper, of course. Taking pity, poor fools, the Wizards offer to employ the penniless spook to help build their machine ('More hehs!'). It is quickly built, wound up – being clockwork, of course – and the magic spell is said backwards (well, the shop only had clocks that go forwards). But they haven't spotted the Innkeeper creeping up ('Lots of really evil hehs!'); and even as they press the button, he resets the timer from 1000 years to 36 hours – and they find themselves back at the evening before, just about to attempt their night at the Inn. So here they are, again, arriving at the Inn: 'Jane Winwood of Whitchurch in the fair county of Shropshire hath suggested a wizard should try . . .' But what's this? The pattern's broken! This time the Inn is surrounded with placards: 'Closed for staff holidays', 'Business not at all as usual', 'Cook on strike', 'Under quarantine' . . .

It was a false ending. The struggle merely transferred to another place, time, and form. The nature of the challengers set this up – they were wizards, attempting time-travel, so must be defeated by self-inflicted time-travel. In the second phase, they are literally building their own defeat. A natty and unusual solution, even for this innovative strip. But the innovations offer us more markers for further investigation. Note these as: the curious ability to cross between comic-strips – at once so obvious and easy, and yet worth a pause. Imagine its equivalent, that Shakespeare had, halfway through *A Mid-summer's Night Dream*, had a guest appearance of King Lear . . . Of course not, we say. But on what do we base our knowledge of this appropriateness/inappropriateness? Note also that convention used at the false ending, where the Innkeeper invites us, the readers, to accompany him to another strip. This prompts a closer look at the strip's relations with its readers.

3. Actions take place regardless of motivations. This parallels Propp exactly:

> Thus once again we come upon the phenomenon that the will of personages, their intentions, cannot be considered an essential motif for their definition. The important thing is not what they want to do, nor how they feel, but their deeds as such, evaluated and defined from the viewpoint of their meanings for the hero and for the course of the action. Here we obtain the same picture as that in analysing motivations: the feelings of a dispatcher (be they hostile, neutral or friendly) do not influence the course of the action. (p. 81)

On 27 April 1974, the challenger was a disguise artist. The spooks don't know.

As each goes up to do its bit of scaring, it's confronted by a different figure. First, he's a relative of Bertie Bedsheet; but by the time Bertie arrives, he's become a bomb-throwing spy. Confused, they all go together, and his special talent is revealed. Boney challenges him: could he disguise himself even as a great fat ugly toad? of course, he just happens to have that disguise in his bag. But the moment he dons it, enters Cookie. 'Tiddles! What are you doing in here?' Mistaking the disguised artist for her pet, she berates him and boots him downstairs. Of course the other spooks planned it – but precisely because they couldn't just kick him out on their own – that would be cheating. It is not cheating because Cookie doesn't know what she's doing. She performs the function without understanding that she is. To this extent, then, Propp's theorem applies perfectly.

But our spooks are not ciphers. True, they don't need a motive; they just act, and the inevitable happens. But sometimes they had a go at thwarting it. Consider the episode where a retired ghost turns up. They positively rebel against having to get rid of him – they feel too sorry for him. Again, it takes action by the Innkeeper to put matters right (31 May 1975). Or recall the episode already cited where the coward is almost nursed by the spooks – and he and they together are made to flee as a result. In fact, whenever they show independent motivation, they are as likely as not to be on the wrong side, and must share in the consequences. Which raises the question: just what is the relationship between the characters, and the formula of the story?

Note also how the Innkeeper can never lack for an idea. A good example is the way the Innkeeper handled the writer of Scream Inn who turned up in Shiver & Shake (7 July 1973) at the invitation of Mark Rothwell. (Mark had asked for a thriller-writer, but as the writer says (nose in air): 'Well, I'm a thriller-writer, aren't I?') 'Here you are, matey! You can spend the night in your own creation!' says the cross-looking Innkeeper, who has just been written as 'standing on his head, singing a silly song', and of course had had to do just that! 'Crumbs! What a grotty room!' says the writer, 'whatever made me dream this up?'. He quickly reimagines it as a luxury hotel room. When the ghost come haunting, he rewrites them as beautiful dancing girls (they have mixed feelings about this. . .). The Innkeeper is getting desperate, so he asks: 'What would happen if you wrote 'Scream Inn never existed at all'?' Unable to resist a challenge, the writer seizes his pad and tries it. The next frame is no frame, just an empty area with the writer falling through it. And in a 'Thinks' balloon above his very cross head, the Innkeeper appears: 'This is the Innkeeper speaking to you from deep in your imagination! Heh, heh, and heh again! What fool thought of a fool that made a fool out of you? (Even more hehs!)' And shedding pages as he goes, the writer rushes off the side of the page, yelling 'Bah! I'll make you lot suffer for this, next week!' (See Fig. 9 for a full reproduction of this strip.)

To me, this was the apex of Scream Inn. Others are funny, but this was

Fig 9 The scriptwriter's set, from *Shiver & Shake*, 7 July 1973. © IPC Magazines 1974.

exceptional. Having to his chagrin been manipulated, the Innkeeper manipulates his manipulator to use the idea of manipulation to manipulate himself into self-defeat. That is what I call neat! But that solution shows a real complexity over the reality/unreality of the Inn. Perhaps it is atypical, because of the unusual relation the 'writer' has to the story. Perhaps, none the less, we can use it to learn more about the 'formula' of the story, and its relations to readers.

4. Whatever a challenger does is done to her or him in return. It is as if a proper *Scream Inn* story contains a *balance*. But it is more than this. A Girl Guider can be got rid of by being sent off on a badge hunt, a character from a painting can be 'framed', Sweeney Toddler (the hyperdigestive comic child) can be propelled out by a giant burp. But beyond that, the strip also integrates as much else as it can. Language, for example. The disguise artist set, for example, rounds off with dreadful puns that are more than puns – they are word plays about the challenge: 'Heh, heh, and heh again! *Dis guy's* certainly getting *toad* off by cookey – just as planned!' A typical feature.

Or consider the *Whoopee!* (16 October 1976) set with an unusual challenger – a terrifying piglet, sent by Ann Lock of Croxley Green. The handling of this was delicious . . . Piggy arrives; but his initial sweet appearance turns out sour as the Innkeeper has to flee up a rope, and the other spooks discorporate through the nearest wall. A very one-sided struggle ensues. Yet little jokes are preparing us for what will come. As piggy settles luxuriantly on to the bed, on the floor a local spider burps loudly. 'Don't be a pig, Sidney!', scolds the other. With the gruesome grunter ensconced, the haunters refuse to go haunting (notice the independent motivation coming in). Piglet rings for room service. 'W-w-what can w-we do for m-my swinish sir?' 'I'm hungry and wish to 'eat like a pig' – let me see the menu.'

Now regular readers knew that at the beginning a menu was usually posted outside the Inn. An array of dastardly delicacies would be listed, including Birds' eyes, Fish and Fingers, Vampire Stake and Gang Greens, and Slime Juice. Particular characters got their own appropriate listings: the Laughing Policeman was offered a pot of tea-hee-hee, while a spaceman was informed that 'Launcheon Vouchers' were acceptable. When pernicious piglet arrived, the notice was covered by a sign declaring 'To be announced later – Cookie's in a tizz'. Guess what she came up with now: bacon sandwiches, ham salad, pork pies, pigs' trotters . . . A rampaging porker chases the Innkeeper – right out of the room and the Inn.

I want to argue that the best sets are those where the greatest number of aspects have been fused in this balance and unity of the story. Humorous touches such as these are not incidental, but incremental. They add to the feeling of closure. Obviously, the inventiveness of writer and artist varies from set to set. But the humour they bring in is no longer just humour. It is integral to the form and meaning of the whole. I stress this because I want to counter the obvious reaction, that these stories are just absurd, or just funny. On the contrary, the humour and absurdity are an organising feature of the form. The artistry consists in mobilising them effectively. What comes from this mobilisation? In the end, what kind of absurd unity and closure does *Scream Inn* offer?

Beyond Propp

Out of thinking about Proppian functions at the Inn, seven points have arisen:

1. It appears that there is some kind of logic in the stories. This logic determines the kinds of events which can happen. What kind of logic is this, and what is its significance?

2. The challengers have a peculiar status. Even when they are recogniseable individuals, they are transformed for the purposes of fitting the strip and its formula. What status do they thus have, and how does that status relate to their other existence?

3. In some sense *Scream Inn* creates/inhabits its own comic world, with its own geography, internal relations, and so on. How does this relate to children's 'real' world?

4. Readers are not simply external to the strip. Their relationship to it is structured by the strip itself. In what ways, and with what consequences, does the strip set a particular role for its readers?

5. The characters have to act out the functions set for them. Yet they often nearly fail, or rebel. They exist in some sort of tension with the rules of that formula. What does that tell us about the formula that rules them?

6. There is a very complex relationship in some cases between the reality and fantasy of the Inn. What does that complexity also tell us about the formula?

7. In sum, what is the significance of the tight unity of the strip, its endless variation within rigorous invariability?

It is not a kind of pedantry that makes me take this analysis slowly and by small steps. It is because I want to penetrate the *obviousness* of the strip. Not that there is more than meets the eye; it is that in meeting the eye it can too easily get taken for granted. Deconstructing the obvious is risky, with a great danger of speculative leaps. So I beg patience as I take these points singly.

1. *The logic of a comic strip.* The strips of which *Scream Inn* is representative acknowledge no stable physical laws. Characters are quite welcome to do impossible things, without explanation. They can create props, machines, and bits and pieces out of nothing. There is no contradiction in the disguise artists having a small bag, and a whole wardrobe of disguises. The Sergeant-Major not only happens to have about his person his own full kit but also all the equipment needing for polishing and blancoing. And the Innkeeper can, at no-frame's

Fig 10 The terrifying piglet set, from *Whoopee!*, 16 October 1974. © IPC Magazines 1974.

Who COULD stay the night at Scream Inn? Tell us the type of person you think might succeed . . . and we'll pay £1.00 if we write a story from your suggestion (first come first served in cases of duplication). Drop a card to "Scream Inn" at the WHOOPEE! ADDRESS!

notice, summon up a bath-on-wheels, a steamroller, what-he-wills: provided only that the logic of the story requires it.

He summons the old-fashioned steamroller because it's needed to iron the armour of a mediaeval knight. Why? Well, before they can get down to a good night's haunting, the chores must be done. Sir Stinkalot has left his armour outside the Haunted Room (he, thinking it will deter them from entering). They presume he wants it polished and pressed. And of course a steamroller will put nice sharp creases in his halberk. Brave Sir Stinkalot, waking and hearing the racket, assumes it must be a dragon, and leaps out of the room to challenge it. Poor fool (10 November 1973).

Anything is permissible provided it advances the story. The world of the Inn has no dependable laws, either physical or moral. It has only *rules*. It is important to stress that this is not the same as magic. There is no hint of surprise, or anything unusual, when the impossible occurs. Compare a *Scream Inn* situation with other, magical ones:

(a) Recall the Man From Outer Space episode (12 May 1973) whose appearance was so terrifying that the haunters couldn't bear to go near him ('I want my Mummy, bandages and all!', wailed Bertie), but who finds the ghosts a real tasty bunch. The Innkeeper goes to the phone: 'Huh! (Gripe) I'd better ring that Yorkshire twit D'Souza and tell him his money's as good as won!' In the next frame young D'Souza is knocking at the door – to terrify the alien with his rank ugliness.

(b) Compare now the fairytale *The Six Swans*, the story of a king forced to marry a witch's daughter. The new Queen is jealous, and searches out where he has hidden his six sons and one daughter. Secretly she sews magic shirts to capture them, and tracks them to their hiding place: 'When they saw that someone was coming, as usual, on the lonely path that led to their hiding place, they supposed it must be their father, so that all six ran joyfully out. But alas! as each came up, the wicked Queen threw one of the little shirts over him, and no sooner had she done that than each boy was turned into a swan which immeidately spread its great wings and, first wheeling over the castle, flew far away – over trees, seas, and mountains.'[6] And so the scene is set for the daughter to search for them and, by sewing coats of nettles for them, to rescue them.

(c) Consider finally a child's trick where the aim is to fool the eyes. A card, let's say, is produced, or something disappears – and the cry is 'It's magic!'

Three different cases of the impossible. The third is easiest. The cry 'It's magic' is a way of accentuating the mysterious surprise. It emphasises its inexplicability, and hopefully turns us away from looking for an explanation. This is the enjoyment of the impossible for its own sake. The second case is different. In folk-tales, natural laws are suspended; and magic enters as a new universe of laws. Magic is part of the moral fabric of the tale: quest, test, and rescue. We don't think to ask why the swans didn't immediately fly to their sister for help. They have to fly away (ritually, over trees, seas, and mountains) so that she can search, suffer and thus prove herself. Magic here, then, is part of a new world of moral laws.

But in our case something different happens. In one sense it is magical that Clifford D'Souza can translate from Yorkshire to the no-place of Scream Inn in one frame. But it would never occur to us to call it that. It isn't the substitution, as in fairy tales, of a new set of laws. Simply, laws are suspended. Where folk-tales use magic to remove absurdity, to conceal its possibility, these strips welcome it, and multiply it. They delight in the ridiculousness of their solutions. In folktales the absurd can happen, but will seem sad, frightening, amazing. The juvenile strips make absurdity serve a cause. A Proppian structure inheres in *Scream Inn*. And the absurd is part of the character of that structure.

2. What clues can we get from the nature of the challengers and the ghosts? We've seen already that they exist in tension with the rules. They would never heroically do what is necessary (as the little Princess does, sewing nettle shirts to rescue her brothers). They are a mockery of their roles, incompetent, easily seduced. Only the Innkeeper sticks to his last; and even he has bad moments. Consider when Kim Manvill sent an electric eel to the hotel (1 June 1974). It's all a bit of a shock for them when they try to tie it in knots. In despair at its size and power, the Innkeeper plugs a light into it to write the cheque for £1 million – and it subsides to the floor in a heap. It was a Japanese transistorised eel, and the batteries are drained! The last frame shows a twenty-foot-long parcel being posed in the pillar box that has (magically) appeared outside the inn. (And one local snake says to the other: 'They did my uncle up like that when he joined the army and got posted overseas.')

The rules determine the events, but the characters make a hash of following the rules. Often, it is their very incompetence that guarantees the rules. They would never weakly submit, or bravely pursue. Things happen with an absurd fate-like assurance, no matter what they do.

3. Where does it all take place? It has its own absurd geography. Bryan Walker told me with (justifiable) pride that the Inn was drawn with great care to continuity. But this didn't stop bus-stops appearing outside on occasion, or cars managing to drive to it through the bogs outside. The Inn is simultaneously very close to us, and far off. It is untouchable by anything in readers' ordinary lives. Yet characters can be there in a trice. It is as though the Inn occupied a place in a world parallel with our own, always near at hand, yet requiring special means to gain access. Reaching it, you don't altogether leave behind what you were. There are still corporation dustmen, or teachers, or interior decorators trying to behave as always. In short, it is a world in itself, a comic world, which ordinary people can visit with ease – but at a price. The price is

the shedding of all individuality, and the loss of all control over one's own fate.

4. The geography, then, and the transformation of characters as they enter the world of *Scream Inn* are already indicators of the kind of relationship readers may have with it. It helps to think of this as being like a conversation. Although characters may not often look directly out and 'speak to us' (a device that is, though, quite common in related strips), we do still regularly 'overhear' words and thoughts, as though they were intended for us. On the many occasions when the Innkeeper delivers one of his 'Heh! heh! and heh again!'s, it is as if we were being invited to join in. And always at the end, the reader is directly addressed with the revival of the challenge – who will try next week? Who might succeed?

There are two kinds of conversation here. The characters, when we hear their words and thoughts, are discussing the state of this week's struggle. The comic itself speaks of the formula and of the (im)possibility of beating it. In this tension between the characters and the formula lies our relationship.

5. The editor's challenge reveals the ambivalent status of challengers. He was not just a fantasy editor – if he had been, the end could not have worked. For it depended on the real self-defeating logic of an editor having to pay himself. No, this was the real editor, transformed and subject to the absurd logic of the strip, but with the residual relation to his origin.

The status of this parallel world can be played on. It is one among the fields of possibilities of action. This is not limited to exceptional characters like the editor. Cliff Brown, besides writing *Scream Inn*, also drew *Timothy Tester* for IPC's *Whizzer & Chips*. Timothy tested everything – to the point of destruction! In the 2 March 1974 issue, Timothy paid a visit to Scream Inn – the artists doing a special composite drawing for the occasion. Such guest appearances are not unusual – they are a form of cheap cross-advertising for the publishers. But look at the effect on the relations between 'reality' and 'fantasy', or between the inside and the outside of the strip.

Timothy Tester had an arch-sparring partner, Constable Flatfoot; at the start (F1) Flatfoot is reading *Whizzer & Chips* when out of its pages leaps Timothy with a brand new camera that he's off to test. He's on his way to *Shiver & Shake* – F2 shows him leaping into its pages (after taking a quick snap of the Constable). Blessing his luck at landing right in the *Scream Inn* pages, he sets up his equipment. The ghosts are annoyed at being interrupted in their reading of *Whizzer & Chips*. Now Timothy is easy meat for them. Having snapped the haunters to see if they really are ghosts (and therefore shouldn't show up on his film), he's persuaded to go and check if his film was OK. Once out, he'd lost.

But just opposite the Inn now, appear the *Shiver & Shake* editorial offices. Timothy calls on the editor, hoping perhaps to salvage something from his trip, by selling him a 'Creepy Creation'. These were mock-horrific drawings contributed by the late great Ken Reid to the comic's back cover, with names like 'The Venomous Vacuum from Ventnor' and 'Shiverpool Docks'. Getting the statutory £1 that real readers got for their ideas, he skips back to his own comic, where Flatfoot is awaiting him. But Flatfoot discovers that the 'Creepy Creation' was himself, snapped in mid-comic. Timothy has to depart fast, muttering: 'Ooer! I wonder if Corr! are looking for a guest!'

Though more elaborated than most, this set uses no rules that are not implicit in all the other sets. Yet look at the stunning complexity of the relations of real/imaginary in it – quite bewildering when set out formally, yet so ordinary (and so funny) to read:

a. The Constable – a comic character – appears outside his own comic, reading it.

b. Timothy comes alive out of his own pages, photographing the Constable in no-comic-land.

c. He enters another comic, as though it were another world, commenting that he is lucky to land in the right bit of it.

d. He interacts with the characters in those pages.

e. Leaving the room (part of the geography of those pages), he goes to a chemist, which is not part of the geography of those pages.

f. The editorial offices that produce those pages and that comic appear on those pages, not 100 yards from the Inn.

g. The editor of this comic meets Timothy, a character from another comic, on the pages of his comic, and buys a photo from him to put on its back page.

h. Timothy pockets £1 as though he were a normal reader of Shiver & Shake.

i. Returning through no-comic-land, he meets the Constable, still reading himself in Whizzer & Chips.

j. They both enter their comic, and discuss Timothy's visit outside.

k. Flatfoot sees the photo (as do we) that was taken outside Whizzer & Chips (except that was really on a page of Shiver & Shake) which was developed in the Haunted Bedroom of Scream Inn, and then taken to editorial office that produces Shiver & Shake (including of course Scream Inn), where the editor bought it for use on the back page of Shiver & Shake (except of course it could/would never appear) – all this now coming to a head on the pages of Whizzer & Chips, except that it is really the pages of Shiver & Shake (which we have never really left).

l. Timothy starts to run off the page of Whizzer & Chips, except that it is really Shiver & Shake, in order to try a guest appearance in Corr!.

Cor!

Each step remodels the relations of real and imaginary, playing with layer upon layer. But for all the complexity, nothing out of the ordinary is going on. And readers have not the slightest trouble following it. If this is simple, may the editor save me from complexity!

The point is that the relation between real and fantastic is not simply made complicated, it is *played with*. The formula, as the sum of the functions of the strip works by combining two styles: at one and the same time, wholly anarchic, and wholly rule-governed. Anything can happen, you can break what rules you like, the limits of rebellion and chaos are the limits of your imagination. But beware – in the end, the very same rule-breakings will return to defeat you. Is that real? Is that fantasy? Who knows? Play with the whole mad thing and find out.

6. Let me summarise what I have been saying: Scream Inn simultaneously is, and inhabits, a parallel world to ours. Anything from our world can enter it; but it immediately becomes subject to the absurd logic that rules there. It is inevitable that characters will struggle; and it is just as inevitable that they will be defeated. The manner of their defeat will be a ridiculous version of their own struggle. This world is neither near nor far: everything in it is recognisable. But it has become chaotic. Yet no matter how chaotic, still, by the end of each set, inevitability has been returned from chaos. The strip constantly acknowledges its own absurd, impossible relation to us and our world – and plays with that endlessly. No great planning goes into making sure that no one wins; the spooks do not even have much motive for wanting to defeat them, except a general dislike for giving the £1 million – though the Innkeeper on at least one occasion says he doesn't care even about that, since it is not his money anyway!

The sum total is absurdity. The child-readers of *Scream Inn* are having a daft conversation about something ridiculous in their lives. What? A crowning moment came when the Innkeeper was required to find a *normal person* to try to stay the night (23 February 1974): 'Well, no normal person would be daft enough to come here off his own bat – so I'd better go out and look for one!' And off he goes. His first stop is to ask a country man where he might find someone normal . . . 'If you'm tryin' to suggest that I ain't normal you'll 'ave this little lot up yer 'ooter!' Picking himself up, the Innkeeper proceeds more cautiously. Ah, here's a man kissing his wife goodbye as he sets out for the city. The Innkeeper follows to make sure. On the bus he looks normal. Yes, he's going to work in a bank. But no, he's pulled a gun out and is holding it up! Leave that one alone. Well, what about this nice lady with her children? 'Oh, I'm so pleased you like them', she says, 'I made them out of bits of old radios, motor cars, cocoa tins . . .' Robots, all. Suddenly, in a boxless frame, it is all too much for the Innkeeper. Ridiculous people are moving around him in all directions. He heads for the safety of Scream Inn. 'Normal person!', he mutters. 'Don't ever use those words in hear again! – I've come to the conclusion that everyone's raving bonkers!'

The mad formula of *Scream Inn* is sanity compared with the anarchic world

outside. To be a reader of Scream Inn is to have a measure of the madness of
the world outside. But it is also to be offered a possible mode of response to
that madness, a response that I call the 'trick-relation'. It is this relation, and
its operation that makes the strips transcend 'mere humour', and makes them
into a distinct genre. For the component missing from my picture of Scream
Inn is the recognition that the relation between characters and formula is a
relationship of power, and response to power. The formula exercises an absurd
power over the characters – even those who are 'on its side'; and the characters,
of course, have no option but to attempt to defeat that power. Battle, struggle
and defeat are all alike: the victory is as absurd as the struggle. In thinking out
the implications of this, we reach the politics of this genre.

The trick-relation

Look back at the strip I have reproduced, where the writer was the challenger
– suppose it hadn't ended in the way it does. Suppose for example that when
the Innkeeper sneaked in with his suggestion one of the following had
happened:
  – the scriptwriter turned him into a glass of limejuice and drank him;
  – he saw through the trick, refused to listen, and just carried on with what
he was doing;
  – he fell for the trick, fell through the 'air', but just in time managed to rewrite
the script to restore things.
  – or suppose the Innkeeper summoned the comic's editor and had the writer
thrown out. (Spend a happy few minutes inventing your own possibilities –
it's fun.)
  It wouldn't be the same kind of strip anymore, would it? Something which
is of the essence of this genre is lost in each case. It has to do with the balance
of powers. For every trick a counter-trick, for every scheme a counter-scheme.
For every absurd exercise of power, a matching one. Stories will always close
as they began, with initial situations and relations restored. Yet something is
transformed along the way.
  At this point Scream Inn can no longer provide all our answers, and for a
reason. I want to argue that these strips are about children's experience of adult
power and authority, and in themselves constitute a form of response to that
power. There is a problem about adult readings of such strips because, even
though we can enjoy them, we read them with a sophistication of response
that sets us apart from their natural audience. I invite my readers to watch the
way children will read strips of this kind. They will read with a degree of
concentration, but without a flicker of a smile. At the end, they will tell you
that they found them very funny. These strips are read by children at an age
when they are increasingly aware of forms of adult authority, both at home

and school, which must seem (and sometimes unquestionably are) arbitrary. That authority appeals to rules and proscriptions which are simply given. In engaging with these strips, children are finding ways to think these relations of power. They are learning distinctions between what can be done about authority in fantasy, and what in reality. In other words, they are gaining from these comics some of the mental resources they need to cope with the living reality of the power we adults routinely hold over their lives. These strips offer insight, and a form of control over the situation: through *the game of absurdity*.

These things are not explicit in *Scream Inn*. They are there as a set of possibilities. But *Scream Inn* existed alongside strips where these themes were much closer to the surface. In *Shiver & Shake* were to be found: *Frankie Stein* (the lad with the mad Dad), *Tough Nutt & Softy Centre* (a battle between the hard and the soft), *Fuss Pott* (the kid who always wanted his/her own way – the gender isn't totally clear, interestingly); and *Whacky* (guess who that was . . .). *Whoopee!* had *Lolly Pop* (the kid – again, almost sexless – with the mean Dad), *Sweeney Toddler* (the demonic baby), and *Scared-Stiff Sam* (a big softie). Each dealt explicitly with issues of power and adequacy, and using the same formula. But IPC's comics never dealt as openly with these matters as D C Thomson's. IPC always compromised more. D C Thomson, by contrast, precisely because of its greater secretiveness, produced comics which conspired more directly with their readers the children. And no comic more so than the *Beano*. The extent to which the names of characters from D C Thomson comics have gone on to become legends, is a testimony to the clarity, directness and completeness of their comics: Roger the Dodger, Minnie the Minx, Dennis the Menace, Beryl the Peril, the Bash Street Kids. Let me use one example, simply a personal favourite, to illustrate how the same formula can become an exercise in children's handling of the 'hidden curriculum' of adult power.

The menace of poetry

On 30 July 1979 on the front and back pages of the *Beano* appeared a set of *Dennis* which brought to the surface a number of the structuring rules of our formula. It is school – but Dennis is not there. Teacher is about to begin. 'Today I would like you to write some poetry.' Good curriculum stuff. Walter (Prince of the Softies), bootlicking as ever, asks: 'Sir! What will we write about?' just at the moment Dennis enters. Teacher looks up sternly: 'Dennis!' Walter obligingly misunderstands and starts writing a poem about him:

Dennis is a frightful scruff,
A nasty beastly horrid tough.
He's all these things, and that's the truth –
I've never known one so uncouth.

(Dennis, still half-asleep, manages to exclaim 'Cheek!'. Teacher (clapping glee-fully) lets out: 'Titter! Jolly good, Waltie – you've got the idea!' Walter: 'Simper!')
Pieface is Dennis' mate, and he's got a poem. Teacher looks dubious:

> Ah, what a simply scrumptious treat,
> Full of lovely juicy meat!
> You look so good, I think I must . . . (*and a new frame has us there*)
> Sink my gnashers in your crust!

On to the back page, and Walter is walking the fields after school, clutching his teddy: 'I've made up another poem. Perhaps I'll be poet laureate one day!':

> Oh, sweet and cuddly darling Teddy,
> You keep me cosy in my beddy.
> You are my dearest little chummy,
> My favourite pal next to my Mummy.

The sheet is surrounded with flowers and hearts.

But from behind a hedge comes a poem of a different kind. Dennis lassoes Walter ('I'm the poet lariat!', he chuckles evilly), and addresses his verse to a squealing Walter:

> O softest of the softy breed,
> You are a soppy little weed!
> So come to Dennis, puny Walter,
> Your features I would like to alter!

But as Dennis utters a terrible 'Prepare to go into orbit, Walter!' and his arm begins to whirlwind, a hand grasps him and . . . 'I've got a poem too!' It's Dennis' Dad, with his poem printed on the bottom of his slipper:

> Oh tough and springy carpet slipper,
> Do your stuff on my young nipper!
> I look on you with fond devotion –
> This will be poetry in motion!

Dennis is spreadeagled over a convenient log, Gnasher covers his eyes and . . . Walter tee-hees: 'Poetic justice, Dennis!'. Yes indeed!

This is a glorious strip, and one that I still laugh at each time I read it. But what is it about? Surely the struggle between teacher, Walter, Dennis and Dennis' Dad is over the control of language. Poems are things of the curriculum, par excellence. But they can be subverted. Because Walter is an 'ear-'ole', a teacher's pet, he plays to the curriculum's expectations by producing an anti-Dennis poem.[7] It means siding with the teacher. Dennis takes them all on, and of course loses. Or does he? Though the slipper descending with Dad's ode is testimony in one sense to his defeat, in another he has not lost. For the language has been subverted. The very fact of playing with the language, the use of poems as puns and puns as poems, is an upsidedowning of the mores of official schooling. Even if Dennis has lost, the formula has won. In the very form of his defeat is his victory.

Check. Suppose that instead of slippering Dennis with a verse, Dad had taken him aside for a severe 'talking to'. Suppose the teacher had come along at the end and advised Dennis that he'd never get a job when he grew up unless he changed his ways. (Dennis . . . grow up? You must be joking . . .) It's not just that these aren't funny any more, but that the whole story-form and expectations have changed too. No, the very form of his defeat subverts the official approach, and is a mock-defeat of authority. It is a defeat within the game-like structure of the trick.

What does this structure do, then? It offers a shape for what must be for children an experience of chaotic power. At school, a great deal of children's lives is incredibly regimented. Yet to the child there can be little logic or reason to that regimentation. It is organised chaos, an incomprehensible order. More than this, the comics' readers are at an age where they are increasingly aware of being defined, institutionally, as children. That is, they cannot be expected to understand the logic of such things, they must just submit to them. This is the 'nature of childhood'. What these strips do is to impose a 'child-like' logic on that disorder. They use the main resource acknowledged to be theirs as children, and turn it into a weapon of response to the very authorities that define them as children: that resource is the area called 'play' or 'fantasy'. Childhood is turned into a mode of response to the very forms of power that each day reproduce it.

If I seem to have left *Scream Inn* behind at this point, that is because it only partially reveals response-to-power. IPC's compromises, plus the particular format of this story, mean that *Scream Inn* plays with the formula of absurdity for its own sake. It is a practice piece, a virtuoso performance perhaps, but not the real thing. For this reason, it isn't possible to map *Scream Inn's* five functions directly on to *Dennis the Menace*. Nor does it matter. We have left Propp quite a way behind. As I shall argue in Chapter 6, it is a problem in his argument that he left the unity of functions as an unexplained 'given'. We can see now how those functions only have meaning by virtue of their connection with children's social situation. The connection between the Innkeeper's world and Dennis' is not a sequence of story-functions, but the formula of which they are each an expression. And that formula has to be understood as a historically and socially specific contract between publisher, genre, and audience that makes possible a range of formats for stories. It is a game they have agreed to play together.

Games have rules that enable them to be played. They are not always written down – especially in children's games. Sometimes it is possible to write them down. The act of writing them down can wipe out a lot of their fluidity – a fluidity that can be important to their functioning. Despite these risks, I have had a go at transcribing the rules of the game in the juvenile comics, and what they mean for their players. I have called it:

THE GAME OF TRICKS 'N' JOKES

The A – Z of powers and strategies for children

The aim of the game is to have fun, despite everything. Fun is had in particular by winning or losing with the maximum absurdity. Therefore almost every rule below may be broken, provided only that the effect is ridiculous enough. The winners are those who score the most points in this way. Points are directly cashable as reader-loyalty. Government Health Warning: You are warned that anyone playing should suffer fantastic injuries. This game is therefore not suitable for those with weak imaginations.

Rules:

1. All real players are children. All other players are there on sufferance and, if possible, to suffer. The only hope for other players who want to avoid pain is to pretend to be a child.

2. Each player must adopt a character which tells him or her how to behave. Preferably choose one whose name warns others what you're likely to be like. Once chosen, you must behave like that – or else.

3. Failure to observe Rule 2 will bring the sky down on your head. Behaving out of character is extremely dangerous, and you had better have an extremely silly reason for doing so. Any attempt by another character to make you act out of character will bring the sky down on their heads.

4. Any player who looks or acts the least bit pleasant, or rational, is a cissy, a softy and a teacher's pet, and has only him/herself to blame for what happens.

5. Players play tricks on each other. The first one to play a trick will get his/her comeuppance, unless s/he is clever enough to get away with it. (NB Players who get away with it too often run the risk of appearing too clever. See Rule 10 for what happens then.)

6. You score points by making comeuppances happen appropriately. The more appropriate absurdities you can build into the punishment, the better.

7. No player behaves rationally. Any player caught behaving sensibly will be immediately flogged, beaten up, or otherwise hospitalised. Alternatively Rule 10 may be cited immediately.

8. Everything happens too fast. All true players suffer from hyperactivity and minimal brain dysfunction. Being slow is a symptom of a sickness known as adulthood; any adult players are advised to hide their advancing slowness.

9. Any adult permitted to play should be as horrible as possible, or else should simply pretend to be a child. Adults who play at being children will

receive all known punishments, but will also have fun.

10. More points are deducted for being boring than for anything else. Any player caught being boring several times, will cease to be.

11. No one ever wins. All players must be fit to play again within a week. Players can win extra points by staging miraculous recoveries from the point of death at the end of one game.

12. Any player who uses power of any kind is nasty, and will be dealt with accordingly.

13. Everyone hates power-users. Any player who adopts such a role had better arm him/herself well. But I don't fancy your chances.

14. No holds are barred, provided they are absurd enough.

15. If the going gets too hard, any player may ask the Games Master (i.e., the artist, not the school kind . . .) to cheat on his/her behalf.

16. Use of Rule 15 will automatically bring the sky down on your head, unless you are very tricky. However, successful use of this Rule automatically scores extra points.

17. A player may appeal to the onlookers at any time. They like this. But players would do well to remember that onlookers like a nicely-balanced, ridiculous game. They also like things to go hopelessly wrong. So don't expect the crowd to be on your side.

18. Any natural law may be suspended for the duration of the game. Any new law may be invented, provided it is inventive enough. Extra points can be won for particularly impossible laws. But watch out – suspended laws may be switched back on at any time.

19. Onlookers are invited to heckle at any time. Players score extra if they manage to answer the hecklers well.

20. To all the above Rules, exceptions are permitted, provided they prove the Rule.

21. Once a player has started, s/he carries on playing until s/he gets boring, or bored.

22. A game is over as quickly as possible. Points are awarded for packing as much stuff into the smallest possible space.

23. Players may invent each other for the purpose of playing tricks on.

24. All the above Rules are subject to alteration without notice. Anyone who takes them seriously is a boring old fart, probably an adult, and will be suitably dealt with. Anyone who argues that the Rules are unfair is right, but is automatically disqualified.

25. Every player should bear the following in mind, as they come under the hammer for the nth time. Rules Rule OK. This game is about being a typical child. A typical child is at odds with everything and everyone, finds the world a quite nonsensical place, and would love to think s/he can win even though s/he knows she can't. Therefore all players must remember that this is a very

serious game of absurdity. Overt laughter results in instant disqualification. Failure to abide by this rule, which is non-negotiable, will result in one of the following: loss of innocence; deviance; growing up; a great deal of pain.

26. If you understand these Rules, it is almost certainly long past time for you to have moved on to one of our further exciting Games of Life.

I mean these Rules quite seriously, and I invite my readers to look at some 'live' strips, and see them through the eyes of the Rules.

In closing this chapter, I want briefly to draw attention to one point inherent in my account, which I feel is important. On the one hand, *Scream Inn* and all strips like it are closed texts; their end is their rebeginning and there can be no development or progress. On the other hand, my conclusion is that *because of their relations to their readers* the enclosedness of the text does not imply the enclosing of the readers. The assumption that readers must somehow be being 'made' to parallel the form of a text is a highly misleading one. With this rider, let us turn to how others have looked at these kinds of strip.

The vicissitudes of identification

Scream Inn is from that genre of comics known either as the 'juveniles' or simply the 'funnies'. Most people do treat them just as that – silly, funny, harmless things quite suitable for young children. Every now and then, dissenting voices are raised, pointing to their possible harm. It is tempting to smother those voices with reassertions that these are 'just fun'. But that is to take a risk – of being once again trapped within a picture of comics as 'either harmful or harmless'. The danger, in other words, is of accepting terms for the discussion that stop us looking positively at the ways kids use their comics. I want therefore seriously to review the criticisms made even of these comics.

Many of them occur in very journalistic contexts (something very common with critiques of the media in general, of course). In different ways, each criticism tries to suggest that the very innocence of the juvenile comics is a mask over some worrying influences. The criticisms range from the very traditional to the relatively sophisticated.

The critics' voice

At the traditional end stands Clare Dellino who in a newspaper opinion article suggested that the *Beano* directly incited imitation of its pranks, its dangerous jokes, and its criminal acts.[1] She particularly addressed an episode of *Babyface Finlayson*, the manic infant with a motorised pram who terrorises all his locals. In her chosen illustration he was raiding the local toy shop. Her argument was trapped in that harmless/harmful opposition; she accepted unwillingly that 'the gooey romance stories are harmless enough, I suppose', but then counter-posed comics like the *Beano* which 'glorify' causing trouble – 'these so-called 'comics' are a major influence on the attitudes and behaviour of children today'. She ended by calling on the publishers to 'realise the damage their "harmless" publications can do'. Dellino's argument, very brief and much of it implicit, is at the 'standard' end of the dimension. I have reviewed her use of examples elsewhere.[2] Much the same is George Gale who, in a debate on comics, concluded that the funnies encourage the infliction of pain, and laughing at the results:

> While violence is the main feature of these children's comics, the systematic destruction of the English language runs it a close second. The blows, falls, shrieks, crunches etc are accompanied by a proliferation of non-words . . . A regular survey

of these and similar comics would show that week after week children are invited to laugh at people who are fat, deformed, handicapped or ugly, especially when pain is being inflicted. This is accompanied throughout by crude, ugly language. Such a regular diet can do nothing but harm to children.[3]

The worry about deformation of language is part of a syndrome of worries going back to the 1950s. (See Chapter 12 for a discussion of these ideas.)

Next come those who argue that comics such as these do harm through the accumulated images they leave behind. Judith O'Connell, for example, in a dissertation on sexism in comics and television, counted how frequently male and female characters appeared in a sample of comics and TV programmes, and related this to the reading and viewing habits of 244 children.[4] She found, for example, that the *Beano* had around 60% male to 15% female characters (the remainder being ungendered – animals, for example) – 'an overpowering imbalance', as she calls it: 'Girls are the readers in schools, but they do not read comics. Why? I am forced to the conclusion that it is because comics seem to set out either deliberately to exclude them or to exploit them. The girls may be relatively unaffected by comics that they don't read anyway but what does a weekly diet of *Beano*, *Shoot* et al do to the boys?' Her empirical survey of the *Beano*, chosen because of its longstanding popularity, ends with a revealing remark. 'Of 714 representations of character in its 20 pages, only 112 are female, a percentage of 15%. Hardly a fair representation of modern society' (p. 19).

Note her assumptions. Comics, she thinks, ought to be reflections of society. If there is a gender imbalance of characters, that is a deviation from the norm, because in the society beyond the comics that proportion does not hold. It is an argument that would not bear extension. Is the proportion of pets correct? I won't even dare to ask whether the ratio of humans to non-human species is right – where would I begin? But stick with pets. Dogs feature hugely, hopelessly out of proportion with the number of gerbils and hamsters actually owned. Does that also constitute a distortion? Hardly, because such an 'imbalance' has no relevance. How do we know that the gender-imbalance is 'relevant' to the comics? O'Connell, I'm afraid, mainly takes this for granted, with just one argument to support her case – that the imbalance of characters is mirrored in the imbalance of readers (in her sample, 42% of boys, to only 25% of girls, read the *Beano*). The implication is made clear; girls lack models for identifying with the *Beano* and are presumably therefore being denied its pleasures. All of which is premised on a second, deeper assumption that readers of the *Beano* relate to them as boys or girls. What would happen to her case if it was shown that the comic invites them to relate, not as boys/girls, but as children? We will return to this. Similar to O'Connell's approach is Pat Isiorho's, who looked at images of black people in the same comics. Both see it as possible to count images across a range of genres (juvenile, boys' adventure, war comics, etc) to produce a general picture of the 'stereotypes' in comics. Isiorho again found an imbalance in the numbers of black characters, and also claims that 'when they are featured, they are stereotyped'.[5]

These four are representative of a corpus of criticism which has several recurring elements. First, there is a claim that the humour and the innocence is a disguise, or mask, concealing unpleasant things going on. Worse, the 'harmlessness' helps transport the harmful contents to the minds of the readers. Perhaps the harmless/harmful pair is not so much an opposition as a linked pair, the one making the other palateable. There follows a claim that things like the *Beano* can be analytically separated into two elements: messages, and parts that help the messages stick. Another such critic, Bob Dixon, not in general quite as judgemental as the others, still voices this view: 'The main aim of the creators of these comics, almost to the exclusion of all others, is to give rise to fun and humour. This is of the knockabout, farcical type though verbal humour, mainly in the form of puns, is also important. The humour nearly always arises through someone getting hurt though this isn't peculiar to these comics. It's the most common form of humour and it's a sobering thought.'[6] On this view, the worst kind of media must be those with a veneer of fun and innocence but with devices to encourage loyalty and identification. Purveying such images cumulatively amounts to a 'diet that can do nothing but harm to children'.

We might summarise these standard claims as follows: the comics 'ought to be' harmless fun, but aren't. Instead, (1) they destroy good language habits, and hence are anti-educational; (2) they embody stereotypes. At their worst, these teach bad attitudes to authority, to women and girls, to black people, to people with disabilities; (3) what they leave out is as bad as what they put in; (4) they may directly encourage dangerous practical joking, even illegal behaviour; (5) they take pleasure in pain, and thus brutalise their readers. Some critics might want to distance themselves from some of these charges. But the point is that all are arrived at by the same procedures, and all start from the same assumptions. One key assumption, rarely brought into view, is instantly recognisable in a recent exchange on the role of children's comics. Mary Whitehouse's pontifications about the dangers of the *Beano* and *Dandy* were pegged to two academics who gave 'scientific' credence to her 'fears': 'Two consultant child psychiatrists, Dr Kay MacLachan, of Cambridge University, and Dr Carol Sheldrick, of London's Maudsley Hospital, say that reading comics like the *Beano* and the *Dandy* could, in certain circumstances, contribute to behavioural problems. Dr Sheldrick stresses that there is particular danger where a character with whom children are likely to identify – such as Desperate Dan – is depicted as behaving violently.[7] Of course, that makes sense of it all ... children, perhaps already unhappy, led on to worse things by something smuggled into their brains by almost a trick process: 'identification'.

Here is a concept needing our close attention. It is by far the most commonly used for explaining how the mass media, including comics, are supposed to affect their audiences. Uses of it are so common that it is pointless singling out one or two examples for quotation. The media are said to offer 'aids to identification', or 'targets for identification', even 'devices for identification'; audiences 'identify' with main characters. The point is that, in identifying, audiences make themselves vulnerable. This is the route whereby they are prone to being influenced by whatever messages lurk 'out there' in the media. So: a boy watches *Starsky and Hutch*. He identifies with the character played by Nathan Glazer. This means that he enters into the programme, 'playing the role of' Starsky. And thus, if only for a moment, he takes on the values – macho, authoritarian – that go with that character. And the chances are that a trace, a residue of this will be left behind. So the story runs.

Or: a girl reads *Jackie*. She identifies with the main character in a romance strip. For that time she 'sees the world through the eyes' of the heroine, participates in her interests (boys), her problems (how to get at least one and keep him), her solutions (making herself into a 'proper girl' so as to get and keep a boy). Through the reader's entanglement with her, the spirit of *Jackie* enters her soul, and leaves footprints of stereotypes, narrow aspirations in her, deep and largely beyond consciousness. So the story runs. And the more they do it, the more they will be influenced.

Those who use the concept will, of course, cover themselves. They will make strong claims for what can happen when audiences, and especially young ones, 'identify': they will 'imitate their behaviour in a crisis',[8] they will 'copy actions of a character with whom they are in sympathy';[9] when they identify with a full-length film there is 'a heightened degree of realism'.[10] They may be specially vulnerable at certain points in our life: 'if, in the search for masculinity, young males identify with the male 'violents' in television, they may be more likely to imitate the attitudes and behaviour found in the TV world of violence'.[11] But these strong claims are always protected by codicils saying that other factors may, of course, abet this process. Personality, friends, family, education and many other influences will affect how far identification leaves its dirty residues. All of which makes 'identification' virtually unmeasurable, and experimentally unverifiable.

That is a worry, but not my main one. The main problem is the curious silence over this supposed process. A review of the literature reveals very few which investigate the meaning, validity and applicability of the claim that audiences typically relate to TV, comics, films by 'identifying'. Still less has there been discussion of how the media are supposed to do this to us. What little there is, points us away from 'identification'. There was a splendid essay by Horton and Wohl which suggested – for TV programmes which use 'personae' as presenters – that we cannot lose ourselves in the programmes. They make us relate to them as to another person, and to have pseudo-conversations.[12] Drawing on them, Grant Noble suggested that that there are two distinct ways of relating to the media.[13] Television, he argues, does not involve loss of self-awareness, because (unlike cinema) we watch in ordinary social settings, with the light on, among people we know. Accordingly he distinguished a second process 'recognition'. This meant that viewers look at people on TV for their likeness to others they already know. Noble used this to make sense of some real differences among the children he researched. But then there is a puzzle.

His own research, plus his re-evaluation of previous work, leads him to doubt the applicability of 'identification' to TV. But even when he expresses concern over the inadequacies of previous research, this never leads him to question the concept itself. This is the status he accords it: 'There seems little doubt intuitively that identification is a meaningful concept, because cinema viewers are often carried away while viewing' (p. 42). I don't want to deny the second half of that sentence – though I am quite certain that the same happens when audiences encounter poetry, or music, or a good programme on gardening. But that makes me want to ask: how does that lead to 'intuitive acceptance' of 'identification'? Try substituting any of the following: 'absorption', 'concentrated attention', 'suspension of disbelief', 'intense involvement', 'deep interest'. Each is as capable of accounting for audiences' 'getting carried away'; but none of them carries with it the sorts of implications that 'identification' has – vulnerability to messages, loss of our own identity, submergence in the identity of a media character, with a residue of influence. Why Noble was so sure? Even he somehow 'knew in advance' that something more was going on. We need to inquire into that false confidence.

One rare piece of research directly tested one implication of 'identification'. If viewers identify with a character, they ought to evaluate situations and other characters' actions from their character's perspective. Howitt and Cumberbatch tested whether those whom measures showed to be 'heavy identifiers' became more favourable to the 'bad actions' of the characters they had 'identified' with. Listen to their conclusion:

> There is no evidence in the present experiment or in the others of the series that identification with a film character influences children's moral judgements of that character's aggression. There are a number of points raised by this research.
>
> The first is that there would seem little likelihood of behaviour modification resulting from identification given the absence of any demonstrated attitude change [because a great deal of psychological research shows attitudes to be more easily modifiable than behaviour – MB].
>
> The second point concerns the internalisation of attitudes and behaviour modelled on television. It would seem reasonable to assume that this may take place and the present research was designed to examine one process whereby this was achieved and analyse some components of moral judgement. The failure to discover any effect of identification in the area may merely suggest that identification is not the appropriate parameter. If this is true then there is an urgent need

for theoretical investigation as well as empirical investigation.[14]

Yes indeed! Of course their results may not be conclusive (though they have been replicated). There can be still be argument over their interpretation. But the point is there is a *total absence of such arguments*. It is hard to think of another concept so frequently used, yet so little discussed. Yet this has not altered the confidence with which it is held. This confidence is virtually in inverse ratio to the amount of investigation into its validity. I want to show that this is not simply a lack but a *significant absence*. 'Identification' is in fact a concept borrowed from political commonsense but deployed without recognition of its origins. More than that, it is not properly a concept, but a focal point where a number of social and political concerns have come together, and have found this term to express them.

ଠା9b

Brutalising the young

It is a real problem that most uses of 'identification' are so casual and incidental. It makes it very hard to examine their logic. Two rare exceptions to this casualness are Fredric Wertham's (1954) *Seduction of the Innocent*,[15] and an essay by Irish historian Owen Dudley Edwards. As I have already discussed Wertham's book at length in my *A Haunt of Fears*,[16] I am going to use Edwards' essay because it starkly reveals both the concept and the problems it embodies.[17] The essay is a witty, sharp-tongued assault on D C Thomson's *Beano* and *Dandy*. Edwards close-read a number of editions between 1975 and 1977, and makes some strong claims about their possible impact. He begins with their odd names, *Beano* and *Dandy*. As he says, 'they mean nothing and their meaninglessness means nothing' (p. 86). For Edwards this links with an odd timelessness in the comics, hardly qualified by recent small concessions to TV culture, or to children's greater sophistication about science. The point is that this blandness is a screen for the transmission of a set of themes and values which are anything but timeless: 'practical joking, greed, revenge, acquisitiveness, laziness' (p. 89), the 'preoccupation with corporal punishment' and 'heavy allowances of sadism' (p. 94): in sum, the teaching of a 'Hobbesian realism: the life of man is solitary, poor nasty, brutish and short. They create in brief, a world of unhealthy acts of violence and malice with even more unhealthy punishments: a conditions of barbarism deemed satisfactory for proletarians to inhabit' (p. 98). Edwards is not ignoring their fun. No, he is only too well aware of that side of them. In fact, it is part of their power, that they have humour, often subtle and engaging. As he says:

> It is, in a sense, a tribute – of one kind – to the *Beano* and the *Dandy* that I do believe them to be influential, to have a brutalising effect, and to be socially reprehensible in part if not in their entirety. The makers have gone to remarkable lengths to

achieve reader-identification, and while traditional in their ways of doing so, have in some cases shown a rich imagination. Series characters going to retirement or 'rest' conclude by saying farewell to readers or directly announcing their successors; the editor, the artist and occasionally other members of staff can flicker into view or near-view for a moment; the artist's pen or pencil may be borrowed with important effects on the story – a device which the comics in question have been using for thirty years. *In these various ways, the reader becomes more directly implicated, and thereby participates more directly in the value-structure which the* Beano *and the* Dandy *impose on him.* (p. 102, my emphasis, MB)

And there we have it again. The greater the humour, the more the devices for making us laugh and respond, the more likely we are to be influenced. It is the very cleverness of the Beano that is the problem. And this is all done by means of 'identification'. The very clarity with which Edwards uses the concept helps us. It is not that Edwards looks at the Beano and Dandy, finds a series of disturbing features in it, and then applies the concept of identification to explain their danger. No, the concept of 'identification' has *already given him the key for sifting the comics for those features which he will then claim to be damaging. It even tells him how the damage is done.*

How does this work? It is concealed within his language, but in a patterned way. Edwards starts by retelling stories from the Beano or Dandy. He then reads off the meanings of the stories, using significant link-words and phrases: 'the story implies', 'it contains assumptions', 'values', 'the implications are'. All these point us to 'themes' which, if lived by, would make for a nasty society:

> The social consequences – if any – of this sort of thing must be the inculcation of standards in children's minds of a wholly anti-social kind. There is utter contempt for education, and the life of the mind. It is largely assumed that school-teachers are sadists, and frequently they are snobs or crooks as well. Both explicitly and implicitly the very nasty habit of practical joking is given constant encouragement. Almost every story turns on efforts at revenge, frequently within the same family. The causing of pain is assumed to be a primary motive of human nature. (p. 98)

My complaint is not simply about a 'hastiness' of determining the 'meaning of stories' – though there is no doubt about that. It is, more, that in discovering these Edwards has already separated out some bits of the stories which are not part of those 'values', 'implications, 'preoccupations'. These parts are the devices that make sure the reader gets these nasty messages. (Note here the ambiguity of some his terms: a story has 'implications'; we become 'implicated'.) For 'identification' to work, the media always have to have two aspects. One makes us vulnerable, the other is slipped in under. How do we know which is which? The simple truth is, it requires a quite arbitrary division of the text into messages and devices.

Because of this, a pragmatic rules turns out to be operating. Those elements we dislike, for whatever reasons, are unacceptable 'messages'. Those which are not part of that dislike are a disguise put over the text and a mode of entrapment. It is by this means that, side by side, Edwards can claim that the *Beano* and *Dandy* make 'claims to realism' (p. 98), yet list a series of features (artist appearing, characters talking to audience, reader's voice replying, character altering his/her own story) which, under any definition of 'realism', are anything but that. I want to say that they are, in fact, simultaneously *modifications of the story and modifications of the relations of the readers to the story*. But once allow that as a possibility, and the concept of 'identification' collapses. Edwards' essay is useful for bring just that to the surface.

Thoroughly 'dreadful' influences

Recapitulate. 'Identification' is supposedly something we do, but its point is to explain how something is done to us. It is not something we can choose to do or not; we are hooked into identifying, and thus are made vulnerable. This is how we are got at by the media, and their more doubtful contents are inserted into our heads. But it seems that all this can be said, or implied, without using the word 'identification' at all. It is as though the concept is there before the terminology. Where has this come from? It is first to be found in the language of the moral campaigners of the last century expressing their fears about the impact of the Penny Dreadfuls on their (predominantly working class) readers. This was the first major campaign against a mass medium for 'corrupting the young'.

What were the Penny Dreadfuls?[18] They were serialised tales sold at a penny an issue, mainly in the major cities. The earliest were gruesome retellings of crimes, arrests, and punishments, as in *The Newgate Calendar* and *The Police Calendar*. Then there were a number of anti-aristocratic melodramas of which the most famous are those written by Chartist sympathiser G W M Reynolds. His 'dreadfuls' included *The Courts of London*, *The Mysteries of the Court of London*, and even a sentimental romance of the peasants' revolt, *Wat Tyler*. In this period (1840-60) also appear the classic romances of lawlessness, such as *Black Bess*, *Claude Duval*, and *Spring-heeled Jack*; and the derivatives of the popular Gothic novels, such as *Sweeney Todd, the Demon Barber* and *Varney the Vampire*. These were reprinted and added to right through the remainder of the nineteenth century, with the appearance, late in the century, of the 'outrageous' *Wild Boys of London* (1866, and reprinted 1873) which was suppressed by the London police. Towards the end of the century, a change took place; and the anxieties of the campaigners diminished despite the continued popularity of the penny-part novels. Now, instead of setting their melodramas at home, the heroes took them abroad. Instead of domestic violence, it became a matter of killing 'natives'. In the later writings of Bracebridge Hemynge, for example, the imperialist adventure somehow sanitised these publications in the eyes of those who, before, had worried deeply about their influence.

Ninteenth-century campaigners assaulted the 'Dreadfuls' with a powerful language. Take as a first sample an article in the *Edinburgh Review*. It drew a distinction between middle class and working class reading habits:

> [Among novelists and novel-readers] they who choose trash do so of their own freewill and choice. But the case of those for whom this article pleads is wholly different. To them no choice whatever is allowed. They must be content with the garbage of the 'Penny Dreadfuls' or nothing. Yet the fancy and the imagination, the innate thirst for novelty and excitement, for a touch of sympathy or of tender passion, are as potent and as true in the heart of every street Arab or the shopgirl as in the fiercest devourer of romance. . . But their desire can be gratified in one way alone. The feast spread for them is ready and abundant; but every dish is poisoned, unclean and shameful. Every flavour is a false one, every condiment vile. Every morsel of food is doctored, every draught of wine is drugged; no true hunger is satisfied, no true thirst quenched; and the hapless guests depart with a depraved appetite, and a palate more than ever dead to every pure taste, and every perception of what is good and true. Thus entertained and equipped, the wide army of the children of the poor are sent on their way to take part in the great battle of life, with false views, false impressions, and foul aims.[19]

I could spend a long time on this as it reveals an awful lot of their assumptions. Begin with the peculiar use of the language of eating. There is a curious insistence that the 'people' didn't really choose this muck. They 'eat' it, and come back for more – but only because it is 'drug-like'. This poison, unlike ordinary ones, doesn't make them sick, or make them avoid it. Instead it somehow makes them poisonous. They cannot help themselves, therefore 'we' must, paternalistically, save them from themselves.

This paternalism is the first piece of a jigsaw. An opposition is being set up between a 'vulnerable' working class and a safe middle class (though we will see the limits of that safety in a moment). This is all set in the context of a fear about the 'future of the nation':

> Surely it is not for a moment to be tolerated that the poor children of our great towns and cities should be trained on a mental diet specially adapted to lure them onto a course of crime, or be driven to find their only amusement in the exploits of thieves and assassins, and the lying chronicles of scoundrelism at sea or on shore . . . To do this is no less than to deliberately poison the springs of a nation's life, by leaving the future fathers and mothers of the next generation of the working class in a worse condition than that in which we found them. (*Ibid.*)

'The people' are out there, volatile, dangerous to the nation, in need of our care and protection. Society is on the edge of doom,[20] because of the power of these publications to bypass Reason. Hear one of the great campaigning journalists of the nineteenth century inveighing against the Dreadfuls. Comparing them with the safe imperialist literature then just emerging, he wrote: 'Neither in number nor in sale can the best periodicals be compared with the Dreadfuls, and these latter are reinforced by penny weekly numbers, which run through the hugest of editions. Is it surprising that the 'pales and forts of reason' should fall before the vicious onslaught?'[21] Reason is collapsing, then, and the people are getting out of hand. Their behaviour is such a puzzle and a worry. One can't help hearing a kind of worried fascination with 'the people' and their inexplicable likes and tendencies in the following, admittedly very late, piece:

> Travelling northward from London I met with a man of the labouring class, warmly and sufficiently clad, but collarless and with a great bottle sticking out of his pocket. With him was a girl of about fifteen, a pretty girl, but slovenly and unkempt, dressed in smart, but very dirty, clothing. A lady in the far corner of the carriage eyed the couple suspiciously as they entered; the man looked rough, and she made as if to change her carriage; but it was too late, and she sat 'on guard', watching every movement uneasily. But as the train left the station, man and girl, after refreshing themselves from the bottle, produced from their pockets two soiled and tattered penny novelettes, which they thenceforth read with slow and persistent diligence. The lady sank back in comfortable relief, and I fell to pondering over the universal reign of cheap literature. What do the people read?[22]

As the author Helen Bosanquet goes on remind us, 'a study of what they will read is really a study of an important part of their minds'. A fascination/fear, then, of the minds of the poor, the people, the working class. What is it that is feared? Just occasionally what seems to me the real core of this fear/fascination rises to the surface, as in Edward Salmon's discussion of the Dreadful's impact on working class girls:

> With girls the injury is more insidious and subtle. It is almost exclusively domestic. We do not often see an account of a girl committing any serious fault through her reading. But let us go into the houses of the poor, and try to discover what is the effect on the maiden mind of the trash the maiden buys. If we were to trace the matter to its source, we should probably find that the higher-flown conceits and pretensions of the young girls of the period, their dislike of manual work and love of freedom, spring largely from notions imbibed in the course of a perusal of their penny fictions.[23]

Impudent, uppity young wenches: where else could they have derived such dangerous notions than by 'imbibing' them from bad reading? The politics of this are all too evident. Somehow, inexplicably, young working class people are getting above themselves – and there is even a danger that this contagion could spread to other sections of society. This fear is particularly acutely expressed by another crusader James Greenwood in a particularly revealing style:

> Granted, my dear sir, that your young Jack, or my twelve year old Robert, have minds too pure either to seek or or crave after literature of the sort in question, but not infrequently it is found without seeking. It is a contagious disease, just as cholera and typhus and the plague are contagious, and, as everybody is aware, it needs not personal contact with a body stricken to convey either of these frightful maladies to the hale and hearty. A tainted scrap of rag has been known to spread plague and death through an entire village, just as a stray leaf of *Panther Bill* or *Tyburn Tree* may sow the seeds of immorality amongst as many boys as a town may produce.[24]

Don't dismiss this just for exaggerated language. That is fundamentally part of the argument; it holds conceptualisation and emotion together. For these are not just arguments, they are calls to action. The threat is so immediate, and can spread so fast, that no delays can be brooked. But where in the texts, exactly, does the threat reside? How do they get their effect? That is surprisingly hard to state. Here is a representative passage: 'The boys' stories stand on an altogether lower plane [than the girls'] . . . (T)hey are so overloaded with incident that the adult mind is bewildered in the attempt to trace the story, while no absurdity or exaggeration seens too gross.[25] Now you might think that literature of such puor quality might therefore have limited influence. After all if it is so bad that people can hardly understand it, surely it cannot affect them. Not so:

> It is not merely the amount of unnecessary bloodshed which is objectionable. There is far more actual killing in *King Solomon's Mines* or *Treasure Island*, but no one objects to it there. It must be the want of skill and imagination which leaves us absolutely indifferent as to who is killed or how . . . Perhaps it is in this mechanical and unconvincing treatment of the horrors of violent death that we may find some justification for the view that they suggest brutalities to our London "Hooligans". Their lack of imagination, which is always mainly responsible for purposeless cruelty, will certainly not be helped by literature of this kind. (*Ibid*)

Notice that. It is not just the amount of violence. Their very poor unimaginative nature is the cause of concern. That does not prevent, it accentuates their likely influence. Yet contrast that with the following, written of G W M Reynolds: 'His tales are the more likely to prove harmful, because of the talent employed in their construction, and the fluency with which they are written. Their very excellence, as specimens of literary work, is one of the main elements of their danger.'[26] If they are badly written, that badness reproduces itself as a moral weakness in the readers' heads. If they are well written, their quality is just a trap to ensnare their minds; thus the bad messages are more surely inserted. Heads they win, tails we lose. This division between the messages in the texts, and their tricks and devices is absolutely continuous with our concept of 'identification'. What is most curious is to find that the division can be reproduced within the readers themselves. Hear, finally, the *Edinburgh Review* for a second time:

> Of such trash as this it is impossible to exaggerate the worthlessness, both as regards style of composition and moral drift. Not only is the picture false from beginning to end, but the incidents are hopelessly, ludicrously impossible. . . The author is totally ignorant of the subject with which he deals, he knows nothing of the usages of decent life, or even of the habits and speech of Bill Sykes and his companions. The whole thing is unreal. Yet this is the intolerable stuff that finds tens of thousands of juvenile readers, gilds the byways of crime, and helps to fill our reformatories with precocious gaolbirds of the worst class. Of the worst class, as being not only bereft of all moral sense, and vitiated in mind, taste and affection, but possessing a cunning intelligence how to turn their knowledge to the vilest use. (pp. 49-50)

The Dreadfuls can not only send particular dangerous messages into the readers, they can even reproduce their own split structure in their readers' heads!

These samples from the anti-Dreadful writings resolve themselves into a series of oppositions: the Penny Dreadfuls are both narrow and fantastical; unimaginative and wildly fanciful; they appeal to the emotions but are also clever, tricky and cunning; they are poison and drug, stimulant and addictive. The texts are a combination of evil messages, and trap-like devices for making the messages work. The traps will work either by cunning or by total lack of it. Each of these oppositions has been at work in every other anti-media panic I have looked at. Each was paralleled in the arguments of Edwards. The concept of 'identification' emerged to give weight to a social and political panic with a century of emotion behind it. Indeed 'identification' is less a concept, more a focal point for a series of worries. They are worries about the behaviour of the 'masses', and their inexplicable volatility. The irony is that the same concept serves a writer like Edwards, who ostensibly stands on the Left – but that sort of Left that sees the working class as prone to being manipulated by the media, in need of a bit of rescuing.

We need a history of these ideas. Leo Lowenthal has provided the beginnings of this.[27] He shows how it is embroidered into a debate about 'popular' and 'high' culture, which began to emerge in the mid-eighteenth century. At first it was moderated by a hope that 'the people' could be redeemed by the educative influence of the media. This meant that writers of the time held a different view of 'identification'. Samuel Johnson, for instance, in a 1750 essay wrote on the text-reader relation:

> In the romances formerly written, every transaction and sentiment was so remote from all that passes among men, that the reader was in very little danger of making any application to himself . . . But when an adventurer is levelled with the rest of the world in such scenes of the universal drama, as may be the lot of any young

man; young spectators fix their eyes upon him with closer attention, and hope, by observing his behaviour and success, to regulate their own practices, when they shall be engaged in like part.[28]

This at least acknowledges there are differences among the texts, that readers are not simply vulnerable, and it connects readers' responses to the rest of their lives.

What changed, first, was the rise of fears of uncontrollable action from below. Geoffrey Pearson has depicted this brilliantly in his study of the history of fears about the decline of national life and morals.[29] He outlines a cyclical history over more than two hundred years of 'morally-minded people' worrying about a collapse of the family, decline in religion and morals, loss of respect for parents, and a looming crisis of civilisation. At each point people thought that thirty years earlier it had of course all been so much better (at which time the same kind of people had been bemoaning the collapse of the family, decline in religion and morals. . .).

The second element is the degree to which popular culture is distinguished along class lines. In a study of popular culture in the eighteenth century, Pat Rogers comments on the way intellectuals, artists and other spokespeople for the gentry related to popular theatre, masquerades, and street entertainments:

> (I)t was the diversions of the gentry which set the tone; which fuelled building, landscaping and what we might call environmental design; which helped to mould the perceptions even of the least privileged strata of the population. Middle class aped those of the rich, or vulgarised high forms of art, or produced genteel versions of lower-class fun. Popular recreations often took the form of galas organised by the gentry; otherwise they tended to be localised and indeed resolutely provincial. They attracted little or no publicity in the new organs of information and opinion. They were more commonly participatory events rather than spectator-sports, another mark of their rusticity. They had a strong component of ritual: consequently, they did not need to be advertised. . . Before the end of the eighteenth century there were comparatively few attempts by the authorities to suppress the popular pastimes of the common people. Until the work-discipline of the Industrial Revolution arrived, it was considered no bad thing for the poor to enjoy themselves in agreed ways. It was safe for them to have a good time because, socially, it meant just that and nothing else. In the early Georgian period there was no symbolic or ideological meaning in the recreations of the people: only the pastimes of the well-to-do possessed recogniseable cultural valency.[30]

But by the time of the Penny Dreadfuls, an ideology is articulated which put a stamp of 'danger' on the literature of the common people. The industrial revolution, the consolidation of factory capitalism had made social, political and intellectual discipline a more crucial feature. From here on, censorship of the imaginative lives and pleasures of the working class grew apace. The concept of 'identification' was in on that attempt from the word go, and took its meaning and its structure of implications direct from there. Though it gained a name, nothing really changed when the concept emerged and took on a 'scientific' appearance.

Identification enters science

Between the campaign against the 'Dreadfuls' and the likes of Owen Dudley Edwards, 'identification' went through a long and complicated process. Baldly, in the 1920-30s the science of psychology was increasingly recruited, especially in the United States, to validate the worries of those who felt that first cinema, then television, were corrupting the population. Psychologists sought to name the mechanism of influence. Although often suspicious of psychoanalysis, they borrowed terms from there: notably 'vicarious learning', and then 'identification'. There is nothing intrinsically wrong with borrowing concepts from other fields, or with giving names to processes you want to investigate. But what if your interests skew your research? Let us look at one piece of research, conducted in the 1950s, which everyone working in the field cites. Till now it has largely gone unexamined – which is of a piece, of course, with how this whole area seems to operate.

It is extraordinary to find, on a close reading of Maccoby and Wilson's classic study, that it is a farrago of unquestioned assumptions, unwarranted methodological moves, and results which actually contradict their hypotheses. Yet not once do the authors query the concept which underpins their assumptions and provides the entire framework for their experiments.[31] The authors set out to test some consequences entailed by 'identification'. From the start this is framed paradoxically. Psychologists have long known that people learn most readily when they are *doing*, rather than just *seeing*. That would seem to militate against TV or films being influential. Yet after noting just this, Maccoby and Wilson open by asserting (p. 76) that 'it is evident' that audiences do learn a great deal, both by remembering content and by incorporating it into their behaviour. They introduce 'identification' to fill the gap they have created. 'Identification' becomes a piece of *covert doing*. Audiences won't be aware that they are doing this – indeed, they may well deny it. It will take experts to tell them.

> We assume that when a viewer becomes absorbed in a dramatic production, he *identifies* himself, at least momentarily, with one or more of the characters. By identification we mean that the viewer, in fantasy, puts himself in the place of a character and momentarily feels that what is happening to that character is happening to himself. In this process, we assume that although he may reproduce very little of the gross motor behaviour of his screen character he does reproduce covertly many elements of the behaviour including the *emotions* he attributes to the character, so that when the character with whom he identifies himself is in a

dangerous situation for example, the viewer feels fear, and when the character escapes danger, the viewer feels vicarious relief. (p. 76)

These are the first of nine major assumptions, which inflect their whole programme of investigation. Among the others are that we tend to identify with the 'main protagonist' (p. 76) of a film. They add to these that 'identification' can vary in intensity, but that the deeper it is, the greater its effect on our memory and our subsequent behaviour. Finally who we identify with controls what we learn and copy:

> We assume that the nature of the content a viewer learns is in part determined by the choice of identificand, for the viewer presumably focusses his attention upon the stimuli that are relevant for his own character, and shares vicariously the experiences of that character rather than those of the people playing opposite him. Thus if A assaults B on the screen, the viewers who are identified with A should feel anger and dominance, while those identified with B should feel fear, and those differential experiences at the time of viewing should be reflected in the nature of the movie content that is learned. (pp. 76-7)

Let me briefly illustrate the problems with a couple of these assumptions. Consider a film device whereby we see a threat building up for a character we like (or even one we don't, come to that). But the character is not aware of what is looming. S/he walks on innocently, unaware that the incidental music is rising, that the camera is cutting to a threatening figure lurking round the next corner. Do we, because we have 'identified' with this character, wait to feel fear until s/he does? Of course not. This is because our relation with the character is always mediated by the point of view from which s/he is presented. It takes specific effort to ensure that we only ever know just as much as the character. A classic example of this was the film Rosemary's Baby where, with great care and subtlety, Roman Polanski made sure we never saw anything which 'Rosemary' wasn't seeing.

Or take the assumption that the deeper the identification, the greater the likely residue of learning and copying. Imagine a film in which we have 'identified' with a character who suffers terribly and is defeated. Would it not be more likely that such a film would move us, if we were strongly affected by it, to avoid any situation that might involve us in their kind of suffering? Examples like these reveal a basic flaw in this whole approach: stating the notion of 'identification' abstractly, without reference to any particular film or whatever, gives it an apparent coherence which dissolves at first touch of actual media content. The trouble is that the concept of 'identification' requires them to work in this way.

In order to test consequences, there has to be a measure of whether 'identification' has taken place at all:

> As we defined the term, identification meant the viewer's putting himself in the

place of a given character as he experienced the story. Clearly, it is difficult to obtain a direct measure of this process. There was an attempt made to get an indirect measure of this process by asking several questions concerning the S's reactions to the main characters. We reasoned that a child would not be likely to "put himself in the place of" a character whom he did not like and admire, since to do so would be to share disapproved characteristics. We also felt that the process of a viewer's imagining himself in a particular role is facilitated if the character playing the role behaves as the viewer himself would behave in a similar situation. We therefore asked three questions for our indirect measure of identification:

1. Which one of the two main characters did you like best?
2. Which one the two main characters would you like to be like?
3. Which of the two main characters do you feel is most like you?

The answers to these three items were combined in to an identification index. (pp. 78-9)

This was all they needed, apparently, to spot an 'identifier'. Interesting, then, that when they moved from Study 1 (on the effects of social class) to Study 2 (on the effects of gender on identification and recall), they report as follows: 'Since we found in the first study that the question "which character did you like the best" was not as useful in predicting the recall of movie content as the other items in our identification index, we omitted this question and used the following questions: (a) "Which character is most like you?"; (b) "Which character would you like to be in real life?"; (c) "Which part would you like to play in the movie?"' (p. 82) Are these new questions simply technical exchanges for the first set? If I were to answer the question in their first index, I would be thinking which character I could most consider as a possible friend or companion. But if I were answering the replacement question, different thoughts would condition my answer. What sorts of things did the characters have to do? Were any of them beyond my competence? Did they have to do anything I would find hard or shameful? Did I think it would be a 'fun' part to play? And so on. Why don't such possible considerations occur to Maccoby and Wilson? It is because they 'know before they start' that they are testing for *symptoms of a single internal process, behind cognition and only unwittingly revealed in answers to questions of this kind*. It does not occur to them that their question was 'not as useful in predicting' because there was actually nothing worth predicting.

Still, even if these are dubious assumptions, we can still ask how well they test them. The striking fact is that on their own account, they have more non-results than results. Their negative results or non-significant results greatly outnumber the results that might seem so support their hypotheses! How do they cope with this fact? Consider just one of their strategies. In Study 1, they had used a 'multiple-choice "recognition" test' (though they give no indication what this involved); but it had not worked: 'In Study 1 there were disappointingly small differences in recall scores between viewers identifying with the two main characters. This fact suggested that our measuring instrument was relatively insensitive, and in Study 2 we therefore tried out two additional kinds of measuring devices in an effort to obtain sharper differences.' (p. 82) Now that is not a wrong procedure, necessarily. Clearly much of science depends on trying again if measuring devices don't give useful answers the first time. But did their sharpened instruments reveal sharpened differences? The fact is that they did not. In Study 2, they made five predictions: that boys should identify with boy-characters, and girls with girl-characters; each should recall the behaviour of their own sex more than the other, except in situations of interaction; each should remember more of the 'stimuli' directed at their own character; they should remember the same proportions of the behaviour of both while they were interacting; but the boys should recall more of the aggressive behaviour, wherever it originated.

Only one of these – the most obvious and most easily interpreted in a thousand other ways – received clear support. Girls do indeed prefer girl characters, and boys prefer boys. In all other respects the results were either highly equivocal, or negative. The predictions simply did not hold. For example, boys remembered boy-aggression, but not girl-aggression. Boys remembered more of girls' behaviour when alone than the girls did – a result to which Maccoby and Wilson do not even draw attention. Girls remember more about boys alone than about girls alone, and more of what is done to girls than what girls do. And so on. The bald fact is that the study disproves its own starting assumptions – but never recognises that fact. This most famous of studies of the process of identification ends by failing to see its own failure – and no one since, as far as I can tell, has noticed their failure. Once again, this time in the guise of a scholarly psychological study, we meet that prior definition of 'identification' blocking questioning, preventing alternative ways of investigating.

Doing away with 'identification'

The concept of 'identification' is both redundant and dangerous. Effectively nothing has changed since the nineteenth century. It might be argued here that I am collapsing modern discussions of 'identification' too much into the rhetoric of the nineteenth century. Are not claims that indiscriminate 'eating' of Penny Dreadfuls is bad for 'the people' significantly modified by saying that we are influenced by relating to particular characters? Are not the modern claims more testable as a result? Am I not in danger of losing all differences by treating 'identification' as just a continuation of old fears?

Very well: let us take 'identification' seriously, as a logical claim. Following Maccoby and Wilson, two consequences are seen to follow from 'identification'. When we 'identify', our self-consciousness is diminished, and our ability to appraise things rationally is reduced. Without these two, the concept could not claim to explain how and why people are influenced 'against their normal will'. But then, what is supposed to happen whilst we are in this state of 'identification'? Presumably, the more complete it is, the more completely we 'take on' the attributes of the character we are identifying with – including, presumably, any self-evaluation and rational judgement that they exhibit. These can't be excluded by fiat, unless something very dubious is going on in the explanatory model. But in that case, the most dangerous characters on television must be bush-babies, wombats and the dog in *Blue Peter* – because they encourage strong 'identification' without the slightest trace of self-awareness or rationality.

Without those assumptions about loss of self-awareness and rationality, all we are left with is 'empathy'. But 'empathy' has none of the power which 'identification' claimed for itself, to demonstrate media influence. 'Identification' claimed that loss of self and or rationality made us vulnerable. That claim only makes sense within a larger model: a model in which rational judgement, self-awareness and critical thinking are seen as a 'veneer' over bubbling primal instincts, pre-rational elements held weakly in check by civilising influences. When we identify, the argument runs, we weaken society's controls over those instincts. And of course 'we know' that some members of our society are less well socialised than others. Once again it will be the task of education and social controls to control such aberrant groups. This is only too popular a commonsense model. 'Identification', far from being an independent scientific concept, is just one extrusion of this political model.

Rather than take longer showing weaknesses and problems, I want now to lay out some general claims, making no apology for their scope:

1. The concept of identification has no scientific validity as one for understanding the relationship between media and audiences.

2. Its use results in arbitrary readings of the media texts about which it makes claims. In particular, it enforces an unsupportable distinction between textual messages and devices.

3. Historically, it arose from a set of fears about working class behaviour. However, it displaced those fears and misidentified them. Under a veil of paternalism, it coded working class resistance and rebellion as 'violence', as an individual phenomenon, resulting from 'bad media', rather than a collective phenomenon, resulting from collective responses to people's conditions of life.

4. It can also however take a 'radical' form, as a fear that the working class are being 'restrained' from being radical enough.

5. Although it has on occasion been used in other contexts, it never sheds the assumptions which prompted its formation and original use. Those assumptions are linked to the commonsense model of human behaviour which sees us as devils constrained by a veneer of civilisation.

6. The implicit politics of 'identification', therefore, is that access to imagina

Fig 11 The witchdoctor set, from *Shiver & Shake*, 4 August 1973. © IPC Magazines.

tive media should always be mediated and controlled by those who 'know better'. And here we have to nod at least in the direction of the puzzle: why is the greatest fear of media influence always directed towards stories?

7. In sum, it is reactionary, unscientific, and has no further place in serious studies of the possible influences of the mass media.

Back to the critics

These theses are directed against the full-blown concept of 'identification'. But as I've suggested, it is rare for it to be so elaborated. It is therefore time to return to the specific complaints noted earlier, to apply them to *Scream Inn*, and to test them in the light of all we've seen.

I don't want to nit-pick over each mistaken understanding. Rather, I want to use problems in critics' objections to bring out shared assumptions, and to counterpose my own approach. Still, the notion of poverty of language would simply not apply – Cliff and Bryan were too inventive for that. But other worries about language could just about have found purchase on this strip: the complaints about 'sound-effects' language, for example. A particularly humourless critic could no doubt have worried about the presentation of 'violence'; George Gale would fit that niche. More significantly, the arguments about stereotyping would have locked on with ease. Imagine Pat Isiorho's likely comment on the 'witchdoctor' *Scream Inn* set (Fig. 11): surely as bad an example as one could wish to avoid of racist stereotyping – and made palatable by the humour, no doubt. This is an important and controversial area, and I want to argue carefully that there is a serious misunderstanding of these comics. Parallel to this is the issue of sexist stereotypes, on which recall Judith O'Connell's very typical argument. Her case was that the absence of girl characters made it hard for girls to identify with the comic, thus explaining the much lower proportion of girl readers. The evidence about girl-readership of *Scream Inn* can help us with both issues. Distributing children's applications by gender, we find the results set out in Table 5. On a first reading, the ratio of girls' to boys' applications looks like a vindication of O'Connell's argument. There were far more male challengers than female; and here is Table 5 showing that, on the (admittedly inadequate) measure of those willing to write letters, the ratio of boys to girls writing to *Scream Inn* was almost exactly 60-40%. But that leaves some strange internal differences, which are all the more striking when we map them onto a curious difference in age-distributions of boy vs girl-applicants.

In some cases, girls' choices of kinds of characters are proportionately the same as boys' (for example, Legendary figures: boys = 4.5%, girls = 5%; Activity types: boys = 15%, girls = 16%). However in one or two areas, there is a marked discrepancy. When we look at applications for Self and/or friends, the girls' number is proportionately increased to the extent that they actually over

Table 5 Girls' and boys' responses to *Scream Inn*.

	Girls	Boys		Girls	Boys
Other comic characters	83 33%	137 37%	Personality types	1 0.5%	2 0.7%
Strip-related characters	5 2%	17 4.5%	Activity types	40 16%	55 15%
Other media characters	26 10.5%	45 12%	Animals and other non-humans	2 1%	1 0.3%
Legendary figures	12 5%	17 4.5%	Self/friends friends	41 16%	37 10%
Real named individuals	23 9%	26 7%	No character suggested	15 6%	33 9%
			TOTAL	248	370

take the gross number for boys, even though their overall percentage is 20% lower. How should we explain these variations? Here, we need to recall the argument that these stories address young people via the category of childhood.

Childhood in this sense is a socially-defined period when young people are most subject to forms of adult authority (at home, at school, etc); they are innocent and in need of protection, and adults lay down rules for them which have an appearance of arbitrariness. However, the crucial element is the child's own response to this. *Scream Inn*, I tried to show, embodies a play with those arbitrary rules, a form of opposition, subversion and appropriation of adult rules into a child's game-world. To enter the world of *Scream Inn* or of other juvenile comics, a child agrees to a game with the adult rules. Therefore the most likely players are those who are at that time most aware of their place in the world in terms of an opposition of adults vs children.

We can therefore form two hypotheses. Children's readiness to submit applications ought to be related, among other things, to the points in their lives when they are most aware of their membership of the category 'childhood'. And at those points, the content of the applications should most closely relate to the implied game of the strip. Table 6 therefore is very interesting. For it shows that while girls' applications may have an overall lower rate, they are distributed differently to boys'. They peak much more sharply around the ages 10-11. It is not simply that fewer girls read (or write in to) the comic, but more that they read it for a shorter period. And the one category in which their gross applications outstrip the boys' is in the one which acknowledges the existence of other social relations than that between adults and children: the relation to friends, and to self. (It is not silly to cite relation to self as outside the normal terms of the social relations of adult-child, since 'children' are almost by definition not fully self-conscious.)

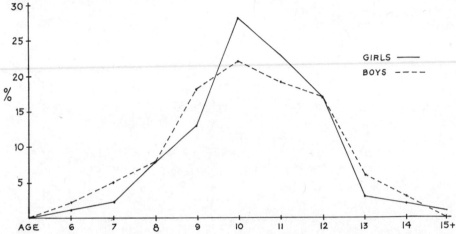

Table 6   A comparison of the ages at which girls and boys wrote making suggestions for characters for *Scream Inn*. The Table shows the percentage by age for each sex (girls, 100% = 248, boys, 100% = 370. The graph shows that, while fewer girls than boys wrote, their suggestions cluster within a smaller age-band than boys'.

The interpretation I offer can't rely on these fragmentary statistics alone, I acknowledge. Yet it feels right, for a number of reasons. I suggest that girls apply less than boys because they feel themselves to be caught within the constraining category 'childhood' less than boys. It is not enough to be defined as a 'child'. They have to be aware of it as a constraint, and also wish to use the 'rules of childhood' as the basis for their resistance. Boys in general (and especially working class boys) are encouraged early to show independence. Yet they are also subject to arbitrary brakes on that independence, 'rules' from parents and teachers. Girls are not encouraged to think of themselves as independent. Battles with parents and teachers tend to be delayed until a little older than boys. Not only that, but girls much sooner (for both biological and social reasons) begin to think of themselves within the categories of adolescence and femininity. Hence they pass out of the simple adult-child relationship sooner, and start other forms of response and resistance, of both fantasy and real kinds.

Now consider the category 'Other characters from the comic' which, I argued, signalled readers' affiliation to the 'comic world' called *Shiver & Shake*. It was also the one revealing the wholesale discrepancy between kids' requests and producers' responses. We might expect, then, that if girls relate more briefly to this world, their choices within this category should also be more concentrated. And so it is. Even though the numbers are getting dangerously small for statistical purposes, Table 7 shows the age distributions of girls' applications in this category. The results are striking, for all their small numbers. There is a sudden peaking, between 9 and 11 years old, supporting the notion that in that brief period girls fit more closely to the overall pattern of applications.

Table 7 Age-distribution of girls' 'comic world' responses

Age	6	7	8	9	10	11	12	13	14
No. of applications	1	0	4	14	27	26	7	4	3

Judith O'Connell's argument was that girls are not reading such comics because of an absence of girl characters. On this analysis, they are reading the comics less because the comics are addressing their readers as 'children'; girls enter that role more briefly than boys. It is not that boys remain children longer; it is that they spend longer reacting in response to perceived adult definitions of them as 'children'.[32]

The problem with both O'Connell and Isiorho is their assumption that the elements they as critics find relevant are also relevant to readers' typical experience of them. They take a 'problem' externally defined, and then search the comics for evidence of their response to that problem. To see the error in this, imagine for a moment a new campaigning society, called MANGY (or, the Movement for the Abolition of Nasty Grins in the Young). A concern with bad manners has led to a search for possible causes of the plague of grins seen on young people's insolent faces. Looking at the comics, they throw up their hands and call for the matches. Aren't there awful grins on every page? Aren't they therefore teaching children to grin? The sheer weight of repetition, and the absence of people smiling normally (except for inverted tokenism, where a 'weak' character is shown simpering) – plus of course the work put in to make sure that we 'identify' with the grinners – all are causing grins. Some luckily manage to resist the influence. Other individuals, the less confident, the less able, are infected and corrupted. At the least we are desensitised to this absurd mouth-stretching; at the worst, we copy it ourselves. Why not?

It is not just because it is hard to conceive 'grinning' becoming a social problem (though not impossible . . .). It is because we can easily grasp, in this case, the function of grins in these stories. They are elements necessary for the unfolding of the action. If Dennis didn't grin manically at Walter, his character as trickster would not be clearly established. The grinning therefore has neither negative nor positive meaning in abstraction. Nor does the absence of 'normal smiling'. We would find it hard to accept that comics contain a secret Cheshire Cat waiting to corrupt us, because we find it hard to conceive of the grins as disembodied from the stories. Exactly the same has to be said of the 'themes' that so many of our critics find present, or even worse absent, from these comics. When Tom Scott of the Society of Teachers Opposed to Physical Punishment (STOPP) argued that the *Beano* was 'putting forward the false idea that there is something funny about child-beating',[33] he was doing the same thing as MANGY. When Bob Dixon looks at such stories, and declares them collectively classist, racist and sexist, because they don't embody the themes he requires, he also is being MANGY.[34]

But all these are still aspects of the syndrome of which 'identification' is the organised apex. For every form of Manginess involves distinguishing 'bits' that worry us (the 'messages') from the 'bits' that are acting as 'devices'. If therefore someone looked at the 'Witchdoctor' strip, and argued that it is purveying a stereotype of black people, the answer can only be: certainly, it is a stereotype, but then the whole point of *Scream Inn* is to play with stereotypes. It makes no difference whether it is a stereotype of a plumber, a tax inspector, a policeman, a black person, a demented pig or a coward. For purposes of the strip, all are equalised. Therefore they are not just 'stereotypes', they are much more; they are *types for the purposes of the formula of the stories*. In the light of which, it seems appropriate to return to closer consideration of what is involved in the methods suggested by Vladimir Propp.

The legacy of Vladimir Propp

How can we validly investigate a story-form like *Scream Inn*? My approach starts from the simple observation that it is a highly repetitive kind of story. Week in, week out, the same kinds of things would happen, with the same kind of outcome. It was, in a word, a 'formulaic' story. How does one investigate formulae in stories? The work that first opened up ways of exploring formulaic story-forms was the work of Vladimir Propp. I want to look at his ideas and at the debates that have followed them.

Vladimir Propp (1895-1970) was a Russian folklorist whose fame rests almost entirely on the book which he published in 1929, just before the Stalinist clampdown on all independent, critical thinking. In *The Morphology of The Folk Tale*,[1] Propp worked out a way of analysing folk-tales. Propp noticed that in his 'wondertales', for all their variety and colour certain elements seemed to be copies of each other. Propp argued that their role within the story is identical. Here is Propp's own retrospective account of this crucial insight:

> In a series of wondertales about the persecuted stepdaughter I noted an interesting fact: In 'Morozko' [Frost] . . . the stepmother sends her daughter into the woods to Morozko. He tries to freeze her to death, but she speaks to him so sweetly and so humbly that he spares her, gives her a reward, and lets her go. The old woman's daughter, however, fails the test and perishes. In another tale the stepdaughter encounters not Morozko but a lesij [a wood goblin], in still another, a bear. But surely it is the same tale! Morozko, the lesij, and the bear test the stepdaughter and reward each in his own way, but the plot does not change. . . . To me they were identical because the actions of the characters were the same. The idea seemed interesting, and I began to examine other wondertales from the point of view of the actions performed by the characters. As a result of studying the material (and not through abstract reasoning), I devised a very simple method of analyzing wondertales in accordance with the characters' actions – regardless of their concrete form. To designate these actions I adopted the term 'functions'. My observations of the tale of the persecuted stepdaughter allowed me to get hold of the end of the thread and unravel the entire spool. It turned out that the other plots were also based on the recurrence of functions and had identical structure.[2]

Propp analysed a group of some 150 wondertales, and found a common pattern underlying them all. What kind of a pattern is this? And what does it mean to have found one? Let us take an example of a non-Russian tale, which still (this would not have surprised Propp) shares many of the characteristics he discovered: Rapunzel.

A woman becomes pregnant after many years of trying. One day while her husband is away, she sees some beautiful herbs in a neighbouring garden which belongs to a witch. When he returns, she demands he go and steal some for her. Very unwillingly he goes. But when he goes a second time, he is caught by the witch who threatens him. He is given a choice: either die, or agree that in return for the herbs he will give the baby to the witch when it is born. In terror he agrees. When the baby is born, the witch appears and takes it away, christening it 'Rapunzel' after the herbs – and the parents never see it again. When Rapunzel grows up, she is locked in a tower by the witch, a tower with no door in the middle of a forest. Now it happens one day that the king's son rides near the tower and is attracted by the sound of Rapunzel singing to herself. He watches to find out who she is, and eventually sees the witch arrive and call out 'Rapunzel, Rapunzel, let down thy hair / That I may climb without a stair'. Rapunzel looks over the balcony and the Prince, seeing her, instantly falls in love with her. He returns on another day, and pretending to be the witch calls out the rhyme; Rapunzel gets the shock of her life when instead of an ugly old witch, the Prince enters her high room. He continues to visit her, indeed 'takes her as his wife', while they plan her escape. But on one of the witch's visits, Rapunzel inadvertently lets slip about the Prince. The witch sets a trap for him ... and here an interesting problem arises. There are at least two, quite different versions of what follows. In one, the witch banishes Rapunzel to a desert where she lives in a hovel and produces twin children. Meanwhile, the witch has lain in waiting for the Prince and catches him as he climbs up the hair (which the witch has now cut off). Horrified, he jumps out of the window of the tower and crashes into a thorn bush which so badly scratches his eyes that he is blinded. Then he wanders for seven years until he comes to the desert where Rapunzel is living. Then he again hears her singing, recognises her voice and is reunited with her – and the tears of her joy cure his eyes.

There is a quite different version in which Rapunzel and the Prince manage to escape from the witch. They are chased, but an old man whom they have helped rewards them with three coloured balls. They throw a green one over their shoulders, and a forest springs up which delays the witch; then a blue one becomes a river, and she has to swim it; finally a red one turns into a wall of fire and burns her to a crisp. Then the Prince and Rapunzel return to his father's kingdom, to marry.

What is the difference between the two versions? If we applied Propp's findings, we would have a problem. Using his technique mechanically, neither obviously fits his functions better than the other. For a great deal of the story, they follow the same pattern: a family member departs (what Propp called *Absentation*), something forbidden is done – the herbs are stolen (Propp's *Interdiction* and *Violation*), the villain reconnoitres, and causes harm (*Loss*). A hero appears, and is *tested* (he manages the task of getting into the tower) and thus comes near *the object of search. Combat* takes place between the hero and villain.

Then our disjuncture occurs. In version 1, the hero is *branded*, but eventually the *misfortune is liquidated*. Each of these is a function within Propp's scheme. In version 2, some of Propp's rules seem to be broken. In Propp's account, the functions dealing with meeting a donor, being tested and giving a gift should precede coming near the valued object and combat with the villain. It would take a great deal of 'stretching' to make this work; we would have to ignore all the 'coming near' that goes on in the tower (which was sufficiently interesting in version 1 to produce twins . . .), and have to count it as referring to their *flight* together. Yet version 2 clearly incorporates many more and important functions than version 1; it includes the *acquisition of a magic agent*, after the meeting with the old man (*Donor*). It includes (what is extraordinarily missing from version 1) the *defeat of the villain*. But at the level of mechanical application of Propp's functions, both can be made to 'fit'.

At quite another level, it is evident that something is wrong with version 1. All this stuff about being blinded, then wandering until he bumps into Rapunzel sitting around in the desert with the twins: somehow it just doesn't feel authentic. And indeed it is almost certainly a late, corrupted version, contaminated with a very literary, pessimistic sentimentalism.[3] Does this mean then that we should abandon Propp's approach and prefer other less formal approaches? My answer is: no. But to know why, we need to answer a question: what have we 'found' when we discover a set of functions or a formula such as Propp's? In most recent discussions one answer has been offered which has been linked with difficult but important criticisms of Propp. I disagree with both the criticisms and the answer. I will therefore defend Propp against that line of criticism, in order to unfold my own development of his ideas.

Propp and Formalism

Vladimir Propp is often thought of as a Formalist. Formalism was a school of literary theory and criticism which emerged in Russia around 1915. Centred on the charismatic figure of Victor Schklovsky, the Formalists began their intellectual careers by doing battle with the Symbolists, a popular school of poets and theorists of poetry. The Symbolists believed that the essence of poetry lay in its imagery. Imagery gave us access to a realm of higher meanings, a semi-mystical world of greater Reality than our mundane one. Art was a way of commenting on our world and we should study it so it could help us rise above our world's ordinariness. The Formalists disagreed with the Symbolists about the relation between our living world and the 'worlds' that are created in works of art. Their central beliefs were two (and somewhat at odds with each other). First, they believed that any event or character that appears within a work of art can only be understood in terms of its place within that context.

For example a murder that takes place within a novel can't be held up against the world outside the novel to see, for instance, how 'realistic' it is or if it might 'incite' violence there. For the murder in the novel gains its meaning from all the ways the novel is *put together*: its place in the flow of the narrative, its context in the relations of the characters the novel creates, the way it is told to us, our understanding of the motives for it, and so on. A novel is a form, something made by a composite of rules of 'novelising' as we might call them. The task of the investigator of novels is to uncover those rules. In this sense, a work of art – be it a novel or a comic – is a self-contained construct, governed by rules and conventions which are strictly artistic/literary/musical.

The second belief of the Formalists seemed to amend part of this. They criticised the Symbolists specifically over their views of imagery. The function of artistic images is not to get us closer to the world or to familiarise us with some deep essence of Reality. Exactly the opposite: their function was to *defamiliarise* what we had tended to take for granted, to renew our perceptions by making us see things in new ways. So, if in a novel or poem we found a murder described as 'a tender act', this connecting of murder with tenderness could be startling enough to make us reopen our categorisations. Defamiliarisation became a watchword for the Formalists; but it does sit uneasily with the idea that art is entirely 'internal', and does not comment on the world. For if art defamiliarises our habitual ideas about the world, it is still commenting on it. The tensions here have led to disagreement on whether we should compare the Formalists with the 'art for art's sake' movement of the nineteenth century.[4]

The Formalist movement coincided with the powerful intellectual currents of the Russian Revolution, and through the 1920s up to the time of Stalin's suppression of all independent thought, the Formalists found themselves debating with the Marxists over the social functions of literature. Some of the Formalists were themselves enthusiastic Bolsheviks; and certainly the aspect of their thought which emphasised art's critical edge became more prominent. Even so, there were many Marxists who saw Formalism as reactionary, teaching that literature and art were outside social considerations, even above them.[5] Some of them argued it with great crudity and dogmatism, simply asserting, for example, that there were obviously bourgeois and proletarian forms of art and literature. But towards the end of the 1920s, an extremely subtle theory of literature (and with it, a theory of language and ideology) began to emerge. This was associated with the names of Mikhail Bakhtin and Valentin Volosinov, and I shall have to return to their ideas later (see Chapter 12). What is important here is that Propp's book was produced at the height of these debates.

There has been an almost automatic tendency for commentators to treat Propp as a Formalist. Of course he was influenced by them. But there are grounds for not grouping Propp with them. Propp himself insisted that his views on the functions governing wondertales were simply a discovery. He did not know until he looked that there would be such a system to find. He did not have a prior theory requiring him to find such rules and functions. The other, much more important reason is this: nowhere in Propp's work is there any suggestion of a process like defamiliarisation. Propp simply and only investigates the formal elements in wondertales and then stops. He does not attempt to answer the question which I want to pose: what have we found when we have discovered a formula? This is very relevant to the acrimonious debate that went on between Propp, late in his life, and Claude Lévi-Strauss.

Lévi-Strauss on Propp

With the violent hand of Stalinism squashing critical thought after 1930, the word Formalism became synonymous with 'bourgeois-reactionary infection'. Elsewhere virtually all interest in the ideas also died. Propp's work along with much else that was important vanished. It was rediscovered in the West in the thaw of the 1950s. This coincided with the rise of structuralism. Claude Lévi-Strauss the structuralist anthropologist came across Propp's work and reviewed it in 1960. In many respects it is a glowing review; it acknowledges Propp as a lost forerunner, invaluable for structuralist investigations of forms of culture. What enraged Propp were the criticisms which followed, criticisms which came from contrasting Propp the Formalist unfavourably with structuralism. At stake between them are some difficult but crucial ideas; and I will pin my tail to the donkey, and say now that in this debate I find myself mostly on Propp's side, not at all on Lévi-Strauss'.[6] The main thrust of Lévi-Strauss's critique is presented at the opening of his review:

> The supporters of structural analysis in linguistics and anthropology are often accused of formalism. The accusers forget that structuralism exists as an independent doctrine which, indeed, owes a great deal to formalism but differs from formalism in the attitude it has adopted towards the concrete. Contrary to formalism, structuralism refuses to set the concrete against the abstract and to ascribe greater significance to the latter. Form is defined by opposition to content, an entity in its own right, but *structure* has no distinct content: it is content itself, and the logical organisation in which it is arrested is conceived as a property of the real.(p. 167)

This is not all that clear. It seems to be saying that Propp, as a Formalist, sets up 'form' as something opposed to 'content'; whereas structuralism does not. In my example of how a murder might be looked at, I tried to show that the interest of the Formalists would be in investigating how the murder was presented, because they see the meaning of the murder as a function of its place and presentation in the text. Is that a dismissal of content?

It might seem he has a point. After all Propp consciously strips away the particular qualities of character, for example, to get his Hero or Villain. He abstracts the qualities of particular encounters to get his Reconnaissance or Combat. And there's not much left, it seems, of the merchant saying goodbye to his three daughters and going on a long journey in Absentation (which is different from the departure of the Hero on his quest, only because they come at different functional points in the narrative). Does this mean Propp is opposing form to content? No. It would only mean this if Propp seriously meant that *anything* or *anyone* could take the place of the merchant. But he nowhere suggests that. Indeed, he spends a lot of space discussing what kinds of characters do appear. In fact some structuralist critics (including Lévi-Strauss, p. 179) have actually complained about this, saying this is evidence that Propp has not gone far enough from the surface content. This is how Fredric Jameson summarises this objection:

> The theoretical weaknesses of Propp's model (Lévi-Strauss has already given an account of them in his important review article) may be summed up in a two-fold and paradoxical way: on the one hand, his model is insufficiently disengaged from the surface of the narrative text; his abstractions still entertain as it were too great a complicity with the conscious story-telling categories, and this is nowhere quite so strikingly demonstrated . . . as in his retention of the notion of a 'character'. To sum up this aspect of the critique, then, we might suggest that Propp's series of functions is *still too meaningful*, is insufficiently formalized or abstracted, has not placed sufficient methodological distance between its own operative categories and the official claims of the text for itself.
>
> The other reproach one can make about Propp's methods and procedures suggests that on the contrary his analysis is *not yet meaningful enough*. This is the sense of the charge of empiricism which Lévi-Strauss levels against Propp's conclusions, and which . . . takes as its object the point at which Propp is content to stop work, namely, the establishment of a series of functions whose reason for being is subsumed under the simple observation that they turn out to exist, that the functions of the fairytale are 'thus and not otherwise'. Propp's model tends to fall apart into a relatively random sequence of events, united only by the inexplicable fact of a certain fixed order; and to juxtapose such analysis with that which his structuralist critic makes of, say, the Oedipus myth . . . is to measure the distance between Propp's relatively empirical approach and a type of analysis which aims at seeing the entire narrative in terms of a single mechanism, or in other words, of tying beginning and end, digression and climax, together in the unity of a single overall process . . .[7]

Something very unclear is going on here. We may make headway in understanding the clash if we start by asking a superficially simple question: how do we know when we have finished an analysis of something like a wondertale? In other words, how do we know when the answer we have is a reliable one which does not leave whole layers unexplored which might undermine the validity of what we think we've shown? Lévi-Strauss, along with other structuralists, is looking for universal structures which underlie all kinds of stories. These are 'archetypes', that is, base models which form the starting points for all particular kinds. What they think of the significance of these varies. Lévi-Strauss believes that they express some fundamental non-logical tendencies of the human mind. Others are looking for very general forms of 'storying'. The point is that, as structuralists, they cannot rest content until they have found these archetypical forms.

So among Lévi-Strauss' criticisms is a claim that Propp does not understand the relations between wondertales and myths. Myths are very important to Lévi-Strauss, because they are our most direct evidence of universal tendencies in our thinking. He is particularly unhappy with one sentence of Propp's that 'Everyday life and religion die away, while their contents turn into a folk-tale' (cited, p. 178). This is unacceptable to Lévi-Strauss, for whom folk-tales must be understood as 'pale shadows' of the myths from which they are descended. They are myths that have lost their motivation, as it were. Lévi-Strauss' one argument for this is that there are a number of societies in which myths and tales coexist, therefore the tales cannot be survivals of 'lost myths'. But Propp is precisely not arguing that they are survivals. He is arguing that some of the content of myths has reappeared within a different narrative form to perform there a different function.

Theory and method are here entangled. The argument between Propp and Lévi-Strauss is not over whether Propp has gone far enough or too far; it is over whether he was looking for the right things in the first place. Structuralism and Formalism do this in very different ways. Realising this, we can see the direction Jameson's criticisms are taking us. Propp didn't go 'far enough' in his analysis of character. He should have gone on to reduce 'characters' to 'structurally defined initiators of events'. He should have gone on to find a system of meanings in the specific content of the tales – the witches, the faraway lands, the houses on chickens' legs. When should he have stopped? When he had unearthed these systems; when he had found the underlying universals, the archetypical story-forms. And if he claimed they weren't there to be found? Then he hadn't looked hard enough, his procedures weren't yet good enough.

In this argument I find myself wholly on Propp's side. One good reason comes from looking at what actually happens when we compare them in action. It has been argued that Propp has overstated the fixity of his functions. There are for example cases where their order gets inverted. That is important, and needs careful checking. But what follows if it is true? Nothing would prevent Propp's ghost saying: 'Fine, I must now amend my thesis to take account of what you say. We will have to look and see if this is true of all the functions, or is it only certain groups of functions which can be inverted?' This invites closer attention to the things being studied. With Lévi-Strauss on the other hand we meet a cavalier attitude to details. If Propp might be open to the charge of minimising the content of his wondertales, Lévi-Strauss is open to the much more serious charge of completely destroying all the narrative form of the myths he studies. Robert Scholes among others well sets out the ways in which he bends the material of the Oedipus myth in order to fit it to his assumptions.[8]

Barthes' politics of narrative

So how do structuralists know when an analysis is 'complete'? We can learn something more by a close look at Roland Barthes' famous essay on the structuralist approach to narrative.[9] Barthes begins by paralleling the position of narrative study, with linguistics. Linguistics, he says, made its great stride forwards when it stopped trying to study languages empirically and comparatively and turned instead to a deductive approach. This meant a study of the first principles of what it means to have a word, a sign, a language. (See Chapter 7 for a discussion of some of these ideas.) In the same way, he argues, we need to look at stories deductively and find out what principles underlie all storytelling. His exploration of these is fascinating, though difficult. First, he says, any story-telling involves putting events in sequence. It isn't enough that one just follows another. There has to be a sense of a connection between them. If I say to you: 'I see the price of butter has gone up in China. I am going to the bank in a minute', these two sentences are in danger of appearing random. It can move towards being a story, if you can make a connection between them (for example, am I panic-buying butter against a world shortage?) The sentences must be causally sequenced in some way to become a story. Barthes calls the way one event generates others a 'function'.

But causal sequence is not enough. If I tell you that 'two amino-acids combined and an oxidase was deposited', we have events-in-sequence. But hardly a story. More, a scientific report. Again, it is very easy to add the necessary element to make it a story. It passes beyond being a scientific report, the moment we put it into the life of the scientist doing the experiment ('I stepped back from the microscope, astonished'); or if we set it in a detective novel where that deposit becomes, say, evidence on a crime; or even, making it a science fiction story, that the end-product of that chemical process now becomes aware of its surroundings! What is added in each case is a 'motivating element'. We must not assume that these are 'characters', as the science fiction example shows. They are motivated reasons for things happening. Barthes simply calls these 'actions'.

Barthes finds a third level in the fact that a story always has to be told in some way. It has a 'narration'. This does not mean only that if I tell you a story, I have a certain style: a pace of telling, a rise and fall of my voice, and so on. It encompasses also the point of view from which I tell it – do I make you fill in some bits ('Well, you can guess what happened next . . .'), do I use devices to make you listen in a certain way ('Once upon a time in a faraway land . . .'), do I give or withhold information you need to follow the story, and so on?

Barthes shows how we might use these three to get inside how stories work. Thus far, they are as available to a Propp as to a structuralist. But a shift takes place in Barthes' argument. He asks whether anything could ever be discounted in our investigation of a story:

> Is everything in a narrative functional? Does everything, down to the slightest detail, have a meaning? Can narrative be divided up entirely into functional units? We shall see in a moment that there are several kinds of functions . . . but this does not alter the fact that a narrative is never made up of anything other than functions: in varying degrees, everything in it signifies. This is not a matter of art (on the part of the narrator) but of structure, in the realm of discourse; what is noted is by definition notable. Even were a detail to appear irretrievably insignifi- cant, resistant to all functionality, it would nonetheless end up with precisely the meaning of absurdity or uselessness: everything has a meaning or nothing has. To put it another way, one could say that art is without noise. (p. 90)

The implication is that there can never be a way of deciding that some bits might be irrelevant. The problem with this is two-fold. It becomes hard to conceive something as a combination of discourses. A naive example to illus- trate my meaning: I am a fan of *Cagney & Lacey*, the US TV series with the two women cops. Over its lifespan, it has become more and more questioning of the role of the police to the point where in the 1987 series one dramatic episode explored the problem of racism among the police. As these developments took place, episodes tended more and more to end with dramatic freeze-frames on one of the characters looking anguished. But the series still retained its theme-tune from the first series, a loud, raucous, punchy one suggesting adven- ture and action. I would want to say that this was a collision of two systems. It's not at all clear that I am allowed to, on Barthes' assumption.

Second there cannot be a 'principle of significance' which can sort meaningful from irrelevant elements in a story-form. We have already seen the need for such a principle in our investigation of *Scream Inn*. Recall the Edward Lear set, and my discussion of why it would have been unacceptable for the Innkeeper to have ejected Lear without a limerick. That surely is to say that the elements are not simply associated in a system, but control and shape each other.

The second shift in Barthes' argument comes when he asks how we move from looking at narratives to asking about audiences. Barthes is definite – this is another whole level of investigation: 'Just as linguistics stops at the sentence, so narrative analysis stops at discourse – from there it is necessary to shift to another semiotics' (pp. 105-6). So our knowledge of texts must be completed without yet considering the receiving audience. Note this for now, and pass on.

Finally, Barthes takes a step that draws a politics out of his apparently technical argument:

> Generally . . . our society takes the greatest pains to conjure away the coding of
> the narrative situation: there is no counting the number of narrational devices
> which seek to naturalise the subsequent narrative by feigning to make it the out-
> come of some natural circumstance and thus, as it were, 'disinaugurating' it: epis-
> tolary novels, supposedly rediscovered manuscripts, an author who met the nar-
> rator, films which begin the plot before the credits. The reluctance to declare its
> codes characterises bourgeois society and the mass culture arising from it: both
> demand signs which do not look like signs. (p. 116)

How has he got here? He is now arguing that we need to distinguish two kinds
of story: one, a masking kind in which the 'author' is concealed; another, a
self-revealing kind which constantly admits its own 'producedness'. The former
is deceptive; its conceits are also deceits. The latter is open and honest. The
former therefore is the ideological. It is not that it is more influential; it is that
its influence is bad because it hides by 'naturalising'.[10] But Barthes can only
reach this conclusion by way of knowing-in-advance what kind of structure is
found by his way of looking. Such structures must contain a tendency to reproduce themselves in us – unless something in them reveals them to us. This is
the self-unmasking aspect. Except for that (or because of other influences having
nothing to do with the story, such as social bases for resistance), the story of
itself will transfer its structure of ideas into us.

Suddenly we are no longer getting innocent useful techniques, but conclusions with political consequences. We will see in the next chapter how each
of these steps in Barthes' argument is reproduced in McRobbie's use of his
ideas on Jackie, and what problems they create in practice.

Time for structures

Whatever the differences between Barthes and Lévi-Strauss, in one very strange
way they agree. Again at first sight, it looks like a technical issue. Here is Barthes
talking about the question of time in stories: 'Is there an atemporal logic lying
behind the temporality of narrative? Researchers were still quite recently
divided on this point. Propp, whose analytic study of the folk-tale paved the
way for the work going on today, is totally committed to the idea of the irreduci-
bility of the chronological order: he sees time as reality and for this reason is
convinced of the necessity for rooting the tale in temporality' (p. 98). Just what
is at stake here? What difference does it make whether we regard time in a
story as a 'chronological illusion' (Barthes' words)? To understand this issue,
we need to pull into focus the different ways structuralists and Propp think
about 'structure'. An analogy may help. Structuralists view structures as being
like those we see in kaleidoscopes. Structure is an outcome of the interrelation-

ships of all parts. No one part determines any other. Just the way they fall in relation to each other makes the structure. The fact that a kaleidoscopic pattern is randomly produced by shaking all the particles, whereas a story is written by an author, is irrelevant for this purpose. The meaning is produced not by the intentions of the author but by the combination of elements produced. Time, then, for the structuralists, is just another element in the pattern, and has no significance for time in the living world. It just is a relation of elements. Of course a story can telescope time: one chapter ends, and the next starts five years later, no problem. That is not all of what Barthes means. More, it is that the end is already contained in the beginning; and so everything that happens is following a predetermined logic – except of course for those stories which 'reveal their authorship'.

This is just not the case for Propp, and Barthes is right to see the difference. The difference is not just about the tales themselves. It is true that once you begin to tell one of his wondertales, you are 'bound' to go on to a certain kind of ending. And time can certainly get telescoped. In one sentence a hero can fly over seven seas and seven deserts. It is only in the different view of 'structure' that we will understand the clash of opinions. If the nearest analogy for Barthes and Lévi-Strauss is a kaleidoscope, for Propp it would have to be a plant. A plant is a structure, a living one. The parts interrelate but their pattern is not just a function of how that happens. The parts are interdependent. The roots supply sap to the leaves, but are also sheltered by the leaves which also act to funnel raindrops towards the root-structure. Not only that, but there are rules governing the way the plant may develop: conditions of its success or failure. It has, in other words, a generative structure. This is the point underlying a vital footnote in Propp's *Morphology*, when he says: 'At this point the following proposition may be stated: everything drawn into a tale from outside is subject to its norms and laws' (p. 116).[11] A wondertale takes over elements that enter it and converts them into elements-in-a-wondertale. Thereafter they take their meaning from their place within that structure. This is, of course, what I was arguing about 'stereotypes' appearing within *Scream Inn*. Just because a witch-doctor appears, it does not mean he can be directly related to the mythical witch-doctor of racist legend; he is a witch-doctor within the transforming laws and structure of *Scream Inn*. Therefore he can 'reinforce' nothing.

How does this relate to the discussion of 'time' in narratives? It does not primarily relate to what either side would say about particular stories. They can agree in a lot of their description of the 'functions' in a group of tales. It has to do with how such revealed structures relate to living social groups. For the structuralists, time in narratives is an 'illusion', or 'only a structural category of narrative'. This therefore means that the *structure* has no meaningful relation to specific times and places. We cannot see narrative structures as embodying historical possibilities. Either they are to be seen as timeless expressions of basic human mental tendencies (Lévi-Strauss). Or they are to be seen as *imposed ideologies*: alien patterns of thought impressed on us (Barthes). These are the only possibilities structuralism permits; and writers within that tradition manoeuvre between them.

   Propp by contrast wants to insist that wondertales embody in their very form peasants thinking about their social lives. In and through the tales they were thinking futures for themselves. Though it may be that the space for social transformations is small for them, none the less, it is real. Wondertales are peasant dreams of justice, escape, and the triumph of the small person. Their life as stories is already a difference to the people's lives. That is the difference between him and the structuralists for whom (as we shall see) stories are ordinarily conservative. And these apparently highly theoretical differences make real practical differences to how they look at structures as I will show in the next two chapters.

A radical critique of Propp

Was Propp, then, a Formalist? On my view, hardly at all. His starting intuition is that the form of stories affects the meaning of their elements. There are criticisms that can fairly be launched at his idea of 'form', quite apart from specialist criticisms from folklorists. But these should lead us away from structuralism, not towards it. Propp argues, for example, that the specific content of a story is a valid field for stylistics to study. But he is interested in story-form and for that purpose style is irrelevant. To him it is like the coat of paint on a car: no manufacturer will leave it off entirely, nor will they randomly spray different colours and thicknesses of it over the body. But its particular colour can be decided independently of the car, its performance or price. In like manner, story-tellers, Propp thought, were free to amend the style of a wondertale. To an extent this is surely true. Individual story-tellers do stamp their personality on the tales they tell. But it is the sheer fact of them being oral tradition that we must consider. I am much persuaded by Jack Zipes' argument that there is a watershed at the moment when folk-tales begin to be written down.[12] In one way, transforming them into literary objects is only an alteration of the style of their telling; at another level it marks a whole change in the social relations within which they exist. It is in this light that we can understand those two different versions of Rapunzel. With some torture we can fit the first version into Propp's functions; but the solution feels wrong. We can sense that it has become literary, sentimentalised. The second version, on the other hand, has that spare unornamented feel that is typical of folk-tales. The implication of this is that 'style' is not a secondary, separate matter. Indeed, it is not just 'style'. It becomes a question of the *mode of use in people's lives*.

   This is perhaps best explained by a further analogy. I suggested that to the structuralists, 'form' is like the pattern in a kaleidoscope. To Propp on the other hand, a plant would be a better analogy. My analysis of *Scream Inn* lines me up on Propp's side, with this alteration. The best analogy for grasping the kind of form we saw there is a symbiote. A symbiote is an organism which lives in a relationship of mutual dependence with another. Although it is possible to study it separately, any full account of its structure and its behaviour depends upon studying it as an organism-in-relation. Symbiotic relationships do not have to be equal. Certain pine trees, for example, exist in a symbiotic relationship with a fungal growth around their roots. In warm months, the fungus benefits from the sugary products of the trees' sap; in winter the tree benefits from the fungus' ability to convert foods in low temperatures. Both benefit from the relationship but the tree is the more capable of surviving without the fungus than vice versa. I am arguing that there is a symbiotic relationship between formulaic narratives and particular social groups. To the extent that a narrative formula emerges, that signifies the existence of such a group. The formula expresses the typified social life of its symbiotic group, both in the way it is internally organised and in the way it relates symbiotically to it.

This is really the substance of my second criticism of Propp. Once he has identified his sequence of functions in wondertales, he simply stops. Because he did so, he is vulnerable to the kinds of criticism Lévi-Strauss among others offered. But Lévi-Strauss' complaints lead in the opposite direction to mine. To extend Propp's analysis along the lines I am suggesting would not lead to seeing wondertales as declining myths. To the contrary, they would have to be seen as the embodiment of the typified experience of a rising social group. Their form is symbiotically related to that group's social location. But that inevitably changes our view of 'form'. It cannot be just a string of functions. There has to be a governing set of rules which commands the functions and their sequence. And changes in those forms will signify changes in the social meaning of the tales.

There is a danger in this. If we treat narrative forms as living organisms, with their own structuring principles independent of the minds of their producers, isn't that rampant mysticism? If the intention is to root such stories back in the lives of their producers and hearers or readers, what is the advantage any more of talking of 'form' at all? Why not turn directly to the ways those peoples tell the stories and listen to them, and look at how they are produced and used? This is in effect what the radical investigator of folk-tales Jack Zipes has done.

Zipes' work is not a direct critique of Propp, in the way that Lévi-Strauss' review is. But it carries critical implications for him. Its main purpose is to rescue a radical reading of folk-tales. His strategy is to recover the history of the tales, and to show the transformations they underwent. Originally folk-tales were part of oral tradition and as such were the communal property of their tellers and hearers. But when they were written down, 'ownership' of them changed; and the stories themselves changed as well. A good illustration is *Little Red Riding Hood* whose history Zipes has retraced. The original oral version, reconstructed from various sources, is very different from later versions. It tells of an girl who, sent to visit her grandmother, meets a wolf on the way. The wolf asks her which way she is going: by the way of the pins, or the way of the needles? The girl elects the way of the needles, and the wolf runs ahead by the other route. Getting there first, the wolf kills the grandmother and puts some of her flesh into a cake, and some of her blood into a bottle. When the girl arrives, she is told to eat the cake and drink from the bottle. Then the wolf, disguised as granny, tells her to undress. As each garment comes off she is told to throw it in the fire, since she won't need it any more. They go to bed, and the ritual exchanges take place – 'What big eyes you have', etc until the wolf is ready to eat her up. But the girl pleads that she 'needs to go'. Eventually the wolf lets her out, with a tape tied to her ankle. But the girl ties the tape to a tree, and runs away.[13] Zipes points out that this version arose in areas of France where needlecraftwork enabled some women to lead independent lives. The tale tells of the transition from puberty to womanhood in a metaphor of drinking the grandmother's blood, but also via the path of the needles. And the threat of the male's rape – explicit here – is avoided by the guile of the girl herself. The name 'Little Red Riding Hood' originally may have referred to the clothing worn by independent women. But the changes to the tale as it came down to us strip it of its original meanings of female independence. First, the warning is made explicit – beware the wolf. The references to the pins and needles vanish. In later versions still the girl is eaten. And the Brothers Grimm introduce the hunter, another male figure, to rescue the girl and her granny from the wolf's stomach. Over this period and in line with the change from being called a 'folk-tale' to being a 'fairy-tale', the girl gets younger. By a process of attrition it passes from an oral tale of women's independence – no doubt primarily told by women to girls – to a tale of moral warnings, extending control over women. Zipes is urging us to pay attention to the implicit politics of the stories which he links to their way of telling. He draws a sharp contrast between folklore and literature, in terms of their social production and consumption:

Folklore	Literature
Oral	Written
Performance	Text
Face-to-face communication	Indirect communication
Ephemeral	Permanent
Communal event	Individual event
Re-creation	Creation
Variation	Revision
Tradition	Innovation
Unconscious structure	Conscious design

Collective representation	Selective representation
Public ownership	Private ownership
Diffusion	Distribution
Memory	Re-reading

Commenting on these, Zipes remarks: 'In studying the lists, it becomes clear that folklore thrives on the collective, active participation of the people who control their own expressions.'

Now a careful look at this table reveals something curious. Whatever may be said about its left-hand side, the right-hand side is clearly aimed at the novelistic tradition; and there, mainly that kind of novel traditionally thought to be the 'creative expression' of unique artists. A lot of the characteristics ascribed to literature simply do not apply to genre-products. A romance story, for example, is not innovative nor does it involve a revision of past models. It most commonly conserves known-to-succeed models. Zipes shows a misleading tendency to treat the loss of the oral tradition's radical potential as the fault simply of stories being written down. This error this shows dramatically in relation to comics.

Consider again *Scream Inn*. It is a printed text in Zipes' sense. At a technical level it might be said to communicate indirectly; the producers do not know their audience personally, or socially. But in other more important senses it does not. For the children's responses show that they are capable of participating directly in its 'play'. Again in one sense it looks like the conscious design of the publishers; but at a more significant level, they are aware of creating it *under the constraints of an existing relationship of this comic with its readers*. Artist, scriptwiter and story-originator all told me, in interviews, that *Scream Inn* worked according to a formula.[14] Yet none was able to say what that formula was. It was a unconscious constraint on their conscious work. It seems to me that Zipes has confused the material existence of the printed form with the implied relationship of a story to its audience. It is still possible for a printed story to express an authentic collective representation, even though it is privately owned and produced. It is this misunderstanding that leads to his dismissing Ernst Bloch's view that folk-tales have always carried a utopian element. For Zipes, that was entirely a function of their being oral:

> What kept the utopian aspect alive was the context in which the tales were actively received and retold by the common people. It is the socio-historical context of the folk and fairy-tale which Bloch fails to take into account in his positive analysis of the utopian elements in this genre. Today the audience for fairytales, whether they be transmitted as a literary text, film, play, advertisement, or TV show, has become passive, and the narrative perspective and voice are generally provided by commercial interests. (p. 123)

Certainly the Disneyfication of many traditional tales, for example, or their use in adverts has subverted their original meaning. But those changes also involved tampering with their original spare form. Zipes' error, I believe, is in thinking that the form-as-such of the stories could not play an independent role in resisting that seizure. All I need to protect Propp's approach is this: to make folk-tales serve oppressive, commercialised uses, their form has to be subverted. There are many ways this could be done – by moralising commentary (Disney's unctuous voice-overs) for example, or by alteration of sequence of events (where the hell did that hunter come from?). No doubt these seizures were made easier by the fact that the 'natural audience' for the folk-tale – a society of peasants, with heavily circumscribed hopes and knowledge – has largely passed away. But the sheer survival of the tales at all is testimony to the residual power of the form. And there has to be a form with its own tendencies, to need subversion. The oral element had long since gone before Disney or J Walter Thompson came along.

There is in Zipes' account the base for another view. He gives an excellent account of the processes by which folk-tales were neutralised into the 'fairytale', with its moralistic elements and emphasis on childishness. He then gives this account of the reasons why even these were frequently condemned, particularly in the nineteenth century:

> The emphasis on play, alternative forms of living, pursuing dreams and daydreams, experimentation, striving for the golden age – this stuff of which fairytales were (and are) made challenged the rationalistic purpose and regimentation of life to produce for profit and expansion of capitalist industry. Therefore, the bourgeois establishment had to make it seem that the fairytales were immoral, trivial, useless and harmful if an affirmative culture of commodity values supportive of elite interests were to take root in the public sphere. (p. 14)

Capitalism sought to change the relationship between public and private spheres, and especially in the early nineteenth century tried to make the private sphere directly serve the interests of 'rational production'. Accordingly any form of free fantasy was dangerous. Later there was acceptance that there had to be a private sphere. But it was to be neutralised by defining it as 'only fantasy'. In their personal lives people could have fantasy and entertainment (colonised if possible); but the price was that it would be defined as 'only' these things. This same process is at work when the mass media, including comics, are judged as being 'either harmful, or harmless'. The unstated criterion is of social usefulness.

Having acknowledged that there is a private sphere even within strict limits (you can have some dreams, but not others . . .), it is not one to be directly controlled. Indeed, the very fact that it is regularly worried over is evidence of this. My argument is simply that forms could emerge in this private sphere that in small ways embody resistances to the prevalent forms of public authority.

Indeed the very fact that they occur as forms, not as overt arguments, may be evidence of their coded nature. Potentially then we could have the ironic situation that capitalism, acknowledging a private sphere but marginalising it, produces for that private sphere forms which embody resistances to its own authority.

The problem with Propp is that, having found a form, he passes beyond it into history. This could mean one of two things: either the form is sufficient in itself to tell us its significance – in which case we don't need the history; or it is the history that can tell us the significance of the tale – in which case the form is irrelevant. Either way, as it stands, there is no way to bridge between them. I am arguing for a third option which builds on from Propp. The strength of his work is that he doesn't foreclose against this development whereas structuralism does. Developing his account of 'form' can enable us to link the internal structures of the stories, with the social possibilities of its use. This is what I have tried to show in my analysis of Scream Inn in Chapter 4. In short, it is this:

A narrative form is a living form, embodying the rules of a 'contract' between itself and an audience with a determinate social location. The form is not an 'essence' with a life of its own. It lives in the unconscious assumptions of producers within the production system. A form does not mechanically take its audience through its predetermined sequence of elements. It positions them in typified social relations to itself – lays down invitations on how they should relate to itself – such that the meaning of the text is not simply in the form, its elements and their ordering but is a function of the kind of relationship into which the reader is invited. This means that the form is not an automatic 'unity' to which all parts contribute equally. Because it is a living organism, it contains principles of significance. An analogy with biological organisms helps. Organisms have mechanisms for converting to their own uses and purposes things which they absorb. Equally, some things cannot be converted and are irrelevant to the organism's life – some are even poisonous. That does not automatically stop them entering the organism's system. In like manner the formula of a narrative such as Scream Inn obeys rules which determine what is relevant or irrelevant to its working, what will count as a successful versus an unsuccessful expression of its contract with its readers. And the readership are already included as part of the definition of its form and its meaning.

This idea needs a great deal of clarification. It is for example the basis for explaining how 'time' in narrative can be real, not simply a category of the narrative. Rather than elaborate further in the abstract here, I want first to illustrate its meaning through my remaining case-studies, before returning to its general meaning in my final chapters.

"They all hate me':
Jackie and the problem of romance

On the alternative comedy show *Saturday Live* (7 March 1987) a comedian stepped to the microphone, following a buzz intro from radical man of the moment Ben Elton. She launched into a series of jokes about how women are led to look at their own bodies, how terrified they can be about getting overweight. But of course, she laughed (and the audience laughed with her) we all know why – we all read *Jackie*, didn't we? That explains everything. 'Everyone knows' that magazines like *Jackie*, but perhaps that one especially, have done long-term damage to girls' psyches. These magazines have subtly preached at girls about boys, romance, beauty, boys, fashion, their bodies, their desires, boys, everything in fact that will help fit them for a future as worried but passive women, everything 'right' to think and think about.

That joke crystallises the topic of this chapter. 'Everyone knows' these things. This view is remarkably ingrained. This makes it very hard to challenge without simply inviting the wrath of women who are rightly concerned to identify those things which are influencing girls into a 'feminine career'. Nevertheless I do want to challenge this radical commonsense about *Jackie*, which has been expressed in a thousand jokes, a hundred articles, and quite a few academic analyses. I don't wish to present the magazine as a source of hidden virtues. Simply, I think it is far more complicated than the critics have made out. My worry has several aspects. First their methods of understanding how an 'ideology of femininity' might be embodied in such magazines are grossly unsatisfactory. Second, there are politics implicit in their accounts, tightly related to those inadequate methods. And third all the accounts I have looked at just cannot account for the enormous changes that *Jackie* has undergone. There is a total absence of history in all the varieties of feminist work on teenage romances – and that is both disturbing and revealing.

My way of working has been, in each case, to revisit the particular issues of *Jackie* (or other magazine) discussed, to see how critics' methods make them work on the texts. But doing so has brought to the surface two major problems. First, typically, critics do not bother to give proper references when they criticise popular materials of this kind. Yes, we will find a nice list of academic secondary sources. But all too frequently I have had to hunt through many months' editions in order to locate, say, a small piece of dialogue presented as decisive evidence. I had thought of simply footnoting a rude remark on this. But I now think it is of quite critical importance since it reveals a cavalier attitude to the material – as though it hardly matters since 'we all know' what dangerous junk it is. Then, almost invariably I would find that a story was either only retold in part or, if fully recounted, was done in a way that already fitted it to the assumptions of the critic. But that would be all we had to go on. There was no way to check whether the evidence really did support the critique being (usually) so powerfully expressed. We are thus very dependent on the manner of retellings.

This double dependence has effects. Since we only get fragments of stories, we tend to 'fill in' what they must be like to qualify for the critics' outraged response. Here, we are told, is a story which restricts girls, or stereotypes them, or enforces a powerful ideology of femininity, tells them that a boy is the only important thing in life and other girls are never to be trusted. Very well then, let's play that game. In researching these chapters, I sample-read one month of every year of Jackie since its start in 1964. I was able to identify some fairly typical story-openings. I have chosen two and I invite you, my readers, to complete the stories so that they become attempts to 'stereotype' girls, restrict them to feminine careers, enforce an ideology of romance on them. My characters Jane and Peter are now grown up a little and of course (in the light of what they might get up to) not sister and brother.

> Our story opens with Jane wondering what she should do. She is in love with Peter, but . . . (flashback) Peter is a wild one. He drives a fast motorbike, dangerously (we see them in one frame swerving down the road, with Jane hanging on unhappily). Then we see them in a café, and he is planning a wild holiday for just the two of them – they can go picking grapes in the South of France. Next frame shows Peter impulsively leaning over the table and kissing Jane. A thought balloon ascends from her head: 'This is what I love him for . . . Mmmm. At times like this I think I couldn't live without him'. But then we learn that Peter has had to go away for a time, because of his job. This ends the flashback, for now Jane is expecting Peter's return . . .

How should this continue and end? I have constructed this opening as a collage from some fifteen years of Jackie stories. Please note I am not asking how it ought to end. Indeed, therein lies a problem. I often feel, when reading critics' accounts, that they begin from a model of what ought to happen in stories for girls – the kind of anti-sexist messages that they want put across. Anything that does not conform to that is then accused of doing the opposite.

I offer my second unfinished story in a different way: first, the opening, and then, a list of possible completions, for you to decide which you might object to, and why:

> It is mid-summer's eve. The story opens with a picture of Jane standing under an old tree, beside a river. She is thinking to herself: where did our love go? How did we come to lose it? Again we go into flashback, and we see that this is where,

a year ago, she first met Peter. She had been sitting on the bank, sad, and he had come and comforted her. Gradually, they had got to know, then fallen in love with, each other. They had had wonderful times together, wild free times which had made them both ecstatically happy. But then . . .

What went wrong? And how was it dealt with? How did the story continue, and end? Here are some possible versions:

1. Though they go on meeting, Jane becomes unhappy because she feels they are living in a dream. She tries to make Peter see that they must come out into 'reality' – and so, one day after their meeting by the river, she follows him home – to find him working in a grotty café, tied by feelings of guilt to a girl whom he evidently doesn't like. Next time they meet in the woods, she tells him know she now knows, and that they can't go on in 'dream-style'. Peter suddenly asks her to wait – he has to go home to sort out something he should have done years ago. The story ends with Jane waiting, wondering will he return? Will he manage to sort out his life at home, and come back so that they can build a real relationship, not just a dream one?

2. As Jane stands there, she suddenly hears Peter approaching – with another girl! Slipping behind a tree she hears them talking, about why Peter likes coming here, to remember Jane whom he used to love. But she went away to London, and there was killed in a road accident. Now all he has left is the memory. The new girl says he mustn't worry – she isn't jealous. She is just glad that Jane once made him happy. At the end we see that Jane is fading away like a ghost, saying to herself as she goes: Now I can rest happy . . .

3. Jane recalls that they began arguing over little things, and the arguments got out of hand – like, her being late for dates, or because she once kissed another boy. Peter had got upset, and she hadn't seen why she should apologise. So, at a disco, they had a terrible row, and Peter walked out on her. They had both been terribly unhappy – Jane had cried herself to sleep at nights – but neither would apologise. Now a strange figure appears at the 'haunt' and tells her a parable about how she had lost someone she loved by being too proud. Jane suddenly under- stands, and we last see her rushing off to find Peter to apologise.

4. In the 'present' of the story we see Jane has a letter in her hand, but she can't bring herself to read it. Why? We go into flashback again – to learn that Jane had spent a lot of time encouraging Peter in his ambitions, to become a fashion designer. Eventually he had succeeded, and had grabbed at a chance to go to America. But his letters tailed off, and now at last the promised one had come to say whether he was coming back. She opens it . . . he's not coming. It's all over. Now the story ends with her thinking to herself: I encouraged him in his dreams, and look where that got me. Can I find the courage to go and realise my own dreams?

Four possible endings. Which ones do you find objectionable? and which ones do you think actually appeared in *Jackie*? So that your eyes can't slide ahead before you have thought it out for yourself, I have sneakily put the answer to the second question in the notes.[1] Now return to the first 'opener'. Here are two examples of how *Jackie* actually completes such a story-form. Are they anything like the endings you thought out?

> While he is away, she realises that, however strong her feelings for him, she can't just carry on with him the way he is. When he comes back, she tries to tell him, but he won't ever keep still to listen. She gets swept along again for a while, until the day when – doing his daredevil bit again – he almost kills an old man. Peter laughs it off, assuring her he had it all under control. Anyway, he says, you can't go through life never taking risks. She now tells him he'll have to go his way, while she goes hers. They just are too different. 'I don't understand you', Peter says to Jane in the final frame. 'That's why it's over', she replies. (See *Jackie*, No. 104, 1 January 1966: 'He Mustn't Guess My Secret')
>
> The next frame shows Jane reading a letter, and remembering, in flashback, all their good times together – the fun, the kisses, the adventure. Above, a narrator's comment tells us that they had promised to write to each other. We see some of their good times together, and how good they were for each other – each one introduced as something that's recalled in a letter he has written her. But after these frames, we see that she is crying; and now we learn that this letter is from a friend, to tell her that Peter has been killed in a motorbike accident. Jane is left, weeping at her loss. (See *Jackie*, No. 678, 1 January 1977: 'Tell Me You Love Me')

Whatever we might want to say about such stories, they do not simply fall into a class called 'ideology-purveyors'. If critics insist they do, they lose the distinction between these and, for example, endings which work straight to a moral point. Suppose, for example, Jane had met a nice 'boy-next-door' type while Peter was away, and discovered that this was True Love compared to her earlier infatuation . . . or suppose she had written to Peter saying it was 'all over' unless he agreed to sell his motorbike and he had come home and promised – reformed by the 'love of a good woman' . . . or suppose Peter had come back, and despite promises to herself, she had gone on going out with him and someone had been killed, perhaps Peter, too – and we saw Jane in the last frame condemning herself for not sticking to her principles. All these would have their moral points printed on their faces. Real stories are rarely so self-evident. In order to extract their meaning, we need subtle and cautious research-instruments, able to grasp the flow and stresses of these stories to bring out the manoeuvres and moments of decision that make the stories meaningful.

I say this because I am puzzled. The most striking thing about the over two hundred stories I sampled was how many of them seemed almost wholly unmotivated. Yet it is in that, in the end, that I think their significance lies. They were unmotivated in the sense that the incidents in them were not causally or purposefully connected with each other. They just occurred. Take the following example, from *Jackie*, No. 107, 22 January 1966: 'A Kiss, A Dream, A Bunch of Roses'. It's wedding day. The story opens with our seeing the heroine/narrator worrying how she will cope with the day. Why? We see, in her flashback, how she fell in love with David while she was in London. David was a married man, with a wife and child whom he had left. But just because of them she couldn't stay with him. She had left and had now met someone else whom she was about to marry. As the moment to commit herself approaches she is haunted by memories, and wonders if she is free of him. In the excitement of getting ready, her mind is temporarily cleared. But as they are setting out for the church a large bunch of yellow roses is delivered – just the same as he once bought her in London. Immediately she understands their meaning. They are saying 'Be happy. Forget me. I am happy.' Now she can go unreservedly to Simon, her new love, to 'create new memories'.

The striking thing about this story is just how unconnected the events are – with one crucial exception. We're given no reason why she should suddenly remember, even be obsessed by David. She just does, and is. We're not told why he should have sent her the roses or, indeed, how he knew she was getting married. They just arrive. In a story where things just seem to happen in a sequence, one transition stands out, and everything else seems to assemble round it. It is the point where, having (how did she do it?) immediately 'under-stood' the message of the flowers, the story can say 'Now she could go to Simon ...' What seems to happen is a releasing, a *transformation of the emotions*. One might even say that the rest of the story is given its point by this moment. Realising something, she is able to change herself, modify her emotions. A moment before she was still half in love with David. Now understanding his message, she can instantly redirect that love to its 'proper object', Simon. But there is something particular here which we mustn't lose. She 'understands the meaning' of the roses. Fine. But it is very easy to see other possible 'under-standings'. David could have been saying 'Don't do it. I love you still. Here is my token'. Or he could have been saying 'You'll never be happy with anyone else. You know you love only me. Remember ... remember ...' The endings would have had to be quite different in each case, and certainly neither would let her just go off to Simon, purified of her past. We have to agree to see her as a particular young woman in order to restrict the interpretation of the roses to what she 'instantly' sees in them. This is why I think that the research instru-ments used by other investigators have been mallet-like. They haven't so much opened up the stories, as crushed them. They have found morals in the stories by treating individual characters as instant moral fables. They have looked on the stories as no different from parables. I hope you can begin to see that they are not obviously like that.

To extract their meaning, we need fine-grained analysis. Most of the time, leading characters retain their individuality and are not simply lessons for read-ers. In that case, we need to make a collage of many individuals' stories. We need to glean from each one its vital motivated element. Often, I shall argue, this turns out to be some transformation of emotions. Where can this get us? Consider a story which certainly is offering a very traditional, conservative picture of women, from the very first edition of Jackie (No. 1, 11 January 1964: 'The Fifth Proposal'). The story begins with Julia announcing that she has already had four proposals of marriage. She is an air hostess whose pilot – a classic handsome type – keeps proposing to her. Very tempted, she promises she won't keep him waiting long for an answer. But she is suddenly asked to crew an emergency flight to Monte Carlo – where she is approached in a casino by the bewitchingly rich Paul Roget who courts her furiously. He flies back to London with her, hoping for an answer to his proposal. Still worrying whom to accept, she goes off on a visit. In a hospital we see her talking to a young doctor, Neil, who is so glad she has come back. He had encouraged her to go off, but only because she said she wanted 'glamour' in her life. A struggling hospital doctor can't give that. Suddenly she realises that it is him she will marry. The pilot and Paul only want her because she 'fits' their wishes. But Neil is different. Now she loves him – 'because he needs ME'.

This is a thoroughly reactionary story. Not because she ends up preferring a hospital doctor to an airline pilot or an arrogant French man – that is the level of particularity in the story. It may be a bit homely, but it is not intrinsically wrong – especially if the other two are, as presented, so very selfish. No, the reactionary element lies in how the story reaches its solution. Julia doesn't judge whom to marry by her own emotions. She reorganises her own emotions in the light of the situation. It is almost strategic. Because Neil is a 'nice guy', and needs her, immediately it is him she loves. It is this element, and this alone, that once again lifts it out of being merely a story of one woman. Without that self-transformation the story just seems arbitrary. To identify the ideological elements in such stories, we must start from how sequences of incidents, otherwise disconnected, relate to kinds of emotional self-realisation in their women-characters.

With these points in mind, I want now to discuss the main critics of Jackie. Each is representative of a way of analysing such texts to determine their 'ideological significance'. There are in fact many discussions of girls' romance comics, almost all hostile.[2] They share several features. Foremost, all our critics assume that these comics form a unity: in two senses. The comics include fiction, editorial chat, readers' letters, a lot of information about pop and fashion. The critics take it for granted that somehow all the various parts accumulate and form a pattern to make up a single kind of influence. If there are tensions and clashes, they are of small significance compared with the overwhelming pressure of their 'ideology of femininity'. Second (though one or two of the critics might demur), there are really no important differences among the various comics which have been on offer now for around thirty years. Of course superficial differences can be found; but the underlying message, it seems, is unaltering: 'being a proper woman means preparing yourself, making yourself attractive and suitable to finding and keeping a mate.' We will need to question these assumptions.

It is also common to think that there is something disturbing, even devious, about these comics' singleminded interest in 'love'. Frequently, this is expressed as a belief that the concentration on romance is a *systematic exclusion* of all else – a way of saying to young girls that nothing else matters in life. This is how Hollings expresses this view: 'The outstanding thing about the portrayal of women in romance comic strips is not really what is shown so much as what is not shown.'[3] Hollings is saying that the comics are not just narrow, but therefore dangerous. Much the same view is expressed by most of the other investigators. I find this view strange, and I will try to show why.

Another shared assumption is that the audience for these comics is particularly vulnerable. Toynbee, for example, calls the magazines' readers 'impressionable'.[4] Girls in the typical age-range of 12-16 are pictured as 'incomplete'. They are still forming their sexual and personal identities, it is suggested; and this makes them prone to absorbing the image of themselves offered by these magazines. I don't so much want to reject as refine this argument. I think there is an important grain of truth in these ideas; but it does not lead to the kinds of conclusion which the critics reach.

Still for all the things they agree on, the critics also differ. And more than any other, *Jackie* has given me a chance to review a number of different approaches to how the media might influence their audiences. Therefore I want to consider each approach in turn. I will be looking at each theory in its own right, and at how it leads them to 'read' particular stories.

'It's all simply mass culture'

The earliest work to note is Connie Alderson's.[5] Alderson starts by assuming that the main romance comics of her time, *Jackie*, *Valentine*, and *Trend* are effectively identical. The fact that they have very different backgrounds and traditions doesn't matter to her because they all are simply pieces of 'mass culture'. There is an unspoken criterion in her account measuring the comics against what they ought to be doing. So these comics are bad-for-girls because they are 'amoral' ('The heroines of the stories are never really involved in a moral decision' (p. 26)), 'anti-intellectual' ('Studying is definitely equated with having no social life and not being available for constant dating' (p. 27)), and 'emotionally immature'. The language is constricted, and so confuses thought; it is banal, simple and hackneyed. The plots use simple psychology ('Just one feeling motivates action: "The wedding's off. No girl keeps me waiting"' (p. 67)). They create 'a world of simple dualities – boys vs girls; like vs dislike; homely vs sophistication; free vs tied down; boy-next-door vs boy in an exciting way-out job' (p. 70). And each of these is obviously damaging. No girl should be possibly allowed to think like that.

She suggests their tattiness is all a function of 'Big Business'. It is all just a device for selling goods to girls and young women. The 'businessmen and promoters' who lurk behind them are selling their wares through the very nature of the magazines (pp. 106-7). The picture she gives us of romance comics is of dull, repetitive, motiveless crap, narrow in conception, and routine in performance. The wonder is that girls could be got to keep reading such pathetic stuff! And predictably, at this point, an 'explanation' enters. Woman are encouraged like mad to 'identify' with these magazines: 'All stories contain strong reader-identification' (p. 11).

> The stories contain positive and negative elements in common. Reader-identification has been mentioned, and this is a common denominator. There are certain forbidden subjects which are never mentioned. These are common to the romantic stories in the cheaper women's weekly magazines, but the boundaries in the teenage magazines are even narrower. Anne Britton and Marion Collins, who have both been fiction editors of women's magazines, advise in their guide to would-be writers of Romantic Fiction that reader-identification is the most important aspect of women's magazine stories. They point out that most women like a story with an escapist quality, yet the plots must not exceed the realms of possibility. (p. 13)

We have looked (in Chapter 5) at the general problems with 'identification'. How do they apply to Alderson? There are two elements in her account. First, 'identification' means that the comics reflect the narrowness of women and their lives, and don't 'broaden' them. These magazines ought to educate, but don't:

> (T)he allegiance that girls and women give to women's magazines is pernicious. It is because they are magazines for women that they are pernicious. . . . In our machine age it is vital for women to keep up the traditional arts of being able to run a home well, be able to cook and sit down and make a child a fancy dress. But if women are not to be second-class citizens, and looking at the figures for women's entries into the universities and the professions it is plain that women are underprivileged in this respect . . . , they must be able to play their part in the community and to be in a position to voice their own special needs and those of their children. (p. 108)

Alderson is criticising the comics for not doing what she wants. She is one of those who think that women must be prepared for the double work of being wives and mothers and also public people. Because the comics are not readying women for that, they are bad. In her scheme of things, not to be doing this is to be actively blocking it. If Alderson accuses the comics of setting up 'simple dualities', she is not above those herself. So, education and broadening the

mind is opposed to 'escapism'. Odd things do appear under the 'broadening'
heading: for example, 'False as they may have been, the romantic pulp
magazines of pre-war days did introduce their readers to the 'enchanted East',
but the identification level in teenage magazines is kept within tight and narrows
bounds' (p. 13). So narrow dreams are more insidious than far-flung fantasies:
'the harm from this kind of literature is the persistent encouragement to
"dream" rather than to "do" or to participate'. Apparently, dreaming about the
East is at least partly educational (not a lingering relic of imperialist fantasies
about exotic natives), whereas dreaming about a boy-in-a-café is dreadfully
dangerous.

This argument only makes sense because she assumes young women are
anyway prone to this kind of dreaming. The sin of *Jackie*, in other words, is to
connect too successfully with women's natural tendencies. It should have
fought against them; women should be 'forced to be free'. Hence the citation
from the Newsom Report: 'All children, including those of very limited attain-
ments, need the broadening experience of contact with great literature' (cited,
p. 2). And of course great literature and *Jackie* are mutually exclusive. The former
is unquestionably good for you. You may be bored by it. You may feel it is
irrelevant to your life. That is a problem to be overcome. *Jackie* is unquestionably
bad for you. You may enjoy it. You may feel it helps to answer problems you
are having. That is another problem to be overcome. Readers of these things
are so 'emotionally and mentally unformed' (p. 41) that they are incapable of
sensible judgements for themselves. There are even suggestions that they will
lose touch with the 'real world'. 'Values of the real world do not exist. The
background of the girls working in offices is monotonous. The reader is seldom
told the type of industry' (p. 17). Now that would be exciting! And would, of
course, begin the transformation of readers' lives! If only they had known that
Helen, the heroine, worked in a *solicitor*'s office . . . typing, filing, running errands
. . . they'd begin to understand that 'doing' is better than 'dreaming'. It is hard
not to pour scorn on the appalling elitism in her argument. Education = good
(where education feels like a combination of MSC schemes plus travel
brochures); fantasy = bad (and especially so when it stays close to their lives).

The second element in her notion of 'identification' is the 'story-devices'
that make the reader feel part of the story. So, the majority of stories are 'written
from a woman's angle' (p. 16). This has the power to convert what would be
boring pap into an addictive drug. How otherwise do we make sense of this
paradoxical argument? 'The effect of the thin, superficial structure of the stories
with a choice of two endings, either catching the right boy or of being resigned
to tears until the right boy comes along, is one of frustration and leads to the
desire to read to another story in the hope that it might prove more interesting'
(p. 23). If so boring, why not throw the bloody thing away? Ah, because of
'identification'. It ensnares them. They are caught, unable to make any critical

response. The 'less educated, the less articulate and the unprivileged' will thus be confirmed in their unfortunate stupidity – thinking their office job dull, not thinking about what industry they work in, not knowing about the mysterious East.

What picture do we get of the individual stories? We have already seen the main components: amorality; anti-intellectualism; rejection of complexity, plus that 'the word "love" is thoroughly debased in the context of the stories'. (p. 11) (What undebased love is like, we can only guess . . .) But as we've seen, all these depend on external criteria about what the stories ought to do, but don't. Let us then consider a story she does cite as evidence: 'Time To Say Goodbye' (No. 99, 27 November 1965). It is one of the few of her *Jackie* references I have been able to track down. The story opens with narrator Judy standing uncertainly by her door. She is thinking: what will she say to Bill when she opens it? She'll tell him she won't be seeing him again . . .. but when she opens it, in he rushes and sweeps her off her feet, insisting on taking her for a fast drive. ('Life's never dull with him, but I wish . . .') At the coast they go for a swim. He lifts out of the water on to a rock and tells her he'd like to keep her there, safe, forever, just loving him. Love him? Oh yes, but that doesn't help her – she must give him up. After a good day, they drive slowly home, savouring each other's company. As she gets out of the car, he promises to be round tomorrow. She doesn't say goodbye . . . 'and now I never will say it because tomorrow I'm going away . . . tomorrow he'll find this note telling him'. She'll be gone for two years.

Why must she go? Think what you would expect, given Alderson's picture of 'amorality'. Again, I've 'hidden' the answer in the footnotes, so you can think it for yourselves first.[6] When you have looked, you will see that there is a real problem. The story expresses the early deep conservatism of *Jackie*. But that took the form of urging women to be too moral, dismissing their own desires and goals for others. The problem is not simply that Alderson is wrong. Rather, in measuring such a story by her external criteria she judges without understanding. Because the decision isn't moral in her sense of the word, it isn't moral at all.

In one sense Alderson is atypical, her politics are so markedly pre-feminist. Yet she is still frequently cited, no one having thought to go back and check her readings of the stories. Those who refer to her tend to dismiss her 'mass culture' theorising on its own as though it wouldn't have affected her interpretation of the stories themselves. It's not at all that she wants women returned to the home – far from it. True, they must have those 'home-making skills'. But they also need to be broadened; they must get out into the world of men, run a home, bring up the children, read great literature, go to university, learn about the worlds of intellect, politics and work. With all this to do, there simply isn't time for diversions like romance. I am not caricaturing, only spelling out what she has left implicit. If the resultant picture is awful, that is her problem, not mine.

Subsequent analysts of romance comics have been much more influenced by the arguments of the women's movement. They share Alderson's dislike of Jackie and its equivalents and judge their influence baleful. But Alderson's insistence on women keeping their home-making skills now becomes part of the problem – to which Jackie contributes. These critiques have been of two main kinds: those using the idea of 'stereotyping', and those using a semiological approach.

Jackie and 'stereotyping'

Through books and other literature, and the great expansion of mass media, ideal images are created and reflected which force comparison on their recipients.[7]

Sue Sharpe's is a classic study of the ways female infants are transformed into 'ideal daughters and wives'. It is in the 'stereotyping' tradition. The mass media are seen as bearing a sizeable responsibility for maintaining the passivity and social inequality of women. They do this by producing simplified ideal 'images': 'The implications of both male and female ideals and stereotypes are not beneficial to those striving to follow them' (p. 68). Sharpe does not study girls' comics and magazines alone. She paints a general picture of the unfolding influences a girl meets as she grows up, goes to school, learns to read, begins to form sexual ideas, and so on. The influences are unidirectional and cumulative. The unifying factor is a division between the sexes into active and passive roles, well summarised in the following: 'The active and passive dimensions of traditional male and female roles can be seen clearly in the way that a man's major activities are outward-directed and a woman's inner-directed. He goes out to confront and capture the outside world while she constructs a cosy inside shelter for them both' (p. 68). It is not easy reviewing Sharpe's argument about Jackie since she gives no references at all. At one level it would be easy to cite stories where a girl is actively interested in more than 'constructing cosy shelters', but that would not be very effective. These could be exceptions, perhaps. And anyway I have a suspicion that 'active' isn't being used with quite its literal meaning. I want to begin, instead, by tackling Sharpe's conceptualisation.

There are a number of implications in that quotation. The first is that Jackie is really an element in a larger process. We may point to a particular magazine like Jackie and criticise its role in reproducing stereotypes, but it is not the source of them. Stereotypes have a life beyond the particular magazine. So if Jackie stories do not end in marriage, that is no reason to think that the magazine is not still part of the stereotype; it is merely limited to one or two aspects of it.

The Cathy & Claire columns may regularly tell girls that they should enjoy romance widely, have loads of boyfriends and see what happens rather than seeking out a permanent relationship. This doesn't alter the picture. It is still a component in a larger unity: the all-embracing stereotypes of male activity and female passivity. The magazine must be read for its part in this. This shows the importance of reviewing the construct 'stereotype'. Jackie alone can neither prove nor refute it, since it overrides the particularity of the magazine. We can concern ourselves with what is different about Jackie if we like. But the parts that matter are those which contribute to the wider stereotypes or ideal images.

Add in that word 'traditional'. It is as if these 'stereotypes' are relics of a bad past, still hanging on and infecting our present lives. Sharpe is not alone in suggesting this. Polly Toynbee, for example, talked of 'the stultifying role stereotypes of the past' – as if they correspond to nothing in the present. But Sharpe is more ambivalent about that. Compare these two quotations:

> Reading primers usually focus on a family, especially the children and their activities. They are meant to seem 'normal' and because of this, they present people who are exaggerated and even caricatured: for instance mothers who seldom go outside the home and never have any sort of job, and working class women with hair tied up in Mrs-Mop-style scarves. Since life appears largely like this anyway, sexism is not always obvious. (p. 92)

> The heroes and heroines of these books are found living happily and peacefully in sunny suburbia . . . They occupy a large roomy house . . . Their toys are large and expensive . . . Jane . . . seems to be a very well-brought up middle class girl . . . Her brother Peter, however, is just the opposite. He is a very active and assertive little rascal . . . In this unreal world neither of them appears to encounter the day to day problems of living and there is no conflict. They have parents with the temperaments of saints whose patience and understanding is limitless. It is hardly a reflection of average family life. (p. 93)

Note that Sharpe condemns the books she is discussing both for being too like 'real life', and for being 'unreal'. If they are unreal, they are selling false images. If they are real and reflect the world as it is, they are disguisedly reinforcing. How does one escape this? Heads, you are too unreal – you are selling an unreal ideal; tails, you are not unreal enough – you are normalising the world as it is. When we look at the general concept of a 'stereotype', we will see that this is a particular example of a general problem.

The problem with this is how Sharpe's idea of the 'real' relates to her idea of 'images'. Anything not openly acknowledging those things of which Sharpe is convinced, is (almost deliberately) hiding them. So: 'People's real life problems are very specific and personal, and those besetting the love story couples are less ordinary and more glamorous and mysterious. But the solutions described for all of them share a common failing in not considering the more basic social problems that many are facing with low wages, bad housing, and

unemployment. Evil is always lurking within people rather than within a system'
(p. 106). It must take a very specific kind of magazine not to reinforce stereotypes
or disguise reality, then. Yup: 'Compared with these [Honey, Jackie etc] Spare Rib
magazine is specifically feminist and devotes its pages to issues of far greater
relevance to the situation of ordinary girls and women'. (p. 107) I am not
criticising Spare Rib, but more relevant on whose criteria? If Jackie readers disagree, and argue that there are other things of relevance to them – like, how
to handle difficult romantic relationships – Sharpe, I suppose, can always reply
that they have been conned. That's possible, but it only goes to reinforce the
centrality of her notion of 'stereotype'. Now it must do circular service, defending itself by showing that people who dismiss its objections have already been
'influenced'. They can't give evidence, because they are part of the problem.

The fact is that there is a jump in Sharpe's argument, as in so many others'
– from absence to exclusion. Presenting her account of influence, she writes
that 'This literature probably only acts as a reinforcement to the limited views
and interests that have already developed, but it is important for what it omits
from its content. Like much of the mass media, it endorses the status quo by
leaving out any suggestions for the possibility or desirability of change' (pp.
106-7). To leave out is to deny what is left out. Not to mention change is to
deny its possibility. How? Sharpe does actually come close to answering, but
in a way which gets stranger the longer you look at it. It is given in two passages,
the first of which is discussing comics for younger girls:

> In these comics, girls are seen as rehearsing for their future roles in the family . . .
> Characteristically, these comics never reveal what becomes of their bright, ingeni-
> ous and persevering heroines when they get older. If these publications, unlike
> comic fantasy for boys, are trying to be realistic, then perhaps they are right. There
> are very few successful women in our society and it is difficult to write drama
> and adventure stories about housewives and mothers. But whatever the reasons,
> the future for these heroines is always left blank. (p. 100)

I'm sorry if it seems fussy, but this does need unpicking. Sharpe has described
the stereotype for girls as passivity. Yet in these pre-teen comics, the girls are
active and clever. How to square this circle? Well, they never tell us what
happened after the end of the story . . . Now that is true, almost a tautology.
But then, when did we ever demand of any other kind of story that it tells us
the remainder of its characters' lives? Of course, this connects with her main
argument that the 'stereotype' of femininity is bigger than any instance. A
'stereotype' is a sort of Platonic unIdeal determining instances. So what would
happen after the end of the story, would be a bit more of the stereotype,
wouldn't it? But then she goes on to say that 'if these publications are trying
to be realistic', then they can't show us the real endings, because there is no
adventure in the lives of real women. Sharpe has walked into a trap of her own

making. No one except critics of her kind ever thought these stories were trying to be 'realistic'. For she and other critics are those who insist that either a story is realistic (and therefore should talk about unemployment, abortion, sexism etc), or it is fantastic (in which case it has to be seen as a disguise over reality). The only other alternative they allow is to be openly oppositional.

In the second passage, Sharpe is considering romance comics in particular. In oracular fashion, we are told that 'The plots (if they can be called that) unfailingly contain some perspective on love' (p. 101). From this alone, Sharpe knows that they must 'obviously run counter to all notions of Women's Liberation. They obliterate any idea of girls as independent individuals having interests of their own' (p. 101). I'm afraid that this syllogism is only valid if (and I would want to deny it most strongly) love and women's liberation are mutually exclusive. It also requires equating the independence of women's liberation with not having 'involving relationships' – something else I would want to question.[8] But I also wonder at the difficulty she finds in comics like Jackie 'unfailingly containing some perspective on love'. If we were to say of detective novels that they 'unfailingly' contain some perspective on crime and its discovery, or of science fiction that it always presented some view of other times and places, would we feel we had learnt much? With Sharpe, we feel the condemnation, and a sense of something dubious having been perpetrated. Why? There is no answer.

We can see that Sharpe overlaps importantly with Alderson. Both 'knew in advance' what was wrong with the magazine. It didn't do what they wanted. Therefore it was not only inadequate, it was working against what they wanted. In both, this is poor theory and even poorer analysis. My one regret is that I am unable to show how Sharpe then works on particular stories. This is simply because I haven't been able to find a single story she (usually very vaguely) cites. Perhaps that in itself tells us something.

McRobbie's semiological analysis

Surely the most influential analysis of girls' romance comics has to be Angela McRobbie's. Published originally in 1979, then updated by a further discussion in her co-edited Feminism For Girls (with a report of her research on Jackie readers in between), it is often seen as the definitive study of Jackie.[9] Only the first piece is explicitly semiological in orientation; but the difference is hard to detect. The first study sees Jackie as mapping out the feminine career 'in such all-embracing terms, there is little or no space allowed for alternatives' (1, p. 3). In the third piece, she writes of all other ideas being 'eliminated' (3, p. 120), of readers being 'denied any choice' (3, p. 125), 'allowed no time off from' romance (3, p. 124). Romances are 'the only attachments worth forming'; any other kind 'don't find a place' (3, p. 119): 'Instead of having hobbies, instead of going fishing, learning to play the guitar, or even learning to swim or play tennis, the girl is encouraged to load all her eggs in the basket of romance and hope it pays off' (3, p. 118). Once again, the language of 'limits' leads to the language of 'restriction' leads to the language of 'exclusion'. It would be easy to show that this is actually untrue. *Jackie* does encourage its readers to have other interests; it regularly advises girls that romance is not the only thing that matters in their lives. But to reply thus would only suggest that McRobbie has overstated her case a bit. We need to look at how she uses a theory and a method to reach these conclusions.

McRobbie combines a semiological way of looking at meanings with a view of young girls' especial marginality and vulnerability. So, *Jackie* is popular: '. . . not because it furnishes its readers with any positive self-image, not because it encourages them to value themselves and each other, but because it offers its exclusive attention to an already powerless group, to a group which receives little public attention and which is already, from an early age, systematically denied any real sense of identity, creativity, or control' (3, p. 128). I don't want to deny this. Young girls, particularly young working class girls, are marginalised in our society. But that doesn't necessarily mean that they are more vulnerable to media influence. McRobbie thinks it does: '*Jackie* is so definitive about its dealing with youth and femininity, it's so authoritative (in the friendliest way), it implies ultimately that it's all "sewn up", all dealt with here. This makes it difficult for readers to imagine alternatives' (3, p. 115). Ironically as we will see in the next chapter, the period she samples is one in which the magazine was losing confidence in its own view of romance. But let that wait. I am interested in her bracketed reference to *Jackie's* friendly tone, a point repeated from the first study. By comparison, earlier magazines were much more preachy and dictatorial. *Marilyn*, for example, one of its immediate predecessors used to run a strip-column headed 'Mum Knows Best' which gave direct instructions on behaviour. It looks very much as though on McRobbie's theory *Jackie* is more dangerous since it is friendlier than the older overtly conservative magazines. She could be right, but we need to know how she reaches this conclusion. To understand, we need to consider the theory of semiology.

Semiology is an approach to understanding how meanings are generated and communicated; it derives ultimately from the work of the Swiss linguist Ferdinand de Saussure. I will only state the theory briefly here, enough hopefully to make clear how it is used on *Jackie*. Semiology argues that while language is clearly the most important system of meanings, it is not unique. There are many other equivalent systems, for example, clothing, food, furniture, gestures and facial expressions. We don't wear clothes only to keep warm, or eat food only to satisfy hunger; we choose clothes to convey a self-image, a social status, our choice of foods expresses all kinds of social ideas. They are all rich in meanings, are 'languages' in their own right. Thus all of them share certain features:

1. Any 'language' is composed of *signs*: road-signs, at one extreme, which exist purely for the sake of conveying a message. At the other extreme, a car, a pet, a jacket, a hairdo all also convey meanings; but they do other jobs as well. In each case, though, we have a sign. Signs, say semiologists, are a combination of two elements: a signifier – whatever is used to convey the meaning; and the signified – this is the concept conveyed. This is an important step in their argument. The signified of 'dog' is not the animal. It is the concept of a dog. When we name something we are assigning it to a category, saying what kind of thing it is. If not, we couldn't make any sense of the following. I go into a house, and I see two orange boxes upturned and side by side. Someone asks me to put something on 'the table', and points to the boxes. 'That's hardly a proper table', I think – and thus I reveal that 'table' is a category with criteria to be met before something is assigned to it. My concept of a table was offended by the boxes. But the implication is that words do not directly depict the world; they cut it up into categories.

2. No single unit of a 'language' can produce meaning on its own. Each unit, says semiology, gets its meaning by being different from the other units surrounding it. An example: 'woman' is a concept with many associations. To call someone 'womanly' is traditionally to think of them as supportive, motherly, attractive. But to call a man a 'woman' would be an insult, implying lack of proper qualities. He is being called weak, emotional, dependent, and so on. To call a woman 'manly' is more equivocal, suggesting strength and independence, but perhaps 'not properly female'. The point the semiologists want to make is that the meanings of 'woman' can't be understood except through its difference from/relation to 'man'. They define each other by their differences. Thus language is a system of differences.

3. A sign then has two elements. It also does two jobs. It denotes – that is, it points towards those things in the world which fall under it. But it also connotes – that is, it links the things it denotes by association with other things. A standard example is 'rose'. 'Rose' denotes a range of flowers. But in our culture, it has taken on connotations of romance. Other flowers have taken on different connotations, though few quite as definitely: 'buttercups' with innocence and childhood, 'orchids' with luxury. The important thing is that connotations reflect cultural ideas and practices. It is here we begin to see why semiology can have political implications.

Let us try out its distinction on a more significant example. Take the word 'democracy'. In our culture, 'democracy' occupies a very special place in our 'system of differences', somewhat like this:

DEMOCRACY		TYRANNY		
=	versus	AUTOCRACY	=	BAD
GOOD		TOTALITARIANISM		

Democracy is clearly a good thing – but what kind of a good thing is it? It is a state of affairs, a political arrangement. It is good, almost by definition, to live in 'a democracy'. But compare 'Western democracy', or 'political democracy' which sound right, with 'school democracy' or 'industrial democracy' or 'prison democracy'. The last three sound awkward. 'Democracy' is not simply a term which depicts clearly, and adds on a glow of rightness; it is rather complicated. It is a good state of affairs within certain spheres. And it has other implications, too. The following was a news trailer on Radio 4 during 1986: 'Today the Queen visits China, the country which tried to step from feudalism to socialism without going through democracy. Today, it is trying to mend its ways.'[10] Democracy is apparently a 'good in itself'. It is a 'system' without which societies can't achieve anything, apparently . . .

This has not always been so. Consider the following quotation from a nineteenth-century essay prompted by concerns over the newly enfranchised working class, and their penchant for 'Dreadful' reading matter:

> The penny novelette has probably much more effect on the women members of the working classes than the newspaper has on the men . . . In the majority of instances the objects held up to the derision of the people are the aristocracy, the plutocracy, and sometimes even the monarchy itself . . . Capital and birth are the two themes on which the democratic journalist never tires of expatiating. By deriding the governing classes he hopes to arouse the enthusiasm of the public. He is, however, victim of the delusion that the democracy is primarily moved by enmity towards the aristocracy.[11]

Here 'democracy' is not a state of affairs. It is a definite group of people, a dangerous, unpredictable mass; and they stand opposite aristocracy, security, rationality. Try inserting that meaning of 'democracy' into Brian Redhead's comments on China, and it looks decidedly odd. Or try to talk of a 'property-owning democracy' in the nineteenth century meaning. It becomes a contradiction in terms!

In any 'language', then, units get their meaning from their difference from/relation to all the other elements around them.

4. We don't just see differences, we see relationships. If a 'language' cuts up its world, it also puts it back together again to form a system. Meanings form patterns. So, we don't just see women as different from men, but as having particular kinds of relationships to them. To be a 'woman' in our society's main cultural definition is to stand in particular relationships to men, to children, to politics, to work, to nature and so on. When I was a child, I well remember learning an expression for when everyone significant was at some gathering: we said 'all the world and his wife were there' . . . Think about it. This reassembling in distinct patterns is what is meant by the semiological terms 'code' and 'myth'.

5. The next element is the separation of 'langue' and 'parole'. 'Langue' is language as a system, pre-existing any individual who may use it. A child learning to speak misstates the past tense of 'come' as 'comed'. It is corrected. Its use (parole) of the language is measured against certain rules which make up the 'langue'. People of course do both make mistakes and deliberately break the rules. But you can only make mistakes and break rules if there are rules to be broken. This is (crudely) the distinction between 'langue', the system of words and their meanings at any time; and 'parole', the way an individual uses (or misuses) that system.

6. Lastly comes the element in semiological thought that is surely the most important for its theory of ideology. It is also the most troublesome. This is the 'arbitrariness' of languages. 'Language is an arbitrary system of differences with no positive term', wrote Saussure. This is not the place for a full discussion of this. But some discussion is necessary. First, it has more levels of meaning than are usually acknowledged. Normally, commentators discuss only two meanings of 'arbitrary':

a. *The choice of signifier is arbitrary.* It does not matter what sound is used to signify four-legged, hooved animals used for riding. The fact that the English language uses 'horse' whereas French uses 'cheval' is irrelevant – each works equally well as signifier. The only (partial) exceptions are onomatopoeic words, like 'hiss', where (perhaps) a sound may have evolved as signifier because of its similarity to the concept it is depicting. This notion of arbitrariness poses no problem, as far as I can see.

b. *The relation of signifier to signified is arbitrary.* In English we separate the concepts of 'tree' and 'bush'. French does not – but it does distinguish (as Jonathan Culler points out) between rivers flowing to the sea, and those that flow into lakes.[12] The argument of the semiologists is that there are no self-evident classifications which impose themselves on language. Language carves up the world, not the other way round. This is a highly contentious claim, but one which I am not discussing directly in this book. I note it particularly because it connects with a third meaning of 'arbitrariness', one that is relevant to how we should understand 'ideology'. This third meaning is missing from most discussions of semiology:

c. *The 'system of differences' that is a 'language' imposes itself on us in arbitrary fashion.* The best way to understand this is to see what is excluded by it. There are in theory plenty of reasons why we might accept a claim about the world. It could be because it is the only view we have ever come across, or because it seems to make sense of our experience, or because, after evidence and arguments, it seems the most plausible. It could be enforced on us, by fear or threat, or because the ideas have some pleasing quality. None of these is necessarily innocent. But the mode of persuasion, as we might call it, is quite different in each case.

Now semiology is not only a theory dealing with how meanings are produced. It already contains a theory of influence. Language is a system governed
by rules before we use it. The world only falls into categories of meaning
because language imposes them on it. Because of these ideas, semiology has
to assert that any 'language' works on us by imposing itself on us, in effect, by
gridding us. Of course semiologists say that we can and do resist this influence.
But their theory already tells them how that influence must work. It tells them
what sort of effect it must have. Put crudely, their idea is that we do not accept
ideas because they make sense of our world for us; they make sense of our
world because we have been influenced by them. We do not accept them
because they appear to us rational and intelligible; they appear rational and
intelligible because we have been moulded in that system's image. The theory
of ideology implied by semiology is a grossly anti-rational one.

It was Saussure who coined the term 'semiology' for a future science of
meanings. This science would encompass all sign-systems including language.
But Saussure's particular view of language would have made it hard for him to
have applied his ideas to systems like fashion, or cars. This was because he
thought of each 'language' coinciding with the boundaries of a natural language.
French was a 'langue', so were English, Dutch, Arabic. It was hard on such an
account to make much sense of dialects or local variations. It was still harder
to be able to think of ideologies. For to think about ideology in his way, you
need to be able to think of a 'local system'. This might then 'belong to' or 'fit
the interests of' some social group. It took Barthes' reworking of Saussure's
ideas to make that possible. He dropped the assumption that we 'already know'
the boundaries of a sign-system; that became a problem to be solved.

But that left him in a difficult situation. Saussure could perhaps not deal
adequately with social difference within a language. But at least his approach
made it clear how we would know the boundaries of a system. Look at a
dictionary. But once stop identifying the system with natural language, and the
problem arises: how do we identify the limits of a system? And if we are doing
research how do we know when we have a sample that will enable us to grasp
the whole system? We do need to know if we are going to investigate, say,
Jackie. For semiology requires us to look for a complete 'system' in it. How
exactly are we to do this? What in fact happens is that these Saussurean assumptions change into something just as worrying. They become *methodological commands.* I want to show what these are, and then illustrate their workings on *Jackie*:

1. *The surface features of a cultural object like Jackie must be understood as expressions of
an underlying pattern or structure.* Semiology says meanings are created in systems.
But systems are not apparent on the surface of a culture. We have to look
beyond the surface to the way all the elements interrelate. But straightaway this
command sets up a problem. Which surface elements should we focus on? A
concrete case: during the 1960-70s D C Thomson, publishers of *Jackie*, became

dependent for much of their artwork on Spanish artists. This had effects on how the characters looked. They tended to be highly idealised, postdated copies of images from other British media. Long after Twiggy and Jean Shrimpton had left the advertising scene, their lookalikes graced the pages of *Jackie*. How should we interpret this? On one interpretation this is an accident of the production history of the magazine, a curious but not very revealing fact. It might even be seen as a barrier to what *Jackie* was trying to say. When in 1978/9 D C Thomson adopted photostrip techniques, perhaps that was a solution to the problem of having to use overseas artists.

Another interpretation favoured by both McRobbie and Sharpe is that the drawings by the foreign artists expressed the comic's fundamental ideology: an idealisation of romance, a highly selected range of physical and personality types, narrowing the possibilities for self-images. How should we decide between these? Following the methodological command, we have to go for the second explanation. The command 'treat surface features as expressive of a deeper pattern' means that in principle we must treat every single surface feature as part of the 'system'. Drawing styles, print styles, paper quality, size, format, price, sectioning, editorial matter, quizzes, stories, references to the 'stars' (and perhaps a schematism of metaphorical connection between 'stars' (= horoscopes) and 'stars' (= pop idols) could be built . . . ?), letters, and so on ad infinitum. Everything must count. As I tried to show (in Chapter 6), there can be no principle for distinguishing relevant from irrelevant surface features. Everything is equally meaningful. The result is that the decision about what to attend to, must be a function of the investigator's own prejudgements. Because of the other methodological commands, it can only confirm her or his hunches. It can never challenge them.

2. *Look for a system, a unified system of differences.* Here further aspects of the first command come to light. First, *Jackie* for example must be a complete system. This is how the problem of the adequacy of a sample comes back as practical problem. It must be enough just to look at the comic by itself. That alone should reveal the 'system of differences'. Second, *Jackie* must be coherent. If there are contradictory elements, they must be simply differences within the (unified) system. The methodological command to find a system of differences turns into a command to carry on researching until we have found a complete, coherent system. We will know when our research is complete, by the 'discovery' of a system. Afterwards we might want to look at how people use it. But that is a separate study. And you can't even begin on that until you have met the third demand

3. *Explore how the system works to impose itself.* This command comes out of Barthes' modification of Saussure's theory. On Barthes' view a system can embody a socially-inflected view of the world. To do this effectively, it must disguise its own origins. Recall Barthes' claim that if something is disguised, it will be more

effective in persuading us than if it reveals its nature; and this leads to some curious claims about disguises. McRobbie for example claims that *Jackie* is somehow concealing its nature as commodity:

> One of the most immediate and outstanding features of *Jackie* as it is displayed on bookstalls, newspaper stands and counters, up and down the country, is its ability to look 'natural'. It takes its place easily within that whole range of women's magazines which rarely change their format and which (despite new arrivals which quickly achieve this solidity if they are to succeed) always seem to have been there! Its existence is taken for granted. Yet this front obscures the 'artificiality' of the magazine, its 'productness' and its existence as a commodity. It also obscures the nature of the processes by which it is produced. (1, p. 11-12)

I always find myself wanting to ask silly questions when confronted with claims like this: like, would it be hiding or revealing its existence-as-commodity more if the price was covered up? I honestly do not know what is meant by this kind of claim that 'appearing natural' is a disguise for the processes of production. What would have to change to make it untrue? It seems to me a simple confusion between something being recognisable and being naturalised. Just because *Jackie* looks like other magazines, I can see no reason why this should make us confused about how or why it is produced.

The problem is the way semiologists know what they must find. It is a game of Hunt-The-Thimble where you know there must be one. Keep looking long enough, and eventually, something will be found that you can call a thimble. In McRobbie this goes one stage further. She not only knew in advance that there must be a unified system in *Jackie*; she also knew what kind of system it must be and what jobs it would do. This is because the take-up of semiology in the 1970s was not 'innocent'. It was taken up because it offered a way of investigating 'culture' that fitted the needs of post-1968 radical suspicions. Disappointed hopes led to a search for the villains who were restraining workers, women, black people from radical action. One of the main blackguards had to be the media. People had been bought off mentally as well as materially. The most recent phase of capitalism (now also called patriarchal) was one that 'positioned people as consumers'; it produced the goods and pseudo-goods to sell to its populace; it produced pseudo-leisure in which to use those goods; and it produced the pseudo-ideas to tie us into consuming. To understand it all, we had to give particular attention to the processes of masking and directing our wishes. At the macro-level the arguments of Louis Althusser told of the 'construction of the subject' as an essential stage of the reproduction of labour.

Semiology neatly dropped into place in this explanation; we 'already know' that consumerist capitalism depends on our willing self-subjugation to being used in certain ways. Now we could show how this was done. This is how McRobbie can begin her essay on *Jackie* with her conclusions: that *Jackie* is involved with consumerist capitalism at three levels. It is a product (but 'hides' the fact); it sells products; and it sells an all-consuming involvement with leisure which is the necessary ideology to maintain the other two. These between them construct Jackie. And though McRobbie insists (1, p. 2) that hers is not a conspiracy model, that denial sits uneasily with claims like the following: 'a concerted effort is . . . made to win and shape the consent of the readers to a particular set of values' (ibid).

Reading Jackie semiologically

I want to show how McRobbie's semiological premises control her approach, and the problems that arise from this. She finds four 'codes': of romance, fashion and beauty, pop, and personal and domestic life. This means much more to her than that there is a lot about each of these in Jackie. These codes combine to present young girls with 'an ideological bloc of mammoth proportions' (1, p. 3). They bind together despite tensions between them. The stories may be idealised and fantastic. But then the problem pages in their grim black and white make sure both that you connect it with your own life and that you can't escape its messages: 'The problem page invariably occupies the same place in all women's magazines, i.e. the inside back page. Comfortably apart from the more light-hearted articles, and set amidst the less flamboyant and colourful small advertisements, it regenerates a flagging interest and also sums up the ideological content of the magazine. It hammers home, on the last but one page, all those ideas and values prevalent in the other sections, but this time in unambiguous black and white' (1, p. 29).

Pause on this. (1) She assumes (wrongly) that the problem page always appears in that position in Jackie – and that is part of its meaning. (2) She assumes that, though set apart, the problem pages still combine with the rest to form a unified message. (3) She assumes that being set inside the back page is 'motivated' by a need to retain interest. (4) She assumes that black and white print is a meaningful feature rather than, say, a cost-saving feature given that some other parts of the magazine would just not look good in black and white. There are other assumptions also – each in itself tiny and not very important. All are products of those methodological commands.

This all adds up to a potential for influence even though the magazine might be used subversively: 'Clearly, girls do use it as a means of signalling their boredom and disaffection, in the school, for example. The point here is that despite these possible uses, the magazine itself has a powerful presence as a form, and as such demands analyses carried out apart from these uses of "readings"' (1, p. 6). Remember that for semiology 'form' has a special meaning; it is the system of differences, the deep structure constructing the surface expressions. 'Form' is what arbitrarily imposes itself on us. To say that Jackie has this form, then, is already to have identified its ideology – which we must study *apart* from how it is used. What is the ideology, then? McRobbie states it in two ways. First she accuses *Jackie* of creating a 'false totality' (1, p. 3) in which class and racial differences among girls are elided for the sake of an ideology of ageness, creating a natural biological grouping of adolescent girls, all with the same interests: 'Thus we *all* want to know how to catch a man, lose weight, look our best, or cook well! Having mapped out the 'feminine 'career' in such all-embracing terms, there is little or no space allowed for alternatives. Should the present stage be unsatisfactory the reader is merely encouraged to look forward to the next. Two things are happening here. 1) The girls are being invited to join a close, intimate sorority where secrets can be exchanged and advice given; and 2) they are also being presented with an ideological bloc of mammoth proportions, one which *imprisons* them in a claustrophobic world of jealousy and competitiveness, the most unsisterly of emotions, to say the least' (1, p. 3). In her second summary she specifies more closely. After noting the fake slangy language used in both the magazine and a lot of adverts, she writes:

> The characters in *Jackie* stories and in Coca Cola TV adverts at least seem to be getting things done. They are constantly seen 'raving it up' at discos, going for trips in boyfriends' cars, or else going on holiday. And yet as we shall see, the female and male characters in *Jackie* are simultaneously doing nothing but pursuing each other, and far from being a pleasure-seeking *group*: in fact these stories consist of isolated individuals, distrusting even their best friends and in search of fulfilment only through a partner. The anonymity of the language then parallels the strangely amorphous *Jackie* girls. Marked by a rootlessness, lack of ties or sense of region, the reader is unable to 'locate' them in any social context. They are devoid of history. Bound together by an invisible 'generational consciousness' they inhabit a world where no disruptive values exist. At the 'heart' of this world is the individual girl looking for romance. But romance is not itself an unproblematic category and what I will be arguing here is that its central contradiction is glaringly clear and unavoidable even to the girl herself who is so devoted to its cause. This contradiction is based round the fact that the *romantic moment*, its central 'core', cannot be reconciled with its promise for *eternity*. To put it another way, the code of romance realises, but cannot accept, that the man can adore, love, 'cherish' and be sexually attracted to his girlfriend and simultaneously be 'aroused' by other girls. . . It is the recognition of this fact that sets all girls against each other, and forms the central theme in the picture stories. Hence the girl's constant worries, as she is passionately embraced: 'can it last?' or 'how can I be sure his love is for ever?'. (1, pp. 17-18)

I have quoted this at length, because it reveals a lot about McRobbie's account. She begins from a claim about a division between surface and depth. On the surface, they're doing things in groups. But underneath, they're alone and doing nothing. How is this move sanctioned? It is done by a number of steps: (a) the surface is contradicted by a deeper pattern; (b) but the surface does not draw attention to this. Its role is to disguise the pattern; (c) it is the deeper pattern that has the effects – the masking surface merely acts like a carrier-wave. The surface elements are in fact a 'trap' to deceive readers into accepting *Jackie's* message; (d) the underlying form, in focussing on romance, works systematically to exclude all alternatives; (e) the organising motif of the stories is the romantic moment. This motif is strengthened by the fact that the characters have no history or social location. This introduces the idea of eternal bliss; (f) however this is a problem, since in the world outside the magazine boys can be sexually attracted to many girls; (g) this contradiction, though experienced by the girl-characters, cannot be understood by the readers because of the magazine's deceits. They can only turn jealously against other girls. Therefore the magazine is teaching jealousy and competitiveness. (Call each of these points a 'move'.)

Wheels within wheels, and assumptions within assumptions. We need to examine these steps. First there are real problems just about her factual claims. Cathy and Claire for example have regularly changed their location within the magazine. But wherever they have appeared, they have always stressed the importance of female friendships and have encouraged girls not to give up female friends because of a romance. Would these challenge McRobbie? Probably not. She might reply that 'stories never end with two girls together'. That is, I agree, by and large true. But it is no reply, unless you add in two further points. First, the stories and the problem pages must be working in the same direction; they must form a single whole (moves (a-c)); and in merging, the stories must win out over Cathy and Claire, which must be purely surface gloss. Second, in showing a boy/girl couple as the end of stories, girl/girl couples must be being excluded – not only from the stories but from the whole of girls' lives (move (d)). Suppose I added that I have found very few stories, even among her own sample, where one girl's romantic ambitions threatened to founder on another's and even fewer where a girl is shown having to 'break friends' with another over a boy – must that worry her? Again, no. On her account, it does not have to be directly said or shown. It can be implied. So, how do we know when a story is implying competition between girls over boys?

The issue for her turns on that unspoken threat, boys' sexuality. This is something which McRobbie has brought in from outside – she herself says it rarely appears in the stories. It is, she feels, being contained in silence (move (f)). But if this was just the magazine sharing a secret with its readers ('boys don't half try it on'), then their solution ('believe in romance and the ideal boy, don't ever trust your female friends') would surely collapse into ashes at the next boy with overactive hands. Or if it meant that girls should set up an image of an ideal boy who doesn't try it on but is interested like the girls in romance: that ought to lead to them being very choosy and demanding of their boys –

hardly the model of the passive, vulnerable girl that McRobbie presents us with. And it wouldn't certainly lead to distrusting other girls. It would be real boys who could not be trusted. No, McRobbie has to mean that Jackie takes in but hides boys' sexuality. (Moves (b, c, h))

How does Jackie do this? McRobbie simply does not tell us. She just assumes it happens. Instead she answers another question: how is the magazine able to be influential? Her answer is revealing. First, the girls are just very vulnerable, and Jackie alone seems to take them seriously (I will return to this point in Chapter 11). Second, Jackie is so 'all-embracing' that it simply excludes all other possibilities. Again, this is assumed to be a powerful thing to do despite the large amount of psychological evidence that, for example, propaganda that ignores and discounts alternatives is nowhere near as effective as that which confronts and argues against those alternatives. (I am being charitable – McRobbie simply equates 'leaving out' with 'excluding', for example in the three words 'ignored or dismissed' (1, p. 50).)

But most significantly, she argues that the magazine has ways to entrap the reader (move (d) again). She distinguishes between the surface-elements of Jackie that link with the deep 'form'; and those which try to sell it to us. The latter are not part of the ideology of Jackie. They are the guise in which that ideology is packaged to us to make it palatable, like a sugar coating. And the main element she says does this job is the way it *appears to be fun*: 'What then are the key features which characterise Jackie? First there is a "lightness" of tone, a non-urgency, which holds true right through the magazine particularly in the use of colour, graphics and advertisements. It asks to be read at a leisurely pace indicating that its subject matter is not wholly serious, is certainly not "news"' (1, p. 9). Now why shouldn't we take this as a hint from Jackie not to become too engrossed, to take its pronouncements with a pinch of salt? In other words, why should it not be a *modification* of the message? That interpretation would surely gain merit if we recall that one section of the magazine is kept separate from the lightness of tone: the problem pages. Not only are they always serious, they are also held separate from the rest of the magazine in another way: when the rest of the editorial staff engage in banter, Cathy and Claire never join in. There is a serious aura which doesn't occur elsewhere. But once note this, and the 'unity' of the magazine starts decomposing. Perhaps then the 'non-urgent tone' is not a ploy for making the serious messages acceptable. Maybe it actually is a declaration that it is *not wholly* serious.

This is a good example of semiology's becoming unassailable through making arbitrary distinctions, then declaring these arbitrary elements to have coded significance.[13] Semiology requires this division of the surface features into those containing the ideology, and those which disguise it and act as transmission aids. There are no objective ways of deciding which is which. Therefore the method can only prove whatever the analyst 'knew in advance'. McRobbie knew that *Jackie* does not paint a feminist picture. Thus she was bound to discover in it an anti-feminist message. Before we can understand the resulting readings of the stories, we need to look at the history of *Jackie* stories.

Conclusion

All these analyses of *Jackie* start from unsatisfactory theories of influence and ideology. I am aware of a real danger of appearing arrogant in this dismissal. At least they have tried, and sometimes under difficult circumstances. My only answer can be to do better myself. I want to argue that to understand *Jackie*, we must not assume that it forms a 'unified' text. Rather, the relations between parts are tricky. The place to start is the problem pages.

'But how can I ever be sure?': revisiting *Jackie*

Compare the following:

> Dear C & C, I'm mixed up, in love and desperate. The boy is 18 – and only out for one thing. He never takes me out on a real date, like to a party or to the pictures or dancing. Please don't lecture me. I'm a girl who listens to her heart and not her head. If you could see him you'd understand. He's a combination of Paul McCartney and Billy J Kramer. Don't tell me to stop seeing him.
>
> *We've no advice for a girl who says she listens to her heart instead of her head. These affairs always wind up the same way. The boy will drop you when he gets bored. If you think you're being used now – just wait.* (Letter and reply by Cathy & Claire, 25 January 1964)

> Lynda is being offered promotion at work, but it means moving to Birmingham and away from her boyfriend. When told, he simply congratulates her and then gets on to telling her about his own plans. He thinks it's obvious she should go – so she does, miserably. In Birmingham, she is lonely and can't enjoy herself at all; she refuses to answer his letters, or speak to him on the phone – until he eventually travels to Birmingham to seek her out for himself. Whereupon all comes right again because 'now our heads weren't ruling our hearts'. ('Give Me An Answer By Monday', No. 261, 4 January 1969)

According to standard accounts of *Jackie*, all the aspects of the magazine add together to make a single message. I have come to reject that view. Of course, the contrast between the two above could be explained away; but I believe it points up a division between the kind of knowledge offered by answers to readers' problems, and the approach inherent in the picture stories.

In one sense critics are right who say that the *Jackie* letters page deals only with a narrow range of problems. Consistently the largest category is problems in relationships with boys (though these decline curiously between 1979 and 1981). These range from not being able to get a boyfriend, through how to start a relationship, how to handle misunderstandings (with the boy, with parents, etc), how to interpret one's own feelings, and how to end it cleanly. Beyond these, there are all kinds of problems about parents, siblings, health, beauty and bodies, occasional issues of sex, and a range of requests for information (about holidays, jobs and the like). It isn't easy to know if this restricted range is the result of editorial staff selecting only those within agreed boundaries, or whether readers have become sufficiently awake to the limits that this is all they now write about. In the end it makes little difference.

A good deal of the advice C & C give is specific and commonsensical. Talk to your parents about this, think about ending that relationship, try the following practical things, go out and have some fun. In small respects, advice has changed over the years. In the 2 January 1965 issue, for example, in answer to a question about how to approach two boys the enquirers fancied, the answer was to leave it, 'It's the boys who are supposed to do the chasing, you know'. By 1980 this was acknowledged to have changed: 'Nowadays we're able to do more, so keep plugging away. Maybe it'll happen' (26 January 1980). But these changes are exceptional. In most respects C & C's specific advice hasn't changed. They are not always on parents' side against girls, they don't recommend that girls just give way to boys' wishes; romance is set in a context of other activities like other (female) friendships, schoolwork, hobbies. It is never suggested that boys are the most important thing in a girls' life. (I couldn't find a single scrap of evidence for this common claim.) But it is not at this level of specific advice that we will discover the importance of the problem pages.

A first clue can be gleaned from their (rare, in my sample) response to queries about sexual affairs. In No. 2, 18 January 1964, a letter asked how a girl should respond to a boyfriend who asked here to 'prove her love for him'. Replied C & C: 'I'd say "Why should I be a mug? I've more self-respect". And I'd think twice before calling him boyfriend, too!' It isn't the advice to say 'no' that we need to think about – young girls can come under a lot of pressure to agree to sex and advising them not to give in is not at all bad. No, it is that notion of 'self-respect'. It was deployed on other occasions, for example as the reason for owning up to having damaged a boyfriend's car. I draw attention to it because it is quite uncharacteristic. For example when much the same question arose in 1980, C & C answered differently. A reader asked what to do about petting that was 'going too far'. At the time she had enjoyed it but had felt 'dirty' afterwards. Their reply was to say that she had answered her own question – she wasn't happy about it. That must be the decider. She should discuss it with her boy. The important point is the way the girl's own feelings have become the test. Jackie's problem pages probably focus on that more than anything else. That early answer about self-respect is in this sense out of line, since that is a criterion independent of how the girl feels. It is something she ought to acknowledge, irrespective of how she feels. If she doesn't, C & C believe there will be unpleasant consequences. Feelings are dealt with differently.

Consider two responses given to readers: the first from 22 January 1966. A reader was bemoaning her bad relations with her parents. They give her presents, but they seem to expect more than a hug and a kiss in return. Cathy and Claire are very stern in their reply – re-read your own letter, they say; you must be very hard to love. You come across as very selfish. They are not always as brutally critical as this. On 9 January 1971 a reader told of her boyfriend Brian who comes from a very unhappy home. She wants to marry him, but her parents think Brian may just be using her as an escape. Their reply is judicious: maybe he is. The important thing is, how do you feel about him? The fact that you have written indicates you're not sure. These are two examples of what I want to call 'meta-replies'. They don't answer the specific points raised by the readers, but reach behind and comment on the reasons for writing, or on what is implied by the letter. Of necessity, these meta-replies put great emphasis on self-evaluation, on looking at yourself and seeing what you are doing and why.

There are two sides to *Jackie*'s recommendations. On the positive side is the advice that the best thing you can do, is to try on all occasions to be 'natural'. Being natural involves relaxing even if you're tense – just do it. It means not trying to force things in a direction they won't go – wait for the right feelings to come. This is seen as an essential part of 'growing up'. For example one reader aged 14 wrote in worried that she had no interest in boys. Don't worry, she was told, it'll come – 'it's a natural thing'. Meaning: there is nothing you can do about it. In its own good time, you will come to it. In the meantime, all you can do is be 'yourself'. The content of this is remarkably imprecise – but it does not mean simply carrying on as before. Indeed, the overtly conservative elements that do slip into *Jackie* come precisely as demands to change. The reader who told of her loneliness and inability to get to know boys was told just how to change herself:

> Your trouble is not your gorgeous friends, but feeling inferior. You'd be amazed how many people feel inferior – probably even some of your gorgeous friends do, too. What can you do about it? First, stop looking at those friends. We just don't believe they're that gorgeous. Instead, look at someone more interesting – yourself. Start with the looks side first. Change your hair style, experiment with make-up, lash out on something that makes you feel a million dollars.
> But far more important – your personality. You may not be the world's greatest wit or conversationalist, but boys don't want wit or chat. What most of them want (girls, too, for that matter) is a *listener*. Find out what a boy's most interested in – and listen to him talking about it. You may be the first person ever to do that – and he'll think you're great even though you've hardly said a word. And finally, if you do get bouts of the blues again, *don't* sit at home brooding about it. Go out, however hard it is. It'll be worth it.

For all the bracketed qualification, this is not good – but also rare. The point is that this still counts as an example of being 'natural', 'being yourself'. 'Naturalness' is a strategic operation. It is creating the situation where you can without evident falsehood achieve what you want. Thus the girl who desperately wants her shy boy to kiss her is advised to let it happen 'naturally' – like, by waiting for the clinch moment in the next film and seeming to get carried away with the same . . . Along with 'naturalness' and 'being yourself' come 'confidence' and, as we have seen, 'personality'. Personality is something which you have but must cultivate. Again, it is part of its meaning that it is difficult to give it a specific content. This paradox inherent is best shown by 'confidence'. A reader wrote in (20 January 1970) about that classic problem, overweight. Now, they replied, is the time to start again since you are about to move to a new job and a new town. But weight is not really the issue, confidence is, and feeling worried. The answer is to tell yourself everything is going to get better, and that will give you the confidence to lose the weight.

We should not make the mistake of thinking that such appeals to 'confidence' are simply editorial ploys for selling traditional ideas about women needing to be slim and beautiful. They have enormous importance in their own right. 'Naturalness' is, it is true, a 'look' to be achieved; and make-up and clothes, subtly used, are part of this. But it is more than a look. It is also an internal organisation of emotions, desires, and attitudes; a way of considering oneself. This intersects with Jackie's prohibitions. Readers are frequently told off for selfishness, for vanity, for being difficult to live with, bad-tempered and thought-less. This is done through meta-replies, with their implicit demands for self-reevaluation. A reader is told in effect: look again at what you have said, think why you wrote that. Therein lies your problem.

I am suggesting that the significance of Cathy and Claire revolves around reevaluating oneself. But this comes in several different forms. There are first the specific suggestions, pragmatic and sensible, for considering just what you do feel in a particular situation. For example (16 January 1971) a reader reports that her boyfriend (over whom she is rapidly cooling) is buying her a bracelet for her birthday. Should she offer to buy it? No, say C & C, first sort out your feelings – do you want to go on with him? When you're clear, make sure he knows well before your birthday. This is local practical advice. Quite different is the advice to have another look at your self-confidence and personality, as though these are manipulable entities inside us.

But there is a third element, another criterion which in the end provides the goal and the measure for all the rest. Frequently, there is in Jackie letters an unspoken but implicit problem: simply, am I in love? How do I gauge whether this is 'real love' that I feel? Such problems are implicit in the tangles of feelings many girls report. Occasionally it comes right to the surface in a question or answer. In the 20 January 1979 edition, a sad letter appeared from a girl for whom everything was going wrong. Sympathetically, C & C tell her that she mustn't think she is alone in this – many more relationships go wrong than right. But one day, she will meet someone for whom there can be no obstacles – and then she will know. 'Love' is inexplicable. It can only be experienced. When you are 'in' it, you will know. Or rather, you may. Here is a Cathy and Claire Special ('Are You In Love?', No. 575, 11 January 1975) honestly admitting the problem: 'Assuming you've been going out with the same guy for a while, and you know you feel more for him than any other boy, how do you tell whether you're really in love? We're afraid there's no surefire answer. There are no rules to love, there's no checklists you can tick off saying I feel this and this, so I must be in love'. And of course paradoxically, 'protesting that you're not in love is often a pretty sure sign that you ARE!'

If it is so unclear, and 'love' will feel the same as a plain mix of fancying plus affection, why worry about the distinction? I believe that this is the heart of the *Jackie* ideology. *Jackie* is about 'love' and its part in girls' lives. Though it never says that love replaces work, fun, hobbies or intellectual achievement, these are just important but plain activities. But 'love' in the *Jackie* dictionary is the one sure thing that will complete a girl: her personality, her sense of self. You can get there by emotional preparation – not by self-sacrifice, not by ceasing to be 'yourself', but by being ready to see its importance to you. In fact, it comes remarkably close to some descriptions of religious experience. Thus it is surely noteworthy that after 1979 there is a sharp decline both in features, and answers to letters reflecting on the mysterious character of 'love'.

How do the problem pages as we now see them tie in with the picture stories? As I noted earlier, a common assumption of critics was that *Jackie* must be a unified whole; its elements must cohere to present young girls with a single ideology. This prejudgement blinded them to the possibility that *Jackie* might be composed of elements relating differently to girls, which might change at different paces and therefore show at times signs of tension and ambivalence. In the problem pages, specific problems of how to cope with relationships are handled. Advice is given, usually (I have to say) of very wise and sensible kinds. I am sure exceptions can be found, but most show acute perception of what is likely to work for readers. Some of the problems are particular. What should I do in this particular situation? How can I communicate my wishes and feelings not just to the love-object, but to parents, friends etc? And how can I trust the feelings I find inside myself? Their answers to the third set of questions set up the relationship with the picture stories. 'Love' is a mysterious unknown. It is preternaturally important, natural but unforeseeable. It also requires right now a kind of emotional economy. Through this *Jackie* offers its readers a conception of their future. But it is not a known future, it is future-as-problem. It is future as expressed in the following questions:

1. *What can I do, must I do, to get 'love'?*
2. *How will I know when it has come?*
3. *What problems will I face on the way?*
4. *What will it do to me? How will I be different then?*
5. *What else will change as a result of finding 'love'?*
6. *How secure will it be, once achieved?*

Jackie does not offer solutions, it poses dilemmas. 'Love' seem so good but so difficult to get. It is in the nature of the beast that there cannot be answers. Like life after death, we can only know it when we are there – or perhaps from 'spirit-writing'. And this is where the stories come in. For it helps to think of them as spirit-written exemplifications what 'love' will be like. They hint at the answers to those six questions. They come, as it were, from the future; they show *what cannot be said*. From this angle we can make sense of the history of the stories; for there have been important changes to the answers to those questions.

But what is it in young girls' lives that *Jackie* addresses? What kind of girls is this agenda of questions speaking to? The implication behind my idea of an agenda is that *Jackie* is living out an unwritten contract with its readers. To explore this idea of a 'contract' we need to conceive that there is a kind of reader who spontaneously recognises that *Jackie* is speaking to issues in her life. We are not yet in a position to deal with this notion of a 'natural reader'. In later chapters we will come back to it, via a study by George Gerbner on the American confession magazines.[1] Gerbner suggests a way to study the links between the social characteristics of his readers and the particular kind of stories. How he does this will help us considerably.

The stages of Jackie

Telling the history of *Jackie* stories isn't easy. As I said earlier, they tend to collapse into dust in the face of the very crude tools of analysis used by most critics. The stories are like fragments. No individual story will reveal enough. The principles behind the narratives can only emerge through collages of periods. Then we will see the very significant changes in *Jackie*'s stories. And we will see how differently at different times the comic has met its agenda.

Between 1964 and 1968 there is a deep conservatism in *Jackie*. Its central tenets are: self-sacrifice, trusting your man even where it conflicts with your own desires, and reorganising your emotions and wishes according to his needs. Thus will happiness be discovered. These ideas are not preached; they are revealed in story-transformations. We have already seen 'The Fifth Proposal', with its instant reorganisation of desires once the heroine realises who 'really needs her'. Even cruder is 'A World of My Own' (No. 52, 2 January 1965). This opens with Joan shouting at her man Ritchie to hurry up with the car or she will be late for her skiing contest. Of course she wins. That evening she just seems to forget to dance with him – and has also forgotten to ask how his job interview went ('for the Board'). Realising, she murmurs to him 'You're always making excuses for me, aren't you?' 'I love you, Joan. It's as simple as that', he replies. Thus they are reconciled. But when her next big contest comes round, he can't drive her there – it's his final interview. Mad, she slams the phone down on him. Her father agrees to drive her there instead, but lectures her gently on the way. 'Don't you think Ritchie needs you today, too? He's in for a nerve-racking time, but he didn't ask you to put off your skiing'. Then as they

Fig 12 From *Jackie* No. 105, 8 January 1966. © D C Thomson & Co. Ltd, 1966. *Jackie* in its early conservative mode.

Barry was one of those dashing young men about town, I suppose . . .

I'M OFF TO THE INTERNATIONAL FOLK CONCERT TONIGHT. GOING?

OH—YOU'RE LUCKY. THAT'S THE ONE I WANTED TO GO TO—REMEMBER, PETE?

I had spoken without thinking, almost admitting we hadn't been able to afford tickets . . .

TELL YOU WHAT—I HATE TO SEE BEAUTIFUL GIRLS UNHAPPY AND I CAN GET ANOTHER TICKET. COME WITH ME—IF OLD PETE DOESN'T MIND.

I "Old Pete" did, so I started to explain . . .

PETE, COULD I GO? IT'S JUST THAT I'VE BEEN NOWHERE REALLY SINCE I CAME TO LONDON, AND...

THIS IS WHERE I GET OUT, BARRY. YOU DO WHAT YOU WANT, JUDY. I UNDERSTAND.

I really thought he meant it. I thought they both understood perfectly — until after the show . . .

IT WAS FABULOUS, BARRY— THANKS FOR TAKING ME. I'LL SEE YOU AROUND SOMETIME WITH PETE.

HEY, WAIT A MINUTE. WHAT ABOUT ANOTHER DATE?

A DATE? OH, NO. PETE'S MY BOYFRIEND. I LOVE HIM.

WELL, YOU COULD HAVE FOOLED ME, DITCHING HIM TO SPEND THE EVENING WITH THE FIRST GUY HE INTRODUCES YOU TO.

Crazy, isn't it, but at the time I just didn't see it like that. I didn't think Pete would—until next day when the quarrel started . . .

WELL, LITTLE MISS BRIGHT-LIGHTS! AREN'T YOU OUT ON THE TOWN WITH YOUR NEW, WEALTHY BOY FRIEND TONIGHT?

I . . . I WAS COMING TO COOK TEA FOR YOU, BUT IF THAT'S WHAT YOU THINK, YOU CAN STARVE!

We both said some pretty nasty things.

I'M GOING HOME, PETE. I NEVER WANT TO SEE YOU AGAIN.

O K, MAYBE I'LL STILL BE HERE WHEN YOU REALISE IT'S YOUR FAULT AND WANT TO SAY YOU'RE SORRY!

That would be never, I thought. I went home, played at having a good time and waited for the heartache to fade . . .

But it didn't. And finally, one morning, this morning, I woke up knowing that I still loved him and wanted him back.

I caught the first train—to say I was sorry, to start all over again . . .

HE'LL STILL BE AT COLLEGE. IT WILL BE JUST LIKE THE MARVELLOUS OLD HARD-UP DAYS...

LOOKING FOR SOMEONE OR DO YOU ALWAYS DAY-DREAM ON DOORSTEPS?

OH, I'M LOOKING FOR A FRIEND WHO LIVES HERE—PETE NICHOLLS.

YOU WON'T FIND HIM. PETE CHUCKED IN COLLEGE LAST MONTH AND WENT UP NORTH TO GET A JOB AND GET MARRIED. A GIRL HE MET ON HOLIDAY—THEY'LL BE IN PARIS ON THEIR HONEMOON BY NOW.

OH, NO...

I'M SORRY—I SEE I'VE SAID THE WRONG THING. COME INSIDE—I'LL GET YOU A CUP OF TEA.

If only I had thought about it, been a little prepared—but I wasn't . . .

YOU MUST HAVE BEEN KEEN ON HIM?

Continued on page 14.

11

Continued from page 11.

drive past Ritchie's office, 'something made me cry 'Stop!''. She has to be with
him. Ritchie is so pleased and – to her own surprise – she finds that she wants
to wait for him. 'But skiing – you live for it!', says a stunned Ritchie. 'Not any
more. From now on I live for you, Ritchie. I'll still ski, but only when you don't
need me'. The story ends on a joke about her again forgetting to ask about his
interview; and with a wedding.

This must seem so obvious that subtleties of analysis would be irrelevant.
But 'A World of My Own' is unusual in its crudeness. The same set of ideas
can be more subtly expressed, as in '(Tommy Quickly and) The Topsy-Turvy
Romance' (No. 55, 23 January 1965). This opens with Irene Nicoll walking into
a recording studio to find Tommy Q (then, a minor pop star) doing yoga before
a recording session. He says she looks as if she could do with a little relaxation
– yes, it's 'boy trouble'. Her bloke Vic had cancelled a date, and had been seen
with a 'pretty blonde'. And there they are, in the recording booth. They have
a row and she won't give him a chance to explain. That night, she writes to
apologise but can't bring herself to post it, pockets it instead. She tries yoga,
standing on her head like Tommy to relax. Next day, she can't find the letter
– it must have fallen out during her acrobatics and been posted for her. Now
Vic appears – he'd been applying for a job in TV, and the girl had been from

the company. The last frame is mutual congratulations to Tommy on his new disc and to them on their engagement. Her error was lack of trust, which is liquidated by accident. She should have trusted him, that's all. The idea of 'trusting your man' took a different form in 'Words of Love' (No. 54, 16 January 1965), a story revealing about the nature of this conservatism. It is about Audrey's anguish that Bill will never say 'I love you' to her. When they go to see a love film, he tells her afterwards that he only took her because he knew she'd enjoy it. She challenges him – doesn't he like the word 'love'? 'I want to marry you one day', he replies; but his refusal to say he loves her leads to them breaking up. But now she starts to realise that Bill conveys his love in deeds, not words; and she hurries back to the park where they had parted. He's still there, rehearsing how to say it but telling himself it really is a tired-out little word. Appearing from behind a tree, she makes an apologetic speech about it only having the meaning that they give it. 'Hey!', says Bill, 'that's a big wise speech from such a pretty face!' 'Sorry, it won't happen again – promise'. The end is a smacking kiss. What should we say about that humiliating exchange? In many respects it seems an unpleasant intrusion, a put-down quite irrelevant to the narrative direction. The story without it could have been about the difficulties of communication of emotions. But with it, it surely is another case of self-sacrifice and self-diminution by the woman. This kind of conservatism does tend to be very preachy in these intrusive ways. But it does not survive the first changes in *Jackie's* stories.

A quarter of the stories in my sample of the 1964-8 period are of this kind. They are supplemented by another kind, compatible with it but equally capable of fitting with other definitions of romance. This is the happy accident story exemplified by 'Yesterday' (No. 105, 8 January 1966, reproduced below – Fig. 12). I find this a curious story in several respects. At one level it is surely dead right; we can't allow our past mistakes to dominate our futures. Sometimes we must wipe our canvas clean and start again, trying to learn from our mistakes. Judy probably was unwise to go for the instant glamour. I would not be convinced by an interpretation of this story in the mode that it is teaching 'limit yourself to the boy next door'. That is not something ever stressed about the lost Pete – it was his fun-spoiling poverty that initiated her discontent. No, the curious aspects of this are the use of this parable-within technique (not uncommon in the early years) and the instant change this induces. As soon as you understand, you can change. This is why this story fits my conservative collage.

What are women allowed to do, in these conservative stories? They can use stratagems or ploys, little love-gambits to get things going. These are risky. Take 'The Taming of Johnny' (No. 54, 16 January 1965): Kim is jealous that her guitarist boyfriend takes her for granted. So at a dance she tries to annoy him by dancing with others. Eric the loathsome road manager – he really does look grotty – muscles in, half-throttling her with his embraces, till he is dragged off by a huge hunk whom she now (successfully) uses to make Dave jealous. Dave tries to thump the hunk who gently restrains him. With this bright start, they sign up the hunk to be their new manager, get rid of Eric – and Dave learns his lesson. He keeps his eyes off the pretty ones out front. It was a close-run thing, wasn't it? It just worked out for Kim but could easily have gone wrong. It does go wrong in 'Surprise, Surprise!' (No. 4, 1 February 1964) where our unnamed heroine has two boyfriends. The story opens with her reading a romantic story about Amelia trying to choose between bold passionate Jonathan and shy tender Spencer. While she's enjoying the book, Doug (her 'Jonathan') arrives and asks what she is doing. She is so engrossed, she almost gives the game away. Doug chucks the book out of the window straight on to 'Spencer' Bobby, just arriving. They soon realise her game – and leave together. Now, says our heroine, how did Amelia cope with this one? In this jokey story, we meet not only the risks of stratagems but also their second allowed area of activity: fantasy. Fantasy was not recommended by Jackie in this period – in fact, not until very recently. It was risky, and destructive of relationships. And the magazine itself comes into that category. Over the years, there have been a few reflexive stories in which reading Jackie itself has been part of the plot. They have always presented that as something not to be taken too seriously.

This broadly depicts the early conservatism. To questions about what 'real love' is like and how to get it, Jackie's answer was: you will know it when your man shows his need for you, and you will get it by self-sacrifice. There is little you can do to prepare yourself, except by setting up little gambits (risky, but possible) and by enjoying the idea of it in fantasy (but these must not replace your readiness for the real thing). Your problem is that you may misunderstand your feelings, so be ready to admit your mistakes – and then keep silent afterwards. This traditional conservatism did not last.

The 'freedom' of Jackie

By 1969 the conservatism is well on the wane. This is not a strict periodisation. As early as 1965 a problem in the conservative version flickered into view. If you'll only know the true man when he expresses his need for you, what are you allowed to do to find him? Take 'Tell Me My Faults' (No. 55, 23 January 1965), about Millie's longstanding relationship with Danny, with whom she feels rut-bound. Her friend Doris persuades her that Danny really isn't the answer – she should look elsewhere; and Millie meets Ray – wow! Well, wow, that is, until she sees him with another. She can't take that so she chucks him; and Doris persuades her to try her luck again. And so the story ends with her back at the Flamingo disco where the following dialogue is projected out to us by Millie: 'So it was thanks to Doris . . . thanks for getting me out of the rut I was in! Thanks for making it possible for me to meet the most wonderful boy in the world . . . one who really loves me . . . It hasn't happened – not yet. But I will meet a wonderful boy some day! Doris was right . . . wasn't she?'

There is an uncertainty here that analysis should not lose. How it developed, is revealed by the contrast between two stories. First, 'Deep In My Heart' (No. 106, 15 January 1966), the 'story' of Patti staff nurse on a serious injuries ward. It is a flashback story recalling how Mike was brought in after a serious accident. She had coaxed him back to life, sometimes having to shout at him to make him work his damaged legs – a little falling in love with him the while. Now when he is about to leave hospital, she can't be there because she is on duty. She sees him out of a window going off with a girl he had meet at a dance while convalescing. 'Goodbye, Mike . . . another little piece of my heart . . . there have been so many of you . . .' And another young boy, another fifty/fifty survivor, is wheeled in. Some day her boy will come; in the meantime there is so much to do. This story is not automatically conservative, but it surely fits that collage. Patti's work is essentially emotional preparation, practice if you like for when she will 'nurse' her own boy. She will serve him as truly as she has served all her patients. Now compare the attitudes to girls' emotions here with those embedded in 'Did I Make The Right Decision?' (No. 262, 11 January 1969). Amy, driving, has offered a lift to a young man. They talk and she realises he is repeating a mistake she made. Flashback to her former life with Ma and Pa (always arguing) in a small Irish village. One day in drove a tall and handsome Canadian Jon who, after staying a month, whisked her off to Canada – where she is set up in a dream-like world where everyone is kind to her – until the day she hears his parents arguing just as hers had, and saying that Jon is being overprotective of Amy, hiding her from the real world. Now she realises she has been coddled. Jon explains. He'd hoped to protect her like a tender plant. She couldn't stay and returned to Ireland – where she meets this young man en route to the same mistake, wanting to live an illusion. She warns him, but knows he must discover it for himself. At the end she settles back to wait for her real Prince Charming.

The end of course is still passivity. But the fact that she must face up to the reality of her own emotions marks the beginning of the change in Jackie. A new element emerges, of truth to oneself. It is still essentially emotional, but without being self-sacrificial. Thus 'Give Me An Answer By Monday' (No. 261, 4 January 1969), précised at the beginning of the chapter. There is no suggestion that Lynda should not have gone – in fact the opposite. But they had to admit the strength of their emotions – and then the transformation occurs. The important thing is that they have to take responsibility for their own emotions; they can't simply be determined by someone else's needs. 'Take Me In Your Arms' (No. 158, 14 January 1967) is an early example of this. It opens with a flashback: will he be the same now on his return from abroad? They had met when he had come to London (at the urging of his mates) to try to make it as a DJ. When interview after interview failed, he got depressed – until they met and she encouraged and bolstered him, and fell for him. Now successful, he began to ignore her, then took a chance of a year in the States. His letters were few and far between. Now returning, he can't get the words out (there are many thought-balloons of her thinking 'Oh please say it!'). Finally he announces he's staying in America and has come to say goodbye. Though desperately upset, she hand-les it with white lies about another boyfriend. The story ends with her now thinking about herself – will she now have the courage to find freedom and happiness for herself, just as he has?

It is possible to read this as her sacrificing herself, and having nothing in return. He uses her, dumps her, she has no more at the end than she had at the start. This reading depends on denying the transformation implicit in the ending. (Here we meet that issue of time and transformation in narrative again.) At the end she is different from the beginning, because she understands a possibility for herself not visible before. Will she/we take it? That is undecided. But with this new ill-defined arena opening up, the use of stratagems declines. In a story mentioned by Jacqueline Sarsby we see this change: 'Kiss Me – Or I'll Burst' (No. 370, 6 February 1971). Tina, at the start, is remarking on the difficulties girls can face in getting dates to go right. For example, she fancies the bloke in the office opposite, but how to get to know him? She and her friends fake a kitten-rescue-gone-wrong, which requires him to rescue Tina, and thus they start dating. But she can never get him to kiss her. She and her friends devise ever more devious ploys, but none work. Finally, taken to a football match, in despair she is standing thinking how impossible it all is – when his team scores; instant osculation, to the point where they are still at it an hour later, on an empty terrace. Ploys don't work. It wasn't (yet) wrong to try them; but love will take its natural course. After 1971 the ploys virtually vanish.

In the early years, reorganising the emotions was an instant process once she found her 'right man'. In the new collage this also shifts. Now a theme of overcoming one's past emerges. The past is a trap; its experiences will block us. We must overcome the hold of their 'tradition'. I believe that this was the beginning of Jackie's response to the politics of the 1960s. Still expressed as personal re-examination, none the less, old experiences and past learning are no longer sources of morals. Consider, first, 'The Girl On His Mind' (No. 261, 4 January 1969), about Gail who works in a boutique; enter Derek Gibson, dress designer of some handsomeness. But Gail, because of a bad past experi-ence, won't touch relationships just now. Which is a pity, because we see from Derek's sketches that he has been drawing an imaginary girl just like Gail. He asks her out, she declines. But that night she cries, wishes she could have said yes, thinks she has lost him. Next day he re-enters; and now melted as it were by the tears, she can say yes.

By 1971 this theme of overcoming your past had generalised. It was no longer just fears over relationships. Several of the stories Sarsby cites are of just this kind. Out of 'Shadow Of A Past Love' (No. 356, 31 October 1970), 'Keep Quite Calm And Don't Scream' (No. 365, 2 January 1971), and 'The Dream' (No. 368, 23 January 1971), let's examine the first. Kate, in love with Jim, can't bring herself to marry him because of something in her past. Her Mum had struggled to bring her up after Dad had deserted them. The story backtracks (when she goes to revisit their old home) to her parents meeting in the blitz, Dad being injured in rescuing Mum and falling for her. After they married, he suddenly and inexplicably left. Back in the present, she is recognised by the local vicar, who now tells her the story. Dad had suffered gas poisoning in rescuing Mum and had quietly gone away so that they wouldn't have to suffer his dying. Now understanding, she goes to find her Mum to tell her and to marry Jim, because the past is now cleared up. Other 'pasts' that had to be overcome included a nostalgia for one's country ('Bottled Memories', No. 370, 6 February 1971), a fear of the city (the second Sarsby reference above), and a harsh childhood (in the third reference above and also in 'Memory Of Last Summer', No. 366, 9 January 1971). What is curious is the spread of this theme, to the point where its content could be wholly unspecific as in 'No Time Like The Future' (No. 472, 20 January 1973). Liz has gone to a school reunion, even though she doesn't enjoy them. Fewer and fewer of her friends are there. Escaping the dance, she does meet an old flame Jimmy Spencer sitting in their old classroom. He tells her that people come to these reunions to find something, then never come again, that she mustn't 'cling to the past'. He wishes they could talk longer, but that's not possible. She doesn't much like being lectured at like this, and leaves – only to learn on returning to the dance that Jimmy had been killed a week before on his motorbike. Of course when she rushes back to the classroom he's not there. She thinks: 'Maybe I do need to look a long, long way beyond these four walls to find whatever it is I'm trying to find . . . I took everything I could out of this place when I was here and I'm grateful. But this is a launch pad, not a permanent mooring.' But we know nothing about this 'past' that is holding her back.

The past must not be a hiding place; we must search on, even if we're no longer clear what we are looking for. It is a new sense of self, a yearning, inchoate and shapeless. This is how the search for forms of freedom entered Jackie from the politics of the 1960s. It reached its high point in a fascinating story in 1971 (and perhaps only conceivable then): 'Take Me Away From All This' (No. 367, 16 January 1971, reproduced below – Fig. 13).

This is a really odd story. Not many years before, she just couldn't have been allowed that much freedom; and the outcome would have had her adjusting to him, along with a lot more direct interest in romance. By the mid-1970s, such a good relationship would have had to lead to disaster, as we shall see.

Fig 13 From *Jackie* No. 367, 16 January 1971. © D C Thomson & Co. Ltd, 1971. The brief flowering of 'freedom'.

By the end of the decade, no way would a story have allowed such dangerous activities as 'going off to a cave with a man you don't know'. A new 'realism' came in then, we shall find. Only really in 1971, and then delicately like a bud that never opened, is there this sense of hope and social yearning. In other stories, the student movements of the 1960s provided the setting for events, without being approved or disapproved. In 'Day Of The Demo', for example (No. 367, 16 January 1971) a couple meet on a demo, he as participant, she caught up in it. She agrees to meet him on another the next day, but nearly misses him in the crowd. When they meet eventually, they decide on a 'long walk' together – and it's not clear whether this is the demo or not. Such stories never do anything as crude as offering romance as an alternative to 'irrelevant' activities like marching. They are much more ambivalent. The same is true with respect to the women's movement in 'Who Do You Think I Am?' (same issue), in which the girl, though fancying him, decides to teach her boy a lesson for assuming she'll always do things like his washing. It ends with him learning his lesson, though still . . .just a little . . . leaning on her – to which her friend comments: 'I've got a feeling she can't win – still, as long as she enjoys herself'. As a criterion of acceptance this is new in *Jackie*, but its politics are not obvious.

From conservative beginnings in 1964 then, up to 1971 a creeping freedom, a questioning of the need for girls to spreadeagle their emotions before their men. The same period saw the emergence of the jokey story, in which romance is qualified with a 'don't take it all too seriously' codicil. These become common after 1970, as in 'My Great Romance' another Sarsby reference (No. 370, 6 February 1971). The story is told by a girl who is looking at her photographic album. She tells of her encounters with Ray and Max, wildly different characters. How she didn't manage to keep the two balls in the air at the same time, so moved on through several others, which all went wrong – but all are recorded in her album. Now she has her 'love of loves' . . . Gerry the photographer who snapped all those others who now has her, but whose 'business has now dropped a bit'!

The decline of romance

From being self-sacrificial or victims of one's emotions, via having to take responsibility for their own feelings and facing up to their past, to an acknowledgement that women can and must, in some ways, choose. From women's work in relationships being love-stratagems plus self-denigration, via self-examination and the growth of possibilities of self-confidence, to a shapeless wish for freedom and even a slight acknowledgement of real constraints. This is *Jackie* over its first seven years. Then began a backlash. It is not as simple as a return to the conservatism of the 1960s stories. Consider, first, 'Crazy To Love Him' (No. 473, 27 January 1973), the story of Meg who quite loves Geoff – except he is such an 'action man'. We see her dangling at the end of a rope half way up a mountain, and terrified to continue. Before this it had been motor racing – except she had thought they were just going for a drive. Then it was sailing – on a windy river where she got soaked. She dumps him, and goes for a quiet lad instead. But the country walks he takes her on are too dull for words; and after she has nearly drowned from swimming on her own when he refuses to join her, she drops him too. Now she realises why she fancied Geoff all along, and phones him up – and at the end we see them celebrating by 'dropping in' at the Walnut Tree restaurant – in parachutes. Now Meg did not have to reorganise her emotions or change herself. True, she has to 'fit in' – and in that lies the backlash. The vague desire for freedom is disappearing fast; girls are back to adapting themselves to boys, but now with a kind of shrug of the shoulders. And this is no longer just about romance; its problem lies in the way it is generalised to anything a girl might do.

'Once Upon A Time' (same issue) is the meanest version of this, in which the romance aspect become a peg for a highly restrictive social message. Maxine is buying an old typewriter; she wants to write 'her first novel'. What will it be, asks salesman Pete who carries the bulky thing home for her? She doesn't know. She'll just write it – and he can come round in a week for a paella and the first six chapters. Of course when he comes she is still on page one, and has quite forgotten about him. They talk about themselves. She is a hairdresser who wants to be 'creative, remembered'. There follows a nasty, preachy dialogue, Pete telling her he used to want to be an Egyptologist but found he was good at being a salesman. When she moans about her job being boring, he reminds her that her customers must think her good or they wouldn't come back. So be realistic, accept what you are and have. They end kissing, with her thinking this is good enough to make a full novel out of, not just a short story. I dislike this story intensely, for its invitation to narrow the sense of your possibilities. Horns are being pulled in, horizons narrowed. But this doesn't lead to greater investment in the importance of romance. It has often been suggested that restriction of the social and political horizons of women is coupled with a renewed 'hearth and home' ideology, of which the mobilisation of romance is logically a part. This doesn't happen in *Jackie*.

On the contrary, after the reaction of 1973 comes the death-theme. This is a puzzling development, not easy to understand. Take 'A Love To Last Forever' (No. 574, 4 January 1975), a story cited by McRobbie as an example that love is unable to breach social, class, or national boundaries. It is the story of Janet, a World War II nurse who has no time for Germans. A young Zepellin survivor is brought in. Despite being reminded by her ward sister that her job is to help all patients, she can't stop herself being harsh to him. But he gradually wins her over; he does a lovely drawing of her, and she learns that he too has lost brothers in the war. When convalescing, though, he tries to declare his love for her. She slaps his face, and goes back to telling him he is her enemy. All this is seen. He is readied for return to the POW camp, she is reassigned to other duties. That night she tosses and turns, unable to sort her emotions. The next morning she sees him being loaded into the camp lorry, and rushes over to kiss him goodbye (while those around her make harsh comments about collaborators). She never sees him again. 'That's the end of my story', she tells us. Later in the war he is killed. Now 'every time I see a happy couple, every time I see a new love starting with the New Year, I remember my love . . . my love which could not be'. McRobbie's interpretation depends on the context of the story being all important; the fact that it is set in World War II is the point of it on her account. But even if it were so, the story is far more ambivalent than she acknowledges. Is it their situation that means that their love is 'not to be'? Is her own behaviour to blame for its failure? Or is it just a sad case where love is too fragile to surmount the difficulties it faces, whatever they are? What attitude are we being asked to take to all those 'new loves' just starting up?

The fact is that from 1975 onwards there is a real decline in confidence in romance's possibilities. The year 1975 is a crucial transitional one in this respect, paving the way to the development in 1978 of the worried, unhappy *Reader's True Experience* stories. This poses real problems for McRobbie's account. Recall that she saw in Jackie a monolithic ideology of real power, trapping girls into a false sisterhood of jealousy. Her sample (scattered through 1974-5) was her evidence of this. Her sample, though drawn without any reference to the history of Jackie, had to be treated as 'typical'; how else could she justify drawing such large implications about Jackie's role in selling young girls the 'appropriate ideology of consumerist capitalism'. But even so there is no justification for the way she draws conclusions from her examples. As with the other critics, she 'knew in advance' what kind of ideology Jackie must be purveying, and the function of the stories is merely to exemplify what was already known. Let us see how this worked in a particular case.

McRobbie has argued that the essence of Jackie is the creation of a false sisterhood in which all girls are rendered the same, irrespective of class, race and other social divisions, and then turned against each other as competitors. She has a potential problem, then, with a story which seems premised precisely on such social distinctions; or a story about poverty and the meanness of the rich. How does she cope with these? She argues that their message is rendered hollow by being set in another time. History becomes a 'moral lesson' for us, but at a distance which renders the issues safe:

> . . . history is not just novelty, it is also used to demonstrate the intransigeance of much-hallowed social values, and 'natural resistance' to change. When a patrician (in the setting of Ancient Rome) falls for a slave girl he can only die for her, thereby allowing her to escape with her slave boyfriend; he cannot escape or be paired off with her . . . A 19th century woman and her child arrive at the doorstep one Christmas and are turned away. Two guests help her and it emerges that the woman is the disinherited daughter of a wealthy man . . . The messages are clear: love conquers and simultaneously renders unimportant poverty – which at any rate only 'exists' in the past (and is thus contained and manageable). People marry into their own social class and race. (When a nurse falls for a wounded German prisoner in wartime Britain she knows her love cannot be fulfilled . . . and the prisoner returns to Germany).[2]

There is a real illogicality in this quite apart from how the stories have been read. On the one hand we're told that history negates and diminishes the issue of poverty, so that it has no moral lessons for us. On the other hand history reinforces class and race restrictions on marriage. 'Messages' are being selectively discovered according to what she already knew 'must be there'. But a look at the actual stories redoubles the problems. Consider, first, 'A New Love For Christmas' (No. 572, 21 December 1974). This is the story of Lucy whom we see in Victorian times getting ready for a ball. She is going to it with her handsome, impendingly famous (surgeon) boyfriend Robert and that is all she can think about. Lucy is presented as a 'butterfly', light and breezy but incapable of being serious. On the way to the ball they pass a series of destitute-looking people, out in the snow – until Robert stops the carriage for one of them, a young woman clearly in distress. It turns out she is about to give birth and Robert bundles her into the carriage to take her to the house where they are going. Lucy thinks they should have left her, not through meanness but because she thinks nothing can be done to help them. On arrival the butler, seeing the young woman, hustles them to the back door – she is the ostracised daughter of the house. There follow some barbed comments about the contrast between the public generosity of their hosts and their private meanness and unkindness. In the kitchen, Lucy is left to ponder while Robert is helping with the birth. Hearing the cry of the baby, she suddenly realises how selfish she herself has been and, realising it, thinks she must have lost her Robert. Now she has truly grown up, and has to prepare for a life without him – she cannot think he will forgive her unkindness. But of course he returns and forgives her without a moment's hesitation; and they prepare for a Christmas and a new adult life together, with a kiss.

It is really very hard to read this story in McRobbie's way. The messages are not 'clear'. If the woman had not been the disinherited daughter, the point about meanness would have been lessened. The contrast between public show and private misery is being emphasised. But actually the story does not centre on that. It centres on Lucy whose infatuated innocence almost personifies *Jackie*'s own earlier attitude to romance: love as an ideal, a self-completion. Now Lucy has to grow up, to realise that love precisely does not conquer all. Only with this new knowledge that love is not the complete answer, can she hope for a love with Robert at all. But then, why the history? Why the setting of this in the past? It certainly is a departure for *Jackie*. Until this point very few stories were set outside a vague 'present'. What exactly does this signify?

We can understand this by examining the other story here referred to by McRobbie, 'A Time To Love, A Time To Die' (a three-part serial in January 1975). Set in Roman times, it has two central characters Melissa and Casso as Christians being sold as slaves. He, to work in the fields and gardens, she to be a maid. Casso is violently anti-Roman, and gets beaten for his trouble. In the first episode Melissa finds herself serving wine to Nero himself, and then catching the eye of a handsome Captain, Marcus, whom she meets again in town the next day. He rescues her from a crowd, after she has been sent to buy cloth. Mocking her Christian beliefs gently, he tells her he serves the gods of love and war and steals a kiss. Both their hearts are set pounding by this. In episode two we see Casso and Melissa agonising over the growing reports of Christians being killed. Now Marcus comes courting and Casso, seeing it, thumps him. The penalty is death. At Melissa's plea Marcus agrees to try to save him, and manages to get his death commuted to serving as a gladiator. Part two ends with Melissa and Marcus entering the arena to watch his fight. In the third part, we see Casso win his fight but refuse to kill his opponent – and now there is no escape from death. Realising this, Melissa throws herself into the ring to die with him. They are endungeoned together, to await death the next morning. We follow Marcus' thought: 'You are a fool, Nero. Their love is stronger than anything you can face them with. I – I only wish she felt that way about me . . . but she goes with her Casso to die . . . and I stand alone and die for a love I cannot have.' That night Nero fiddles while Rome burns, and Marcus breaks into the dungeon and rescues them, but is wounded in the attempt. They see him die, and have to flee alone. The story ends with their escape, and a caption wondering 'Perhaps a new Rome will rise from the ashes' where love is once again possible.

We cannot understand this story without following the switch of narrative angle to Marcus' thoughts. Without that, his actions would lack point. He does indeed die for love, but more important he dies for the idea of a love he cannot match. Seeing his thoughts turns the story into a contest of conceptions of love. It becomes a melodrama of these conceptions in which motives come conveniently packaged in the rhetoric of the time. Rome was anti-Christian, Marcus embodies nobility plus the problem of Rome's attitude; so he can't win. The whole story turns on the social distinction between them. Slavery is not rendered unimportant by the story (which is the logic of McRobbie's reading); it provides the scenario for a melodrama of love and death. It is in other words a further confirmation of what I have been arguing: that 1975 is a year in which commitment to an ideal of love turned rhetorical.

In one respect McRobbie is right, and that is in seeing significance in the shift into history. But the meaning of this shift is the opposite of what she argues. It is not a strengthening of romance by draining off politics into the past; it is a weakening of it by melodramatising it at a distance. Almost the only stories permitted in this period to stay close to home are the joke stories in which everything is starred as absurd from the start. Just one example (again, one which McRobbie cites), 'Meet Me On The Corner' (No. 582, 5 March 1975), whose premise is a camel escaped from the zoo. Scenes of low farce (with the camel running amok and carrying off a zealous policeman) lead to the girl rowing with her fuddy-duddy boyfriend in perfect time to be free to go out with the hunky zookeeper. This poking fun is the other side of the same coin of a new dismissiveness towards romance.

As a last illustration of the problems with McRobbie's analysis, look for yourselves at a story which she cites and from which she reproduces one frame. To her, it is the exact embodiment of her 'ideology of romance'. It is 'Where Have All The Flowers Gone?' (Fig. 14). Rather than have my account of it, make your own analysis of what 'messages' might be got from this sad story.

Fig 14 From *Jackie* No. 584, 15 March 1975. © D C Thomson & Co. Ltd, 1975. The coming of the 'death'-theme.

184

Death, doom and dire warnings

By 1977, the trends that opened in 1975 have set in with a vengeance. Now, to be in love is to be at risk – of being deeply hurt, of doing something wrong and suffering. This is all done melodramatically. Consider 'I Won't Forget You' (No. 680, 15 January 1977) – one of my last chapter's variations-on-the-wild-boy theme. Brian won't stop following Sue around even though she has finished with him. The story flashbacks to him rescuing her from a load of local yobbos and their romance starting. But he is so wild on his motorbike. It gets too much for her when they nearly have an accident which could have killed someone. But he won't let her go. Sue meets Roy – gentle, unpossessive, nice. At the youth club, Brian gets into a fight with Roy and thumps him. This time Sue really tells him. Convinced at last, he roars off on his bike – only to have a terrible crash. In hospital he's dying, with all the fight taken out of him now. The story ends with Roy assuring Sue Brian's death is not her fault – he had really known long ago that it was all over. 'But in my heart I knew the real answer', thinks Sue. 'You really loved me, Brian. You died because you loved me. And I'll never forget you.'

Lest anyone think this is just a way of 'putting blame' on the woman, in some subtle way, compare another even more explicit story: 'Tell Me You Love Me' (No. 678, 1 January 1977). On a day truanting from the office, Sue meets Steve. They like each other and begin to have a fling, doing silly things together and steadily falling in love. Then by chance Sue finds out that Steve has to go away shortly. Yes, he admits, it's true; for a whole year. But he promises to write before the year is out, to say if he'll be coming back to her. And this is how we saw her at the beginning, letter in hand, wondering what the letter would be saying. At the end she opens it – yes, he was returning to her. But now, she says, I know you won't be coming. Your letter came today – but your friend Mike's telegram came yesterday. 'Steve was killed in a car crash'. As unmotivated tragedy, this takes some beating.

There is a spectrum of stories involving death or equivalent loss; from what I would call 'logic of perfect love' stories in which a romance is too good to last and is 'bound' to self-immolate, to those stories where a character's actions explain the disaster that follows. But neither bespeaks much confidence in romance's possibilities for girls.

Learning the lessons

If one end of a spectrum has the logic-of-perfect-love story, at the other end begins to emerge, around 1977, a 'logic of responsibility' story which finally demolishes the ideal of love. Take 'I'll Never Let You Down' (No. 679, 8 January 1977), one of the occasional stories told from a boy's point of view. Kevin rescues Irena from the attentions of some 'rough types'. Damn. He hadn't intended to get involved again . . . Flashback to when, as a wild boy on a motorbike, he was a hero to all around him – including the lovely Helen. Helen's Dad did not approve of him, thought he would prove unreliable; and he did, going out with other girls who all thought him marvellous. He and Helen had argued and he had walked out – and Helen in distress had got herself killed. Knowing he was to blame, he had settled down, determined never to be anyone's hero again. So after buying Irena a coffee, he leaves the café pronto – only to run into the rough types who work him over. Irena finds him, and this time he can't just walk away. And so it ends with him saying: 'If things work out for us, I'll never let her down . . . and some day, perhaps, I'll know that Helen's forgiven me – and that I can love again.' This notion of learning lessons from relationships grew and transformed. Also with the declining faith

Fig 15 From *Jackie* No. 784, 13 January 1979. © D C Thomson & Co. Ltd, 1979. Warning! Life is very dangerous . . .

Continued on page 15

13

in ideal love, the scene was set for a new form of picture story in *Jackie*: first, the *Reader's True Experience*, then supplemented by *What's Your Problem?*. In the latter, the moralising became explicit. A story would be told with an ending; but then an alternative ending would be spelt out, showing how it might have been if the heroine had acted differently. By 1980 the combination of these had swept the board.

The first picture *Reader's True Experience* appeared on 11 November 1978 (although they had been appearing for years as the much less popular written stories). At first they had an opening photographic frame, with the remainder drawn 'in style'. By mid-1979 the changeover to photostrip was complete – first, in the *Reader's True Experience* stories. It is clear that the change in the stories predated the change in pictorial form. I am going to suggest it also determined it. Obviously, once adopted the use of photos imposes its own constraints. For cheapness of production, there will be few special location shots, no top-class models, no action photography. In short, the change to photostrip encouraged a greater localisation; the stories were about particular girls in specific social and geographical locales, rather than about ideas of love and romance.

But another change followed, a corollary to the others. The stories began to acknowledge how romance fitted in the rest of young girls' lives. Begin with the starkest: 'I Didn't Stop To Think' (No. 784, 13 January 1979 – Fig. 15), a grimly realistic story. If the starkest, this story is none the less of a kind with many others in this period. Such stories in my sample covered issues of drink, of setting yourself up to be used, of using someone yourself and ending up feeling ashamed, how you can benefit from taking good advice, handling the impact of parents' divorce or remarriage, or being a child of elderly parents.

The morality implied in these stories is interesting. Partly they are just cautionary. In the one reproduced, for example, there are no instructions on what Julie and Mandy should have done, except that they should not have hitched on their own and lied to their parents. In other tales the morals are more specific, but they do not add up to some obvious whole. Compare three: first 'They Didn't Understand About Us' (No. 887, 3 January 1981), an RTE story about Julie who has been going steady with Mick steadily for ages; but now she has switched her fancies to Billy. The trouble is she finds it hard to tell Mick. Her parents also are very assuming about it all and invite Mick to go on holiday with them without asking Julie. This forces her to tell them the real situation, whereupon her parents declare their 'disappointment' in her. But when she tells Mick, he accepts it. He also had felt they had gone a bit stale. They'll stay friends. The end has her saying to herself: 'I know I've done the right thing, no matter what anyone says'. The second story is a *What's Your Problem?*, entitled 'I Couldn't Give Him Up'. Nicola and Jayne have been best friends for ages, inseparable in fact – until at a disco Nicola meets Kenny, who is luvverly. She hardly thinks about Jayne, even when Kenny meets her outside her school while they are together. But then she realises how unhappy Jayne is. Nicola rings Kenny to ask if he would mind Jayne coming to the youth club with them. Kenny does not mind at all, and Jayne starts meeting a few boys herself. Nicola realises she has gained too because she isn't only ever being romantic with Kenny. In the 'It could have been otherwise' ending, the dangers of losing girl-friends are discussed.

The third story, an RTE, was called 'They Didn't Care About Me!' (No. 890, 24 January 1981). Mum and Dad are having a child late in life, and June feels horribly left out. When the baby is born, and her parents just don't notice her, she decides to go her own way. This involves lingering on the way home from her youth club and getting involved with a gang. One of them fancies her and they agree to meet for a snog behind the pavilion next day. But she gets landed with the baby. In the park the boy persuades her to leave the pram for a few minutes while they're busy. But when she returns, it's gone. The boy disappears. Luckily the pram has been taken by a worried old lady who thought it abandoned. After a ticking off she gets it back, and June promises herself 'I'll never do anything so stupid and selfish again'.

These three, though they don't contradict each other, hardly form some obvious pattern. The first clearly recommends being honest with yourself and true to yourself, whatever the pressures. The second recommends sensible strategies for keeping your best friend. The third is more obviously 'moral'. If there is a pattern, it is that they are cautionary tales; life is not always safe, you should stop and think before doing things. It is, if you like, a loss of confidence not only in romance, but in the world in which the girls live. The stories are at last reflecting what had been the typical topics of the Cathy & Claire columns since 1964. It is important to emphasise this. Up until 1978, Jackie keeps a large gap between the topics and tone of the picture stories and the concerns of the Cathy & Claire columns. The gap can be set out thus:

Problem Pages	Picture Stories
Present time	Future time
Context-aware	Context-blind
Real relationships	Ideal relationships
Pragmatic solutions	Transformation solutions
Unchanging	Substantially changing
Recommendation of self-examination	Results of self-examination

After 1978 the gap declined; only whereas the problem pages gave direct advice to individuals, the stories deal with exemplary problems embodied in narrative form. But it was to mark the 'beginning of the end', and begin a wholesale change in the stories. To understand this fully, we need to reflect more directly on the methods that have been at work in my analysis.

Finding the themes in Jackie

In the course of this chapter and the last, I have pointed to a number of typical story-features, but without making explicit my method. In fact, this has involved distinguishing different kinds of motifs within the stories. By a 'motif', I mean a small-scale organising feature which enables a typical move to take place, or a typical relationship between parts to be suggested. I do not want to propose some general technical terminology, for reasons which will become apparent in a moment. But it can help if we approach Jackie stories with these distinctions in mind:

Sets. These are typical places for kinds of encounter; they come endowed with certain possibilities. For example parks, coffee bars and discos are territories where new relationships can begin. They are places for encounters. It is no accident that open countryside is less commonly the place for this kind of accidental encounter. Or perhaps better, if such an encounter takes place in a wild place, it will somehow be a wild encounter. Places, in other words, come coded with possibilities of relationships.

Story-enablers. Of these the most obvious is flash-back, which enables us to see a problem, and work back to its cause and outcome. A story-enabler is a procedure whereby the romance-agenda is helped into story-form. A quite different example of a story-enabler is a switch in narrative perspective (see for example 'A Time To Love, A Time To Die' in the preceding section).

Theme-markers. These are motifs which provide points of tension, but which also incline the story to resolve itself in a particular direction. For example, a separation between boy and girl often sets off a series of events through the rest of the story. Suppose a character gets a new job – whether explicitly or implicitly, the question will have been posed: will s/he return to the relationship?

Emotional foci. These are moments of high drama which mobilise the energy of the stories. A number of people have commented on the 'clinch' as the climactic goal of the story; and often this is true. But the point to note is that sometimes the clinch happens early in the story, and is merely a launching pad for subsequent moves. Compare, for example, the story where the girl cannot get her boy to kiss her – until he gets carried away at a football match – with one in which a couple meet and kiss (symbolising the achievement of romance) but then separate. Only in the first is the clinch an 'emotional focus' in my sense. (I have not had the chance to test this, but I have a strong hunch that emotional foci in *Jackie* are associated with a rise in the number of thought-balloons.)

These different kinds of story-motifs are both sequentially and hierarchically organised. A 'set' on its own is a low-level motif, merely broadly indicating a field of possibility of encounters. On its own it carries little or no emotional charge. 'Story-enablers' facilitate the assembling of tension and uncertainty, but on their own do not determine the content of that tension. 'Theme-markers' begin to organise the movement of events through the stories, and can condition the use of sets and story-enablers. And 'emotional foci' provide a rhythm of movement through a story, between high and low tension.

I want to propose that *Jackie's* agenda of questions largely determines the forms and combinations of these motifs.[3] They make possible the translation of romance into stories revealing the meanings of 'love', its problems and pleasures. They take these forms precisely because that agenda is concerned with the logic of emotions. And I offer (for testing) the proposition that the more tightly organised a story is, the more meaningful it will be to its readers. By 'tightly organised' I mean that the lower-level motifs become embraced with the higher-level motifs.[4] Let me illustrate this. In her study of romance comics Julie Hollings tabulates in various graphs their changes over a thirty-year period. Among these is a graph indicating the frequency of happy and unhappy endings.[5] The problem is that 'reading-off' the endings in this fashion assumes that that they always constitute the same 'theme' in stories. Take 'The Dream' (No. 381, 23 January 1971), and think its difference from other stories I have looked at in which 'death' comes to a principal character. At a lonely house a young woman, Becky, arrives out of the snow, to be taken in and revived with hot drinks. But she keeps lapsing into a 'dream' in which she flashes back into her childhood. We see her parents, brutal and unfair – until she discovers they are not her real parents. She ran away, took a job – but her employer also was cruel towards her. Then she met Luke, who at last showed her some kindness. She flickers out of her 'dream', half-thinking that her rescuer is somehow connected with it all. And now she realises, he is Luke's brother Rod. This tips her back into her dream, where we see her happiness with Luke – except that she can't quite shake off her past. She can't surrender her emotions completely, for fear that he is only pitying her. Rod now talks to her, and convinces her that Luke really does love her. But even as she comes to believe him, she hears someone calling to Rod . . . and the house dissolves away. It is Luke looking for her. They had had a row, and she had run off. And now both Rod and Luke find her – dead in an icy stream. Now Rod has to convince Luke that she died happy. For look, poor Becky has a smile on her face. Though all her life before had been terrible, still for eighteen months Luke had made her happy. And as Luke accepts this, Becky knows she doesn't feel cold any more.

What is the meaning of the 'death' here? Seen as I am suggesting, it sits among those stories which deal with the past-as-problem. And it is actually not clear whether this should count as a happy or sad ending. The 'dream' is interesting, since it assembles and organises two distinct motifs: it is both a story-enabler, in that it regulates the movement between past and present, and also a theme-marker in gathering tension around whether or not her thoughts are real. It plays a complex role in evoking the overall theme of past-as-problem. The meaning of her 'death', then, cannot be determined except through the full interplay of the romance-agenda and the motif-devices turning that into a story.

Now see the difference with 'Forever And Ever' (No. 681, 22 January 1977). It illustrates particularly well how the answers to the romance-agenda can be embroidered within the fabric of a story. The tale opens with a young woman, Kathie, standing by a river bank, recalling how it all began. Immediately flipping into flashback, we see how she had sat crying on that spot when a boy (Terry) had come and comforted her; how gently he had led her out of her depression, and their romance had started. But even as they are happy together, she has slight premonitions that all is tentative, fragile: '. . . as if all the happiness I'd ever known was about to . . . to slip away from me'. Then back in her present we learn that this is somehow where it ended, their last kiss under this tree. 'Where did our dream go?' she wonders. As she stands wondering, she hears voices – and it is Terry, with another girl! He is telling her why this place is so special to him, how it recalls Kathie and his happy times with her. He goes on to recall their love, and how – just for a few days – Kathie had to go away to London; how she was hit by a car on a crossing. Now all that is left is his memories of her, and this place. The new girl Linda understands – Kathie will

always be a part of him, but there is room for her, too. And she is grateful to
Kathie for having made him happy for that time. Now at the end we return to
Kathie who is fading from the frames, looking content, knowing both that she
is remembered and that Terry is happy. (Incidentally, we would have trouble
making a case that this one was 'teaching jealousy'!)

How should we understand this? Its motifs are not difficult to see. The use
of flashback, without which this story would not hold together, melds with
the use of the theme of 'haunting': that a place can in some sense 'hold the
spirit' of a relationship that blossomed there. 'Haunting' is a good example of
a 'set' (low-level device) turned into a theme-marker (higher-level device).
More important is the theme of separation. The fragility of their love,
foreshadowed in her fears, is brought to them by her having to go to London.
London in Jackie is the exact opposite of their 'haunt'. It is where all their
absenting heroes and heroines go, for jobs, bright lights, adventures, and disasters. But here the theme of separation is doubled and made tragic. She not
only goes away, she also 'goes away' permanently, by dying. It is more than an
event, it is a crucial motif – one that is regularly repeated in this period. Love
that is flawless and pure is therefore vulnerable. When romantic couples go
apart, they are not just physically separating. They are poised on the brink of
disaster; but it is just this which allows the intense 'spirit' of their love to remain
and 'haunt'. If Kathie had died in their town, she could not have returned to
find this peace. All these add up to show that what has become fragile here is
an idealised romantic love. In Jackie from this time on, confidence in the ideal
of love is waning fast. This only becomes fully evident when we see the way
the motifs of flashback, haunting and separation work together in the particular
tale to produce this sad uncertainty about the future.

The contrast between these two suggests a number of things: first, that in true
Proppian fashion elements within stories take their meaning from their place
within the narrative. But second, the organising motifs should be understood
as temporarily-achieved forms through which the romance agenda can be turned
into stories, and answered. They therefore perhaps contain the main ideological
work of the stories. For they offer condensed forms for thinking the 'unthink-
able'. 'Love' cannot be known in advance; but it can be thought through its
motifs. If the motifs were to disappear, it would signal a whole change in the
stories' relation to that agenda. That is just what happened during 1982.

Decline of the Jackie story

In mid-1982, virtually between issues, both the *What's Your Problem?* and the
Reader's True Experience picture stories vanished. The stories taking their place
were much more episodic. There is virtually no tension in them. There are
therefore no transformations needed to resolve it. Sandra Hebron's example

was of this kind: 'My Lucky Day' (No. 993, 15 January 1983). This is the story of a girl's first day at college. She has a lousy cold, and Mum insists on her taking some of Dad's enormous hankies with her. Pulling one out on the bus, she drops her lucky horseshoe. A passing boy returns it to her and then shares his umbrella with her going into the college. He says he'll show her where to go, as he is going that way to meet his girl-friend – well, nearly ex-girl-friend as he is having difficulties. She lends him her lucky charm, to see if it will help him. Her first day is quite good and she makes some new friends. On the way home they meet again. His girl-friend definitely finished with him – but he doesn't think it's bad luck as (he says, meaningfully) he's already got another in mind. It's her! Quickly she gets her horseshoe back, for the luck it brings . . .

The striking thing is that this story is entirely without tension. Girl meets boy, they talk, he is ending one romance, can he start one with her, OK, that's nice, finis. There is nothing remotely approaching tension, transformation, or resolution. It is sequence of uncharged events – and that is surely significant. Any mode of analysis which cannot sense this has something missing.[6] To understand this decline, we need to look at Jackie's production history. Up to the time of writing this, Jackie has had eight editors in all. The earliest editors had been largely trained on the old letterpress magazines on which high priority was given to the stories. In Thomson's production system, outlines for stories are largely written internally, then sent out to writers and on to artists. In the early days it was usual for the editor him/herself to take responsibility for this, and to oversee this aspect of magazines. The first editor of Jackie, Gordon Small, did not himself do this. But his Chief Sub-Editor Gavin MacMillan (who took over the editorship at the end of the 1960s) bore this responsibility. This degree of oversight helps explain the underlying unity of the stories I have been pointing to.

However during the 1970s one editor, Nina Myskow, made a hit with the inclusion of pull-out pop-posters. Under her editorship, sales topped the million mark – and began a shift in the focus of editorial interest. Now more attention was paid to pop, and features. Gradually the status of story-editing declined. This decline was accentuated by the arrival of the photostory, which 'was forced on us by IPC'.[7] IPC had led the way with the introduction of photo-strip techniques in their teenage magazines Oh Boy! and Photo-Love. The success of these left Thomsons with no choice, even though the use of photographs spectacularly narrowed the stories.[8] But the result was a further slippage in the status of the story-editor. Now it is seen as one of the least interesting jobs of the magazine. This is surely a main reason for the decline of the Jackie stories, and their wholesale loss of tension. But equally this means the decline in any possible power to influence readers.[9] The stories became disengaged from the romance agenda. With the passing of the agenda from the stories, the organising motifs also passed away, like lost Proppian functions whose time has gone. This makes it very difficult, for example, to assess part of Liz Frazer's research on *Jackie* readers.[10] She met with mockery and dismissal towards her sample story. But this was taken from 1985, when the stories had long since 'died'. I would hardly have expected anything else. (See Chapter 11 for more discussion of this.)

Conclusions

I have tried to do a number of things in these chapters. First I hope it is clearer why I am dissatisfied with literary-critical, stereotyping, and semiological approaches to the media. I have tried to show their inadequacies as theories, and their inability to capture the nature of the stories. I have also tried to show a curious evolution in Jackie's stories which corresponds to no tidy scheme of ideology: a decline of confidence in romance, followed by a decline in the stories as such. To understand that evolution, we need two interlocking approaches. The first must explore the nature of a 'contract' between readers and the magazine; the second has to consider the production history which enables that contract to be met – or may fail. More than with any other group of comics, we really do not have the materials to produce a meaningful history. But one thing is clear. It was almost by accident that they came to be produced for their current age-range of readers. In the late 1950s the publishers were astonished to find that magazines they thought to be aimed at young married women were being read by young teenagers.[11] In producing theories of ideology, we are at risk if we lose sight of the role of accident in history! Finally, I believe I have drawn out in greater detail my own methods for understanding story-forms. Each of these – 'contract', production history, and appropriate methods – is taken on in later chapters. But first I must step aside to look in more detail at one concept which we have seen at work on *Jackie*. This is the concept of the 'stereotype'. Very like 'identification', it has an influential but lost history that needs recovering.

The lost world of 'stereotypes'

In a recent discussion of girls' magazines, Gillian Murphy concludes from a study of *Jackie* and one of its predecessors, *Peg's Paper*, that really nothing has changed over sixty years: 'In the period 1922-78, the content, style of presentation, topics featured, style of story-writing and the stories' actual content (place, theme, characters, behaviour suggested as appropriate for male and female and roles and interests ascribed to them) in the genre of magazines read by adolescent girls and described in this chapter as 'romance magazines' hardly changed at all despite a period of considerable social, economic, political and moral change between these years'.[1] She concludes this despite noting that in the pre-war *Peg's Paper* women were frequently advised to be passive in various ways, that the pre-war stories often dealt with class and politics (usually preaching love across class but not race lines); but that after the war and particularly by the time of *Jackie*, these all change. She also details changes in the kinds of character assigned to men and women. Somehow, these are irrelevant to the question whether a single view of femininity is being put across. The answer lies in her use of the concept of a 'stereotype'.

What is a stereotype? It is a shorthand image which fills in gaps in our knowledge. Where we do not know the reality, a stereotype gives us apparent knowledge. Their danger lies just in that. If we need to know something but haven't got another source of knowledge, frequently the media can step in with a cartoon-like knowledge which will seem satisfying. Or as Murphy puts it: 'The comic strip tells young teenagers about the world before they experience the situations portrayed. And these preconceptions, unless education has made them aware, govern their whole process of perception' (p. 209). So it is an opposition between (bad) stereotypes, and (good) education – the latter, no doubt, conceived more broadly than school curricula. This model is footnoted to a book which almost every study of stereotypes identifies as ancestor: Walter Lippmann's *Public Opinion*.[2] These critics don't know just how wrong they are in giving Lippmann their faith and footnotes.

Lippmann's 'Great Society'

Walter Lippmann was a radical journalist and writer of a kind that America particularly has produced. Like a number of thinkers of his time, Lippmann was very concerned about how society holds together. There is no magic formula, he argued, that guarantees that all the different opinions in society can be made to coincide and work in one direction. In fact for him, this is the main flaw in democratic theory. It just isn't true that all groups of people, just because they are democratically associated together, will rationally arrive at the same judgements. Yet luckily they mostly do, at least sufficiently for society to function. So how does it happen that one relatively coherent 'will of the people' emerges?

Tyranny is one way. Force, threats, terror and hard propaganda can – for a time – produce a single will: but at terrible cost. War can also do it. Remembering the recent World War I, he recalled the ways national symbols united people together. But Lippmann had a problem – he wanted not only unity of purpose, a common 'public opinion' but also rational unity and opinion. The motivating question behind his enquiry was: how do we achieve sensible cohesion in our society in which people acknowledge the real problems they face and find rational ways to act on them? To understand Lippmann, you have to grasp this founding question and its singular politics. For Lippmann was an early 'mass society' theorist, one of the early prophets of technocracy and the central mediating role of the 'expert': 'the need for interposing some form of expertness between the private citizen and the vast environment in which he is entangled' (p. 378).

Here was his problem. Human beings live by the 'pictures in their heads'. As private citizens (and Lippmann was firmly among those who think we are really only care about what touches our private interests), we have only bounded experience of the world; and within those boundaries we are 'passionately involved'. We are therefore very poor judges of our real situation, because we are too wrapped up in own goals. Beyond those limits, we are the victims of the pictures in our heads we have gleaned, mainly nowadays from the mass media. This was his problem. Modern society increasingly needs central planning, he believed, but the citizenry isn't up to it. We are all too individualised, caught up in our local interest-groups. These are great for mobilising people, but weak on knowledge and understanding.

Lippmann's solution was to separate politics into a special realm. Democracy needs specialist politicians, people who enter politics for its own sake not to grind some private axe – this is the only way, he thought, we can get a little bit of objectivity into decision-making. But even more, we need a whole stratum of specialist knowledge-producers, experts dedicated (with early retirement at 60 on generous pensions . . .) to producing and publicising independent 'facts'. This was his only way to solve the 'problem' of public opinion without recourse to war, tyranny or endless faction-fighting. Bring the experts into everything. Is there a labour dispute? Put in a mediator, with experts who will operationalise (and thus strip of their emotion-content) phrases like 'exploited' or 'over-paid':

There is for example a grave dispute in the steel industry. Each side issues a manifesto full of the highest ideals ... Perhaps those who object to conference do not quite say that. Perhaps they say that the other side is too wicked; they cannot shake hands with traitors. All that public opinion can do then is to organise a hearing by public officials to hear the proof of wickedness. It cannot take the partisans' word for it. But suppose a conference is agreed to, and suppose there is a neutral chairman who has at his beck and call the consulting experts of the corporation, the union, and, let us say, the Department of Labour.

Judge Gary states with perfect sincerity that his men are well paid and not overworked, and then proceeds to sketch the history of Russia from the time of Peter the Great to the murder of the Czar. Mr Foster rises, states with equal sincerity that the men are exploited, and then proceeds to outline the history of human emancipation from Jesus of Nazareth to Abraham Lincoln. At this point the chairman calls upon the intelligence men for wage tables in order to substitute for the words 'well-paid' and 'exploited' a table showing what the different classes are paid. Does Judge Gary think they are all well paid? He does. Does Mr Foster think they are all exploited? No, he thinks that groups C, M, and X are exploited. What does he mean by exploited? He means they are not paid a living wage. They are, says Judge Gary. What can a man buy on that wage, asks the chairman. Nothing, says Mr Foster. Everything he needs, says Judge Gary. The chairman consults the budgets and price statistics of the government. He rules that X can meet an average budget, but that C and M cannot ...

Nevertheless, says Judge Gary, we shall be ruined if we change these wage scales. What do you mean by ruined, asks the chairman, produce your books. I can't, they are private, says Judge Gary. What is private does not interest us, says the chairman, and, therefore, issues a statement to the public announcing that the wages of workers in groups C and M are so-and-so much below the official minimum living wage, and that Judge Gary declines to increase them for reasons that he refuses to state. After a procedure of that sort, a public opinion in the eulogistic sense of the term can exist. The value of expert mediation is not that it sets up opinion to coerce the partisans, but that it disintegrates partisanship. (pp. 403-4)

This lengthy quotation shows Lippmann's thinking. Disinterested experts will have 'facts' at their fingertips. These facts will provide the basis for a neutral resolution between conflicting interests. He didn't want to give to his experts the power to enforce their conclusions. His 'Great Society' was to be built, though, on the dissemination of this knowledge, and a populace informed by the experts will become a 'Public Opinion' – and then let employers and unions dare to carry on so divisively.

Within this framework Lippmann's 'stereotypes' find their place. His account of society entails a tripartite epistemology. The elements are 'interested experience', stereotypes, and expertise. Each relates to a different aspect of our lives: the first with the private individual; the second particularly with the mass media; but the third primarily with the disinterested expert. Our 'interested knowledge' is the limited domain of experience of our jobs, homes, family (which of course can't lead us to more general reliable conceptions . . .); this makes our ideas detailed but too emotionally-involved. We do form stereotypes from this, particularly of those towards whom we are antagonistic, but they are different from the stereotypes we form of those outside our limited experience. Our stereotypes of, let us say, the Japanese are simplified images; but they are not very important – unless, that is, they start governing the formation of political policy or get invested with the power of symbolism. And this is Lippmann's real concern. It is not stereotypes themselves that move us but the emotions that get attached to them by symbolism:

> These great symbols possess by transference all the minute and detailed loyalties of an ancient and stereotyped society. They evoke the feeling that each individual has for the landscape, the furniture, the faces, the memories that are his first and, in a static society, his only reality. That core of images without which he is unthinkable to himself, is nationality. The great symbols take up these devotions, and can arouse them without calling forth the primitive images. The lesser symbols of political debate, the more casual chatter of politics, are always referred back to these proto-symbols, and if possible associated with them. The question of a proper fare on a municipal subway is symbolized as an issue between the People and the Interests, and then the People is inserted in the symbol America, so that finally in the heat of a campaign, an eight cent fare becomes unAmerican . . . Because of its power to siphon emotion out of distinct ideas, the symbol is both a mechanism of solidarity, and a mechanism of exploitation. It enables people to work for a common end, but just because the few who are strategically placed must choose the concrete objectives, the symbol is also an instrument by which a few can fatten on many, different [emotions], and seduce men into facing agony for objects they do not understand. (pp. 235-6)

This is Lippmann trying to reconcile his devotion to nationalism with a fear of its consequences, all too clearly perceived after a world war; and trying to reconcile a liking for democracy with a suspicion of the people. In his account, stereotypes are really not important. They are the inevitable by-product of our limited contact with the world. They do not have any particular power either to transfer themselves, or to arouse action. It is the mixture of interested experience and symbols that is explosive.

Limitations of space and other priorities forbid a proper evaluation of Lippmann's epistemology. But there is a real inconsistency in it. His view was that our understanding of the world is distorted by non-rational factors, like interests, and symbols. Yet his solution is to suppose that more 'facts' could temper our emotions. That is hardly likely on his own premises. The conclusion ought, I suspect, to be quite Hobbesian – nothing short of subordination of the individual could safeguard against these dangerous commitments. I am not just pointing out an inconsistency but suggesting that the opposition Lippmann sets in train, between (bad) stereotypes and (good) knowledge is slippery. His descendants slipped, as we shall see.

But in one respect Lippmann's ideas seem to me clearer than many of his his followers. Lippmann acknowledged that people don't just have experience. Experience is what we gather, sift and react with as we live our lives. It is not therefore an innocent component. The way we see and hear things is affected by who we are, and how we live. So it won't help simply to expand people's 'experience'. Certainly, Lippmann's solution – bring in the experts – is theoretically naive and politically fearsome. But at least Lippmann is clear that, on this whole approach, there is no solution to the bias in knowledge that stereotypes represent, by letting people see their 'experience' more clearly. Not so recent critics of 'stereotyping'.

How did it come about that a concept with such unpromising beginnings became one the main organising concepts for work on the mass media with a completely different motivation and political tendency? And how far have subsequent uses of it freed themselves from the political and epistemological implications in Lippman's account?

'Stereotype' after Lippman

The career of the concept after Lippmann is largely uncharted – and again, I think this is significant. There are some concepts about which users seem to be blind and unself-critical. 'Stereotype' seems to have gone through two main stages. First,it entered social psychology between 1930 and 1960. Then it transferred into 'radical discourse' about texts, particularly after 1970.

One of the things for which Lippmann was justly famous was his assault on the anti-immigrant crusaders of the period 1910-24 in America. In the name of eugenics, IQ testing and race paychology, many psychologists threw their academic weight behind demands for immigration controls, enforced sterilisation of the 'feeble-minded', and segregated education.[3] Lippmann's critique made him a natural ally for those who within psychology began to move the discipline away from 'race-psychology'. 'Race-psychology' asked: what are the differences between different 'racial' groups? In what (biological, cultural) bases are they rooted, and how do they condition relations between groups? The new 'psychology of prejudice' asked quite different questions. Instead of making other 'races' the object of enquiry, the new investigators asked about the sources of our attitudes towards them. The problem did not lie in the despised groups. It lay in us, and in our attitudes to them.

Samelson, an American historian of psychology, has explored this change, showing how quickly and completely it took place.[4] There were a few studies of racial attitudes in the early 1920s but these were usually just demonstrations of the usefulness of a research technique rather than a challenge to 'race psychology'. Yet within a short period, 'Researchers in a score of studies of prejudice sought the intrapsychic roots of bigotry and intolerance, forgetting that not long ago psychological science had certified the inferiority of the rejected groups. The last step was taken; the issue had moved from one pole to the other, from the real race superiority of the Anglo race (and the Anglo psychologists) to the irrational prejudices of the psychologists' new subjects. The superior rationality of the professional researchers had been maintained' (p. 269-70). That last remark expresses Samelson's conviction that psychology has been far too blind and self-satisfied about its own historical role.

The change from race-psychology to prejudice-investigation was linked with several developments: the passing of the restrictionist Immigration Law of 1924 which, for a time, took the sting out of issues of immigration. A lot of the psychologists who inaugurated the study of prejudice were themselves immigrants, often indeed refugees from persecution in Europe. Also, with the arrival of the Depression there was a marked 'swing to the Left' among psychologists. This peaked with World War II, in a determination that psychologists should contribute to building national unity and overcoming internal divisions.

Samelson's analysis is germane to mine. For he shows that psychology did not just 'discover' the stereotype. Psychologists so defined it that they safeguarded their own superiority. They, of course, were not tainted by its irrationalism – and, by extension, they had the key to changing it. It is the nature of this imputed 'irrationalism' that we need to look into.

A stereotype would be defined as: 'A relatively simplex cognition, especially of a social group (e.g., "All Orientals look alike"). Stereotypes tend to be widely shared by members of a given society. Stereotypes may be seen as an instance of the part-whole principle in cognition, in that our judgement of any particular individual member of a group is influenced by our stereotypes of the group to which he belongs.'[5] According to this definition, although 'stereotyping' involves simplification of our ideas about other people, nothing says this is unusual or abnormal. Quite the contrary. Many social psychologists say that this is simply part of our normal tendency to categorise, which we can't do without:

> One line of argument against stereotypes . . . is completely wrong-headed. It has been said, for instance, that the trouble with a stereotype is that it treats a large number of distinguishable persons as equivalent, it is a generalisation and so ignores individual differences. In the ritualistic words of the General Semantics movement: 'Negro$_1$ is not Negro$_2$ is not Negro$_3$'. The implication is that we ought to react to each person and event as a unique entity. This is neither possible nor desirable. If we were to register every discriminable feature of a space-time event, it would indeed be unique. Nothing ever repeats exactly, not even the turning red of the traffic light on the corner. . . . Events or persons in all their detail do not recur but unless we can discover recurrence, we cannot project ahead, we

cannot anticipate the future. To form accurate anticipations is an obvious necessity for survival and we and all the higher animals are continually forming such anticipations.[6]

This sounds acceptable, with a proviso. We form categories to anticipate future encounters. How accurate are our anticipations? Probably not very; but provided they are easily modifiable if our expectations are not fulfilled, stereotypes should be no problem. We form them, they run up against experience, we change them.

But add a new component: that a stereotype might resist change. Gordon Allport, in one of the most influential early studies of prejudice, puts it thus:

> More than a generation ago, Walter Lippmann wrote of stereotypes, calling them simply 'pictures in our heads'. To Lippmann goes credit for establishing the conception in modern social psychology. His treatment, however excellent on the descriptive side, was somewhat loose in theory. For one thing he tends to confuse stereotype with category. A stereotype is not identical with a category; it is rather a fixed idea that accompanies the category. For example, the category 'Negro' can be held in mind simply as a neutral, factual, nonevaluative concept, pertaining merely to a racial stock. Stereotype enters when, and if, the initial category is freighted with 'pictures' and judgements of the Negro as musical, lazy, superstitious, or what not. A stereotype, then, is not a category, but often exists as a fixed mark upon a category . . . It operates . . . *in such a way as to prevent differentiated thinking about the concept.*[7]

A stereotype includes a 'screening' device which enables its holder to ignore contradictory experiences. This is because it carries an evaluative load and a weight of emotion.

Who, then, is prone to them? All of us to some extent. But (the story runs) some of us are better able to overcome this tendency than others. Some individuals are prone to such rigid categories, because of personality defects. It was, therefore, quite logical to find the dynamics of extreme prejudice in an 'authoritarian personality'.[8] The problem is a certain kind of sick individual; and fascism was simply its extreme outcome. Such individuals are incapable of letting experience change their stereotypes; and the problem is compounded by faulty socialisation.

I am not trying to summarise the whole history of such research and theorising in social psychology. Certainly, its reduction of 'prejudice' to a problem of high-stereotyping individuals has been powerfully challenged by empirical research.[9] But just as importantly, the implicit epistemology is borrowed from Lippmann, with that change I indicated. 'Experience' has become a naive encounter with the world in which we learn without preconceptions, 'the facts' speaking to us. The trouble is, some individuals can't do this. These are the ones with emotional problems that make them 'screen' the world, to exclude uncomfortable bits. The rest of us, of course, use categories. We can't do without them. But at least we manage to remain a bit flexible. This is how one social psychology textbook sets up this opposition:

> (T)yping people is almost inevitable, because of its functional usefulness. No one can respond to other persons in all their unique individuality. That form known as stereotyping, however, is generated as exaggerated typing, and has been consistently attacked by social scientists. Stereotyping is a sociocultural phenomenon, in that it is a property characteristic of people sharing a common culture. People do three things in stereotyping: (1) they identify a category of persons (such as policemen or hippies), (2) they agree in attributing sets of traits or characteristics to the category of persons, and (3) they attribute the characteristics to any person belonging to the category.[10]

There is much wrong with this account. First, it is simply a false opposition to say that we either treat people as unique individuals, or treat them as members of categories. This reduces categories to the equivalent of naive bird-spotting. We have a small list of birds (some of which we are keen on, others of which we dislike) and anything we see we force into one or more categories. We don't seem to do this for any reasons, except to keep on spotting. Second, and in the same vein, it sees categories as like limited lists, each constituting an independent fragment which goes out and confronts experience. If they form a 'whole', it is only in our personality. Missing from this account is any sense that people *make sense of the world* via their categorisations, that they constitute an *argument*.

We can see this in the quotation from Secord and Backman who put the categories 'police' or 'hippies' on a par with naming a new breed of grasshoppers. These appear to be history-less, decontextualised groups about whom we have no prior thoughts, arguments, commitments. We seem to come round a corner, see them and react – the trouble being that some of us, with our over-rigid personalities, then attach a lot of emotions to our labels and can't see past them.

If this seems overstated, consider a particular instance. In 1971 a very useful review of almost a hundred psychological studies of 'stereotyping' was published.[11] After reviewing the progress of research in identifying dimensions of stereotypes and describing the methods used (typically by inviting people to assign attributes to photographs, or to assign adjectives to groups), they discuss one particular piece of research:

> Different samples show varying uniformity in assignment of stereotypes. Rice . . . found that Vermont Grange members showed greater uniformity in assigning labels (Businessmen, US Senator, College President) to a series of photographs than did a group of Dartmouth students. Litterer . . . , replicating Rice's study, failed to find a greater uniformity among businessmen than students; he suggested

that Rice's group of Vermont Range members were a more homogeneous group than his group of businessmen. Edwards . . . found that Communist and non-Communist displayed equally high uniformity in stereotyping disapproved Fascism and somewhat less uniformity in stereotyping approved Democracy. Edwards' results suggest that it is not the homogeneity of the group itself that is important, but rather it is the homogeneity of the attitude toward the stereotyped group. (p. 119)

I find this bizarre, but revealing. We are invited to equate assigning adjectives to photographs, with declaring what we think about fascism or democracy. The vital difference, surely, is *argument*. People don't just have 'attitudes' towards such political phenomena; they have more or less articulated views on them. These are elements within their world-views.

'Stereotype' theory relies on an appallingly inadequate epistemology which is directly inherited from Walter Lippmann, and carries the same social and political implications as his original argument: that stereotypes are an unfortunate inevitability, fostered by our limited 'experience' of the world; and that we, the intellectuals, must play a protective role given our relative independence of them. This epistemology instructs researchers how to inquire into 'stereotypes'. The problem with the experimental procedures is that they were incapable of discovering conceptual complexity. Using techniques like adjectival responses, treating pre-existent categories like 'Negroes' as isolable variables towards which 'attitudes', inevitably they failed to discover differences in the way people hold to their views. These will be differences of at least three kinds: in the seriousness with which people assert their attitudes; in the kind of discourse with which believers support their beliefs; and in the role that those opinions play inside systems of rationalised beliefs.

Take the two kinds of example in the last quotation, and think about their differences. It suggests a distinction along new dimensions. People's responses to a photograph might just be a function of an isolated 'attitude', particularly when they are asked to assign adjectives to a photograph of a College President – a role probably not very salient in many lives, and about which we are unlikely to have worked-out opinions. But to extend that to 'attitudes' to communism is absurd. Here, we surely enter a realm of rationalised discourse, of arguments, of generalised views of the world – in which 'communism' is likely to have considerable argumentative saliency. That suggests a distinction which, while it might rescue the concept of a 'stereotype', trivialises it:

Stereotype	*Rationalised opinion*
Resulting from limited interest/ involvement/saliency.	Resulting from greater interest/ involvement/saliency.
Visual/superficial	Conceptual/explanatory
Hardly informing important behaviours	Capable of informing important behaviours

| Simplex, and relatively isolated from other beliefs | Complex, and relatively involved with other beliefs |
| Casually held | Seriously held |

There are real gains from this. With it, we can make sense of the findings of researchers such as Richard LaPière, who have pointed out how unreliably attitudes and actions are correlated.[12] This easily makes sense, where such 'attitudes' are held casually and unconnected with other salient beliefs. But the price is that 'stereotype' loses virtually all its explanatory power.

'Stereotype' and media work

When did 'stereotype' get turned on to the mass media? Bibliographies suggest that it made a definitive appearance in the early 1970s. For example in the mid-1970s Sara Zimet was able to cite more than sixty articles and books published between 1970 and 1975 which use or assume it; and that seems to be representative.[13] Prior to 1970 it is used only spasmodically, so far as I can tell. Perhaps the first use, though, was in the American studies of propaganda of the 1940s. These studies were initiated during World War II with the aim of detecting shifts in German war policy by analysing their propaganda broadcasts.[14] For these purposes, they developed quantitative methods of content-analysis of communications. After the war these ideas were carried into research on the media by people such as Bernard Berelson, for example, in his study (with Salter) of minorities in American romantic fiction.[15]

Berelson and Salter draw directly on psychological attitude-research. Stereotypes, they say, act 'socially as a stimulus to xenophobia' (p. 179). They provide 'mental pictures of what other "different" kinds of people believe and do' (p. 179). Their article is very cautious about effects, suggesting mainly that 'readers with latent tendencies to assign the usual stereotypic descriptions to groups they do not know, or towards whom they are unsympathetic . . . can find support for their convenient tags, labels and aggressions in such magazine fiction' (p. 188). The authors do in fact note that hardly any of their stories discuss minority groups' right to be in America. But in line with so much later theorising, this absence is itself turned into something bad. To miss out discussing the question of why blacks are deprived in America is to deprive them of the right to have this considered.

After this, the concept went largely underground until 1970. The other frequently referenced pre-1970 article is Nancy Larrick's study of American children's books.[16] Larrick powerfully exposes the exclusion of black people from books for children. Along the way, and almost incidentally, her argument uses the concept of a 'stereotype'. But it seems to mean little more than 'stock character'; it does not seem to carry any implications of influence. Her argument is: there is a problem about the way 'negroes' are shown and not shown. For the most part, they are simply absent as if non-existent. Where they are shown, it is almost always as bad characters or with echoes of slavery. The need is to show them as human first, black second. There is a curious tension in her article. The tension is over the ways in which literature (or the media) can or should reflect their society. When she was writing, black people were only too aware that America was not an integrated society. The Civil Rights movement was a living demonstration of their certainty. When, therefore, concern was (quite properly) expressed about the pathetic treatment of black people in books, it could really only be on the political grounds that they *ought not to be so excluded*. There is nothing wrong with such an argument. But using 'stereotype' to express it has the effect of concealing the fact that this was a political demand. Larrick's own political commitments are well captured in the following quotation: 'Across the country, 6,340,000 non-white children are learning to read and to understand the American way of life in books which either omit them entirely or scarcely mention them' (p. 63). Of course the implication of this must be that the 'American way of life' does not really exclude them. That is highly arguable; a case can well be made that their absence from the books accurately reflects their status in that 'way of life'. To have shown them otherwise would have been a distortion. I am not in any way diminishing the importance of a demand for proper presentation of black lives, or women's lives, or gay or disabled people's lives in books, comics, magazines etc. But how we understand the problem changes what counts as its solution; or, what will count as 'proper' versus 'improper' presentation. And when 'stereotype' fully emerges in the 1970s as the organising concept these problems fully surface.

The trouble with 'stereotypes'

The search for 'stereotypes' in the media has become a small industry in its own right. The literature is now so large that it is pointless discussing just one or two. I want, instead, to draw out the main problems I see in its use. There are many, and I cannot deal with them all. Let the following be indications, and invitations to others to take the arguments further.

1. There are real problems with 'stereotyping' theory's demands that the media etc should 'reflect' society. In a society where, for example, black people are disproportionately kept in low-paid jobs and on the dole, or sent to prison, to have this simply 'reflected' in the media would cause outrage. Hence the demand shifts to one that these things should only be shown if they are explained in acceptable ways. I do not want to quarrel with this – only to make clear that thereby 'stereotype' has disappeared as a criterion.

But this isn't just a pragmatic problem. It creates two incompatible yet coexisting demands, as Steve Neale has noted.[17] On the one hand, a regularity may be dubbed a 'stereotype' if it shows a deviation from the 'real world'. So, a great deal of media representation of women is condemned for reinforcing the (false) stereotype that women want sex at any time. Or again, the proportion of black or women characters in the media is greatly out of line with their proportion in the population (or relevant subsection thereof). These are stereotypes as falsehoods, distortions of the world. On the other hand, something may be dubbed a 'stereotype' for the opposite reason, that it is so very like the world outside. Here, a good deal of media representation is condemned for showing women in the home, providing services to men – though of course it is in fact true that very many do. Or again, black people are overwhelmingly shown living in poor conditions, in ghetto areas; books etc have been condemned for showing this even though it is (regrettably) the case. These are stereotypes, this time, as self-fulfilling prophecies.

It ought to be clear that these two are sharply at odds with each other.[18] They would have to work on us in different ways, to be influential. The first has to block our perceiving the world as it really is; the second has to stop us seeing anything but the world as it is. This conflict is important, not just this is an inconsistency. More importantly, if we look behind the conflict, we may find out how it is (silently) resolved, and therefore has largely gone by unnoticed. This needs an understanding of the other main problems with the concept.

2. There is a hidden agenda in here, that it is wrong to present people as 'representatives of categories'. This is a point Richard Dyer makes very effectively. Discussing 'stereotypes' of gays in films, he points out how important it is to the possibilities of collective self-defence that there should be positive group-images.[19] Ellen Seiter takes this a stage further, suggesting that the hidden agenda on images of women is the 'bourgeois career individual', which is every bit as ideological as 'hearth and home' images.[20] The problem arises because the 'stereotyping' tradition grumbles, not about the particular content of a certain category, but about the fact of categorising at all. It is only this that renders that disagreement invisible.

3. Part of that agenda also is a peculiar theorisation of 'influence' which, ironically, in the end does away with the very notions of social power that first stimulated the enquiries. If it has a method, 'stereotyping' depends on content-analysis. The more widespread an image and the more often we encounter it, the argument runs, the greater the likely influence. Otherwise, why worry about frequency of appearance? This very passive view of audiences is a problem in itself. But as R W Connell has pointed out in another context, it has the curious effect of doing away with any reference to power.[21] Recall O'Connell's problem with the *Beano*. It was that girls are under-represented as characters. Suppose we put that right. Still missing from these comics would be any representation of the typical relations between boys and girls. Dealing with that in story-form is a quite different problem from 'getting the balance right'. For 'stereotype'

theory, it would seem that girls learn their self-images only from the proportion-
ate appearance of the sexes, not from how they relate to each other. The power
of men over women has no place in 'stereotyping' theory.

4. There is an unsatisfactory account of how we form categories and use
them. It would seem that categories just 'assemble' out of the balance of influences on us; and then – unless something positively interferes, like a good
radical pointing out the error of our ways – we use them mechanically. There
are a wealth of visual metaphors in this kind of talk: 'images', 'representations',
'pictures in our heads', 'distorting our perceptions of the world'.[22] There is
nothing wrong per se with using metaphorical talk. But it has two results here,
which again help resolve that hidden inconsistency I pointed to earlier. These
'images' stand between us and the world. They mediate between us and the
world, and stop us 'seeing the reality'. They are like sheets of glass which refract
the light and make us see things awry. We can't easily see past them. So, when
one distorts the world (stereotype as falsehood), it prevents us seeing clearly.
But how does that explain the other kind, the too accurate stereotype? Only
because these 'images' are seen as storehouses of the past. The power of the
visual metaphor is to suggest staticness, trapping us in the past. This is the
reason for the obsessive use of words like 'traditional', 'age-old' and 'outdated'
in such work. Take as representative the following quotation: 'After all these
years of battering on for a new deal for women, struggling with Equal Oppor-
tunities, Equal Pay, anti-sex discrimination, equal school curicula, striving to
release young girls from the stultifying role stereotypes of the past, magazines
like these [teenage romance comics] are actually travelling fast in the opposite
direction'.[23] This kind of talk has long struck me as strange. The implication
clearly is that 'stereotypes' have no relevance to the present, and might well
have declined but for their continued media presentation. But also it is implied
that stereotypes draw their power from ideas and images of the past; they are
not creations in the present, fought for and made convincing to us, but residues
of already-existing powers which dull and stultify us, trapping us back into
those power-relations. I want to suggest that this is yet another component of
the peculiar issue of 'time' in theories of ideology. Once again, ideology is seen
as a force from the past, barring our access to a future.

5. The resultant politics are inevitably elitist, in two ways. First, 'stereotypers'
still share Lippmann's assumptions which, from the start, were infected with
elitist politics.[24] They never shed that infection. 'Stereotypes' exist within a
pattern of oppositions:

Stereotype	Non-stereotypes
Pre-cognitive	Cognitive
Fixing the past	Pointing to the future
Typical site: the mass media	Typical site: 'education'

Inevitably we, the ones who have 'seen past them', must play a role in educating and saving others. They need our cognitive protection against these non-cognitive influences.

And just as inevitably, the question hangs in air, why some individuals and groups are more prone to being influenced than others. This brings with it a class dimension. A variety of studies have shown that working class people are more prone to categorical thinking, than 'educated' middle class people.[25] According to the logic of the stereotyping approach, this must show the inferiority of their thinking. I reject that. To understand why, consider one 'stereotype' already mentioned by Cauthen et al.: 'fascism' and the 'fascist'. Suppose we did decide to call our 'attitude to fascism' a stereotype: what might be in it? We might list 'intolerant', 'prejudiced', authoritarian', and 'violent'. Now there are quite a few individuals whose views I regard as fascist who are not personally violent. Does that mean that my 'stereotype' of fascism and fascists as 'violent' is a distortion? At the very best, it would be an exaggeration.

I want to dispute that hard, for reasons that to me do more damage than all other criticisms of 'stereotype'. Part of my conception of fascism concerns its tendencies as an organised political force. I would want to argue that fascism is not just a sum-total of its individual adherents' behaviours. It is a political movement, built round ideas about 'race', conspiracy theories and so on, whose inherent logic leads to class and racial violence. To define my view as a 'stereotype' involves turning fascism into an *aggregate of individuals*; then my 'image' of them is more or less accurate inasmuch as it relates to those individuals. Against this, my conceptualisation of fascism involves treating it as a socially-organised phenomenon, in which individuals are not simply aggregated (with all their particular likenesses and unlikenesses, personal violence or otherwise). They are being mobilised for a socio-political movement; it is the potential of that movement I am assessing in calling fascism 'violent'. I am assessing its future, not just summarising its past.

'Stereotyping' dissolves all sense of social organisation. In protesting against category-inclusions, it dissolves all categories. What kinds of characteristic are seen by 'stereotypers' as the most likely to appear within our 'stereotypes'? They are almost always *individual physical or personality traits*. For example psychologists will ask us if we regard Jews as 'shrewd', 'clannish', 'greedy' etc – all individual personality traits. But how, within such a model, could we encompass the repeated fascist claim that Jews are mounting a world conspiracy, or that mixing their blood with ours will lead to racial degeneration? The whole 'stereotyping' edifice depends on hostility to thinking in group-terms.

Once dismiss that assumption, and the politics no longer flow from it. It is then open to me to argue that working class people are in general *more accurately* aware that the social world is really divided into categories. If they have a 'stereotype' of managers, or employers, as 'exploitative', 'greedy', 'selfish' or etc, that is not a false generalisation. It is an accurate summary of their experience of the inherent tendencies that arise from occupying a concrete social position. It is not a statement about the personality of an individual, but a claim about what follows from occupying a definite position in a class society.[26]

My conclusion is that the concept of a 'stereotype' is useless as a tool for investigation of media texts. It is dangerous on both epistemological and political grounds.[27] Its view of influence and learning is empiricist and individualistic, and leads to the anti-democratic politics which Lippmann first set into it. Finally, it leads to an arbitrary reading of texts which tells us only about the worries of the analyst.

The trouble with Dad:
Bunty, Tracy, and fantasy

In recent years, a new approach to ideology has emerged which seems to escape a lot of the problems of other approaches. It also offers powerful tools for looking at things like comics. 'Post-structuralism', the term usually given to a very mixed set of ideas, is complicated. I am not up to a full discussion and evaluation of them. But I want to study one very thoughtful use of this new approach by Valerie Walkerdine on two pre-adolescent girls' comics, Bunty and Tracy.[1] To understand her argument, we need some understanding of the general position taken by the post-structuralists.

Post-structuralism derives from several sources which don't necessarily sit easily together. After the excitement of structuralism in literary theory, there was a reaction. Structuralism had shown new ways of investigating how texts produce meanings – but always on the assumption that readers would get these meanings. Part of post-structuralism's project was to think again about the 'reader'. Out of this came some striking work on the "implied reader", "ideal reader", "narratee", and so on.[2] A second source was Louis Althusser. He challenged what he saw as a tendency within Marxism to assume an 'essential self' which was repressed, or alienated by capitalism.[3] While 'humanism' might be morally attractive, he regarded it as theoretically and politically dangerous. But if we could not talk of an 'essential self', we needed a new theory of subjectivity. For this he turned to the French psychoanalyst Jacques Lacan. Althusser's call was answered also by a new radical critique of mainstream psychology. An alliance emerged of Marxists, literary critics and psychologists.

There is an oddity about this alliance which has not generally been noted. Here, on the one hand, were the literary analysts trying to rescue the reader from his/her subordination to texts. But then there were the radical psychologists decomposing the concept of 'the subject', and replacing it with an account which stressed how we could be 'constructed' by and within discourses – which includes texts! This odd alliance depends on some curious shared assumptions which are relevant to Walkerdine's discussion of Bunty and Tracy.

It would be irrelevant for me to give my views on all these traditions. I am very hostile to the whole of Althusser's theories. But they are about much more than 'ideology'. Readers may want to think about how my criticisms of Walkerdine might affect the wider theories.

The matter of the 'subject'

A useful introduction to post-structuralist work is given in a book to which
Walkerdine herself contributed, and which she uses in her discussion of the
comics. The book, *Changing the Subject*, offers a wide-ranging critique of psychology from which emerges a retheorisation of the 'subject'.[4] The authors argue
that psychology (and by implication other disciplines, too) has taken for granted
a dualistic model of individual-versus-society. The problem with this is not just
that it is scientifically inadequate. More importantly, the model itself is an
expression of modern bourgeois society and is implicated in the running of
that society. In mental measurement, fitting people appropriately to jobs, defining social problems and shaping responses to them: in these and many more
ways, psychology is not just a science but a functioning set of power-relations.
The way they explain this idea of 'power' gives us the beginnings of their theory.
Following Michel Foucault, they suggest that power is located in ways of talking
about people, ways of investigating them and making them into objects of
knowledge. A quotation from Foucault gives the flavour of this. He is illustrating
the way 'sexuality' was turned into a scientific domain:

> One day in 1867, a farmhand from the village of Lapcourt, who was somewhat
> simple-minded, employed here then there, depending on the season, living hand-
> to-mouth from a little charity or in exchange for the worst sort of labour, sleeping
> in barns and stables, was turned in to the authorities. At the border of a field, he
> had obtained a few caresses from a little girl, just as he had done before and seen
> done by the village urchins round about him; for, at the edge of the wood, or in
> the ditch by the road leading to Saint-Nicolas, they would play the familiar game
> called 'curdled milk'. So he was pointed out by the girl's parents to the mayor of
> the village, reported by the mayor to the gendarmes, led by the gendarmes to the
> judge, who indicted him and turned him over first to a doctor, then to two other
> experts who not only wrote their report but also had it published. What is the
> significant thing about this story? The pettiness of it all; the fact that this everyday
> occurrence of bucolic pleasures, could become, from a certain time, the object
> not only of a collective intolerance but of a judicial action, a medical intervention,
> a careful clinical examination, and an entire theoretical elaboration. The thing to
> note is that they went so far as to measure the brainpan, study the facial bone
> structure, and inspect for possible signs of degenerescence the anatomy of this
> personage who up to that moment had been an integral part of village life; that
> they made him talk; that they questioned him concerning his thoughts, inclina-
> tions, habits, sensations, and opinions. And then, acquitting him of any crime,
> they decided finally to make him into a pure object of medicine and knowledge
> – an object to be shut away till the end of his life in the hospital at Maréville, but
> also one to made known to the world of learning through a detailed analysis. . .
> So it was that our society . . . assembled round these timeless gestures, these barely

furtive pleasures between simple-minded adults and alert children, a whole machinery for speechifying, analyzing, and investigating.[5]

Power, for Foucault, is in the speechifying etc; it is in the way we can be turned into objects to be studied. Our talk becomes a symptom, our dreams, thoughts and sensations become the property of 'experts'. That is power. It is not to deny that there are forms of direct physical control, punishment, armies, police forces. But the first and most common form of power lies in these linkings of power/knowledge.

Whatever the arguments over some of Foucault's particular claims, there is no question but that this way of thinking about power has great potential, and has opened the way to new kinds of research. And his notion of power/know-ledge is central to Henriques et al.'s rethinking of the 'subject'. Two implications, in particular, are taken over. Foucault argues that we have no reason to think of power as centrally unified. Nor need it necessarily have a single purpose (as, for example, in many notions of 'ruling class power'). Rather it is spread out through society, distributed wherever power/knowledge come together (in 'discourses'). These might cohere, but they might also conflict; that is a matter for investigation, not fiat. Foucault also argues that all knowledge of ourselves is implicated in these discourses. In fact we are constituted through them. So we are not pre-given individuals on whom things are foisted by external powers. Power/knowledge now penetrates our very hearts and minds, it defines us. It make us 'subject' to the discourses. And all the ambiguities in the word 'subject' are here consciously played on. Because these many discourses each position us differently, we must give up the illusion of ourselves as 'unitary individuals'.

Henriques et al. argue that psychology itself must be rethought in the light of this. It is itself a powerful discourse defining people, constructing their iden-tities. It participates in the socialisation of children (through, for example, instructional guides to parents), women (Hollway's discussion of the produc-tion of 'hysteria' in the nineteenth century is fascinating), and so on. Thus, they arrive at their own argument which draws on psychoanalytic theory, and in particular Lacan's version of that. They need psychoanalytic theory to provide a general picture of how a human being can be 'constructed by discourses'. According to Freudian theory, the infant at birth is an undifferentiated mass of needs. The way in which the young child experiences a mixture of pleasures and frustrations leads to the division of its mental life into distinct areas. Its hunger is satisfied by its mother, and the mother therefore takes on central importance in the child's primitive conception of the world. But the mother often goes away, causing a sense of loss. In fantasy, the child starts to wish for power over the mother. It is loss that leads to the development of fantasy. But the fantasy is impossible, not least because the mother is 'owned' by the father. So hand in hand with fantasy comes repression. The child becomes aware that it cannot control the whole world, even that it is forbidden to do so. For fear of losing the mother which it needs/loves, it represses its desire to control into other forms. Thus, out of its original need-satisfying contact with its mother, gradually emerge the various components of its mental life: the unconscious was an arena for its repressed desires, fantasy as the way these are 'played out'; the superego, which contains the internalised rules and forbiddings of its parents and others; and its ego, the more-or-less secure conscious persona by which it will know itself. The boundaries between these are never secure, and there is always tension between them.

This dynamic model of the production of human desires – dreadfully over-simplified here – has been the subject of a lot of criticism. A good deal of it has come from people sympathetic with the psychoanalytic project. In recent years, Jacques Lacan's modifications have, it has been argued, overcome the conservative implications in the original. Henriques *et al.* give a very clear pre-sentation of these arguments. They see Lacan as challenging two particular tenets of the original Freudian version. First, the 'hydraulic' model in Freud: the original 'instincts' were thought of like a (biological) head of steam that had to be released somewhere. The task of repression was to redirect that head of steam along socially acceptable paths, and the unconscious was the seat of the repressed desires. Lacan, drawing on Freud's half-drawn distinction between needs (original drives) and desires, argued it was the latter that occupied the unconscious:

> For Freud 'need' derives from a state of internal tension, and it can be satisfied through specific action which procures the adequate object, for example 'food' which satisfies hunger. Needs can thus in principle be fulfilled. Wishes and desires on the other hand are based on needs which have once known satisfaction, to which, as it were, they hark back. . . Wishes and desires are thus relations which are mediated in fantasy. Moreover because the search for an object in the 'real world' which would provide satisfaction is entirely governed by this relationship with signs, wishes and desires involve an inevitable distancing or disjunction from the original esperiences of satisfaction. Later the notion of ideational representa-tives was given central importance by Freud. . . In this account the unconscious is the site of repressed ideas. . . What is crucial in this theoretical development is that the unconscious is not the seat of drives or instincts, but of ideational represen-tatives, signs or memories. (p. 213)

Lacan developed this view, using structural linguistics to explain how wishes and desires gained 'meanings'. From this came his famous saying: 'The uncon-scious is structured like a language'.

He also modifies the theory of the Oedipus Complex which, in Freud, led both to the biologistic view that women lack something by comparison with men. For Lacan, the psychic differences between men and women are not the result of the penis (or its lack), but of the 'phallus', its symbolic version. This is the source of language and all other cultural distinctions: 'From this position, the resolution of the Oedipus Complex, in which the child resolves problems associated with desire for the mother or father by identifying with the same-sexed parent, is the point at which the child becomes a subject according to the cultural laws which preordain it and, to a certain extent, constrain its destiny. Hence gender difference enters into the production of subjectivity in Lacan's account' (p. 215). This achievement is coupled with the mastery of language; 'loss of the mother' occasions the child drawing its first full distinction between 'self' and 'other'. 'In Lacan's account, the child uses his or her first words to establish, in fantasy, control over the loss of the object which gave satisfaction' (ibid.). The outcome of all this is a powerfully explanatory view of desires. They always 'hark back' to that original distinction/attachment. The unconscious, once it has been constituted as a 'site', is composed of representations; and these belong to discourses which position us in a Self/Other relation. Thereafter, that beginning is the source for the child of the shaping of all desires. Each power/knowledge nexus, each discourse in which we are thenceforth caught up, works on us through those desires. It is in following through this view that Walkerdine arrives at her analysis of Bunty and Tracy.

Becoming victims

Walkerdine begins by criticising some assumptions she sees as underlying preceding approaches to media influence. Her comments seem to me very apt. Approaches that talk of the 'power of images', she argues, present a rationalistic picture of readers. We only have to get them past the images, to see the world more accurately and the influence should dissolve away:

> (T)here are at least two difficulties with this position. First, it assumes that by presenting a 'wider range of experience', children's views of themselves and of possible courses of action will change; secondly, that unproblematic transformation will come about through the adoption of non-stereotyped activities. Such an approach assumes a passive learner, or rather a rationalist one, who will change as a result of receiving the correct information about how things *really* are. It assumes that when the little girl sees the veil of distortion lifted from her eyes, she too will want to engage in those activities from which she has been forbidden by virtue of her gender. (p. 164)

Instead, we need to consider the role of these comics (among other influences, of course) in talking to girls' desires. And that means taking seriously that the stories are fantasy. They talk to those areas of girls' lives where dreams, hopes, ambitions, fears, and desires are formed. And, formed with a struggle. There is no reason, she says, to suppose that girls are led passively and without conflict into their 'feminine' self-definition. Regardless of her post-Freudian theory, this is surely wise thinking. For there are strong indications in these kinds of magazines for girls of a debate going on about what a 'good girl' is, how she should cope with 'bad' tendencies inside herself – all indicative of a struggle.

Walkerdine does see these comics as powerful, but not in the traditional sense of forcing themselves on to passive readers. They are powerful by virtue of playing out tensions already present within their (young, working class, female) audience. It is important to be clear about this concept of fantasy. It doesn't mean that the stories are amazing, otherworldly, 'fantastic' – crudely, the meaning it has in 'science fantasy', for example. Nor does it mean the uncontrolled, free-association kind of thinking implied by 'having a fantasy about becoming famous and immensely wealthy'. And we can never attach the word 'only' to fantasy, suggesting an innocent, purely escapist nature: as when people say in commonplace arguments, 'It's not real, it's only fantasy'.

Walkerdine takes fantasy very seriously. It is where desires take shape, where we make images of ourselves, where we face, or hide from fundamental dilemmas. And reading stories provides rich material for giving shape to as-yet-unshaped desires. Hence the importance she sees in Bunty and its stable-mates. Her argument is that these comics can play an important part in shaping the psychic pattern of young girls appropriately for a heterosexual, romantic future – even though they do not explicitly deal with romance or sexuality at all. They deal instead with the desires and emotions which will, in the next phase of their lives, become the sources of responses to sex and romance. They are the effective kind of stories to do this. Where other critics have suggested that setting stories in other places and times is a form of disguise, Walkerdine believes this is an essential distancing device. Put a heroine in Victorian times, remove real parents (substituting, as so many of these stories do, step-parents or orphanages), and the distancing makes it easier to dramatise in fantasy our conflicts of desires about parents, responsibilities, morality. The distance gives safety for playing out the conflicts. But then it becomes very important to know, in what kind of resolution of these conflicts do the comics involve the readers?

Walkerdine argues that the stories typically involve girls in self-sacrifice.[6] The resolution always comes in the form of self-denial, externalising 'bad' (selfish) desires and reinsertion into a proper family. She points in particular to these characteristics:

1. The stories make the heroines into victims, and 'in receipt of gross injustices' (p. 170). A girl is forced to work in a circus, for example, another is hated at school because she works hard, or a third pair of orphan sisters are brutally worked in a Victorian orphanage.

2. The heroines rarely live in a normal family. Orphans and step-parents abound. (In her sample there was one apparent exception. In The Snobby Stantons, Samantha faces the problem that her Mum teaches English at her school and the kids all think her a snob. Sam is always having to rescue Mum from disasters

– but without Mum knowing it. This doesn't really break the pattern of 'non-normal families' since in the logic of the story Sam's family is the problem, and she can't communicate with them.)

3. The heroines respond invariably by being ever-so-good, passive and self-sacrificial. Often they also (wrongly) feel indebted to those who have power over them and abuse them. In *Meg and the Magic Robot*, for example, Meg is trapped by her belief that her cruel uncle and aunt are paying for her brother's hospital treatment. So no matter how cruel they may be, she feels she owes them her submission.

4. It is precisely by being virtuous and self-sacrificial that the heroines are eventually rescued – and returned to a proper family.

5. A number of distancing devices are used so these stories can be held at a distance, as fantasy, and thus can work out displaced emotions and desires. These include the historical and geographical distancing. It is even possible on occasion to use animals as heroines (for example, a horse facing dilemmas about selfishness!) but with the same dramatic conflicts and resolutions.

What gives the stories their magnetism, then? Walkerdine's argument has two stages. First, the stories offer a fantasy dramatisation of girls' situation, in whose solution certain values are embodied. Girls use the stories as the basis for fantasies. In living out the exciting drama of these stories they are internalising values which may then play a part in moulding their desires:

> What seems to me important about this is that if cruelty is seen as exciting and works at the level of fantasy to romanticise difficult practical and emotional circumstances, this suggests a passive and not an active response to the violence (which in psychoanalysis would relate to the displacement of angry and hostile feelings onto others). It also provides the conditions for resolution: selflessness, even though it brings pain and suffering, brings its own rewards (knowledge of good deeds and righteousness). If the heroines are displayed as passive victims of circumstance, all bad and difficult actions and emotions are invested in others. The heroines suffer in silence: they display virtues of patience and forbearance and are rewarded for silence, for selflessness, for helpfulness. Any thought for the self, any wanting, longing, desire or anger is in this way produced within the texts as bad. This provides for the readers a value-system in which certain kinds of emotion are not acceptable, and a set of practices in which their suppression is rewarded by the provision of the longed-for happy family, the perfect bourgeois setting. (pp. 172-3)

Victory comes through passivity and helpfulness. Anger is never shown even in the face of real injustices. It's not that the girls achieve nothing – they must achieve it for others. It is a discourse about the meaning of being a 'good girl', Walkerdine argues, in which 'bad girls'' qualities (like anger and selfishness) are projected on to others. This is what she meant by saying that girls don't achieve the 'right desires' without struggle and conflict. These stories don't do away with 'bad desires', they project them elsewhere. If a girl who takes these fantasy-constructs into herself then feels angry or selfish, she will see that as coming into her from outside, as representing a 'wrong part' of her, stirred up by 'bad influences'. Her 'real self' is helpful, gentle, and selfless.

The outcome of this is emotional reorganisation, 'preparation for the prince' (p. 175). Not that the stories are secretly about heterosexuality. It is the resultant 'regime of meaning': 'Girls are victims of cruelty, but they rise above their circumstances by servicing and being sensitive to others – selflessness. The girl who services is like the beautiful girl whose rewards for her good deeds is to be taken out of her misery; she is freed by the prince. The semiotic chain slides into romance, with the prince as saviour' (p. 175). In reading little dramas in which activity is associated with selfishness and passivity with goodness and eventual success, girls are being offered a shaping of their emotions whose logical outcome is the waiting for the 'prince' who will rescue them, and continue their passivity: emotionally, socially, sexually.

Lost harmonies

There is a long tradition of criticism of psychoanalysis on the grounds that it is far too speculative, and mightily difficult to test. Generally, I don't want to associate with that kind of criticism. It doesn't worry me that some theories require speculative elaboration, and may never be easy to test. But it does worry me if other kinds of test – theoretical tests of coherence, for example – are not used. Adherents of psychoanalysis do need to remember that they are adhering to a *theory*. For example, I have often felt that it is somehow thought unarguable that there is a 'site' which may be called 'the unconscious'. We may discuss the status of its contents, and its relations to other aspects of mental life. But to doubt its existence is bizarre, it seems. I don't agree. It seems to me perfectly valid to want to question the whole notion of a constructed 'geography' of the mind in which there are separate 'sites' (however metaphorical that language may be). I do not accept that I have automatically contradicted myself if I reject the notion of an 'unconscious' but still say that there can be mental processes of which I am not aware. There are other possible accounts of 'unconscious mental activities' which carry none of the psychoanalytic implications. I begin my critique of psychoanalysis with this point for good reasons. I am frequently struck by a curious blindness among the psychoanalytically-minded about the status of their own theory. In Henriques *et al.*, this shows itself in their excusing psychoanalysis from the full rigours of the critique they offer against traditional psychologies.

When they look at traditional psychological theory and research, there is no doubt. It is a 'discourse'. As a form of knowledge-production it is socially-implicated, not only in the uses that might be made of its knowledge (what nasty things might be done with the results of intelligence tests, for example), but also in its own basic models (the implied individual/society opposition), and in its practices (the funding and carrying out of the tests themselves, and the construction of people as test-objects). But when they come to psychoanalysis, although they acknowledge the patriarchal assumptions in Freud and the way his therapeutic practices were involved in the bourgeois society of his time, still excuses are made. It is as though, here, a 'good theory' can be got by cleaning out the unfortunate contaminations – something not allowed to the theories they criticise. Their reasons are revealing. First, we are told, after the force of many of the criticisms has been acknowledged, that one critic, Donzelot, 'has not put in its place any explanation of how individuals are positioned in discourses, or their effectivity at the level of the individual subject' (p. 206). Well, that may be true. But is it not possible that another approach would not need to do this in the first place? Then, we are told that no other theory can do what psychoanalysis does: namely, to account for current conservatism: '(T)he political crises of the present time make it imperative that we develop a clearer understanding of what militates against change, what accounts for reaction and resistance. This has been recognised particularly within feminism' (p. 207). Now there is nothing wrong with a theory setting itself political tasks (if there were, this book would be a bit thin!). But this is a very particular political agenda, and I don't happen to share it. It is , in fact, the hidden model in Lacanian psychoanalysis. Perhaps Lacanianism is itself more of a 'discourse' than it would care to admit!

I will put my case against post-structuralist psychoanalysis in a series of short arguments. I suspect that, if valid, they hold not only against the particular version offered by the radical post-structuralists, but against a great deal of other psychoanalytic thought

1. *The theory distorts its opponents by falsely crystallising them under the headings 'humanism' and 'theories of the unitary self'.* 'Humanism' is a term of abuse, binding together a wide range of different theorists. 'Humanists' are all those who make the mistake of thinking the 'individual' opposed to 'society'. This is bizarre in the extreme. Others have criticised the same tendency in Althusser;[7] here, it results in equating instinctivist psychologists like William MacDougall, Gestalt theorists like Gustav Kohler, behaviourists such as Watson and Skinner, and prejudice theorists like Henri Tajfel. The fact that the first sees the individual primarily in terms of stored-up hereditary group-attributes while the third group see individual simply as a bundle of influences is all lost in this pea-soup of a criticism. Ironically, those who might in truth be said to be humanists – Erich Fromm, say, or Abraham Maslow – were the ones most critical of a denial of the individual in, for example, behaviourist theory.

Now consider their repeated assertion that they are opposing a tradition which treats the individual as a 'unitary, rational subject'. What is meant by this? A casual inspection of the traditions they are criticising would show this to be nonsensical. For example, psychology was greatly influenced by the empiricist tradition, deriving originally from John Locke the seventeenth-century philosopher. But the tradition which Locke began was built on a distinction between human rationality, experience, and passions; and the whole point was to emphasise just how uneasily these were related. The later behaviourists, drawing on nineteenth-century forms of this philosophy, shared the view that a human being is essentially a bundle of responses, not unified by rationality at all. Next, the mental testing tradition insisted on the separateness of various mental skills, and through its connections with social Darwinism and the eugenics movement, it emphasised the non-rational construction of our behaviour. In what sense could any of these be seen as asserting the 'unitary, rational subject'? Are these just careless arguments? I feel they signify something more. They are symptoms of an incoherence brought about by the demands of their own theory. This shows in the problems we meet within their theory and in the way that leads them to misread individual pieces of evidence.

2. *Post-structuralism's account of 'non-unitary' or 'multiple selves' is incoherent.* With the opposition thus labelled, the field is clear for the one possible alternative: a 'non-unitary self'. We learn the meaning of this by seeing what it is opposed to. For example, it is opposed to seeing masculinity and femininity as 'fixed features' (p. 228). (I must dispute that a 'unitary' view must treat them as 'fixed', or that a 'non-unitary view' automatically 'unfixes' them.) They are also opposed to a view of the self as 'rational' (p. 254). (Again, this is unhappy. Even were I sure what a 'unitary' self must be like, I can't automatically associate it with being 'rational'.) Third, they believe there is a (perhaps inevitable) tendency to turn this 'self' into a biological entity (pp. 88-9) – and that makes change difficult to conceive. (It isn't obvious what theories might see human minds as simultaneously rational and biological. These have tended to be very opposed to each other.) The 'non-unitary self' stands opposed to all these.

This 'self' is formed by discourses. Recall that 'discourse' means here what Foucault meant by it: a specific expression of knowledge as power, as in the way children are 'defined' by intelligence and aptitude tests. These discourses don't only measure us externally, as a ruler will measure. They create what are called 'subject-positions'. A problem arises from this, as they acknowledge:

> First, in this view the subject is composed of, or exists as, a set of multiple and contradictory positionings or subjectivities. But how are such fragments held together? Are we to assume, as some applications of post-structuralism have implied, that the individual subject is simply the sum-total of all positions in discourse since birth? If this is the case, what accounts for the continuity of the subject, and the subjective experience of identity? What accounts for the predictability of people's actions, as they repeatedly position themselves within particular discourses? Can people's wishes and desires be encompassed in an account

of discursive relations? (p. 204)

This is a real problem for them. But see how this unity now has to be phrased. It becomes entirely a non-cognitive and non-rational matter. There is no space for such ideas as 'forming a coherent picture of the world', or 'holding a consistent set of beliefs'. Instead, it is 'experience of identity', 'predictability' and 'wishes and desires'. In the Lacanian model, these are par excellence non-rational; experience of 'identity' is an illusion necessary for society's functioning, 'predictability' is an external judge's assessment of our behaviour, and 'wishes and desires' are the repressed expressions of infant loss of the Mother. In other words, from opposing a bogus 'humanist' who believed in the 'rational unity of the self', our authors have ended up with no theoretical space for rational understanding at all.

This isn't to say that they won't smuggle back in some capacity for critical enquiry. But the theory can't justify it. As a result their desire to keep the possibility of change turns to ashes in their hands. One of their own number, Urwin, accepts that their view 'may appear pessimistic' (p. 321) since it sees people as inevitably seeking safety in the familiar, as naturally resisting change. Their picture of humans is so bedevilled by a false spectre of the 'rational humanist' that all capacity for critical understanding becomes impossible. The unity of self, when readmitted, is only unity of emotions, feelings, desires – never of understandings. The need to feel like a single subject is really just an escape from anxiety:

> For instance, a woman academic is in contradictory relations of power and power-lessness by virtue of her positioning as both woman and academic. From this it is possible to argue that such simultaneous positionings of power and powerlessness produce anxiety states resulting from distress at such contradiction, and the consequent desire for wholeness, unitariness – a coherent identity. Such anxiety states can clearly be manifest in a variety of ways, from the denial of contradiction to a variety of mechanisms for apparently achieving conscious 'closure' or coherence. But while we may be positioned in a non-unitary way, the normative practices which fix us produce for us a model of a whole mature 'individual' with an 'identity'. Much is therefore invested in our recognising ourselves as unitary, whole, non-contradictory, mature, rational. (p. 225)

But of course we know that is just illusion. . .

This is terribly unsatisfactory. In the end there is far more opposition of individual to society (now called 'discourses') in their own theory, than ever before. The woman's identity comes from her being positioned as an individual. Her search for an identity is the result of anxieties provoked by individual insertion into contradictory discourses. Suppose she manages to combine with others who are suffering the same? That, of course, has nothing to do with the way the discourses constructed her. No wonder resistance is so difficult. The problem arises because in their general model one important term has become marginalised: activity.

3. *They use a threefold model of how infants become human: power-desire-knowledge.* Missing is a fourth term, 'activity' (or as I would want to call it, 'work' or 'productive activity'). In their account, an infant at birth has only needs, and only looks at the world around it to find sources of satisfaction. It only forms desires when it becomes aware of loss. When the Mother does not automatically satisfy its needs (and she cannot), then enter together gender, desires, and language. Only as a result of these comes activity, work on the world. Work, on this model, is a result of frustrated desires for consumption. Remember that this is not a conclusion reached by empirical research. It is a demand of the theory.

4. *This positions the theory in the sphere of the private, in that the infant is seen first and foremost as frustrated consumer.* This primacy of infant as consumer relegates work/class to a secondary expression of repressions. This will explain its curious role in Walkerdine's discussion of *Bunty* and *Tracy*, as we shall see. It also justifies the virtually exclusive interest in gender-relations. For the approach is premised on this. Lacan's model makes gender the first distinction of meaning, and the one from which all language and all conceptualisation of the world flows.

5. *Post-structuralism shares an assumption with psychoanalysis generally, that our present day desires are stored up versions of our childhood distinctions.* Since these initial distinctions are based on gender, therefore all subsequent desires must also be. This is both an outcome of the theory (here is a model which we find satisfying) and a heuristic demand (go forth and show how subsequent desires are based on that primal gender-distinction). But even if they were right about this first distinction, why should the rest follow? Think, for example, of the way plants grow. The first leaves which plants put out are the cotyleda. These are the ones which break the surface of the soil. They are crude leaves and bear little relation to the complex forms that subsequent leaves take. They do not do the same job, and they do not have the same structure. Why couldn't the same be true of the relationship between first distinctions/desires, and subsequent ones?

The only reason for denying this would be because of a suppressed argument, that the motive-force which produced the original desires (leaves) continues, identically, to produce subsequent desires (leaves). And this assumption is secretly there in psychoanalysis. The original distinction of self and other is motivated by loss of control over the mother. From this follow language, fantasy and desires. What kind of a loss is this, then, that can have so lasting an influence? It is a loss of immediate identity with the mother, a forced separation from her. This is not separation in the sense that the mother deserts her child. It is only that the child is forced to recognise her as an independent being, having her own desires, and other relationships. This model then proceeds to the assertion that this 'loss' and differentiation of self and other remains forever inside us, shaping the form of all our future desires. The logic of this is: that all our desires forever stem from and express a buried wish to return to primordial harmony, lack of differentiation.[8]

6. This is a weird view, with strong elements of utopian nostalgia. Consider some of its implications. Of necessity, power takes on a most peculiar meaning. There were no power-relations in the original unity of mother and child. Power enters along with fantasy and desire. For desires are produced in every encounter between social discourses and our subjectivity. We are 'positioned' – and that is an act of power; and we respond by seeking to fulfil our repressed sense of loss by controlling the world beyond us – and that is also an act of power. In short, there is no longer any space for a distinction between power and an opposite to it. Or rather, the only possible escape from power is a return to undifferentiated unity with mum. Otherwise, everything is power since every encounter between an individual and his/her world is one in which the individual is positioned within discourses. In this model, no space remains for any critique of power-relations – which contradicts the original supposedly radical intentions of the retheorisation. There are merely alternative forms of power, some of which we like or don't like.

7. *Paradoxically, when used as a base for empirical research, this theory enforces a new and troublesome 'unity of the subject'.* All this also has implications for empirical work. At different levels, the assumptions underlying this model guide how evidence is gathered and interpreted. Look, for example, at the way Urwin considers evidence on mother-baby interactions. She is looking, in a fascinating and provocative way, at the processes of children's language development.[9]

Urwin argues, surely rightly, that traditional child psychology has been wrong to see language development as an isolable process, just governed by its own internal logic. Instead she interprets the development of language as an expression of the self/other distinction which follows 'loss of Mother' and the beginnings of of gender-identity. (Note again the curious assumption in this that there is something painful in discovering you are a separate being. Why? Only if you assume that undifferentiated absorption is the lost ideal.) This leads her to see young children's activity as an expression of a 'fight for control over Mother' (see p. 274). I confess to knowing little of this field, but one thing strikes me about Urwin's account. Her theory requires her to treat all children's activity at this time as expressive of this search for control. Paradoxically, she reimposes 'unity' on the child. I am sure that from very early on, part of a child's life involves conflicts with parents. But that does not mean that every other act of the child – absorbed consideration of its own toes, fascination with lights and movements, grasping at objects, even its actual conflicts with parents – have to be seen as resulting from that loss of mum. If anyone here is guilty of a 'unified view of the self', it is Urwin.[10]

There is much more that could be said about the problems with this approach, but it is time to turn back to Walkerdine's use of it on the comics.

224

Fig 16 The final episode of *Cherry and her Chimps*, from *Tracy*, 14 August 1982, illustrating the 'problem of endings'. © D C Thomson & Co. Ltd, 1982.

6   TY. 14.8.82   CH2

226

7

Mavis had been right. The girl in the photo was Mrs Price, as a young girl—the Prices were Cherry's parents! They had survived a plane crash several years previously in Africa and their daughter, just able to walk, had never been found and was presumed dead. The Tanners received long prison sentences for their ill-treatment of Cherry.

The problem of endings

We saw the ways in which Walkerdine thinks girls' 'psychic conflicts' may be channelled by the comics. They will not simply become good and feminine through reading them. But they can learn to distinguish their 'true' from their 'bad' feelings. There is a real subtlety in this argument. The pity is, it just won't work. Begin with one part of her argument. It is vital to her reading of the stories that girls are not only victims trapped with 'wrong' families, but that they will be rescued because of their selflessness and reinserted into 'good' family life. This sets off her 'semiotic chain' which ends with passivity and the wait for the male saviour.

What kinds of endings would we expect, on Walkerdine's approach? She writes that the resolution is equally as important as the suffering: 'Through the narrative device of the inadequate or 'bad' family structure which is also the result of circumstance, not choice, the girls are shown themselves as being able to bring about by their own actions the conditions for the restoration of the *desired* family structure' (p. 173). Therefore restoration of the 'proper family' must be the motivated result of the girls' selflessness. Return to the family is the 'reward' for the selflessness. Take one of her sample stories, *Cherry and the Chimps*. Cherry, a sort of jungle girl, has been found and brought to England by Cyril and Mavis who pretend to be her parents. She is forced to work looking after the chimpanzees in their travelling circus. In the episode Walkerdine sampled, one of the chimps has escaped and Cherry searches for it. She is befriended by an old lady; but Cyril quickly intervenes to hide her backstage again. At the end of the episode, however, Cyril and Mavis are looking decidedly worried because two kind-looking people are taking an interest in Cherry.

How would we expect the story to end, on Walkerdine's account? I invite my readers to pause and work out their own version – for clearly many are possible – bearing in mind that Cherry's selflessness must be the key to her own salvation. In actual fact, the story ended the following week, in the four pages reproduced below (Fig. 16).

Why am I so sure that this ending does not meet the requirements of Walkerdine's arguments? It is not obviously incompatible with her analysis. But the connection between the main thrust of the story and the ending is so thin that her interpretation is at best a weak one. And an alternative reading has much more to support it. First, it is not Cherry's selfless actions that bring about the result. If she does contribute to her own salvation, it is more a result of her ignorance. She is getting on with her oppressed life and, without realising it, she puts herself in the way of being noticed by her real parents. Second, the end has a strong reek of 'deus ex machina'. The crucial transition is not really made in the story at all. It does not occur in any picture-frames but in that guiding caption. I can't help feeling that the story at this point had simply run out of steam. The emotional force of the story is invested in Cherry's victimisation and her powerlessness. When that ran out, it was just stopped, abruptly. *Cherry and the Chimps* is not alone in this. Take the remainder of the stories in her sample issue of *Tracy*, in turn.

Joni the Jinx – Joni's very presence seems to set off rows, usually involving her parents. For example, (in Walkerdine's 7 August issue) both parents arrange tennis partners for her, without telling each other. They then row over the resultant confusion. Both 'partners' walk off and get into a fight – for which Joni gets blamed. As a result, her parents resign from the tennis club. Joni increasingly blamed herself for all the problems that arise. The story eventually ended on 25 September. Joni, in despair, has decided to run away before she destroys her family. But as she is leaving, she meets an elderly man. It turns out to be her grandfather whom she hasn't seen for years. He persuades her that all families have rows, and that she is not to blame – and she returns home.

Polly's Painted Smile – Jane Kent collects glove puppets. From an old aunt she's inherited one very ugly one which she loves and calls 'Polly'. But whenever she puts it on, it makes her behave badly, but forget it all when she takes the glove off. In Walkerdine's episode, a child is visiting with its parents. With the puppet on, she gets it blamed for breaking the best crockery. The visitors are 'asked to leave'. Again and again, Polly gets Jane to do 'wicked' things so even her parents come to doubt her. But it is a long time before Jane can work out what is happening. As the story worked towards its end on 25 September, Jane enters a battle of wills with the doll. She tries to throw it away, but fails. Finally she finds an old diary in their attic. It is the doll's maker's. Jane learns that he had grown bitter, and had left his 'evil will' in Polly. Jane carefully repaints the doll to put a new happy face on it – and the bad magic dissolves away.

Sandra and the Space Invaders – the sample episode was the last, about a girl who has a discovered that ten special 'Space Invader' games are really the means by which aliens are taking control of the world. She has had to find and destroy each of them – getting into a lot of trouble in the process. At the end, the last one very nearly takes control of her; but she just manages to smash it. The moment she does, her parents – who have been very suspicious of her – forget everything, and all becomes well again.

Nothing but the Truth – Georgina Washington has been 'punished' for her 'story-telling' by a witch putting a spell on her: whenever a crescent moon shines on her forehead she'll tell the truth, however inconvenient. The sample episode closed the story. Her family has entered a TV 'Happiest Family' contest, but Georgina (with her 'moon' shining) makes some embarassing revelations. Her family are furious until to their surprise they win, because of her 'frankness'. The story ends with the witch reappearing. She removes the curse, but warns her about exaggerating again. Says G: 'In future, just as I promised the old lady,

I'll use the truth wisely and well!'

'*She'll Stay a Slave*' – Jenny Morris, living with Aunt May and Uncle John, lets herself be treated like a slave by her cousin Paula, and Jenny puts up with it because she thinks that Paula had once saved her life. In this episode, Jenny has a chance of winning a scholarship to an athletics college. But Paula, who wants to keep her doing all the work, thwarts her. After (unsuccessfully) using local yobs to try to make her fail her high jump, Paula tricks her into a cellar and locks her there so she'll miss the relay race. Jenny gets out, but is covered in filth, late, and in trouble ... The story ended abruptly three weeks later, with Jenny accidentally discovering what Paula was doing, getting a confession from her, and a single frame ending it all happily.

Meg and the Magic Robot – Meg Watson is being forced by Uncle Syd and Aunt Maud to play at being a robot in their fairground act, deceiving the public, because she thinks they are paying for her brother Tommy's hospital treatment. They even cheat her of her food. In Walkerdine's episode, she has spotted an escaped criminal posing as a character in the show. She manages to alert the police; but Uncle Syd just clouts her for endangering their act. The story ended on 21 August. Their own meanness rebounded. Starved of food, Meg gets ill; and when they throw water over their 'robot', she sneezes. In the confusion that follows, she escapes and finds a photo of Tommy in their caravan. Running away, she finds him being looked after by an elderly couple, and there is a happy ending.

The Snobby Stantons – Samantha's story about her Mum, the teacher. In this episode, Mum has decided to educate the kids away from pop with a classical music concert. Of course the kids all sneer and say they're not going. So Sam tricks them into thinking a local pop idol is going to be there, and thus saves Mum (who knows nothing of all this) from the embarrassment of having no one at her concert. The final episode (4 September) ends with Mum learning not to be quite so snobby. But she is sacked from the school for 'not understanding the needs of her kids' – whereupon the kids go on strike for her reinstatement and her chief tormentor speaks up on her behalf. Reinstated (of course), she and Sam now begin to be accepted.

Sheila the Sham – Following a road accident, Sheila is being forced to go on pretending to be deaf, in order to get compensation that her Aunt will of course take. In this episode, while out shopping they meet Mr Green whom they're suing – whereupon Auntie marches Sheila out. She makes her walk right across town to another shop and carry it all home. Ending on 14 August, there was a sudden 'revelation', two days before the court-case; and Sheila and her siblings are adopted by the Green family.

Nine stories, then, all pretty typical of this kind of comic. But notice that they have two different kinds of endings. On the one hand there are *Cherry and the Chimps* (saved by the accident of investigation), *Nothing but the Truth* (saved by a witch who decides her lesson has been learnt), *The Snobby Stantons* (saved by the kids deciding that Mum has reformed enough), and *Sheila the Sham* (saved by someone becoming suspicious): in each of these, the 'solution' is a 'deus ex machina' one. An outsider intervenes and solves things. In the remaining cases (bar one), the distinguishing feature is that the heroine herself is *unaware of what is going on*. Here the main narrative and the ending are much more connected. The link is made by the struggle of the heroine to understand what is happening. For example, in *Polly and her Painted Smile*, Jane has to struggle to overcome Polly's influence. But first she has become aware of it. In *Joni the Jinx*, Joni doesn't understand how families work and so runs away – only then to meet her 'deus ex machina' who gives her the consciousness she needs to know what to expect. Meg (of the *Magic Robot*) has been misled about her brother Tommy. It is only when she discovers the truth about him that she can act to find him and save herself. Jenny ('She'll Stay A Slave') doesn't know that Paula is trying to spoil her chances. But once she has found out, she herself can act to bring Paula to book. There is a pattern: the endings are only tightly motivated by the preceding story when the solution involves changing the heroine's understanding. And only in those will her own actions provide the solution.

The apparent exception is *Sandra and the Space Invaders*. I am always fascinated by apparent exceptions for the light they can throw light on organising principles. *Sandra* is tricky because she does know what is going on, and yet she is the one who takes action. Yet here again, the issue turns out to be one of knowledge. Sandra's problem is that no one will believe her about the aliens. She therefore has no option but to act on her own – even though it leads to misunderstandings of her. But the end of the story magically removes those misunderstandings again – the moment the last of the 'Space Invader' games is smashed, her parents forget all the things that they thought she had 'done wrong'.

Living with Anguish

In as much as there may be ideology in these stories, I want to argue that it is in the stressing of self-knowledge. To have self-knowledge is to know what you are capable of. It is to be honest about yourself (as in *Nothing But the Truth*); it is to be aware of other people's intentions towards you (as in *Cherry and the Chimps* and *She'll Stay a Slave*); it is to understand the normal problems of life (as in *Joni the Jinx*); and so on. But we must be careful. For we must remember the extent to which these are 'ex machina' solutions. Sandra Whilding, in her discussion of Bunty stories, developed the idea of an 'energy' in the stories.[11] This, she argued, comes from unresolved tensions which provide our motivation for keeping reading. But the endings we have looked at show those tensions and that 'energy' running out.

Walkerdine's account not only supposes that the ending is motivated by the preceding dilemmas; it also supposes that the ending will seem the natural outcome. A young girl, seeing herself in fantasy within the drama, will feel encouraged to reshape her desires. Without that, there is no influence. Her argument depends on the stories 'fitting' girls' psychic dilemmas at this age. The girls must read these stories because of the state of their psyches. They are in process of making themselves into 'girls', using what cultural materials are available. This is something inevitable. All girls do it. It is only the cultural resources that change. The post-structuralist approach here turns out to be strikingly anti-historical, despite appearances. Yes, it has space for a kind of history of cultural products which then work on us in historically specific ways. But we that are worked on are not historically distinguished at all. At all times and in all societies, the psychic processes will be identical. We are driven by the same forces in all periods. Just, different cultures squeeze those drives into different shapes.

But there is a bigger problem. Post-structuralism scans cultural products for elements that may connect with 'phases of psychic development'. So, in looking at *Bunty* and *Tracy*, Walkerdine searches for what might work on young girls constructing their gender identities. But these comics only really took the form which she describes after 1971. What must have been going on before then? She claims to find a close connection between these stories and a distinctive phase in the 'construction of gender identities'. Up to 1970, then, something must simply have been missing. For these comics are major providers of the fantasy-resources that young girls need for their 'correct' images of the family. Her argument must lead to the conclusion that in some senses these comics were *necessary*.

There is an implicit model of how these comics came to be produced. From the little that is known about this (under-researched) area, the late 1960s saw a steady decline in sales of these girls' comics, as with the boys'. In response, both D C Thomson and IPC started searching for a new formula. It meant creating new comics altogether (the IPC stable of *Tammy*, *Sandy* and so on); it meant revamping those still reminiscent of Angela Brazil. A great many of the previous stories had been set in public schools, with the jolly japes of adventurous girls (*The Three Marys* in *Bunty* long survived to represent this trend). It was writers like Pat Mills who helped effect the transformation. How do we account for it? Walkerdine has put herself in the position of saying one of two things: either the publishers were involved in a conspiracy to refashion young girls' psyches (however they got the knowledge of what would do that – I mean, Lacan was only just publishing his ideas . . .); or, quite accidentally, they hit on a story-formula which the girls wanted. But the implication of that is that the young girl readers welcomed their own massive psychic subjection. And that conclusion would surely be very much against Walkerdine's own intentions.

This, despite her noting herself that the bulk of the readership is pre-adolescent working class girls. In fact, in Walkerdine's account, 'class' becomes just another layer of vulnerability. It contributes nothing, seemingly, to how and why the girls read. It only adds to the difficulty of their lives. They are girls. That they are working class means they have just fewer resources for coping with being girls: this is the logic of Walkerdine's position. Recall why. In Lacanian psychoanalysis, work (and therefore class) is a repressed form of sexuality. It is secondary, where gender is primary. Class, therefore, can 'worsen' gender. But it can't fundamentally alter it.

Without a great deal more research, I can't deal adequately with this. I can offer only the bones of an alternative, in particular by referring to one extraordinary event from these comics' history. It involves reversing Walkerdine's picture of class and gender. To proffer my conclusion first: these stories are unresolved dramas of the class-experience of working class girls. As many researchers have documented, these girls experience multiple constraints. They are expected to take responsibility for housework and other family duties. They are not allowed boys' freedom, either in general activities or in sexual experimentation. They often lack the resources even for those things marked as properly 'female': clothes, make-up and so on. Along with these restrictions goes also an ideological instruction manual telling them that this is their proper lot. I do not know of much evidence that working class girls and young women accept these ideas, forming desires and ambitions around them. They are more the source of frustrations and angers. But very often those frustrations do not have an obvious outlet. These stories, I suggest, dramatise those frustrations, precisely in showing the deeply hopeless lives of young girls. They are endlessly put upon. However hard they take the expected responsibilities, they have no escape. This interpretation focuses on two things about the stories.

First, it is important that, typically, the reader knows more than the heroine. As Tania Modleski has pointed out in relation to Harlequin romances,[12] where a reader knows more than a character, she may relate emotionally to the dilemmas but she is held apart from the character, because the reader understands things the heroine cannot. Indeed, the emotional relationship can be stronger just because the reader can understand the problems more clearly than the heroine. We have seen this gap in our stories. Many of them depend on the heroine's not knowing, or misunderstanding, her position. She cannot escape because she does not understand. But we do. We also saw that the solutions only connected with the stories' 'energy' where they involved changes in understanding. The stories which apparently fitted Walkerdine's case were those where the solution was externally brought about (paralleling her 'Prince'); but in those cases, as we saw, the ending was 'unmotivated' by the story. In other words, the issue in these stories is not desire, as Walkerdine argues, but knowledge and its relation to action. And the readers are not implicated in the stories; they are watchers of the stories, seeing dramatised in front of them their own typified experience.

Thus, the second element. On my account, this kind of story in *Bunty* and *Tracy* depicts the real social barriers for pre-adolescent working class girls. The heroines of the stories are in the worst kinds of situation which their readers typically feel they experience: trapped, helpless, misunderstood, put upon, exploited – even by those who should be loving towards them. But then, why should there be a obvious solution at all, Prince or otherwise? On this scenario, we might predict that the girl-readers would expect no resolution, would prefer an ending which gave no magic rescues. If they are dramas of impossible oppression, their ending might logically be melodramatic death! And one curious event in the recent history of these comics bears this out.

In 1981, *Judy*, a companion comic to Walkerdine's, carried a most unusual story. Drawn by Paddy Brennan, it told the story of Heather Morgan, for whom as the title said *Nothing Ever Goes Right!*. The following introductory frame of one episode gives the flavour perfectly: 'A series of tragic misfortunes had left Heather Morgan with face scarred, her mother dead, and her father without money and a home. Heather was sent to a boarding school for problem girls while her father was recovering in hospital from an accident. Heather escaped from the school – only to discover that her father had died earlier that day' (*Judy*, May 1981). The story ran from April to June that year. It began with Heather having a riding accident, from which came the scarring. She is carrying a heart condition. Then her mother was killed in a road accident. Her father lost his job, and most of his money. They had to leave their home, and search for somewhere to live. Finding a tatty boat, the next accident occurs. Dad falls in, nearly drowns and catches pneumonia. He goes into hospital, Heather into care. But the foster-parents are only in it for the money. So after taking what they can, they have her sent to a tough boarding school for 'difficult girls' – who lock Heather in, stopping her from visiting her father. She runs away to see him, only to find he has died. Now the police are after her. After a couple more tries at finding some friends have turned to dust, Heather is lost, on the streets. The story ended, as you will see, with her helping to rescue two children who are trapped in a demolished house. But her heart gave out in the process, and she died. At the end, we see various people either mourning her death, or wondering what happened to her (Fig. 17).

As the story progresses, then, Heather's problems get steadily worse and worse. Every attempt to do something rebounds. Every attempt to find friends fails, until she is completely alone. At the end, there is nothing left but for her to die. The point is that according to one artist who himself worked on the comic, this story 'remained an all-time favourite among the readers'.[13] Now according to Walkerdine, the point of the stories is to be resolved in the return

Fig 17 The final episode of *Nothing Ever Goes Right!*, from Judy, 13 June 1981. the 'most popular story of all', yet hardly a standard ending... ©D C Thomson & Co. Ltd, 1981.

At the hospital—

The strain has badly affected the girl's weak heart. Her condition is extremely serious. I doubt if she will recover consciousness. Have her relatives been informed?

There was nothing by which we could identify her. We know nothing about her.

An hour later—

She's dead! She helped to rescue those two children and the effort was too much for her. Now we'll never know who she was or where she came from.

A few days later, Heather was buried in a simple grave.

No one was there to mourn Heather's death—but there were many whose lives had been helped by her. Young actress Caroline Newton, for example.

Tonight is my big chance. I'd never have made it without Heather Morgan, the girl who helped me with my first part at school. I wonder what happened to her?

Librarian Barry Reynolds.

An excellent display, my boy! You have some first-class ideas!

Thank you, sir.

It was that girl with the scarred face who helped me at school. She had all the good ideas. What was her name? Heather Morgan! Yes, that's it! If only I'd been nicer to her when I had the chance!

Ballet student Paula Adams.

This cup, for the most outstanding student of the year, is being presented to Paula Adams.

I never dreamt this would ever happen to me! I do wish Heather Morgan could be here now. I know she'd be pleased for me. I wonder what became of her?

Katy Phinn and her brother Sam.

We'd still be living on that filthy barge with our horrible aunt and uncle who bullied and beat us if that girl hadn't seen us stealing in the supermarket and reported us. Do you remember her?

Yes, her name was Heather. I think she did it deliberately to help us. I liked her. She'd like our super foster parents.

And crippled Pauline Richards.

Bravo, Pauline! You've walked the whole way on your own!

I've done it at last, Dad!

If only Heather was here to see me! She helped me so much when I didn't want to try to walk. Whatever became of her and her father, I wonder?

No one would ever know, for Heather's grave was unnamed—but her memorial was the gratitude in the hearts of those who had reason to remember her.

My two children would have died, but for this nameless girl. I'll never forget her, whoever she was.

THE END

N.E.G.R.JDY. 13.6.81

STARTS NEXT WEEK—" THE STRANGE POWERS OF PENNY."

of girls to a proper family. Yet here is an 'all-time favourite' story whose ending is exactly the opposite. Trapped and overwhelmed by her problems, Heather has no future. In the drama offered to her readers, she cannot be rescued. A 'prince' would only misunderstand her and make things worse. She has to die. And the readers loved it.

My interest in this is not only that it offers support to my interpretation. It also throws light on another problem in Walkerdine's approach. She assumes that the stories which appear will relate directly to some psychic structure in the readers. The mistake is in missing out what others have called the 'production history' of the comics.[14] Although this needs researching in detail, it is evident to me that girls' comics are produced within constrained traditions. Publishers were responding to a decline in sales in the late 1960s. But they could not simply recast their comics wholesale and produce a new form of story perfectly matching some psychic need in their audience. It is not just that they would not know how to. There would also be risks of alienating parents. They might produce the kind of hostile public reaction which the publishers were always very careful to avoid. Also, their own staff editors, writers, and artists would have been trained on the previous girls' comics, and their patterns and forms. The combination of these would make for caution, even when a story produced a particular response from their readers. These events therefore do not surprise me. *Nothing Ever Goes Right!* was produced because they just wanted to find out how far the readers wanted them to go. But though it proved so very popular, D C Thomson chose not to make its grim pessimism the basis for subsequent stories. I can only be glad that the one story and readers' response to it occurred to throw light on girls' relations to the comic.

The concept of a 'production history' summarises the way all these factors combine to produce a particular cultural product. There are traditions of production, of marketing, and of audience. Producers are trained to see certain kinds of stories as 'natural'; audiences learn that too. Then there is the constraining hand of a possible 'public reaction', particularly to a 'children's comic' (and both words mark out terrains of danger). These and other factors mean that comics like *Bunty* and *Tracy* are in the end compromises. To study them, without some knowledge of such a production history, is to court disaster.

It also complicates greatly the meaning of being a 'reader'. My next chapter turns to this question, in the light of the various kinds of reader-research.

'Reading' the readers

What do we need to know about comic-readers? If arguments about 'ideology' are to be settled, at some point we have to attend to those who live under its star. There has not been a great deal of research on comic-readers; what there is, is markedly uneven in quality. For a long time, the only things available were some reports telling how many comics were read. These were useful as a bare minimum. From George Pumphrey, for example, we learn that in the 1950s virtually every child in the country was reading at least one comic per week. His figure of 98% readership is striking, and no doubt served to make people worry about comics. But the associated information that children shared and swapped their comics was not really thought about. That each comic might well be read by up to eight others was simply further proof how widespread comic reading was. It did not raise questions about how children might use comics in their wider social relationships.[1]

This kind of research was part of a wider concern, in both Britain and the United States, about the impact of comic-reading on literacy. Were reading skills were being undermined by comics? Was children's time being so taken up with comics that they were turning away from books? Could comic-reading even harm the necessary habits of left-right eye movement? This tradition of research was packed with unargued evaluations. It was assumed that comic-reading was an inferior activity, involving no significant skills. Ideas of visual literacy had yet to make their appearance. Reading was an unquestioned good. The following is a good example of this kind of thinking. Ruth Strang asked children of varying ages why they read comics.[2] She found, hardly surprisingly, that children said they read them for 'adventure', 'excitement', because they were 'funny', but also because they do not 'overtax the mind' and did not 'require much concentration'. You can almost hear the relief in her voice when, in response to one pupil saying that '*Prince Valiant* enhances history even to the most casual student', she says that 'This serious attitude toward the comics is not common. The majority of children read and forget them'. As long as it isn't serious, that's alright . . . But note the assumption that they are only serious if remembered. That puts comics on a par with school text books. We are meant to record their contents. There are in fact many other ways we could seriously relate to a comic. But for Strang, the parallel with school was paramount, and it led her to a significant judgement:

> In conclusion, it might be said, with respect to the reading of the comics, that adults should advocate moderation rather than total abstinence. They should recognise that the values of comics differ for individual children. Undoubtedly the comics meet needs of certain children at certain stages of their development. Thus they serve a useful transitory purpose, often stimulating an initial interest in reading and leading to the reading of books which, although of increasingly better quality, have the comics' appeal of adventure, surprise, plot, life-like characters, humour and action. Realising the power of the comics, the dissenting educator might wisely turn his objections into a positive program for their improvement and utilise them as one avenue of education. He should work with, rather than futilely against, the comic-strip artists and thus mold this naturally attractive medium to educative purposes. (p. 342)

Of course there is nothing wrong with using the comic form in education, and indeed it has over the years been used to great effect (though not without angst on the part of some teachers – I recall the horrified grimaces at the comicbook version of *Macbeth*). It is the assumptions in this which are worthy of comment. Comics fit a 'stage' that children go through. Rather like crushes on teachers, or becoming spotty, as long as they are treated sensibly, the children will out-grow them. But they can hardly have a positive role. They are at best an escape from the serious and life-enhancing pressures of school. So, 'we'll let them' have the comics – for now, in moderation.

There is no scope here for what I argued in Chapter 4, that some comics might be coded forms of resistance to adults, including teachers. That is not surprising – it must be hard for teachers to think of themselves as part of the 'problem' for children. For researchers like this, education means absorbing correct facts and acquiring prescribed skills. Because comics do not fit this mould, they are not educative. The options are to wean the kids off them as quickly as possible (since banning is drastic), or to seize this 'naturally attractive medium' for proper purposes. We should, I suppose, be glad that Strang went for the line of moderation.

This style of research had a long run. Beginning in the 1940s, it petered out in the 1970s.[3] Yet from the earliest days, research showed that 'the reading of comic books seemed to have no effect educationally on the children', and was not correlated with lower levels of intelligence.[4] That did not stop even the same researchers wanting to go back and check if, perhaps, finer research would reveal 'maladjustment' in regular comic readers, or perhaps that comics impede normal personality development. Trapped in their own worries, and arguably contributing to the very problems they claimed to be finding causes for (children's difficulties at school, resistance to teachers, and the like), these researchers kept on publishing their data in educational magazines. This style of research comes close to 'effects' studies. There has been some good critical attention to this kind of research on other media.[5] How far are the problems in this research – exemplified in my study of *Action* – revealed in the one sub-stantial piece of 'effects' research that has been carried out on comics?

The hiding of McCarthyism

Lotte Bailyn's study of boys and girls in Arlington, Massachusetts in the 1950s is a sophisticated one which could put to shame much more recent work on audiences.[6] In fact it almost escapes the limitations of 'effects' theory. But only 'almost'. At vital points, her assumptions prevent her from seeing where she is going. I will risk summarising this very dense piece of research. She and her co-workers first administered a questionnaire on reading and watching habits to 626 children in 1955, divided between boys and girls. From these, she then selected a sample each of 100, evenly split into four groups to represent the possible combinations of high or low exposure to the mass media, and high or low levels of reported life-problems. Then, by a mixture of asking them questions, and getting them to read and respond to one comic, she examined various combinations of factors.

For example, she looked at how exposure related to choices of possible careers, and found that high exposure boys were much more likely to choose what she termed 'fantasy careers'. She measured whether the children tended to blame themselves or others for their problems ('extra-punitiveness vs intra-punitiveness'); and found that boys blaming others also tended to see characters in black and white ('stereotyping').[7] She also found that high exposure boys tended to be more 'passive' than others in projecting their father's job as their own. In her own summary of significant conclusions, she notes that 'Four factors seem related to the amount of exposure to the pictorial media . . . Children whose parents attempt to restrict their exposure time actually see less of the pictorial media; children with high IQs spend less time on this kind of entertainment, as do children whose fathers have white-collar occupations and who are Protestant. Hence, the factors associated with high exposure to the pictorial media are lack of parental restriction, low IQ, fathers with worker or service occupations, and being a Catholic' (p. 32). None of this is terribly sur-prising, except perhaps the correlation with religion. Her results are more interesting when she comes to explore content-preferences among the comics. It is here she starts claiming that her results reveal 'effects'.

She categorises the comics by one element she claims they have in common, that they are of the 'aggressive-hero type' (AH for short). The following factors then seen to link with liking these: first, it is mainly boys who prefer these. Restrictive parents help to limit their choice, but not if they use physical punish-ment – that raises AH preference. Rebelliously independent boys will prefer them, as will boys with lower IQ. High general exposure to pictorial media also associates with preference for AH comics; so does having a lot of problems, and blaming others for those problems. But none of these say anything about effects. All these could simply be the result of boys with these characteristics preferring this kind of comic, as Bailyn herself recognises. To test for 'effects', she studied reactions to the comics. She began with how long children took to read a sample comic. High exposure readers took less time to complete the story. (Bailyn claims her interviewers were also able to distinguish time spent on reading from looking at the pictures. I am intensely sceptical of this.) They were then assessed for level of involvement, by amounts of fidgeting, signs of boredom etc; not surprisingly, high-exposure readers showed greater involvement.

The key step was to find out what they remembered of the stories, and how they assessed characters and situations. Her results are interesting. She found that high exposure readers tended to recall the stories in typified ways. In other words, they read the comic as an example of its kind; whereas low exposure readers recalled specific events in the story. But also, the less involved low exposure readers actually remembered more details of the story than high exposure readers. Bailyn only notes this result. She does not interpret it. But it raises the important possibility that some boys who would normally choose such comics did not take to this one; and so could not recall so much of it. But that did not happen with those who would not normally read these comics in large numbers. There is more than a suggestion here that exposure is not just a matter of amount. It also affects the way they read them, and their way of relating to them.

Bailyn came close to recognising this in that interesting distinction between typified versus unique recall (does a child say Strongman was knocked out, or that he was hit over the head with a pipe?). As she says, we might expect a child familiar with the typical plot moves of a genre to recall it in typified form. But then she jumps to supposing that this is an effect of reading aggressive-hero comics in general. It is this which justifies her conclusion:

> This study indicates that a [boy] with certain psychological characteristics who is highly exposed, picks up certain elements of the mass media, forms these into a picture in his mind, and draws on this picture when asked to express attitudes and desires on related matters. One might speculate, therefore, that in a situation requiring some overt act, which is similar in certain crucial respects to some media-determined picture in his mind, he will also draw on this picture to guide his actions . . . (T)he danger area with regard to overt behaviour lies in the group of boys with a certain combination of social and psychological factors, a group seen, at least in the community of the present study, to be small. It is in this group that the media serve the function of escape and that the cognitive syndrome investigated makes its appearance. At any rate one may safely conclude that any connection between the mass media and overt behaviour will be indirect, mediated by all the factors discussed. (pp. 36-7)

This is cautious and judicious. Why worry about it? Partly because it is yet another claim that a small minority are 'vulnerable' to the generally harmless influences of aggressive materials. More because of the way she has established the connections.

What is this 'cognitive syndrome' of which she speaks? This is how Bailyn puts it: 'High exposure boys, especially when they have many problems and extra-punitive tendencies, see such a comic book more as a type than as a unique story. They are attuned to the typical elements in it; because of the character of the genre, these typical elements stress aggression, threat, a technical view of crime with a lack of concern for the criminal's motivations, and negative attitude toward law enforcement officers. These boys, with high exposure, especially when they have many problems, view the content of such stories as more realistic than do the others. In their way of looking at the people in these stories, their emphasis is on physical characteristics, stereotyped evaluations, and explanations centering on social factors' (p. 32). Notice the implicit explanation. Boys with stressful lives escape into comics, and thus lose the ability to judge them unrealistic. The more they read them, the more they lose their ability to judge reality from fantasy. The shift to giving 'technical' judgements, and the tendency to stereotype is the result of processes triggered off inside the child. The comics are merely a source from which the boy gleans what his psychological profile requires. Why comics, then? Once again we are back to the view that it is because they are 'pictorial'. Pictures, to put her view crudely, are anti-thinking machines. All comics do this, and their particular content is irrelevant for this purpose.

The trouble is that Bailyn's readers knew the comics better than she did. We must look at the comic she asks them to read. The story is 'Strongman and the Red Hand of Moscow'.[8] A 'band of thuggish Reds' are trying to smuggle a defector out of America; only Strongman can stop them. From start to finish, the story assumes the outright nastiness, and stupidity of 'the Reds', and the simple-minded heroism of Strongman. He alone can be trusted to defeat this menace; even the police are incapable. This story reeks of McCarthyite vigilantism; and this sense of threat is mirrored in the second story, 'To Touch The Stars'. A bunch of aliens are seeking to kill an American professor about to solve the problem of space flight, because (as their leader puts it) 'We of Centauri have ruled the galaxy for generations! All the alien cultures that exist on inhabited planets are under our rule! If mankind once reaches the stars, it will bring freedom with him, and challenge our rule!' In these stories, there is indeed a 'cognitive syndrome', and her high exposure readers have more accurately diagnosed it than she has. Such McCarthyite stories are certainly stereotyped. The only unanswered question in them is the technical one of how to dispose of such obviously evil characters.

Bailyn's problems are two-fold. First, she simply assumes that 'stereotyping' is a negative personality trait, and obviously unrealistic (her measure of a 'stereotyped' response is describing a character as 'very bad' (p. 24) – hardly adequate for any purpose). Lacking ways of looking adequately at the comics themselves, she cannot see that the most involved, experienced readers (I substitute 'experienced' for 'high exposure' – look how it changes our sense of them, without altering their amount of reading) might be accurately responding to their invitation. Her second and main problem then lies in her classification of the comics.

Her methods of classification would make Vladimir Propp turn in his urn. In the Introduction to his *Morphology*, Propp inveighed against those who make arbitrary categorisations among folk-tales. Bear that in mind and consider Bailyn's classifications: Animal, Situational, Western (into which, for some reason, are put Jungle comics), Crime, Spy and War, Superforce, Horror, Space, Other. I could spend hours unpicking these categories, showing, for example, that Animal stories of her period included both situational and crime elements; or that Horror sometimes included elements of superforce, sometimes space, sometimes situational crime! Bailyn simply groups them into two kinds: 'aggressive hero', and the rest. This only makes sense if you have made the prior assumption that their only significant content is their aggression.

Here we have the flip-side of *Action*. *Action* was singled out because of its politics, but without admitting that. Here, we have a refusal to distinguish kinds of comics, because that would demand thinking about the nature of McCarthyism. The stories accurately embodied that political view, and invited a related style of thinking. Rather than see that, Bailyn blames it on the medium in general and on the psychological vulnerability of the boys.

Uses and gratifications

Standing opposite the 'effects' tradition is the Uses and Gratifications approach. This approach argues as follows: the 'effects' model treats its subjects as decontextualised, asocial beings who either absorb mass media contents or (luckily) resist. We need instead to recognise that audiences are already members of their society. They don't passively encounter mass media. They choose what they will read or watch, because they want certain things from them. In the slogan which only partly caricatures this approach, it is not what the media do to the audience, but what the audience do with the media. Why do they watch, and what needs do they satisfy? This reorientation of research took audiences seriously, and invited them to give their own perceptions of the media. Developing in America in the late 1940s, it was a reaction against the 'effects' tradition of the 1920-30s, and against the aftermath of the propaganda research of World War II.[9]

One famous piece of research on comics came out of this tradition. Much cited, it has been much less analysed. Wolfe and Fiske investigated a sample of 104 American children, to see what they looked for in their comics, and how they progressed through them.[10] They found distinct stages. In the first, they say, children choose 'Funny Animal' comics, in which the stories are predominantly centred in the home, and the characters are like people they recognise. This does not prevent those characters being animals – the children had no problems declaring animals to be more 'real' than human figures. This ability on the kids' part might have made Wolfe and Fiske cautious in their use of 'real' and 'realistic' elsewhere. It didn't.

Leaving the Animal comics, the children began to read Superman-type comics, taking pleasure in fantasising themselves as able to fly, and having other special powers. Soon, the majority leave these behind, some via a superhero with less extravagent powers, such as Batman. But before long, most have either given up comics altogether, or have turned to the True Comics, educational comics quite common at that time. Wolfe and Fiske's argument is that these three groups of comics – Funny Animal, Superman-type, and True – correspond to distinct phases of children's development. Isn't it lucky, they say, that we have something available to the kids, which corresponds to these phases of their growing needs? Then, like old clothes, they grow out of them. We just need to make sure that none of them cramp their growth by wearing old comics that are too tight for them.

Once again, the smell of a problem. Wolfe and Fiske distinguish kinds of readers: fans, from ordinary, and hostile readers. And of course the first group must be the potential problem, mustn't they? There couldn't be anything abnormal about disliking comics – that could only mean that the children had 'grown up a little faster'. Using very crude measures, they distinguish between 'normal' readers, readers with 'problems', and 'neurotic' and 'psychotic' readers. Disregard all the hesitations I hope you are having over these classifications, and think about why they might want them in the first place. The implication is that most normal children will go through comics like size 5 shoes; a few with problems will be able to use the comics to help them (and that's lucky). The neurotic and psychotic – well, we must worry about those in just a moment. The point is that comics can only be neutral or negative, in this scheme. The best we can hope for is that they will only 'indulge in moderation' and give them up pretty soon. Even as they are saying that the comics 'fulfil children's developmental needs', those needs are being classified as ones to be got over with as soon as possible.

The fans are out of control; therefore by definition they are neurotic, ones 'whose problems had affected their entire behaviour pattern'. More than that, the comics help to trap them in their problems. The comic-reading itself becomes a neurosis: 'The fan does indeed become neurotic, i.e. . . . the habit and characteristics of comic-reading gradually engulf his life and affect his entire behaviour-patterns.' (p. 29) Their argument is a real puzzler. On the one hand they accuse the comics of producing this neurosis. Yet they next tell us that the fans don't read the comics as intended; they skip to the ends, they read the middle bits afterwards, they forget them the moment they have read them, and thus take pleasure in re-readings as if they were for the first time. These two just do not easily fit. But as so often, they can be made to fit if we add in a hidden premise. This concerns the nature of 'fantasy'. Wolfe and Fiske talk of fantasy as something children must go through, on their way to the 'correct attitude' which is a 'realistic' interest in the world. We must of course allow them to go through that fantasy stage. But it is of little value, except to be outgrown. Fantasy is simply escapist. It is not a way of engaging with the world in which we might learn something. It is a phase of hiding from things – hence the need to get children past it as soon as possible.

Being escapist, it is also lawless, and hence potentially dangerous. Anything 'fantastic' that we read, therefore, could link with uncontrolled tendencies in us. So no matter how the kids do it, the sheer fact of reading them at all marks them as being at risk. That hidden premise about fantasy is the hidden organiser in Wolfe and Fiske's argument. It enables them to conclude that:

> For the normal child, then, comics are a means of healthful ego-strengthening and a source of amusement. Other children do not seem to be so eager to fortify themselves for the experience of life. They do not seem to have emancipated themselves from their parents to any great degree ... But their belief in their parents seems nevertheles to have been shaken ... They therefore search for a more perfect father-figure, a being who is omnipotent but, at the same time, tangible and feasible. And such a father-figure they find in Superman. These children become fans ... For normal children, then, the comics function as an adaptation mechanism ... For the maladjusted child, the comics satisfy, just as efficiently, an equally intense emotional need, but here the need itself is not so readily outgrown. The religion of comics is not easily given up ... That he became a fan can no more be blamed upon the comics, than morphine can itself be blamed when a person becomes a drug addict. (pp. 34-5)

Here, as in Uses and Gratifications research generally, we get a potent mix: timeless needs, which 'explain' why people use the media; unargued distinctions between 'reality' and 'fantasy'; and naive classifications of media-content.

These standard traditions of reader-research won't help us. They do not (know how to) analyse the comics themselves. They simply import current 'commonsense' classifications. Whether they then investigate the comics quantitatively (as 'effects' work tends to), or by interviews (as in Uses and Gratifications research), they already embody prejudgements. There can be nuggets of important information; but we will only disentangle these from the dross of poor interpretations with the help of a more satisfactory account of the comics themselves. What would work better? It is not an issue of whether the research is quantitative or qualitative, in laboratories or in live situations, by structured or by open-ended interviews, or any other choices of particular techniques. The issues go deeper. No doubt, in the right framework, any of the above techniques could yield useful information. The problem is the framework. My argument is that the great bulk of existing studies, of both texts and readers, have found only what their theories assumed already to be present. The issue then is to find an approach which cracks that circularity. To put it at its simplest, I want to put back the element of *surprise* into studies of the media and ideology. Research should have the ability to startle us, by throwing up evidence that is hard to explain, or simply requiring us to start again.

As soon as we begin to study a text, we are already making assumptions about its readers. There are no self-evident ways of looking at a comic and knowing what is of significance in it. But the moment we opt for one approach, we have also opted for a view of what is significant in the media. That will contain hints at how its audience might relate to it. I have already tried to show there are good reasons for rejecting many of those theorisations. Some of the reasons are theoretical, concerning internal coherence for example. Some are historical, showing a mismatch between the history implied by the theory and the actual history. Others are analytic, aiming to show that textual features are simply ignored or arbitrarily discounted. And in a few cases I have tried to show how quite detailed evidence about readers favours one interpretation over another.

However, one other important way measure of an approach is its implicit claims about readers. For example, Angela McRobbie's view was that *Jackie* is teaching girls to distrust each other. Suppose we found that many readers share copies and discuss the magazine with each other – would that challenge her account? If not, perhaps it is because those who read it collectively are performing 'negotiated' readings of the comic. But in that case, a study of the sub-set who do read it alone should give us those girls who are being most influenced by it. An investigation of solo-readers as against group-readers should surely give us a direct test of her analysis.

We will only make progress, I believe, if we can uncover such implicit theorisations and develop appropriate tests. The tricky part is that it involves an interplay between studying the texts, and thinking about their readers. Any research which claims to stay on one side of the divide only, will be silently making assumptions – almost certainly borrowed from current 'commonsense' – about the other side.

This was surely the lesson from my brief look at Uses and Gratifications research. At first sight, this tradition seems to sidestep issues about 'influence' altogether. It was certainly intended originally as an alternative to 'effects' theories. But it fails; and we must see why. Uses and Gratifications theory assumes that people come to the media with pre-existent needs. The media, then, either gratify those needs or they fail to. That sounds simple – except that, as we saw with Wolfe and Fiske, we are automatically caught up in a theorisation of needs. Some are 'good' needs, some 'bad'; some are only related to phases of our lives, some are life-long. Some are 'higher', some 'lower'. And some of them are capable of being over-fulfilled. If we use the media to fulfil those kinds, we can become addicted. An approach that apparently ducks all issues of 'effects' and 'influence' has in fact smuggled the whole palaver back in, in just as intractable a form. Ideas about needs are just as prone to external social definitions as ever 'violence' was.

Asking the girls

In recent years, there has been some much more sophisticated and self-critical research on audiences. Largely from within the cultural studies tradition, this work has borrowed techniques from anthropology in order to explore the way people's uses of the media fit into their lives.[11] A good example of such work is McRobbie's study of adolescent girls.[12] This was part of her important critique that previous work on adolescent sub-cultures focused solely on boys.

At first sight this seems to be singularly detached from her study of Jackie. There is only one reference to the magazine, the bulk of it being a careful ethnographic look at how girls respond to the constraints on them: from school, parents and boys. Her conclusion, from listening to their talk about jobs, marriage, sex, babies etc, is that 'the culture of adolescent working class girls can be seen as a response to the material limitations imposed on them as a result of their class position, but also as an index of, and response to their sexual oppression as women. They are both saved by and locked within the culture of femininity' (p. 108). This implies that 'romance', the crucial category in McRobbie's 'culture of femininity', becomes double-edged. It offers a bolt-hole from the pressures of external definitions of the girls, but ultimately repro-duces them within those definitions.

But although Jackie appears only the once, its cameo role is revealing. McRob-bie argues that girls use their collective interest in romance as a basis for resis-tance to teachers, to parents, even to boys. At school, they will bunk off to talk about 'boys', or read magazines (including Jackie) under the desks. They will form very close friendships, from which base they will handle boys' sexual demands. In other words, the key to their resistance is their girl-friendships; and that is where Jackie comes in. Jackie was indicted, recall, for encouraging girls to compete with each other. McRobbie repeats that claim here, that central to Jackie's repertoire are 'problems, romance, jealousy' (p. 99). Jackie's role, then, is to work against their one resource for resistance: their collectivity, their sisterhood.

I have to repeat what I have already argued. In all the issues of Jackie that I have sampled I found no evidence of it fostering suspicion between girls, in any form. Indeed, I found masses of evidence to the contrary. Girls are regularly advised to value their female friendships. In a hundred other ways the magazine also assumes girls read it together. Quizzes will invite girls to fill them in about each other. Going shopping for clothes is talked of as a group-activity. And so on. This parallels what McRobbie herself in another essay tells of meeting a group of Asian girls sagging off from school and doing a Jackie quiz in the ladies' toilet.[13]

What would the publishers have said to those girls? Of a certainty, they'd have been told to get back into school, and to 'keep romance in its place'. Romance must not be allowed to get in the way of getting properly qualified. And that's significant. Contrary to McRobbie, I am convinced that Jackie does relate to girls' culture, but with the proviso that it walks the line of being too close to official views. Its limit is that it takes school too seriously, and talks too hopefully about future careers. These are the very reason why the magazine almost has to be appropriated subversively. The problem with Jackie is not its wholesale concern with love and romance but that it qualifies that with other more 'official' concerns. In other words, it does not enter wholesale into the defensive 'conspiracy' McRobbie's girls have joined. The trouble is that McRobbie's semiological approach disjoins her textual analysis from her more (much more useful) investigation of girls' lives.

The researcher who comes closest to tackling the critical questions here seems to me Jacqueline Sarsby. Sarsby's work has not received the attention it deserves. From an anthropological perspective, she sets out to review the place of 'romance' within our culture, concluding from a review of evidence that there is no reason to suppose 'romantic love' is a specifically modern invention. Her book includes a chapter on women's magazines, including Jackie. Her analysis (based on a 1970-1 sample) points up some contrasts which other analysts have missed. She notes, first, that 'Jackie magazine has on the whole rather independent, carefree heroines, who do not fit the image of the rather unconfident, self-conscious girls which emerged from my survey'.[14] Her survey showed that working class girls (the main readers of Jackie) believed more strongly that love involves being dependent on your partner, and also attached much greater importance to physical pleasure. Neither of these were at work in her sample of Jackie stories.

Sarsby does tentatively tackle how Jackie might relate to girls' lives. In her first version, she stops at two rather weak points. After looking at her stories, she notes that they do not directly reflect their readers' lives; the heroines lead different lives from the readers. Perhaps, she suggests, we should look instead at the 'morality' of the stories (though we are given no indication how to do this). But even then, she found no significant influence, declaring that her evidence 'must lead one to the conclusion that class and schooling have a much more formative role than magazine-reading possibly could have in this sphere'.[15] Thus her argument hangs limply between two bald alternatives: either *Jackie* has an independent influence, or it simply reflects their lives.

But her subsequent book, drawing on the same evidence, suggests a far more interesting approach. Here, she takes 'class' seriously. Linking her discussion with a classic study of working class wives,[16] she suggests a connection between one account of a miner's wife, and *Jackie*. The woman displayed great anger towards her husband who kept his wages secret and gave her too little, who rarely showed any feeling for her, and so on. At the same time, she declared that she couldn't leave him because she 'worshipped' him:

> The conflict of her love and hate came from his refusal to respond to the material and emotional needs of her children and herself. His stage was the pit and the pub, hers was the home and her contact with neighbours and relations. She could gain no esteem with them, however, because Vince refusd to make her a 'nice home' or to spend any time in it. Elsie's 'I love him' was synonymous with 'I need him here'; it was full of desperation. Elsie was no less intelligent, no less able than most people; she was in a predicament of almost total powerlessness, dependence, exploitation and lack of reward. She is an extreme case. The idiom of love is for many such women the only acceptable representation of need. As in the end of the last *Jackie* story, it is the irrational, the inexplicable in the idea of love which lends grace to what is too plain to be spoken.[17]

That story was 'Shadow of a Past Love' (no. 356, 31 October 1970, discussed in Chapter 8) which ended with a narrator's comment: 'Love never dies, not real, true love, because it's not made of flesh and blood – or words or actions even. It's in the heart and it can't be explained.' What is exciting about Sarsby's suggestion is that it invites us to think how 'love' might mobilise different feelings at different points in women's lives. Romance stories like *Jackie*'s would have a complicated, social relationship to readers' lives. But it could be studied.

The discourse strategy

The most recent study of *Jackie* readers is perhaps the boldest. Elizabeth Frazer set out to discover directly how readers responded to its themes.[18] She argues that traditional arguments about *Jackie* and ideology have made assumptions about girls' responses which have not been borne out by investigation. Accordingly she wants to find a replacement for 'ideology'.

She has several complaints against the concept of ideology. First, it implies that ideas have power to reproduce themselves in us; yet no such evidence has been found. Second it assumes without evidence that 'ideology' is unitary, with something like *Jackie* neatly 'fitting in' to a general ideological package. Then she complains (rightly in my view) that 'ideology' is assumed to be hidden behind the backs of texts, affecting us without our seeing what is happening. Frazer's comments on standard uses of 'ideology' seem to me both apt and accurate. I must say what a pleasure it was to find someone else saying what I felt! In place of all these, she wanted to find out how girls themselves talked about *Jackie*. Her method was to discuss one *Jackie* story with seven different groups of girls. From these, she concludes that there is no evidence that they are 'injected' with an ideology. They are always aware that it is a fiction, and maintain a critical distance from its ideas. Yet she thinks that her evidence does show that, in a quite different way, *Jackie* still has a power to inflect the girls' thinking. Accordingly, she introduces from sociolinguistics the idea of a 'discourse register'. This suggests that there are situationally specific ways of talking about topics, which are rule-governed and constraining. Frazer illustrates this by showing how her interviewees are able to shift between some very different ways of talking about problems of love, marriage and related topics. One moment, they will talking in the 'register' of the Cathy and Claire problem pages, offering solutions like 'being brave, putting up a show'. The next moment they may shift to a much more personal 'register' in which problems can be thought through in highly complex ways. She also points to elements of a feminist register (when, for example, talking about male violence towards women), and of one that seems to owe a lot to tabloid newspaper styles (when they talked about child molestors).

The concept of 'discourse' has developed with astonishing speed, to become the most popular means for thinking about the ways meanings are produced and exchanged – but with a host of different definitions and theories.[19] Yet with all the differences, 'discourse' seems always to stand opposed to 'ideology', at least as I want to use it. Therefore an examination, via Frazer, of the notion is useful. A 'discourse register' is a structured, socially-approved way of talking. People sharing a register will talk to each other in particular ways, using shared grammatical and conceptual forms. A register will 'prefer' certain kinds of questions and answers, and make it easier to arrive at some conclusions rather than others. Frazer uses this idea to make sense of the way her girls could switch between different ways of talking about issues affecting them – but seemed to find some easier to use on some topics than others. Thus, she notes that the girls are very critical of *Jackie*'s problem pages. But when asked to invent their own problems and answers, they tended to reproduce *Jackie*'s form and tone.

Frazer acknowledges that she has used the idea of a 'discourse register' loosely. But she thinks that it can be stated with sufficient precision to make it a valuable technical tool. It moves from the speculative, to the testable. If her claim could be substantiated, it would clearly be a major step forward. But in fact there are real difficulties in this concept of a discourse register (henceforth, DR). I have set out my worries serially, for speed's sake:

1. The DR approach has little if anything to say about power. Yet implicitly it has to be using some notion of it. For girls 'pick up' certain registers from around them and find them 'applicable' to *Jackie*. They don't generate these

themselves. But in that case it has to be explained how the girls are persuaded to adopt some rather than others. It is not at all obvious what sort of notion of power will do this.

2. DR theory dissolves the phoney 'unity' of ideology into a multiplicity of discourses. Fine. But then it has little to say, as I understand it, about either the relationships between different registers, or the way we can shift between them. For example, how would we explain how one register might be dominant over others? Presumably it must be accepted that some registers can be more effective, or persuasive, or commanding than others. Again, then, the question of power creeps back in, demanding our attention.

3. A discourse register is an institutionally-defined pattern of approved ways of talking. The implication clearly is that to discover a discourse register is to have a pretty good notion of its source: the institution from which it derives is not going to be hard to find. My problem is that I have a strong suspicion that when, for example, Frazer identifies one of her girls' registers as the 'popular press', this wasn't a discovery based on delineating a distinctive register. Her own knowledge guided her to pick out some bits that do indeed sound like bits of the Sun. That does matter. It reinforces my sense that registers may not be as easy to separate, as the theory suggests. Certainly in practice, her Jackie-readers didn't seem to notice their shifts between them. We need to think about that.

4. It isn't clear what DR thinking has to tell us about registers, except to describe them. It may be perhaps invite interesting questions about their origins, but we need also to be able to ask where they might take us. If people take a discourse seriously, and try to orient some part of their lives by it, what will be the result? To find out, we need to ask different kinds of questions. To answer that, though, we need to go beyond questions about 'discourse' altogether.

5. One of Frazer's strongest points is that all her groups of girls were very critical of Jackie. This was her main reason for rejecting any idea that they were being 'influenced by the ideology' of Jackie. The trouble is that using the notion of 'discourse' to understand this leaves as an odd, almost unanswerable question why they read it at all. This is because it seems to treat discourses as simply happening, and being accepted. There isn't space within this approach for notions like goals in reading, absences in knowledge, and 'contracts' between a magazine and its readers. Imagine an alternative interpretation of the girls' criticisms of Jackie. Could it be that they believed that the magazine would offer certain kinds of involvement, but that they were disappointed when they read it? Once admit such a possibility, and the notion of 'discourse' can't help us any longer.

6. Curiously, in fact, the approach seems to have nothing to say about Jackie itself. What is the point of analysing its meanings, or its messages or proposals,

when responses are all just a function of readers' discourses? Frazer did show her girls a sample story which she clearly finds objectionable. But she seems to have known the meaning of that story without any system of analysis. And anyway her respondents were untouched by it. They simply responded through their various registers. All that is left, then, is to determine the range of responses. Jackie itself has effectively ceased to exist.

7. Finally, the idea of 'discourse' has one important general implication, which surely makes it incompatible with any notion of 'ideology'. One of the motives for its introduction was to 'decentralise' our understanding of power. But this decentralisation has another face. For it can no longer be seen as worrying, or significant, that people have 'decentralised' responses. If Frazer's interviewees switch mode of response with such ease, on a 'discourse' approach that is just the way they are. But an 'ideology' approach might ask whether this fragmentation of their thinking was not itself an ideological effect. The very fact of their inconsistency can be argued to be a symptom of their subordination. 'Discourse' hides that, or makes it meaningless to explore.

Two general issues underpin these worries. First, there is the question of power. Second is the meaning of 'being a reader' of something like Jackie. I need to broach each in turn, as a precursor to returning to reader-research.

Thinking about media power

Consider the following list of possible models of powerful relationships. Each expresses a way of thinking about how the media might be powerful; I think the list encompasses encompasses most kinds of claim about the influence of the mass media.

1. *Direct stimulus approaches*. These are commonly based on claims that there are two tendencies in us – one (weak) one towards rationality, morality and civilised behaviour, the other towards violent, non-rational tendency. The latter (which may be instinctual) can be 'triggered off' by arousing media images.

2. *Physical force models*. At its simplest, this model might apply to straightforward threats, of the kind that, say, Nazi papers made towards the Jews. Outside such totalitarian situations, there might be assaults on our fears of failure, or other very basic 'survival' desires.

3. *Personality-construction models*. These can take several forms: they could be theories of the creation of needs, desires, problems in us; more strongly, theories of the construction of identity, and notions of 'hailing', 'interpellating'. Most generally, they might talk of 'socialisation', at least in the sense that our very ways of responding and patterns of motivation for responding may be worked on by the media.

4. *Rhetorical persuasion*. Under this would come claims that the media are designed deviously, and work on us by deceiving us into accepting their

messages, without realising what we are agreeing to.

5. *False ideals.* This model claims that people need something in their lives to aim at and to organise their emotions; the media can play on those needs by offering images, values and ideals that falsely satisfy them.

6. *Enclosing solutions to problems.* This model starts from the acknowledgement that people have real problems (though perhaps produced out of distorted contexts) but they cannot solve them themselves. However the solutions offered by the media do more than solve the immediate problems, they further entrap them as, for example, a short-term loan to pay a debt can re-entrap a debtor.

7. *Ordering inchoate experience.* This is a claim that people's experience of their world is relatively 'shapeless' or unordered. The media offer a 'language' which orders, interprets and values that experience, but the language is itself value-laden, and thus leads them into ideological paths.

8. *Offering pseudo-sociality.* In this, the media are seen as offering pseudo-social relationships to audiences. These can be influential because people need good social relationships, and the media are able to 'glamorise' what they offer. Thus they can supplant living relationships which could really satisfy needs and solve problems.

Each of these is a potential explanation of how the media might have power. Each, differently, instructs on where to look within the media for the site of that power; and where to look in the receiving audience for the things that make them 'vulnerable'. The models fall naturally into groups. The first four are distinguished by thinking that the media on their own are sufficient for influence. They don't need any particular condition in the audience for their power to become effective. On these approaches, audiences are either influenced by the media, or they resist using resources from the rest of their lives. Thus they all use words like 'direct', 'force', 'construct', 'persuade'. In each, something external imposes itself on us. Such models see the media as working on us, regardless of our original motives for having contact with them. Our role is simply to be 'vulnerable'.

The remaining models assume some definite characteristics already present in us, which the media work on. They use different words: 'false', 'ordering', 'enclosing', 'pseudo-'. But behind each of these is an ethical ideal of how things ought to happen. In these, the media's power is not quite an different, external imposition. It is the same as other kinds of influence, but wants to take us in a wrong direction. We should be getting 'proper' sociality, the right shaping of experience, true ideals, and opening rather than closing; but we aren't.

Seven out of the eight models have been directly used to formulate ideas about 'ideology'. The exception is the direct stimulus model, because this is assumed to work on a below-mental, 'instinctual' level. So ideas – even pseudo-ideas – do not really come into consideration. But all eight assume that when we talk of power, we are talking of something just a little less than human. The 'ideological' works in suspicious ways on those elements in us that do not represent our best. It is dubious, by definition. On these kinds of approach, therefore, everything 'ideological' shares a distinguishing mark. Find that birth-mark, define it, and we'll know when we have 'ideology' – and we'll know how it works. It is a search for a formal distinction, which will show that 'ideology' works on us in different ways from those things which are not ideological. It is a sign of Cain, giving a formal criterion for distinguishing the 'ideological' from the 'non-ideological'. And dogging the footsteps of all work on 'ideology', has been that shadow-partner, non-ideology. Rarely emerging from the gaps, but always entailed, there is an alternative, that which ought to be, accompanying the ideological.[20] At the other end of its leash it tugs im-patiently, reminding us always that the ideology is a restraint on it – if only it could get away.

I want to argue that the distinction between ideology and non-ideology should be ditched. In the main, work on 'ideology' has involved hopeless searches for that distinguishing birth-mark. Its presence would mean bad power; its absence would mean good influence. Every attempt to deal with 'ideology' in this way has foundered on this wretched opposition. We need an approach that positively escapes it. Now, the objection has always been: to have a concept of ideology, without an opposite concept of non-ideology, is to empty 'ideology' of all significant content. If everything is ideological, then it might as well be that nothing is. It becomes as hollow of implications as saying that something exists.

I believe that there are reasons for saying that this is not as hollow as it sounds. I want to argue that it is a 'significant tautology' to say that 'Everything is ideolog-ical'. Certain statements which look like truisms in fact play a role in orienting us; they invite us to ask certain questions, and to investigate, in ways that go far beyond the obvious and the tautological. To say that something is 'ideolog-ical', then, would be to ready ourselves to ask the right questions.

Talking to the readers

This takes us back to Frazer. There is one further point on which I find I disagree with her. She points out that most notions of 'ideology' find it hard to allow for audiences responding critically to the media. It isn't that they deny that people do often have critical responses. But they are not the ones who have been influenced. Therefore when they want to talk about 'ideology', they talk as if somewhere there are other people who don't talk critically. They are the ones who are being influenced. Now Frazer accepts this implication that if an audience is able to discuss critically what the media are doing, they are not being influenced. Criticism excludes influence. So, since the girls she interviews are obviously quite capable of discussing Jackie critically, they can't have been influenced. (We might say that 'lack of critical ability' is one of those supposed birth-marks of 'ideology'.)

But this is still part of that model that sees ideology as a barrier. Frazer is still thinking of it as preventing us doing certain things, stopping us thinking in certain ways. Set that aside, and there is no reason why the influence should not precisely be one of involving us in certain kinds of critical thinking: asking certain questions, inquiring into things in particular ways, even self-critically working on what that medium itself gives us. In fact one of the things I see Jackie as doing, is somewhat obsessively asking young girls to ask questions about themselves. It is for its question-posing role, not for any particular answers it insists on, that I would challenge Jackie.

Given this, let us ask a very different question: what will happen to a girl who becomes involved in a dialogue with Jackie? What will happen if she should try to live through her relationship with it? This sets up a different logic. It would replace questions about Jackie restricting or narrowing or constraining its readers. But then, a comic like Jackie could only connect with young girls because it offers to talk to them about topics which are already significant in their lives. And no matter how 'clever' or 'powerful' a conversation, if they have no interest in listening there can be no influence.

This tells us where Frazer goes wrong. Her misunderstanding (along with so many other people) is to suppose that anyone who reads Jackie is its 'reader'. Just because certain girls in very widely dispersed social locations will pick up the comic and read it – perhaps even regularly – does not mean that they are the ones we need to be studying. To know who we should be studying, we need first to identify the characteristics which the comic supposes its readers to have. In what ways does a comic like Jackie define its own readership? With its regular features, its reliable format, and its repeated ways of dealing with issues, it offers a contract with its readers. And of course, a Jackie reader can be expected to be critical if some part of the contract she feels she has entered into is not being fulfilled. The 'natural readers' will be the most critical.[21]

We need to be able to distinguish different kinds of criticism. Outsiders, who do not want this kind of story at all, may use dismissive criticism. 'Casual' readers, who perhaps enjoy them but to whom the issues are marginal, may half-criticise. But the 'spontaneous' or 'natural' readership will want the stories to live up to the promise of Jackie's contract; and their criticisms will start from there.[22]

The contract

The idea of a 'contract' suggests that a magazine like Jackie is more than just a body of contents looking for a mind to invade. It suggests that it offers a kind of relationship to its readers. We might say that *Jackie* extends an invitation to readers to join in and use its contents in particular ways. In recent years, an idea very like this has been developed in literary theory. This is the idea of the 'implied reader'. Put over-simply, this suggests that any work of fiction (though it need not be limited to those) not only has its story; it also has the way this story is told. It has a narrator, and the way that narrator tells the story.[23] Thus any work of fiction does not just tell a story, it tells it in a particular way to a certain kind of reader. The textual devices give us a sense of who is telling the story, and why. Thereby a role is established: the role of being the reader of that particular story. To read the story, we have to be willing to play that role. A great deal of work has gone on within literary theory, to classify kinds of narrator and narrative strategy. This has led to distinctions between different aspects of the role of 'implied reader'. A useful illustration can be gleaned from Jonathan Culler. Culler uses Jonathan Swift's *A Modest Proposal*. This was Swift's barbed satire on those who blamed the Irish for causing their own famine, by having too many children. Swift makes his satire work by seeming to take this cruel view seriously. Yes, he says, they are to blame; but there is an obvious solution. The famine can be greatly relieved by simply persuading the Irish to eat their own children – at one fell swoop, their hunger and their overpopulation will be removed. To understand this as satire, we have to play several roles together:

> Someone who reads Swift's 'A Modest Proposal' as a masterpiece of irony first postulates an audience that the narrator appears to believe he is addressing: an audience entertaining specific assumptions, inclined to formulate certain objections, but likely to find the narrator's arguments cogent and compelling. The second role the reader postulates is that of an audience attending to a serious proposal for relieving famine in Ireland but finding the values and assumptions of the proposal (and of the 'ideal narrative audience') singularly skewed. Finally, the reader participates in an audience that reads the work not as a narrator's proposal but as an author's ingenious construction, and appreciates its power and skill. Actual readers will combine the roles of authorial, narrative, and even ideal narrative audiences in varying proportions – without embarrassment living in contradiction. One ought perhaps to avoid speaking of the 'implied reader' as a single role that the reader is called upon to play, since the reader's pleasure may well come, as Barthes says, from the interaction of contradictory engagements.[24]

These new approaches to the 'reader' have proved very fruitful, revitalising literary theory. But they have created their own new problem. For what is the relation between 'implied readers' and the real readers who pick up and read the texts? This is a problem that literary theory may be ill-suited to tackle, unfortunately. For the relation between a novel, say, and its 'public' is a particularly distant one. And literary theory tends to be most interested in those novels that are the most distant from their readers.

Consider science fiction for a moment. There are a number of ways in which authors and readers interact, and future writing will be affected by this unfolding relationship. Partly distributed through regular magazines with feedback, there are also Conventions at which authors often meet and talk with their fans. In contrast, typically 'literary' works are produced in a much more individualised way, and indeed there is pressure from publishers, reviewers, etc, for authors to produce unique works, in which the 'voice of the author' can be discerned. To become a reader of works of this kind, then, is also much more individualised, with an emphasis on the readers' 'taste' and 'pleasure'. More even than science fiction, the mass media depend on developing sets of typified expectations. Readers learn what to expect, and what is expected of them. This is how they can recognise when their expectations are being disappointed. And perhaps those disappointments can be our best evidence of what those typified expectations were. If readers of *Jackie* reject one kind of story, and demand another kind of *Jackie* story, maybe they are distinguishing 'contract-fulfilling' stories from those which fail to meet their expectations.

This is why we need to investigate not only implied reader-roles, but the implied social relation to readers. The difference is this. The idea of the 'implied reader' refers only to the text. We can define it purely by reference to textual devices. We do not need any knowledge of the social characteristics of the readers. A novel creates a reader-role. Who (if anyone) can enter this role is another matter altogether. The novel has offered it, and we either agree or not. But if we change the 'implied reader' to the 'proposed social relation to readers', this changes. We still need to study the textual devices. But they will now just be a part of a conversation with some aspect of the readers' lives. And, I want to suggest, the more formulaic the text, the more it has to be a conversation with some typified social experience in their readers. George Gerbner's article (introduced in Chapter 8) exemplifies this.[25]

Gerbner analysed the Confession Magazines which developed in America after World War I. They grew out of readers' accounts of their personal problems written to Bernard Macfadden's *Physical Culture* magazine: ' "Broken-hearted women sent us letters . . ." wrote Mary Macfadden, "after they had done two two hundred knee-bends, twice a day, and had thrown away their corsets, only to find that the Greek gods wouldn't give them a rumble . . . There were girls who confessed their sexual mistakes and thought they were fallen women until they had taken up dumb-bells (the iron kind)" ' (p. 29). By 1950, there were forty titles with a circulation of sixteen million copies. The earliest editions of the first, *True Story* were apparently written directly by readers. But this was soon replaced by formula confessions, still written to give the sense that they came direct from a reader. So (and this is important) Gerbner notes that the stories all had to be first-person tellings:

A recent study by Social Research Inc. found, for example, that the confession reader does not feel as much the center and prime mover of the family as does the white collar reader. She is more emotional about her job as a mother, and is torn by a conflict between that job and her role as a wife to a greater degree than is the middle class woman. Presenting these findings to advertisers, the confession publisher illustrates the difference in social attitudes and values by contrasting 'Built in Baby-sitter' with the confession story, 'I Killed My Child'. The former, taken as a 'representative' story from a white collar woman's magazine is a 'superficial problem, which does an excellent job of entertaining. But inherent in its situation, its manners, its artwork, is a social sophistication that is not to be found in [confession] stories. 'I Killed My Child' is a stark title. It is also the true story of a young mother who saw her child killed by an automobile. Because she has taken the child with her when she left home in a fit of anger after an argument with her husband, she could never thereafter escape the sense of personal guilt she had for her child's death. (p. 32)

These stories are grim. The women find themselves in impossible situations, torn between their roles as mothers, daughters, wives, and wage-earners. When things go wrong, they blame themselves. Only through accepting the blame and being punished for it do they find release. Gerbner cites one which gives this flavour. 'How Can I Face Myself? I Let Him Cheapen Me' tells of Marilyn who lives with Mama after her father and brother had died in a car crash. Weighed down with grief and debts, Mama starts embezzling money from the firm where they both work. The owner Morrison forces Marilyn to submit to him sexually as the price for keeping Mama out of prison. Marilyn feels degraded and in a moment of anger hits Mama – who decides to give herself up. Tortured by all her 'sins', Marilyn finds the courage from this to resist Morrison. At the end he agrees to let them work off the embezzled money.

These are extraordinary stories. They require great suffering of their heroines, who find a whole world outside them loathsome and frightening. Even inside, they find sex a ugly force threatening to break through. When Morrison takes Marilyn, he is transformed from 'a thin, nice-looking guy, not quite as tall as I': 'Passive, I let his hands go where he wanted them to. I saw the awful lust come into his face, making him look like an animal'. Only through suffering is she redeemed. She cannot fight back. Gerbner points out how the first-person telling connects with other aspects. The stories are invariably set in ordinary places, with heroines who are machinists, typists, shop assistants. In short, he argues, they do the job of showing young working class women how other such women cope with the impossible demands made on them. They are not fantasy-material; they are like confidences told over the kitchen table; and the breathless hurry of the style reinforces this.

However dreadful, in some way they 'fitted' their readers' lives. The readers were usually working class from small towns in the South and Mid-West of

America. With little education, they were mostly married with young children, but not so poor that paying the bills was their prime worry. They were more likely to be worried about status and the company their children were keeping. How should we assess the role of such magazines? Gerbner hints at one explanation, a poor one which requires that there was something like a conspiracy between the magazine publishers and the advertisers to trap these women into their hopeless lives. The magazines had to work hard, he argues, to find advertisers. Although such people control a large amount of disposable income, advertisers were not used to crossing 'The Invisible Wall', to reach working class people. The publishers therefore worked very hard and consciously to persuade the advertisers that there was a market, and that it would need a special language to reach it. The task was urgent. Gerbner quotes one Editor-in-Chief ending his 'philosophy for the woman-reader' with a warning: 'She is exposed, far more than her white collar sister, to demagoguery, labor agitators and radical philosophies! Yet American business rarely, if ever, runs its institutional messages in the magazines read by these women . . . I believe it is an economic sin to default in the enlightenment of the more than ten millions of women who live and learn by our behaviour magazines' (cited, p. 32). The advertisers sell their goods to the women. The magazine talks to them about their problems but offers false solutions which leave the women caught in the very position the advertisers want. 'Wage-town protest – in forms disguised, submerged and disoriented – becomes senseless individual sin, socially irrelevant in the world of confessions.' (p. 40)

How is this done? How were they persuaded? For a task of such a magnitude, only one can be called on: our old friend 'identification'. Gerbner claims that this is specially effective because of the first-person narration and the ordinariness of heroines and settings. It allows the readers to imagine it is really them, and come away, feeling that the solution is also theirs. Gerbner's analysis is better than his conclusion.

Aside from general problems with 'identification', there is a real problem here. He himself notes a paradox in the first-person narration. All told in a breathless rush, there is little space for reflection. Indeed, the heroine often does not understand what is happening to her. But we do. There is a gap between her understanding of her situation and ours which debars any simple identification.

Rather than see it that way, I would suggest that we take seriously the sense of dialogue; as Gerbner himself says, 'like a conversation across the kitchen table'. 'Identification' suggests that we are spoken for. 'Dialogue' suggests we are spoken to. If we look at these confession stories as like dialogue, still keeping our sights on the textual elements Gerbner has pointed up – unresolvable conflicts, first person 'common speech' – as well as the class characteristics of the readers, then perhaps we can understand them as public dramatisations of readers' typified experiences. To working class women in parts of America where traditional gender-roles were particularly strong, but with the rising demands of consumerism doubling the pressures on them, the stories could give a comparison with their own lives. The very bleakness of the heroines' lives might allow a sense of shared suffering. The 'contract' then might be seen as providing readers with formularised mirrors of their own lives. I say this tentatively, because it would need different kinds of research to confirm or refute this. But how close Gerbner comes to showing us such a 'contract' between a formulaic text and a quite specific form of social experience!

A 'contract' involves an agreement that a text will talk to us in ways we recognise. It will enter into a dialogue with us. And that dialogue, with its dependable elements and form, will relate to some aspect of our lives in our society. This idea has in fact been at the root of all the chapters so far in this book. In each case, I have been illustrating the way specific comics offer a contract to some aspect of the social lives of their readers. It could be *Action* with its melodramatic mates' conversation about the hardness of modern life. It could be the juvenile comics, with their game-like talk with children about the idea of 'childhood'. It could be *Jackie* with its older-sisterly chat with girls about 'true love', giving them glimpses of something they won't yet be able to experience for themselves. It could be *Bunty* offering fantasy-versions of the double hardness of being a working class girl, and virtually giving body to the despairing cry 'I wish I was dead – then you'd care'. It is from this that I want to formulate the central hypotheses of the book: (1) *that the media are only capable of exerting power over audiences to the extent that there is a 'contract' between texts and audience, which relates to some specifiable aspect(s) of the audience's social lives; and (2) the breadth and direction of the influence is a function of those socially constituted features of the audience's lives, and comes out of the fulfilment of the contract; (3) the power of 'ideology' therefore is not of some single kind, but varies entirely – from rational to emotional, from private to public, from 'harmless' to 'harmful' – according to the nature of the 'contract'.* This is a bare, formal statement of the hypotheses that have been at work throughout this study.

In each case we cannot grasp the contract, except by developing a picture of the reader as well the comic, the reader and her/his relation to the comic. The moment we choose an approach to one, we have implicitly begun to define the other. This is inevitable on my approach. For if all comics, all media, involve a dialogue between text and reader, then to study one side without implicitly assuming the other, would be like listening to one end of a telephone conversation without thinking about the other person's part. That analogy with conversation is deliberate. My argument is that we need to understand ideology as dialogical. This, I believe, is significantly different from other approaches. To pursue it, we need different theoretical resources. It is time to look back at the contribution of one thinker who made the idea of 'dialogue' the basis of his whole theory of language and ideology.

A dialogical approach to ideology

The seeds of the theory of ideology I am propounding are to be found in the ideas of Valentin Volosinov. Volosinov was a theorist of language and member of the group of Russian thinkers to which Vladimir Propp was close. In 1929-30, shortly before the Stalin purges, he published the two parts of a book on the foundations of linguistics.[1] A very difficult book, perhaps this is the reason it was long ignored. Those who have taken note of it have all too often grossly distorted it. It is not uncommon for it to be treated as very close to, for example, Ferdinand de Saussure.[2] Volosinov has a way of saying things that look either trivial or problematic: for example, that all language is ideological. It isn't easy to unpack what he was struggling to say. But it does help to note that he wrote his book in large part as a critique of structuralism, devoting two chapters to its errors. I have not read any other critique as powerful as his. I won't try, here, to summarise that critique, except where it helps to explain his own ideas. The implications of the theory of ideology which I am drawing from Volosinov cannot be limited to comics, or even the mass media generally. Potentially, I believe, Volosinov completely redraws the map of ideology. But it would be daft to keep hinting at how it might be used in other fields (literature, news, science, religion, education, everyday discourse, etc) when I am not competent to expand the hints.

Volosinov argues that before we can have an account of particular ideologies, we need a theory of language, the vehicle of ideologies in general. Thus far, he seems to agree with the structuralists. But thereafter they diverge, first over what will count as a 'language'. For the followers of Saussure, there are many kinds of 'languages'. Any sign-system, be it clothes, foods, elements within the mass media, or whatever, is equally a 'language'. According to the semiologists, they function in much the same way. Volosinov fundamentally disagrees. All signs, he agrees, use one material form (a sound, a shape of print on page, a picture, a cross, a badge, or whatever) to refer to something other than themselves. But they do it in different ways. In Volosinov's words, 'each field of ideological creativity has its own kind of orientation towards reality and each refracts reality in its own way' (p. 10).

Volosinov depicts a number of ways in which words differ from all other sign-systems. One of these differences is of most importance to my argument. To see it significance, it helps to notice how Volosinov rarely talks about 'language' at all, but about *speech*. What is tied up in that difference? Saussure who did talk about 'language' argued that its system of meanings exists before any individual user of it. A child is born, and learns an already-set system of distinctions. The child does not make them; it inherits them. It might contribute a little to changing them; but these will be changes to an established system. The system always comes first. This is the basis for Saussure's distinction between 'langue' and 'parole'. It is social-as-opposed-to-the-individual. Volosinov wholly rejects this. Instead, he argues, all talk is essentially *like dialogue*. I will first state what he means by this, and then hopefully explain with an example.

Understanding words involves much more than just recognising their meaning. That would make language like deciphering a script. In a powerful passage, Volosinov argues that structuralism treats language as a dead thing. Its attitude is that of the philologist to 'alien, defunct languages', 'these cadavers' (p. 71). In fact, he explicitly likens it to the way we might try to understand an alien signal-system. What has gone is any sense of response. We do not understand language (which involves being socially involved in it), we decode it. In this vein, it is worth noting the vast gap between Saussure and Volosinov over the purpose of language: what do we need it for? According to Saussure, the primary function of language seems to be to describe the world, and attach values to its parts. According to Volosinov, the first function of language is to establish social relations between human beings in society. The difference is fundamental. Therefore to understand is to begin to respond. The key to his meaning is this quotation: 'To understand another person's utterance means to orient oneself with respect to it, to find the proper place for it in the corresponding context. For each word of the utterance that we are in process of understanding we, as it were, lay down a set of our own answering words' (p. 102). Think about the meaning of this. To understand what you say to me – whether 'you' are a friend, a stranger, or a magazine – I have to orient myself to you, by finding a context for your utterance. I cannot be trapped by your language. I am an active respondent – or I could not understand you at all.

Try this out on an example: *Can I have an apple?*

Think of some contexts in which this might be asked . . . (1) a child to its parent, while standing in the kitchen; (2) child to parent, but while out shopping; (3) customer to waiter, in restaurant; (4) patient to doctor, during a consultation. What would it mean in each case? For each utterance, we need to know how to identify the *referent* of 'an apple', and the *force* of asking 'can I?'.

1. For the first child, the meaning of 'apple' is likely to be 'one of those four in the fruit bowl'; and 'can' asks permission. If its parent replied 'I don't know, are you tall enough to reach?', the child would guess s/he was playing games.

2. But now out shopping, both referent and force have changed. 'An apple' is now an open class, probably meaning 'one from the greengrocer'. It refers much more indefinitely; and its parent must understand this to be able to respond. 'Can' still involves permission. But unless this is a very burglarious family, the answer 'yes' certainly won't allow the child simply to take one. It

has to be paid for.

3. Now visit the restaurant. All changes here. What context are you filling in imaginatively as you hear the customer say 'Can I have an apple?'. Partly, we need to know a little more – is there a bowl of fruit in sight? Are they on the menu? Suppose neither. In that case, the effective sense of the question is 'Are you able to supply me with an apple as part of my meal?'; and 'can' certainly is not a request for permission. The referent has become even more open-ended. The force of the question is to ask for more information about the range of foods the restaurant can supply.

4. Next come to the surgery. 'Can I have an apple?' Most likely, this is a request for permission to include apples in a prescribed diet. Here 'an apple' wouldn't be a particular one at all, but 'apples-in-general'. And the kind of permission changes. If the patient pulled one from a pocket at that moment and started munching, the doctor might be a touch surprised.

To understand the meaning of the words, then, we need to orient ourselves with regard to the situation. Understanding their meaning is *knowing what would be a relevant response* (Volosinov's 'laying down a set of our own answering words'). This commonplace example has implications. The most significant is that understanding involves placing ourselves socially in relation to the utterer. Speech always occurs within social relations; and it depends on those for its meaning. You cannot first have a system of language, and then uses of it. To Volosinov, in every act of speaking and hearing (or writing and reading), the people involved are already socially-related to each other.[3] Even strangers still relate socially. If you doubt this, try imagining a stranger approaching you and asking: 'Can I have an apple?' Think how force and referent change in each of the following circumstances: (1) a stranger entering a fruit shop (well, most grocers don't know most customers); (2) an Ethopian refugee approaching a relief worker; (3) an author saying it in the middle of a book . . . In each case, we have to fill in a social story in order to gain the meaning of the sentence. This involves giving some history to the people and their relations to each other, and a material-institutional context. This is why Volosinov insists on calling language 'social-ideological'. It must always be both, simultaneously.

This has an odd effect on traditional notions of power in 'ideology'. How, on Volosinov's model, is power-in-language conceivable? If understanding always involves orienting ourselves, it isn't easy to see how another person's language could in any sense control us. Volosinov says very little directly on this. Instead, he talks of language as our 'most sensitive index' of social changes. I believe that in Volosinov's argument there is an implied theory of power. But it emerges as a conclusion of his theory.

When Volosinov writes of words as our 'most sensitive index' of social changes, he points us to a notion which he posits but hardly explores. This is the 'speech genre'. If speech interactions happened as randomly as might be suggested by my 'apple' example, it would be very difficult to study them, or to see how they could be learnt. We do need to make fairly reliable predictions as to how people will speak to us, make demands of us, understand our requests to them. The child will quickly learn from its parent why you cannot just take an apple at the greengrocer's. There are rules governing the interactions which govern the contexts in which words must be understood. These rules in some way link together how we live together, our social system; and our ways of communicating with each other. This is how Volosinov himself establishes this bridge:

> Production relations and the sociopolitical order shaped by these relations deter-
> mine the full range of verbal contacts between people, all the forms and means
> of their verbal communication – at work, in political life, in ideological crativity.
> In turn, from the conditions, forms and types of verbal communication derive
> not only the forms but also the themes of speech performances.
>   Social psychology [by which Volosinov means social psychological behaviour,
> not the study of it] is first and foremost an atmosphere made up of multifarious
> speech performances that engulf and wash over all persistent forms and kinds of
> ideological creativity: unofficial discussions, exchanges of opinion at the theatre
> or a concert or at various kinds of social gathering, purely chance exchanges of
> words, one's manner of verbal reactions to happenings in one's life and daily
> existence, one's inner word-manner of identifying oneself and identifying one's
> position in society. Social psychology exists primarily in a wide variety of forms
> of the 'utterance', of little *speech genres* of internal and external kinds. A *typology of
> these forms* is one of the urgent tasks of Marxism. (pp. 19-20)

There is no getting away from the obscurity of this passage. It begins with a piece of very orthodox-looking marxism: production relations determine everything else in society. It then leaps to talking about commonplace kinds of communication, like discussions at the theatre. Yet it ends back with marxism, with 'one of its urgent tasks'. The bridge, we shall see, is provided by three notions: 'theme', 'speech genre', and 'evaluative accent'.

The dialectic of speech in Volosinov

Language has structures of many different kinds. 'I if can whole dog put why' is nonsensical, because it breaks grammatical rules. But there are other kinds of structure to human communication, as a great deal of recent discourse analysis has made clear. Michael Stubbs' valuable book on discourse analysis contains many examples of how we have to assume structure and coherence, in talk with others.[4] He uses an example from Samuel Beckett's *Endgame*. 'Hamm: 'Why don't you kill me?'; Clov: 'I don't know the combination of the larder'.' Heard out of the context of that play, with its surreal characters and situation, it would be difficult to see a connection between the two sentences. It's not that they can't be linked, but that it is hard. Stubbs' point is that we seek to find a structured link. This is a structure beyond grammar. These structures are situationally specific. Consider, again: (1) 'Hello, John. How are you feeling?'; (2) 'OK, not so bad'. We have no problem in guessing the probable context – casual meetings between people who know each other, but not very intimately. But see what happens if we add (3) 'Can you be a bit more precise?' Either we quickly switch our understanding to this being a doctor's surgery; or there is a strong sense of broken rules, invasion of privacy, excessive intimacy. There is a presumed set of rules, in other words. This much is commonplace to all discourse analysts. In the way Stubbs, for example, discusses it, it has few implications for power, or ideology.[5] This is because, I think, Stubbs has focused primarily on examples where we can't see the form. He has shown that there must be rules, but not tackled how they might arise.

According to Volosinov we need to investigate the rules of speech through their conflicting aspects: 'From what has been said, it follows that social psychology must be studied from two different viewpoints: first, from the viewpoint of content, i.e. the themes pertinent to it at this or that moment in time; and second, from the viewpoint of the forms and types of verbal communication in which the themes in question are implemented (i.e., discussed, expressed, questioned, pondered over, etc)' (p. 20). Though his terminology is not always consistent, Volosinov is indicating the areas of speech we need to study. 'Form' is the difficult one, and I will come to that later. First, 'theme'.

Themes. Another simple example. Compare: *We want a dog* and *We want the dog*. Fill in possible contexts (orient yourselves) in order to understand the referent of 'dog' and the force of 'want'. The first sounds like a pet-shop, perhaps; and that makes it easy to determine referent and force. The second is more tricky – which dog? Perhaps someone demanding the return of something stolen? Or offered a choice between a dog and a toaster, as prizes? Use your imagination. The point is that we are forced to orient ourselves quite differently, just because of the change from an indefinite ('a') to a definite article ('the'). Knowing (having ordinary competence in) the grammar of articles, we are able to orient ourselves to these two statements.

But now compare: *We want a vote* and *We want the vote*. Something more than the switch to an abstract noun has changed. Imagine a context for the first: a meeting, perhaps, and a demand that discussion ends – is someone trying to avoid a decision being made? But among the likely contexts for the second, are some very striking ones. 'We want the vote' is easily imagined as a slogan on a poster or banner. It is, perhaps, the suffragettes. But they were not demanding a specific vote; they were demanding the right to take part in a democratic process. In fact, this pair of examples seem if anything to have reversed the uses of definite and indefinite articles. This is because, on Volosinov's approach, the phrase 'the vote' has been *sedimented into grammar*. A long period of struggle in British history over the right to take part in elections was summarised into 'the vote', and the phrase was in effect seized for radical purposes – amending on the way the normal grammar of the definite article. This means for Volosinov that meanings are not given or fixed; they are 'an arena of class struggle'. This is because languages do not coincide with classes. They couldn't. The relation of employer to worker, of teacher to pupil, of warder to prisoner, of master to slave are all social relations; they have to be able to communicate.[6] But sharing a language does not mean agreeing on its uses. Think of the way the word 'suffragette' has been fought over. Originally, it was a term of belittlement. In the same way that feminine endings to words frequently diminish their objects ('major' vs 'majorette', 'leader' vs 'leaderene', 'mister' vs 'mistress') the word made mock of their demands. But their militancy and their success turned the word into one now associated with militancy and commitment. In Volosinov's terms, they had established a new 'theme'.

Speech genres. 'Themes', then, are meanings with social purposes attached to them that have been sedimented into talk. They are, to an extent, 'accepted'. But that acceptance is always shaky. Consider the idea, much argued over in the early 1980s, of 'secondary picketing'.[7] In Tory hands this was an implement (to be codified into legal talk) for distinguishing picketing that would be (just about) allowable from what was 'evidently' wrong. The choice of the pseudo-neutral 'secondary' obviously helped; had they said 'support picketing', the objection would not have been that obvious. 'Flying picket' would have had worryingly activist associations. But now imagine, say, a strike meeting of ferry workers looking for ways of winning support against sackings. If P & O get away with it, it will be a green light for the others. Obviously it is logical to call the others out, by picketing them out if necessary. In such a debate, the phrase 'secondary picketing' just would not naturally arise. It would have to be introduced from outside – by frightened officials, by the Press, or whomever – as a constraint on actions with another logic. Or, to put it in Volosinov's terms, there would be a struggle between a sedimented theme ('secondary picketing') and a formed speech genre (workers' strike meeting, debating 'how can we win our strike?'). In that clash, the meaning of 'secondary picketing' would be put severely at risk.

'Speech genres' are established ways of talking to each other. They have been formed from shared purposes; and they have rules, conventions, procedures for progress and so on that reflect those purposes. Volosinov has little to say about them, beyond that brief reference to 'little speech genres'. But his meaning can be worked out. Consider 'pub talk'. A prime feature of it is its relaxedness. There is, in fact, a clear difference between 'pub talk' (casual, 'purposeless') and talk that happens to take place in pubs (meetings over a pint, for example).

Think about the form of pub talk between relative strangers, and the way topics are considered 'safe'. We can begin with the weather, the state of the beer. Such talk is also the site where 'commonplaces' can be rehearsed. But what happens when such conversations take a turn to racism – say, in the form 'Well, you know what it is like with those blacks, don't you?' Given pub talk's defining rules of casualness and the commonplace, it is hard to respond by saying 'No, I don't know that', or 'Keep your racist ideas to yourself, will you?'. The difficulty is that you know you are breaking the rules of such talk. Even in the most loosely-organised, relaxed forms of interaction, there are rules with political content and implications. That is never to say they can't be challenged, or changed. But for the theme of race easily to enter the form of talk I am calling 'pub-talk', it has to have entered the commonplace, or 'commonsense'.[8]

Volosinov's approach would generalise an example like this to all other forms of communication. Hear how he relates the idea of a 'speech genre' to written materials:

> Dialogue, in the narrow sense of the word is, of course, only one of the forms – a very important one, to be sure, of verbal interaction. But dialogue can also be understood in a broader sense, meaning not only direct, face-to-face, vocalised verbal interaction between persons, but also verbal communication of any type whatsoever. A book, i.e. a *verbal performance in print*, is also an element of verbal communication. It is something discussable in actual, real-life dialogue, but aside from that, it is calculated for active perception, involving attentive reading and inner responsiveness, and for organised *printed* reaction in the various forms devised by the particular sphere of verbal communication in question (book reviews, critical surveys, defining influence on subsequent works, and so on). Moreover, a verbal performance of this kind also inevitably orients itself with respect to previous performances in the same sphere, both those by the same author and those by other authors ... Thus the printed verbal performance engages, as it were, in ideological colloquy of large scale: it responds to something, objects to something, affirms something, anticipates possible responses and objections, seeks support, and so on. (p. 95)

Books, newspapers, magazines, all written materials are also caught up within speech genres. And that would apply also to other forms of broadcast.

'Speech genre' is Volosinov's key term for linking our material and social lives with the way we talk to each other, and write to each other. Our social world is carved into hundreds of different settings (which of course overlap and conflict), each with its rules which guide how we orient ourselves to each other's speech or writing. How these are carved up is always changing, and is largely determined independently of language. The divisions are the outcome of the social, political and economic processes of our society. The fact that I can (crudely) depict a speech genre I call 'pub talk' is not innocent. It derives from the fact that our society at this time makes certain kinds of division of public and private, work and leisure, serious and non-serious; and marks out spaces and times for engaging typically in different kinds of interaction. It has not always been so. The pub in many places has been the place where news and ideas of particular communities were exchanged (and still is in some places). In the Chartist era, for example, it was the place where people would meet to hear the radical newspapers read.

The idea of the 'speech genre', therefore, is central to Volosinov's theory. It is his link between 'base' and 'superstructure'. But it avoids reductionism, because of the way language is rooted as practically organised responses to material situations. It is the starting point for my own retheorisation of media-influence.

Evaluative accent. Look again at the last sentence I just quoted, about writing and speech genres: 'Thus the printed verbal performance engages, as it were, in ideological colloquy of large scale: it responds to something, objects to something, affirms something, anticipates possible responses and objections, seeks support, and so on.' What do all those forms of communicating have in common – responding, objecting, affirming, anticipating, seeking support etc? They are, for Volosinov, forms of *indirect speech*. In indirect speech, we take hold of someone else's talk, and embed it within our own. In the process, inevitably, we say something about the status we are giving to what we are quoting. Consider: *The actress claimed the Bishop led her to believe that God had instructed him to do it this way.* Now that word 'claimed' would never be the actress' own. It is 'my' way of signalling that, whatever she said, a lingering doubt remains. Her 'claim' was that the Bishop 'led her to believe'; in phrasing it thus, she exonerates herself. Fault is apportioned. The Bishop, meanwhile (if we believe her account), felt 'instructed' – not 'advised' or 'suggested'. But of course these are not separate. In a sentence like this, the initial scepticism expressed in my 'claimed' conditions all subsequently embedded pieces of talk. In short, it proposes how they should be received. (If this seems too silly an example, try 'The National Coal Board today announced that 304 miners had gone back to work; the National Union of Miners disputed their figures, claiming that many more were joining the strike.')

What has all this to do with theorising ideology? It is a curious thing that in a book devoted to developing a new Marxist study of ideology, the only empirical case-study is on just this: indirect speech. This is, I believe, because indirect speech is for Volosinov that 'most sensitive index' of social change that he talked about. And it is that, because indirect speech codifies and reveals the forms of something which has to be present in every kind of speech: an 'evaluative accent'.

Whenever we speak or write, we take part in a speech genre. This means that we share in social situations which have a material and ideological history.

That history is acknowledged and embodied in the rules that structure success-ful communication in each situation. These are rules for the kinds of things that may be said, how they may be said, and the kinds of interest and attention (questioning, doubting, arguing, enjoying, responding) that the others in that situation will give to our contribution. They govern other things also: for exam-ple, who is the 'natural audience' for my communication. Some define this quite closely. Think what assumptions must be shared, for satire to work. Think how a political speech establishes common ground with an audience. Other situations define this much more loosely. My example of pub talk left it open to many people to enter that conversation – as long as they were prepared to adopt the 'relaxed' respondent role. In each case, we can ask: what views, what social circumstances, what gender, etc are assumed as the basis for orienting to and understanding the rules of a speech genre? Also, what are the boundaries of the speech genre? If I visit my doctor, and am told I ought to be getting some exercise, the doctor-patient speech-genre has rules (which I defy at my peril) which tell me to take this seriously, to examine my life-style, to adjust my self-image. I am supposed to turn this into *self-instructions*. The same advice, in a casual conversation, does not have the same force. How far outside the immediate contact between speaker and hearer (reader and writer), then, do the rules apply and orient the participants? And what is implied about how ideas, knowledge etc gained within that situation may be used outside? In communicating, then, we orient ourselves to the rules of that situation. Others, hearing us, orient themselves to our speech in the light of that history and its embodied rules.[9]

Every communication, then, already involves us in taking note of past talk and writing. In this sense, all communication contains indirect speech. To understand, we need to have some sense of the kinds of speech which would have preceded it, and to which it is oriented. Now there are many forms of communication where it is immediately evident how I am orienting myself to others' communication – because I tell you so. Compare:

The miners could have won their strike.
There were some who said that a compromise was inevitable. But the miners could have won their strike.
Some people in key positions sold the pass, saying that a compromise was inevitable. Therefore they didn't organise for all-out support. But for them, the miners could have won their strike.

Each of these orients my claim in relation to past arguments. But each is different in who is its implied audience, and what they are asked to do if they are persuaded. The first simply assumes the context of argument and its rules. Suppose it was my total interjection into a discussion. Either I was being delib-erately provocative, perhaps hoping to be asked to expand; or I was assuming you broadly agree, putting our shared thoughts into words. But it still only makes any sense if there have been disagreements over the miners' defeat. The second explicitly positions itself in relation to other views, but in a neutral, 'transparent' way. I don't say anything to fix the status of those I disagree with. The third does just that. It not only invites you both to disagree with them, it also asks you to see those others as to blame for what happened. In other words, in the third, I have attempted to orient you to the status of the speakers, and by implication offered an alternative orientation to my own views. And in the process, I have 'cut up' the social world into distinct groups: a 'we' and a 'they', and a relation between us. *My speech has offered a little model of our social world.*

In the third example, it is obvious how I have done it. But on Volosinov's approach, this is a feature of every communicative act. In speaking to you, I am not only trying to get you to orient to the meaning of my words. I am also trying to get your agreement to establish a certain social relation between us – and thus, by implication, reorganising your relationship with others. The clue to this, for Volosinov, lay in how I quote other people. And every time I orient myself and you as my hearer to previous talk, I qualify the 'themes' of that past talk by the evaluative accent I use.

An important implication flows from this. Volosinov argues that meaning is not fixed in words, but depends on how we orient ourselves to understand them. He states this as that: 'the meaning of a word is determined entirely by its context', and 'there are as many meanings of a word as there are contexts of its usage'. But that threatens to dump us in the trap of saying that the word itself is empty of meanings. How would we know we were even hearing the same word? His answer is interesting: 'At the same time, however, the word does not cease to be a single entity; it does not, so to speak, break apart into as many separate words as there are contexts of its usage. The word's unity is assured, of course, not only by the unity of its phonetic composition but also by that factor of unity which is common to all its meanings' (p. 80). The first part is easy. The sound or shape of the word remains steady (though this is something I may still have to learn – that, for example, a short Yorkshire 'bath' is the same word as my Southern-drawled 'baath'). But the second 'factor of unity' is quite different. This is its 'theme'. The theme, recall, is the sedimented meaning which has been accepted up to now. Its force as a theme is to guide us into certain ways of talking and thinking. Recall 'secondary picketing'. If accepted, it has several effects. It sets up a legalistic framework of thinking; it neutralises the political activities of picketing; and it divides 'primary' pickets from other workers.

Of course workers may reject that talk, and organise to defeat it both materially and ideologically. But it makes no difference of principle whether it is accepted or rejected. Either way, *the meaning of the words is put at risk every time it is uttered, in a new context.* Of course we inherit words; but to see that as determining meaning is like seeing the tools in a tool-box determining the use I make

of them next time. Yes, they come 'scarred' with previous uses. Successful
thematisations are sedimented in them. But language is not just a re-run of its
past. Every use transforms the word into a new theme, by making a new 'bridge'
to a new hearer.[10] The importance of this is that it points to a major difference
between a Volosinovian theory of ideology and all the others which I have
been criticising in this book.

The implication is that language and therefore ideology is always oriented
to the future. There is not therefore a distinct kind of speech, or discourse, or
communication called 'ideological'. It has no formal differences. It does not
signal a different kind of speech, or knowledge. It is not epistemologically
flawed, or damaged, or substandard. It does not work on us in a different way
from other talk. Therefore if we want a theory of ideology, and a theory of
power in communication (and hence in the media), it can only be formulated
out of the particular combinations of the elements in any language. These are:

1. *Themes* – the sedimented meanings from the past. These carry with them
their proposals for kinds of talk (speech genre), and social relationships;

2. *Speech genres* – the live associations of people with rules and conventions
for talking to each other. These are not simply phenomena of speech and
communication. They are the result of groups of people forming common
purposes within material social situations. Any talk within a speech genre inevitably refers, even if only implicitly, to past speech. It also inevitably draws on
past 'themes', however great or small their importance.

3. *Evaluative accent* – every act of speech not only draws on past themes and
refers to previous talk. It also comments on it, and thus inevitably puts it at
risk. Every new act of speech is a new proposal. For it to be understood, hearers
must newly orient themselves to it, laying down sets of answering words. The
evaluative accent guides us on how we should orient ourselves to the communication. It invites a certain kind of response.

4. *Power in communication*, therefore, has to be a particular unification of themes,
speech genre, and evaluative accent which is able to persuade a particular group
or groups to reorient themselves to become the 'natural audience' of this kind
of talk.

There are many mediating steps between this general approach to ideology,
and the study of comics. As a preliminary illustration of how it would work,
let me briefly return to the issue of racism. Earlier I argued that it was significant
that racist ideas could very easily turn up in the typically relaxed kinds of talk
of which 'pub talk' is one example. The significance, for me, lies in the particular
ways in which racism has been made into 'commonsense'. Effectively beginning with Enoch Powell's speeches in 1968, a new set of 'themes' about race
has been proposed. At one level, they offer concepts to make sense of disorganised experiences of contacts between people of different colours and ethnic
backgrounds: concepts like 'culture', 'way of life'. But Powell argued from this

base that different 'cultures' were incompatible, and that all kinds of explosive and destructive consequences would follow their mixing. Therefore it would be kinder all round to keep them separate.

But this is not the end of the matter. For we can now see that these were not transmitted purely as 'ideas'; they also carried suggestions for how 'we', the recipients, should orient ourselves. So, 'we' are British (even 'English'). As such, it is 'only natural' that we should be upset – and the very fact that we are uneasy/unhappy/angry in our reactions to immigration etc is proof that we are responding as 'members of the British way of life'. In short, such a way of talking not only gives particular arguments; it gives them to us with an invitation that we should respond emotionally; and it validates our 'immediate, common-sense reactions' as 'only natural'. They are the kinds of response which any ordinary British person would have. Not surprising, then, that such a topic should be seen so readily as one for the pub. On a Volosinovian approach, the power of Powellite ideas lay in their simultaneously offering 'themes' which bound together and 'made sense of' a great many experiences, together with proposing that our response to such ideas should be at the level of 'common-sense' and 'gut reactions'. Powell forged a unity of themes and evaluative accents. This made it able to penetrate many live speech genres. I believe this theorisation of power in speech is significantly different from other attempts to understand a phenomenon such as racism.

Volosinov and stories

I set myself the task in this book of reviewing theories of ideology, by looking at how they had looked at comics. Comics, of course, are just one kind of mass medium with particular kinds of stories. Inevitably, there must be mediating steps if Volosinov's general theory is to be applied to comics. Begin, then, by thinking how on his approach we might look at stories.[11]

There is something quite special about story-telling, on a Volosinovian approach. All acts of communication involve proposals. But a fictional story's proposal has two distinctive features. First, the proposal is in the form 'What if. . .'. It invites imaginative projection. A world is offered whose relation to our own lived world is problematic. Second, stories embody change and development. The commonplace that stories move from beginning to end turns out not to be so commonplace. To read a story, therefore, is to agree to orient oneself to its imaginative progression. It is to follow its proposal for kinds of sequence, unfolding, and resolution.

Stories take place within established speech-genres. These are speech genres of many different and overlapping kinds. Children learn, while young, that there are many kinds of stories: moral fables that they are supposed to 'take to heart'; relaxing stories, told for the pleasure of the listening; adventurous stories, showing them their possible futures; and so on. Then there are stories coming via different channels: books (beloved of teachers – and thus accented by that); television (with its distinctions between stories for them, and for adults); comics, watched a little uncertainly but nostalgically by parents; and so on. There are stories asking different skills and kinds of attention of them: some deliberately leave them uncertain, not quite sure what is happening; others give them a secure knowledge of what is going on, and what will happen. This is a tiny sample of the kinds of story any child learns to distinguish. It is impossible, in the light of all these cross-cutting distinctions, that any child should meet a story and orient to it in a singular way.

But every time they meet a new story, they meet something unique, which puts at risk all past orientations. Each new story read makes a proposal to its readers. This proposal is a result both of the themes it embodies, and of the evaluative accent its expresses. In stories, this is our sense of the narrator and the kind of invitation s/he extends. Readers therefore receive the story within those existing conventions, rules, and expectations. Their relation to the story is like dialogue. They have an answering role. The story offers not only a model of a 'what if . . .' world, but with it a proposal how readers should approach that world.

Finally, every story carries its readers through a process. Events unfold, and the readers' relation to those events also unfolds. In creating an imaginary world, the story therefore also creates laws for that world, processes of change, problems, attractions. To be comprehensible at all to a reader, they have to have a logic. (Even apparent absence of logic can be a logic – it is called 'magic'. But magic that could do *anything* would make no stories.) And they have to have a logic to which particular groups of readers are capable of orienting themselves.

A great deal of the complexity of understanding stories seems to me to derive from the last point. Given that they are imaginary projections, it is not easy to know how to investigate how particular kinds of stories might relate to the preoccupations and orientations of particular groups. This is where I feel that Vladimir Propp ought to make his second entrance.

The return of Vladimir Propp

Volosinov's (or Bakhtin's) literary interests led him to look at the rather conscious devices of literature. Propp offers us the other side of the coin: a theory and a method for looking at non-self-conscious fictional forms. On my interpretation (outlined in Chapter 6) Propp was trying to grasp the 'form' of stories in a way remarkably resembling Volosinov. For him as for Volosinov, to find a form is not to find a powerful structure. It is to find a sedimented social relation. We might put it like this. To Propp, folk-tales were themes which so successfully embodied the typical imaginative projections of their 'natural audience' that they became a speech genre in their own right. In studying folk-tales, Propp was exploring the *typified imaginative projections of peasants.* What has always so excited me is the way Propp did this. He does not first go and study the ethnographic evidence about their sources, and then deduce what role folk-tales must play. He is able to study the stories first, and deduce from their structure and transformations the typified social relations which are sedimented in them.

Propp stopped, of course, once he had depicted the form of his stories. Having revealed the pattern, he did not go on to ask what it signified. That pause (and the silencing of further thoughts by Stalin) left the field clear for the structuralists to bend his ideas to quite other purposes. I am not looking at the same forms as Propp. But the method, properly understood, remains the same. I am suggesting that we should see Vladimir Propp's work as the start of an application of the dialogic approach to cultural forms. What are the fundamental principles as I have been using them in this book?

1. *Form in a cultural object is to understood as proposal to a typified kind of imaginative projection.*

2. *Any such form sediments within itself some typified social experience. This means that it has a typified readership, and relates to a determinable aspect of their lives.*

3. *All forms are produced out of determinate production histories. These histories summarise the interactions of producers (their purposes, institutional structures, external constraints, relations with creators, writers, artists etc), their audiences (traditions of reading, definitions of the medium, etc) through which the form is produced and reproduced.*

4. *In investigating the form, therefore, we need to investigate, as Propp did, regularities of transformation; and the ways in which such regularities constrain what actual characters, settings, problems, etc can appear, and how they can behave. It will also mean investigating the kind of proposal for an answering role (how readers should orient themselves to the form) offered in the cultural object's whole presentational process.*

5. *To study readers, we have to begin by identifying the characteristics of a form's 'natural audience'. This requires investigation of both the social characteristics of the audience, and the form of the cultural object, in order to determine the interaction between them engendered by the object's form, and its proposal to readers. We have to discover both who are likely to be willing and able to orient themselves to the dialogue proposed, and what transformations they are thereby involved in.*

6. *Responses other than those of the 'natural' readers themselves represent socially-typified orientations. They should be seen as (not misreadings, but) rejections or avoidances of the proposed dialogic relationship, from other social positions.*

How, in practice, have my own investigations used these approaches?

(A) My argument about the juvenile comics was that they propose a relationship to children, and offer an imaginative conversation with them about 'childhood'. In other words they address that aspect of their readers' lives in which they meet, in typified form, adult authority. The stories' form contains definite transformations. With these, a child can 'play' at challenging adult authority in a way that acknowledges that s/he cannot defeat it. But even in victory, adult authority is subverted; it can only win by the use of the absurd forms of children's fantasy-resistance.

Scream Inn is a compromising version of this. Although it obeys the same general form and rules, it deals with the adult/child clash tangentially. This arises from the differences in the production histories of D C Thomson and IPC. IPC, more conscious of itself as a 'public company', has accepted constraints on its comics which Thomson, being more closed and paternalistic, has not. By an irony, conservative Thomsons can better embody the form of this subversive 'game' with children, because they are so rigid and Victorian.[12]

For all the compromises, the readers of Scream Inn still reveal (in the little bits of evidence I got at) that their relationship to the strip fits my account. Peak-reading is at the point when the clash between adult constraints in the name of 'childhood', and their own aspirations are at their height; girls' reading of it peaks more decisively and for a shorter period, as we would expect, given their earlier move into adolescence. Their preferences for contestants are for the kinds who normally appear, in more uninhibited form, in other comic strips embodying the conflict. This is for them a separable world but one that parallels their own; and characters are able to move across stories within this world, always subject (of course) to its rules.

'Form', then, in Scream Inn is a game of transformations, which we can investigate using this combination of the dialogic and Proppian approaches. These comics, interestingly, virtually refuse any separable presentational process. It is only through the strips themselves that a relationship with readers is established.

(B) Action was produced out of a rather accidental production history, which made its achievement very vulnerable and uncertain. A brief lifting of barriers was made possible by falls in sales, and the need to shatter a unresponsive institutional production set-up of writers, editors etc. Once given the chance, Mills set in train a new way of relating to readers which we are still living in.

The attack on Action was not simply a matter of moral concerns, but the rejection of its political melodramas. Under the guise of attacking 'violence', other 'themes' (childhood, trust of authority, reactions to punk and adolescent rebellion) were being debated. The stories in Action embodied unresolvable dilemmas, therefore in a sense failures of transformations. Their closeness to other contemporary cultural forms (Jaws, Rollerball, Dirty Harry, etc) links with their deliberate 'grottiness' in constraining the kinds of characters who can enter and participate. A dialogue was thus created which made it possible for those close to the 'punk generation' to look on the comic as their 'friend'. And the differences in my readers' questionnaires between the committed and the uncommitted readers bore this out.

(C) *Jackie* stories, I have shown, embody transformations which are the clue to their nature, and to the nature of their 'typical readers'. The stories are formed around a series of questions to which answers in words cannot be given: what is 'true love' like, and how can I recognise it, what must I do to achieve it, and so on? I have not been able to study *Jackie* readers directly. But it would follow from what I have found that the first step must be to identify the characteristics of its 'natural readers', that is, those whose typified life-experience makes them most able to becomes its implied audience.

For most of its history, *Jackie* did not offer a single orientation to its readers. It split its proposal to readers into distinct areas, each with its own kind of knowledge and interaction, and resulting transformations. The only link between them operated at the quite abstract level of 'general interest in self-knowledge'. The problem pages either gave pragmatic 'commonsense' answers; or they invited self-examination and self-criticism. This linked, generally, with the stories' implicit answering questions about girls' evaluation of their emotions and desires. The disappearance of that gap between stories and problem pages signifies, I feel, a loss of projection. Crudely, *Jackie* is now much less able to discuss futures with its readers. I think that is a pity.

(D) *Bunty* and *Tracy*, on my approach, are (melodramatised) versions of working class girls' oppressive class experience, compromised by the constraints placed on them by their production history. In their most common form, in fact, the stories end by magically resolving girls' suffering away. But this is not a genuine transformation of the stories. It is either a full stop superimposed on a story which has no energy to go any further; or it is attached, at the cost of the reader being more knowing than the heroine, who thus only becomes an object-lesson in the need to understand who is being horrible to you. But there is at least a crumb of evidence that the 'natural readers' of these comics would choose, if such were provided, unsullied melodramas with no salvation at the end.

(E) The concepts of 'identification' and 'stereotype', I have argued, are not so much tools of analysis as sedimented social concerns. They disguisedly express themselves as claims about the comics. They are arguments from definable social positions, not methods of cultural analysis. There is, too, in each case even a production history of these ideas, which we need to explain how each came to sediment its 'themes'. Therefore I would want to claim that my discussion of these concepts is not so separate from the discussions of comics as might at first appear.

You now have, as formally laid-out as I can manage, the theory of ideology which underpins the book. I want now to test it openly, by using it directly in a last case-study. It will be a test of its investigative and explanatory power to see what it can say about the controversy that has surrounded the Disney comics, and in particular the weighty argument by Dorfman and Mattelart that the Disney comics represent a form of 'cultural imperialism'.

Deconstructing Donald

Of all analyses of comics, perhaps the most important is Dorfman and Mattelart's study of the Disney comics.[1] Written at the height of Chile's attempts to break free of United States domination, before the US-backed bloody military overthrow of Salvador Allende's socialist government, their book is a damning indictment of Disney as a prime carrier of 'cultural imperialism'. It is well-researched, and well-argued. And not surprisingly, it is often cited as a paradigm of Marxist cultural analysis. I want to use their study of Disney as a test-case for my own approach.

Donald and Uncle Scrooge: colonialists unlimited

Dorfman and Mattelart's argument is multi-faceted. Modern imperialism, they argue, needs not only economic and political power. It also depends on power over people's minds. American capitalism has to persuade the peoples it dominates that the 'American way of life' is what they want, American superiority is natural and in everyone's best interest. This is not a new argument. They begin to differ from other approaches in suggesting that the most effective form for achieving this is the most innocent. Turn your attention from the horror comics or the war comics – look instead at the forms that come girded around with guarantees like 'harmless fun', 'innocent amusement' or 'suitable for children'. There can be no more effective form for propaganda than wholesomenesss. If anyone attacking it can be branded 'anti-children', you have the perfect device. This is Disney, to the T.

In American capitalism's self-image, the 'child' plays a central role. Into the 'child' are projected all the dreams of innocence adults want for themselves. Comics for children embody those dreams:

> Children's comics are devised by adults, whose work is determined and justified by their idea of what a child is or should be . . . (T)he comics show the child as a miniature adult, enjoying an idealised, gilded infancy which is really nothing but the adult projection of some magic era beyond the reach of the harsh discord of daily life . . . Juvenile literature, embodying purity, spontenaity, and natural virtue, while lacking in sex and violence, represents earthly paradise. It guarantees man's own redemption as an adult: as long as there are children, he will have the pretext and means for self-gratification with the spectacle of his own dreams . . . Regaling himself with his own legend, he admires himself in the mirror, thinking it to be a window. But the child playing there in the garden is the purified adult

looking back at himself (p. 30).[2]

The point, to Dorfman and Mattelart, is that these ideas are not simply sad bits of a sick culture. The 'children' grow up within those definitions, find their lives surrounded by them: 'children have been conditioned by the magazines and the culture which spawned them'. In a world which rewards conformity to its 'natural' images, the children learn quickly. 'Considered, by definition, unfit to choose from the alternatives available to adults, the youngsters intuit 'natural' behaviour, happily accepting that their imagination be channeled into incontestable ethical and aesthetic ideals. Juvenile literature is justified by the children it has generated through a vicious circle' (ibid).

Children's literature thus becomes the prime centre for the ideology of American capitalism. It took general shape long before Walt Disney universalised its dreams of innocence. 'Good' children's literature makes childhood a self-enclosed world. Parents will keep discreetly out of the way. But like a garden pruned to make it safe, the only things allowed will be those which the adults see as good for the children. 'The imagination of the child is conceived as the past and future utopia of the adult' (p. 31). And the power of such dreams is enhanced when it takes the form of mass culture. Hence Disney's comics, distributed in their millions in every country where American business interests need a culture to match, are in the perfect position to sell a paternalistic ideology.

The Disney comics were first produced in the late 1930s as reprints of the newspaper strips which carried the increasingly-famous names of their characters. However within a short time, they had run out of strips to reprint and began to commission new work. As this new work found its feet in its format, new characters were added to the Disney lexicon: Uncle Scrooge, the Beagle Boys, Magica da Spell and Gladstone Gander (he of the never-ending luck) and so on. Within a short period, they became immensely popular; and foreign translation editions, usually produced by franchised firms overseas, multiplied their sales. The comics are still being produced today, although the scale of the operation has diminished and many are now reprints of earlier work. The new material is grossly inferior to the heyday of their production.

Dorfman and Mattelart note the curious absence of parents in Disney. No fathers and mothers, only uncles and nephews. In this way, the children's world is kept free of the taint of sexual production. To help this desexualisation, people take the form of animals. Animals, of course, are closer to 'nature'. But it is more than this:

> The use of animals is not in itself either good or bad, it is the use to which they are put, it is the kind of being they incarnate that should be scrutinised. Disney uses animals to trap children. The language he employs is nothing less than a form of manipulation. He invites children into a world that appears to offer free-

dom of movement and creation, into which they enter fearlessly, identifying with creatures as affectionate, trustful and irresponsible as themselves, of whom no betrayal is to be expected, and with whom they can safely play and mingle. Then, once the little readers are caught within the pages of the comic, the doors close behind them. The animals become transformed, under the same zoological form and the same smiling mask, into monstrous human beings. (p. 41)

To be influential, the comics must combine two features. They must speak to some part of their readers' lives. Then, they must effect a transformation, via their story-structure. Thus, all the stories start somewhere very ordinary. At home, at school: somewhere instantly recognisable, typically with Donald and the three nephews (Huey, Dewey and Louie) doing ordinary things, enjoying childish pleasures. Then Uncle Scrooge proposes an adventure. They go off to solve a mystery, to seek out wealth, to find fame and fortune. But their adventures take peculiar forms, and are governed by distinct themes:

1. That absence of parents means that Scrooge, appearing in the guise of an uncle, can behave like the worst kind of employer. Consider 'The Hunka Junka', a story beginning (unusually) with Donald and nephews just back from searching for a rare coin for Scrooge. His only reward is to send them forth again to get the rarest of all coins, the Hunka-Junka from a South Sea island, of which there is only one. After desperate adventures, in which they are nearly killed, they bring back the monstrous coin – it is a huge circle of rock with a hole in it – only to find it is a fake. Does Scrooge reward them for their efforts? Not a bit of it. He orders them to take it back, and get back his money.

Under the guise of a near-natural relationship, Scrooge gets all the power of a parent with none of his affections or responsibilities. He contracts their labour at slave-prices, but can't be challenged because he is their uncle.

2. Just as parents and thus sexual production are absent, so are work and material production. In story after story wealth is just lying around without an owner. Consider 'The Great Rainbow Race', in which Donald and nephews are sent to find the crock of gold at the end of the rainbow (which Scrooge hears is somewhere in Arabia). The evil Magica da Spell overhears. She disguises herself as the stewardess on their plane, sabotaging it and prachuting out. Donald & Co. crawl out of the wreck and make it, parched, to the nearest town – only to discover to their horror that there is no lemonade to drink – it is too expensive. Magica reappears, and the race for the rainbow recommences. To beat them she summons up a storm, then dives headfirst into its rainbow – landing headfirst in a muddy puddle. Furious, she stomps off. Now Scrooge, being scroogish, had economised on the trip by loading their plane with a delivery of special seeds. These had spilled everywhere in the crash; and Magica's storm made them all shoot up in minutes. Now Scrooge arrives and they gather the fruit, to make that missing lemonade – and go home, rich.

No work, no effort, no ownership. Simply, 'by magic', wealth springs out of empty land. And of course the country they are in gets the 'advantages' of lemonade as well (hard to believe it wasn't Coca-Cola).

3. With no work and production, there is no need for workers. Although Donald does in various stories try to get a job (and usually fails), the only way the working class appears, say Dorfman and Mattelart, is as the Beagle Boys. These are the stupid, incompetent criminals, known only by their prison numbers. Always trying to steal Scrooge's wealth, they are the source of many of his anxieties, and make him work ever harder to protect his fantasticatrillions. ('I am satisfied. Donald has at last recognised that the life of millionaires is no bed of roses', he says at one point.[3]) Scrooge's inevitable victory over them represents, say Dorfman and Mattelart, the victory of mental over manual labour.

4. Change is to be laughed at, but revolutionary change is to be feared. In 'The Lemonade Fling', for example, Scrooge has decided to test the honesty of Huey, Dewey and Louie. He has invested in a lemonade stall which they will run, selling drinks to passers-by. So they can't cheat him, he disguises himself as a customer and sits at the stall. Donald meanwhile is sent to tout for business, using some of Scrooge's money as enticement. So, a disorganised march comes past, with placards for 'Peace' and 'Love'. 'Hey, people, throw down your banners and have free lemonades.' With an appeal like that, they can't refuse. All thought of the protest march vanishes, and they rush to the stall. . .

Revolutionary change is a different problem altogether. Disney ran stories about both Cuba (named 'Brutopia' in Disney, but there is no doubt where it is) and Vietnam ('Unsteadystan'). In 'The Treasure of Marco Polo' Scrooge has gone to Vietnam after a jade elephant he bought vanishes, leaving only its tail (with a secret treasure map in it) and an escaped peasant Soy Bheen, who agrees to help him. They find the country under the thumb of a murderous leader of a 'workers' paradise' Wahn Beeg Rhat who does things like ordering his miserable soldiers to shoot Donald with the words: 'Shoot him, don't let him spoil my revolution'. In the end, the rightful ruler of Unsteadystan is proved to be Soy Bheen, who is revealed as Prince Char Ming. He proves himself by appearing 'magically' out of the jade elephant, and all the people welcome him back, turning their cannon on Rhat: 'We suddenly think it'd be nice for Unsteadystan to have a King again – like in the good old days!'

In these ways, power is associated with (childlike) symbols, and change is associated with danger. All people really want is a simple life which of course in no way interferes with Scrooge roaming the world pillaging their wealth for his 'collection'.

5. Which brings us to what is perhaps the most important element in their analysis. Disney writes stories for children. And he writes about children, in the form of Donald and nephews. But also, his vision of Third World peoples

is as children. There are, in fact, two kinds of children. There are Scrooge's relatives, who are learning from Scrooge how to be adult (and that means becoming rich!). There are also the 'children' out there, simple, naive, who don't really want the wealth that is lying around their country. They don't even know its value. So there is no difference, really, between animals, aliens and Third World peoples; they are all there for the taking. Scrooge can go to Tibet and trick the abominable snowman out of fabulous wealth (in 'The Lost Crown of Genghis Khan'). He can justify exchanging a box of dirt for a whole moon made of gold (in 'The Twenty-Four Carat Moon') on the grounds that the Venusian owner of the moon even got the better of the deal; he's 'happier' with his dirt, with which he can create a simple paradise than Scrooge is with his gold. And he can swap Arabian jewels for a bottle of detergent; Donald and Co. blow bubbles which astonish the tribal chief: 'It's real magic! My people are laughing like children' (cited, p. 51 – I do not know the reference for this story).

> But how can this flagrant despoliation pass unperceived, or in other words, how can this inequity be disguised as equity? Why is it that imperialist plunder and colonial subjection, to call them by their proper names, do not appear as such?
> "We have jewels, but they are of no use to us."
> There they are in their desert tents, their caves, their once flourishing cities, their lonely islands, their forbidden fortresses, and they can never leave them. Congealed in their past-historic, their needs defined in function of this past, these underdeveloped peoples are denied the right to build their own future. Their crowns, their raw materials, their soil, their energy, their jade elephants, their fruit, but above all, their gold, can never be turned to any use. For them the progress which comes from abroad in the form of multiplicity of technological artefacts, is a mere toy. It will never penetrate the crystallised defence of the noble savage, who is forbidden to become civilised. He will never be able to join the Club of the Producers, because he does not even understand that these objects have been produced. He sees them as magic elements, arising from the foreigner's mind, from his word, his magic wand.
> Since the noble savage is denied the prospect of future development, plunder never appears as such, for it only eliminates that which is trifling, superfluous, and dispensable. Unbridled capitalist despoliation is programmed with smiles and coquetry. Poor natives. How naive they are. And since they cannot use their gold, it is better to remove it. It can be used elsewhere. (p. 51-2)

These are just snippets of the themes Dorfman and Mattelart detect. Within the sixty or more comics they cite, they uncover a whole network of attitudes to women, the environment, to status and self-image, and to history. Written at the height of Chile's confrontation with America, their book is not a dispassionate analysis. It is a brilliant polemic, but one using a theory to display the comics' message and power.

Making mock of money?

Let me point up some difficulties, by contrasting Dorfman and Mattelart's interpretation with others' on the question of wealth. There is no question, sheer wealth-acquisition is a dominant theme. But what attitude to wealth is being promulgated? Uncle Scrooge is obsessed with it. His giant Money Bin is always bursting at the seams. He takes a sensuous pleasure in it. He can dive into it and swim in it like a porpoise. More than anything else, money motivates adventures. But what convinces Dorfman and Mattelart that wealth in the stories amounts to concealed imperialist plunder is the very form it takes. It is gold: inactive, stored, abstract wealth. It doesn't take work to produce: it is found, it rains from the sky, is dug up, appears 'by magic'. Scrooge is also obsessed in a dozen stories with his 'first dime'. This dime, the first he earned by his own labour, is the talisman enabling him to make more. It is the historical precedent for all subsequent accumulation. He is the 'only truly passionate being' in the world because only to him does wealth matter, for its own sake:

> Here is the basic myth of social mobility in the capitalist system. The self-made man. Equality of opportunity. Absolute democracy. Each child starting from zero and getting what he deserves. Donald is always missing the next rung on the ladder to success. Everyone is born with the same chance of vertical ascent by means of competition and work . . . Scrooge has no advantage over the reader in terms of money, because this money is of no use, indeed, it is more of a liability, like a blind or cripped child. It is an incentive, a goal, but never, once it has been attained, does it determine the next adventure. So there is really no history in these comics, for gold forgotten from the preceding episode cannot be used in the following one. If it could, it would connote a past with influence over the present, and reveal capital and the whole process of accumulation of surplus value as the explanation of Uncle Scrooge's fortune. In these circumstances, the reader could never empathise with him beyond the first episode. And what's more, they are all the first and last episode. They can be read in any order, and are 'timeless': one written in 1950 can be published without any trouble in 1970. (p. 79)

This pinpoints a problem. Their account of the significance of wealth is got by a dangerous move: they theorise significance from what is absent. They jump from noting an absence to claiming an exclusion, as in the following:

no continuity between episodes = absence/denial/hiding of history
no mothers and fathers = absence/denial/hiding of sexuality
no work = absence/denial/hiding of production
no spending of wealth = absence/denial/hiding of capitalist accumulation

Here is a sample of these assumptions at work: 'The pathetic, sentimental solitude of Scrooge is a screen for the class to which he so obviously belongs.

The millionaires reduce themselves by *making themselves appear* as a random, rootless miscellany with no community of interests, and no sense of solidarity, obeying only 'natural' law, as long as this respects the property of others. The story of one eccentric *glosses over* the fact that he is a member of a class, and, moreover, a class which has seized control of social existence' (p. 79, my emphases). Using exactly the same information, other commentators on Disney reach an opposite conclusion. In their history of the American comic book, Reitberger and Fuchs make Scrooge into a form of self-mockery:

> A special fascination attaches to the Uncle Scrooge stories, because Scrooge himself leads Donald and his young nephews, Huey, Dewey and Louie, in a fantastic search for hidden treasure. Their adventures take them to the far corners of the earth, and wherever Uncle Scrooge seeks he finds new riches; whether on the trail of the Ponce de Leon, or discovering El Dorado, Ophir or the mythical Sesven Cities of Cibola, Scrooge never seeks in vain. He finds Montezuma's hoard, King Solomon's Treasure, and the philosopher's stone. In this way Uncle Scrooge and his intrepid followers re-live practically every myth and legend. Robert Louis Stevenson and Enid Blyton mingle happily with the Disney touch and to top it all, every known adventure cliché ever used to dazzle the public is carefully caricatured.
>
> The 'from rags to riches' philosophy and the glorification of free enterprise are combined in Uncle Scrooge, who once stood penniless on the gold fields of the Klondike and, steeled in this hardest of all social Darwinistic schools, can now detect the smell of gold or money from miles away. The hoarding of Scrooge's fantasticatrillions in an enormous 'money silo' runs contrary to the most elementary principles of capitalist investment policy. Why then this mountain of gold? Because Uncle Scrooge loves to plunge into it like a porpoise into water, because he likes to burrow through the coins like a gopher, tossing them high up into the air and letting them hit him on his bald pate like beneficent rain.
>
> This is rampant money-fetishism, an apotheosis of Mammon – it is making fun of wealth in an absurd and at the same time most fetching way.[4]

Another interpreter went one better, finding a closet critique of capitalism in the Disney comics. Dave Wagner[5] illustrated his case with one story 'The Land Beneath The Ground'. This is the story of the Terries and the Fermies, two strange races who, unknown to us, live miles under the earth. They gather once a year to hold a contest. This involves rolling as hard as they can at the pillars which support the world above - hence, earthquakes. Scrooge, worried about the safety of his Money Bin, has sent his nephews down to investigate. Donald is forced into a contest with their best roller and, of course, loses. He escapes with their trophy – an ancient Greek vase which had fallen down a hole centuries before. The Terries and Fermies are so furious they cause a massive earthquake which splits the Bin, and its contents pour down the mine-shaft. But the little creatures are insulted. They have listened to radio programmes which give away money, so they think it worthless. They hurl it back and seal up the hole.

Wagner reads this story as a critique of capitalism. The Terries and Fermies only want to have fun – theirs is a good life, without money. Donald didn't want to compete with the Terry – he only did so because his own home was threatened. But he knew what Scrooge was up to. Then (and this is said as if in the voice of Donald):

> There is a larger unity, though, that has to do with the continuity of our characters from comic to comic. The rubber balls didn't need cash because all they wanted to do was bounce around. Scrooge, as Barks consistently cast him, was actually the same way with his money. All he wanted to do was swim around in it; it was no more an abstraction for him than bouncing was for the Terries, though for the moment in this story he is the butt of the lesson. Barks' characterisation of Scrooge, for that matter, was one of his finest accomplishments. Where I was supposed to play a typically American figure (too individualistic to hold a job for long – which gave us a certain narrative flexibility; always caught in the moral conflict between get-rich-quick schemes and my social responsibility – which pointedly win out in the end), Scrooge was more deliberately balanced as a deeply ambivalent figure.
>
> Above all, he represented a biting parody of the bourgeois entrepreneur in the competitive stage of capitalism . . . Scrooge's personality is . . . torn – between the logic of capital and the ridiculous fetish it creates in him for money form. If he keeps his capital in the money form, he won't be able to expand, and all will be lost, But if he invests he will be deprived of his only source of delight, which is to swim and bathe in piles of the stuff. It's a nicely preposterous contradiction, the source of all Scrooge's endless anxieties. Needless to say, Scrooge is not broken by this state of affairs, or the comedy would be lost. (pp. 9-10)

Finally, Mike Barrier interprets it another way again. He makes the important point that each of the main characters embodies a different attitude to life (Scrooge, money at all costs; Gladstone Gander, an easy life at all costs; Donald, a respectable, lazy life; and the nephews, commonsense and practicality). But Barrier argues that the stories transcend their starting points. Commenting on these kinds of ideological analysis, he says:

> (T)his sort of analysis can be carried too far; Scrooge and Gladstone were much more than ideas with feathers. It was as natural for Carl Barks, in mid-twentieth century America, to write and illustrate stories about money as it was for a Renaissance painter to depict the Madonna and Child. Good artists work with what is around them, but they are not limited by it. Barks used the American preoccupations with wealth and idleness and work; he wasn't imprisonned by them . . . What matters is that he brought them to life in characters who were solid flesh and blood. His real subject-matter was not money, but the ways in which human beings deceive and destroy themselves - and how funny they can be when they

do it. Scrooge's wealth and Gladstone's luck were only stepping stones to that larger theme.[6]

The same information, interpretable four different ways.

'. . . or the comedy would be lost'

These disagreements seem to turn on the role of the humour in the stories. (1) For Dorfman and Mattelart, the humour is a mask, a device for innocenting what would otherwise be open imperialism. Except that their behaviour seems like silly antics, we would have to treat it as vicious exploitation. (2) For Reitberger and Fuchs, the humour is a modification of the message. Capitalist exploitation is mocked by being made absurd. (3) For Wagner it is a way of keeping the butt of our attacks 'alive'. If we were not able to laugh at Scrooge, he could not survive to be the object of our derision. (4) And for Barrier, the humour is a parable of human absurdity. It provides the bridge between the particulars of Scrooge and the larger themes of human obsessions, imaginatively brought to life by these funny stories. How could we ever decide between these three interpretations? They each appeal to exactly the same evidence from the stories.

Little has been written about humour and ideology. What there is tends to be about specific forms of humour, such as jokes[7] or situation comedy as a television form.[8] Behind these stand grand theories of humour such as Freud's, or Koestler's.[9] I have not found this much help in tackling Disney. What is needed is a way of distinguishing the role of humour in particular situations. Let's approach this by a careful comparison of two stories, which Dorfman and Mattelart discuss. First, 'The Lemonade Fling'. This was the story of Scrooge testing his nephews' honesty by funding the lemonade stall. He himself dons a beard as disguise and sits at the counter, checking them. But with the stall getting so busy, Scrooge has to keep buying drinks to keep his seat. Every time he tries to signal to Donald to slow down, the nephews think he wants another drink; and he is getting very fizzed up. Finally, he staggers away. Next day he meets them to check their takings – and finds they have sixpence too much. He is about to round on them for carelessness or dishonesty when they tell him how it happened. This strange man in a beard kept drinking more and more, and at the end looked so ill that he left without collecting his change! Collapse of Unca Scrooge . . .

Dorfman and Mattelart cited the story for its implicit ridicule of the demonstrators. But in the story as a whole, that is a side-show. It would have been possible to delete that part (and its counterpart – the other group Donald attracts is a parading cadets' militia), and the main narrative could have continued. That concerned Scrooge, and how his own obsessive distrust makes him ridiculous. Not in his nephews' eyes, since they don't understand what has gone on; in our eyes, rather. He has set in motion the mechanisms to make himself absurd. This is accentuated by the fact that it is Scrooge's thoughts we follow; we see his fizzed-up angst in the thought-balloons. In other words we watch the progress to destruction of his attempts to be clever.

Compare, then 'The Treasure of Marco Polo', about Vietnam. This story, already briefly outlined, is very different. Scrooge and all go to 'Unsteadystan' with Soy Bheen. But the moment they land, the story ceases to be their adventure. Their plane is shot to pieces. They attempt to leave by boat, and it sinks under them. This is all done humorously - the captain is seen sinking under the waves at an acute angle, with one hand Napoleon-style in his uniform. But it is a different kind of humour. Thus trapped in the country, they decide to seek the treasure. But Soy Bheen manoeuvres Scrooge into play-acting as the lost prince Char Ming, and then tips off the rebel guards (called the 'Rhat Brats'). Scrooge is captured. When the nephews interfere, they only make matters worse – they get captured, and have to be rescued by Soy Bheen. After a long interlude in which things are just getting worse and worse for Scrooge and Donald, they are led out to be shot by the 'Eraser Squad'. In the nick of time, Soy Bheen gets inside the hollow jade elephant, starts its secret mechanism and reveals himself as the true Prince Char Ming. Immediately, the Eraser Squad turn their cannon on Wahn Beeg Rhat, and all is well. Now Scrooge acts quite out of character. Declaring he has lost his taste for treasure, he tells Char Ming: 'I'm giving this hoard and the elephant to Unsteadystan, and when I get back to Duckburg I'll do even more – I'll return that million-dollar jade elephant tail!' Ah yes, adds one of the nephews, 'The tired and hungry people can sure use that wealth!'

What are the differences? The Vietnam story is characterised by chaos. Scrooge and Co. are not in control at all. In fact, they hardly do anything, after the start of the story. And the moment they stop doing, it turns from adventure into near-horror. It is grim enough to make Scrooge act right out of character, giving wealth away. If in 'The Lemonade Fling' the humour is a function of Scrooge's obsessions driving him to self-destruction, in the Vietnam story it is gruesome and bewildering because things are out of his control. What does the difference signify? In the first story, Scrooge's obsession is money. In the second, the force that halts the one obsession is another: power. I want to suggest that these two opposed forces broadly organise the Disney stories. The above stories show the two ends of a possible spectrum. At one extreme, money-obsession is absurd and rebounds on its embodiment. But it embraces a world of 'normal activities'. At the other extreme, where power operates, there is no normal life. In short, I would suggest that the Disney comics do readily consort with capitalism. But they are less easy about power. Business is as usual; it is a normal part of life. Ridiculous, yes, but understandable. And if the natives don't want their things, take 'em away. But if they start playing politics, beware – we've run out of innocence.

The politics of Uncle Walt

There are a number of biographies of Walt Disney, most of them pretty uncritical. Only one – by Richard Schickel – attempts to find the real Walt Disney amid the myths, but understands the importance of those myths themselves.[10] But it is also remarkable that the 'official' biography of Walt Disney doesn't mention the comics once, in its entire 392 pages. The nearest it gets is to note that Disney quickly lost interest in their precursors, the newspaper strips.[11] This is in stark contrast to his obsessive overseeing of his films, both animated and live. Indeed, Schickel mounts a convincing case that this was a hallmark of Disney's cultural politics. These might be summarised as:

1. The desire for control: instanced by his insistence that his name alone, and not his artists' or writers', should appear on his products. Every detail had to be vetted by him. At the same time, he fought tooth and nail against allowing the banks or distribution agencies any control over his flims. This of course was easily mythologised as the 'little man's' battle against the corporations, or the fight for artistic integrity against the money-merchants. But as Schickel points out, the motivation was quite different. For Disney, control meant quite other things:

2. 'Artistic integrity'. Disney was not primarily interested in his films as culture, but as saleable items. He was, Schickel claims, almost hostile to any attempt to see them as 'art': 'Speaking to a magazine journalist some ten months before he died, Disney confided: "I've always had a nightmare. I dream that one of my pictures has ended up in an art theatre. And I wake up shaking".'[12] Instead of art, Disney protested that he spoke the language of the people, directly. He 'knew' that he could produce things that ordinary folks could enjoy. He didn't have to try, it came naturally to him. He was so 'ordinary' inside, he just had to do what came out of him.

3. But that meant working to a 'lowest common denominator' where nothing disturbs or challenges. This has the greatest effect when Disney turns his sights on folk-tales. First, they cease to be their originals. They must become *Walt Disney*'s Snow White and the Seven Dwarfs, *Walt Disney*'s Cinderella, etc. As Gilbert Seldes put it in an early review, Disney reduces the soul of these stories to brilliant technique.[13] Disneyfication of a tale meant its transformation into folksy, gag-ridden, technically brilliant 'innocence'. (Schickel notes that the one occasion when Walt was away from the studio for an extended period while a film was being shaped, resulted in a simpler, less 'clever' film: Dumbo, of all his feature-length cartoons, one of the most straightforward. This absence was a significant moment – it was during the famous strike at the Disney studios.

Persuaded to go away to give negotiators a chance to resolve it, Walt went on a Government-sponsored trip through Latin America. More on that anon.) This drive for technique was Disney's strength. He was one of the first to introduce sound, then colour, to his cartoons. It led to the development of the multiplane camera, which allowed for a much more naturalistic look to movement. It made his films much more expensive than any rival's because he would insist on having slight inaccuracies redrawn and refilmed. It also produced the obsessive style of management which made his studios such a hothouse.

Schickel suggests that this drive for technique was not simply technical perfectionism but almost an ideology. Disney wanted fantasy films that stopped looking like fantasy, cartoons looking so naturalistic, that they were no longer cartoons. In the end, therefore, he had to leave cartoons behind and make live films – but in the process they would become as 'techniquified' as the cartoons. It is this quality in his brilliantly-shot nature films (such as The Living Desert) that has antagonised many people. The animals end up performing to a Disney script with a voice-over narration making them cutely, dehumanised humans. And as Schickel says, when he turned his hand elsewhere to make a 'living statue' of Abraham Lincoln, the result was not awe but a safe cute astonishment. Our 'imagination' has been duly shaped, and the exquisitely precise required response has been called forth.

Finally, in Disney's 'Magic Kingdoms' of Disneyland and Disneyworld, everything is so perfectly controlled that a new utopia appears. A utopia of undemanding pleasure and channelled imagination. There is play, but no free play, because it has all been done for us – and so well done.

4. These qualities in Disney made him uncriticisable. Everything he did was so 'innocent' that 'Disney' became a name not so much for a kind of cultural product as for a form of morality. Which brings us full-circle to Dorfman and Mattelart's beginning. In attacking Disney, they were not seen as criticising a politics or an art-form, but a morality. Disney became the embodiment of the 'American way of life'. And of course the comics coming out under that imprimatur bore both that protection and that responsibility.

This is the context we need to understand something of Disney's role in connection with American foreign politics. It is also the context within which Carl Barks, the 'good artist' of the great bulk of the Disney comics, worked.

The 'good artist' at work

Barks is a key figure in the history of the Disney comics. These were produced by a Disney subsidiary Western Publishing Company. By the early 1940s, WPC had run through the newspaper reprints at least once, and some twice. A demand for new material arose. Around this time, Barks was working as an 'in-betweener' (drawing movement frames) in Disney's animation studios.

Unhappy at the fruitless work and the 'over-the-shoulder' management, he left in 1942 – but not before he had illustrated a new story for the comic *Donald Duck*. The success of that led WPC to ask him to script and illustrate new stories. He stayed at this task until his retirement in 1966. Barks wrote and drew the great bulk of those Donald and Scrooge adventures which Dorfman and Mattelart and others are arguing over. Barks' relationship to the Disney studios is complicated. Like so many Disney artists, he remained completely anonymous until after his retirement. Known to his fans only as 'the good artist', it was fandom that eventually tracked him down and told his story. Even so, he was in an exceptional situation: 'Barks has lived away from Los Angeles since leaving the Disney studio and, in his isolation, he was, in effect, his own editor. No one else saw his scripts or his drawings until he submitted them for publication, and only rarely did Western reject a story or order changes. Barks still had to work within tight restrictions – he was, after all, doing stories for comic books – and sometimes he chafed against them, but fortunately he was given enough breathing space to show what he could do as an individual artist'.[14] Barrier, very much an admirer, argues that Barks' earliest work was the best. After 1953 Barks was pressed by WPC to concentrate on Scrooge for their new comic of that name:

> What was missing from many of these stories was the emotional resonance of Barks' earlier stories. Scrooge was limited, as a character, in ways that Donald was not, and this meant that some of the flexibility and great range that Barks had shown in the late forties and early fifties had to be sacrificed . . . The difference was that Barks wasn't extending himself as he had in his earlier stories. He couldn't; his format in *Uncle Scrooge* didn't allow for it. The publishers had given Scrooge his own magazine because Barks's stories with Scrooge had been so well received, so Barks had really constructed his own prison. (pp. 222-3)

In Barrier's view, then, the great foreign adventures are part of this decline. They still had the special Barks sense of authenticity and non-patronising attitude to readers. But something had gone, as a result of Barks' position within Disney's production system.

Barrier here ducks the issue of the politics of the stories. He acknowledges Barks's personal conservatism (bordering on reaction) and admits its relevance. But he does not allow that to impinge on his celebration of Barks: 'His *real* subject matter was not money, but the ways in which human beings deceive and destroy themselves – and how funny they can be when they do it. Scrooge's wealth and Gladstone's luck were only stepping stones to that larger theme' (p. 220, my emphasis). The giveaway word here is 'real'. In order to celebrate him, he has to distinguish a 'true' Barks story from the rest – and those where the self-mocking has waned leave him uncomfortable. But by 1953, as we will see, any self-mocking reticence about foreign exploitation has gone. Natives are funny, and longing to give up their wealth to Duckburgians.

Still, there is something in Barrier's defence of Barks which rings true. It is hard to see how stories as diverse and changing as these can simply all perform one function. That gives added point to the question: what do we mean by 'cultural imperialism'?

The problem of 'cultural imperialism'

There are hardly any precise definitions of 'cultural imperialism'. It seems to mean that the process of imperialist control is aided and abetted by importing supportive forms of culture. If the imported culture is accepted, imperialism would appear normal. It might even be embraced as a 'good thing'. In a strong version, this might even say that modern imperialism and colonialism cannot survive without such a backup. But what sorts of culture would support imperialism? Simplistically, we might expect the job to be best done by pro-pagandistic materials. So, American domination would be justified by pro-paganda about 'freedom' from communist subversion. News, documentary and political rhetoric would look likely candidates to help spread that. Mean-while, advertising could help by fitting people's consumption patterns to the needs of foreign businesses. Sell 'em Nestlé's baby-milk powder because that is good for profits and will make them dependent on foreign products and markets.

I am sure Dorfman and Mattelart do not want to deny the role played by propaganda and advertising. But they want to say further that Disneyfication of the world also supports American domination. Just how would this support imperialism? What cultural forms would achieve it? Standard works on cultural imperialism hardly help. They are predominantly about, for example, how far Third World television companies, newspapers, radio stations, etc are owned by metropolitan companies or how far American-made films and television series penetrate other countries' networks.[15] This is important, obviously. But it is not enough. We need also a theory that can say: what jobs did these media have to perform to normalise imperialism? and what sorts of cultural forms and products might be capable of performing them? Unfortunately, as Fred Fejes has pointed out, work on cultural imperialism has hardly touched on these.[16] But in the absence of explicit theory, discussions of 'cultural imperialism' still assume answers to these questions. And Dorfman and Mat-telart's reading of Disney is produced from within a definite theory of cultural imperialism – a problematic one. They were closely involved with Salvador Allende's Popular Front government in Chile, which sought to mobilise a move-ment of national independence. As part of this, there was an attempt to produce a *national culture* which would be free of the taint of American domination. To do that, there had to be a critique of the main forms of American culture – and that included Disney. Their critique of Disney was the flip-side of this struggle for a 'national culture'. And in that surely lies the problem. For Allende's movement assumed that there was a single national interest which could unite all Chileans. Their theory of imperialism, in other words, opposed 'the Chilean people' united by their nationhood, to American business and State with their ideology of 'Americanisation'.

Their time saw new ideas developing about the nature of American power. The 'standard' theory that the Third World was being 'developed' by the Metropolitan countries was comprehensively bashed by André Gunder Frank, who argued that America was systematically de-developing the countries it dominated economically.[17] Following his lead, a whole school of theorists sought to explain the persistent economic backwardness of, for example, Latin America, in terms of structural dependency.[18] And there are certainly strong echoes of these ideas in their thinking – with a difference. The difference is that, in their account, imperialism tries to control not only economies and political systems but the *very personalities* of the subordinate countries. This is where their neo-Freudianism comes into play. They damn Disney for reproducing political and economic dependency in the story-form of adult-child relations.

There are many problems with this. I can only deal with two. First, there is a problem in how they conceive the relationship between American political and business interests abroad. For their account to work, there have to be strong links between American attempts to control Latin American economies and their communications policies. Certainly, at times of crisis these links emerged. The CIA and International Telegraph and Telecommunications collaborated closely during the overthrow of Allende's government. But at other times, there are stresses between individual units of American capital and the American State. These tensions were particularly evident between government and the communications industries when the Disney comics were at their height.

Fejes has documented the difficult relationship between firms like NBC and CBS and successive political adminstrations over the control of short-wave radio to Latin America.[19] 'New Deal' policies after 1930 meant that the State switched from open aggression towards a new diplomacy towards Latin America. This was linked, he argues, with a new emphasis on cultural relationships:

(D)espite this sincere belief in their own positive intentions and understanding of the role and nature of cultural exchanges, it is apparent that the United States policy-makers were becoming aware of a lesson learned quickly by every modern empire or imperial system. While an imperial power never absolutely renounces the ultimate sanction of force, it is far more useful, effective, and less costly, to rely upon other seemingly non-coercive control measures . . . As with any imperial

> power, the United States found it necessary to construct mechanisms for the dissemination of a world-view which would justify its position of power and domination ... Such a world-view would seek to convince the client-state that, despite apparent inequalities, the costs and benefits, obligations, and rewards asociated with the imperial system as a whole were evenly distributed. (p. 76)

But while such a policy suited the State's interests, it was resisted by the broadcasters. Even with the approach of war, powerful hostility met new proposed broadcasting regulations which included a clause that 'A licensee of an international broadcasting station shall render only an international broadcasting service which will reflect the culture of this country and which will promote international goodwill, understanding and cooperation' (cited, p. 104). This was an expression of the Government's 'Good Neighbour' policy, designed to make Latin America see itself as 'naturally' linked with the United States. Yet it met with a wave of objections, on a mixture of grounds including censorship fears over their right to be critical of foreign governments, and commercial fears about being forced to invest without a certainty of return. The clause was withdrawn.

With World War II cooperation did increase, coordinated in particular through the Office of the Coordinator of Inter-American Affairs (OCIAA). It was the OCIAA headed by Nelson Rockefeller which organised Disney's trip through Latin American countries in 1941. The trip was openly propagandistic in intent. Disney only wanted to go if he could use the trip to make films. This was precisely Rockefeller's intention – to trade on the popularity of Disney's films for political purposes. Out of that trip came *South of the Border with Disney*, *The Three Caballeros*, *Saludos Amigos*, and a number of shorts – altogether a mix of cartoons and documentary:

> The point of this feature is to make North and South Americans feel comfortable with each other. To display strong cultural differences would be disturbing and would not promote the unity the government hoped for, so instead cultural similarities are accentuated. If Donald Duck is shown having a good time in South American, it implies that many North Americans might like to visit and socialize with their Latin American neighbors.[20]

This was the high-point of State/communications industry cooperation.[21] After the war Disney himself retreated from direct political involvement, though he personally moved rightwards (supporting the ultra-conservative Barry Goldwater in one Presidential campaign).

Several things, then, set the comics apart from simple 'cultural imperialism'. This honeymoon period between business and State was short. When it came, the required message stressed how alike and mutually dependent the USA and Latin America were. But the comics, produced on the margins of the Disney empire, were saying exactly the opposite. Therefore we need to understand their *distance* from direct political processes. Their production history sets them apart; and their content will not neatly dovetail with the perceived needs of American imperialism. How then should we understand the comics?

Retracing Barks

Recently, the American editor of Dorfman and Mattelart's book, David Kunzle, has done a remarkable job in tracing the main stages in Carl Barks' work.[22] A very potted version of this follows. Barks' first independent work for Disney was 'The Mummy's Ring' in 1943. This and other stories through to 1949 hardly showed foreign adventures. 'Latin America is not yet an object of desire – it arouses, rather, a xenophobic revulsion.' So, in stories such as 'Volcano Valley' or 'Mystery of the Swamp', Donald and the nephews may go abroad (even if only as far as Florida), but the peoples they meet thwart them and they return home empty-handed and wiser (at least until the next tale begins).

The change is signalled by the arrival of Uncle Scrooge himself who first appeared as a decrepit old man in 1947, but by 1948 was the 'belligerent, tyrannical capitalist' and by 1950 was spreading his charms abroad. This also brings to Scrooge both his Money Bin (object of his fetishistic love), and the Beagle Boys (embodiment of all threats to that love). This period sees the shadow of McCarthyism in the Disney stories, with a repeated theme of spies (for example, 'The Pixillated Parrot', and 'Dangerous Disguise') and the appearance of the pig-characters representing 'Brutopia' (a Russian/Cuban composite). Once a basic opposition has been set up – Scrooge + money versus the Beagle Boys, Brutopians, and various other enemies – the scene was thus set for various themes to emerge. Capitalist versus socialist economics: Kunzle refers to the story in which an 'act of nature' sprays Scrooge's money over the world.[23] Everyone becomes a millionaire and stops working. Only Scrooge and the nephews work on, growing vegetables. Soon everyone is demanding to buy their (the only remaining) food; and Scrooge quickly reaccumulates all his wealth. This was one of a number of stories in which the 'laws of the capitalist market' were given narrative form.

By the late 1950s explicit anti-communism coincided with the appearance of another character Magica da Spell, also out to deprive Scrooge of his wealth. (Kunzle hints that Magica 'represents' communism.) 'Captain Blight's Mystery Ship' (1964) directly represented the Cuban revolution, which had occurred just two years earlier. In the same way, America's obsession with safeguarding its oil interests provided themes and references for Barks, beginning with 'The Magic Hourglass' (1957) on Mossadeq's nationalist revolt in Iran. Interestingly, Kunzle shows how these early stories deal with the replacement of 'false rulers' or defeat of rebels. Later stories, coinciding with the rise of John Kennedy and his 'New Frontier idealism', back away from this interventionist, exploitative relationship. So in 'Pipeline To Danger', Scrooge at the end agrees not to develop the oilwells that will wreck the villages of the pygmy Arabs. Instead, he provides them with water. 'It was the only way I could ever prove to them that I really am a BIG OPERATOR!'

If oil directly expressed American geopolitics, Kunzle sees more symbolism in the presentation of the space race. 'The Twenty Four Carat Moon', for example, told of a race by Scrooge and others to seize a pure gold moon that had appeared. Scrooge, winning the race, found it occupied by Muchkale a Venusian. But Muchkale is willing to trade his moon for a box of earth that Donald had taken along so that he could 'keep his feet on the ground'. With it Muchkale can rebuild his lost planet. At the end Scrooge is left wondering if Muchkale didn't get the better of the bargain. Kunzle calls this 'a transparent morality tale, gold or the quest for material wealth is ultimately sterile'; but adds the rider that this 'realisation cannot change Scrooge's nature'.[24] In stories of myth and history, Kunzle notes that when Scrooge goes hunting through legends for wealth, he as often as not is thwarted. True, in 'The Lost Crown of Genghis Khan' he may outwit the Abominable Snowman with an old watch-stopping trick. But then in 'The Seven Cities of Cibola' he not only fails to get the wealth, but destroys the city and loses his memory in the process.

Finally, Kunzle deals with the 1960s when, in Africa and South East Asia in particular, wars of independence broke out. The comics' response began with 'Bongo On The Congo' (1961) in which the fears turned out to be misplaced. What they had thought to be war drums of the Mau Mau turned out to be a tsetse fly dancing on a drum of the friendly Qwak Qwaks. And an old Treaty of Friendship makes all well between them. But the portrayal of Asia, where of course US interests were very directly involved, was different. First, 'Monkey Business' (1965) set in 'Siambodia'coincided with Prince Sihanouk's resistance to the American-backed South Vietnam government, the massive bombing of Cambodia and Sihanouk's eventual overthrow. The story reflects this first, in the degree of outright resistance Scrooge meets to his money-making plans; second, in the cynicism of his plans – his plans to sell noisy toy monkeys to the Siambodians causes a war and ruins their crops (twice); but Scrooge still gets away with three barrels full of diamonds. The ultimate story of this kind we have already seen: 'The Treasure Of Marco Polo'. It is one, as Kunzle notes, which breaks many of Disney's studio rules in depicting war, weapons, and fighting.

Kunzle's history is important. It shows how different stages of American foreign policy were refracted in the comics. But curiously, Kunzle himself does not take that opportunity. With the one exception of Barks' very last story before he retired ('King Scrooge The First', which he sees as a satire on Barks' own life in Disney), Kunzle still interprets every story as equally expressing a single 'imperialist ideology': 'Barks, to the American sophisticate, may be a master of satire, or at the very least, of the burlesque. In a larger perspective, this satire is the band-aid of laughter over the gaping wounds of reality. Imperialism is made palatable, attractive, by transformation into fun-filled adventure . . . By making it appear funny, and lending it a commonplace air, Barks normalises cynicism and selfishness.' Once again, humour is all a disguise. Kunzle has hesitated on the brink of seeing that the form of the stories must transform the content. This hesitation allows him to acknowledge their 'perfection of narrative construction and visual montage', their 'felicity of verbal expression and satirical touch'. Yet quite separately he wants to examine their 'content and political implications'. In practice, his examination of the comics is much more subtle than this opposition might suggest. But a barrier remains, which reveals itself in his language.

For example, he repeatedly claims that various characters 'stand for' some real group. So, he suggests that in 'The Land Of The Totem Poles' the Indians 'stand for the virgin peoples of the Third World'. Talking of stories produced towards the end of the 1940s, he remarks that 'the rescue-of-Donald theme may be regarded as a metaphor for the US having to rescue its foolish 'parent', Europe, from fascism'. The Beagle Boys, meanwhile, variously represent Chinese socialism (in that they outnumber Scrooge as the Chinese outnumber Americans), the working class (in being the brawn opposite of capital's 'brains'), various primitive peoples (in that they sometimes dress up in 'native costume'), etc. His implication seems to be that in being thus 'disguised', the implicit persuasion is that much greater. That is an unargued view of influence. What warrants it?

The return of the 'identifiers'

Almost inevitably, Kunzle shares Dorfman and Mattelart's belief that the comics work by making us 'identify'. Therefore only the openly satirical are not promulgating imperialism. His main amendment is to see the time-specific elements in the comics. But he does not see how this challenges their neo-Freudian perspective. They see the comics infantilising Third World peoples, persuading them to identify with their oppressors as substitute father-figures. This power resides in the very form of the comics, for Dorfman and Mattelart. And that form is independent of any particular time-situation:

> Mass culture has granted to contemporary man, in his constant need to visualise the reality about him, the means of feeding on his own problems without having to encounter all the difficulties of form and content presented by the modern art and literature of the elite. Man is offered knowledge without commitment, a self-colonization of his own imagination. By dominating the child, the father dominates himself. The relationship is a sado-masochistic one, not unlike that established between Donald and the nephews . . . The authoritarian relationship

between the real life parent and child is repeated and reinforced within the fantasy world itself, and is the basis for all relations in the entire world of the comics . . . (T)he relationship of child-readers to the magazine they consume is generally based on and echoed in the way the characters experience their own fantasy world within the comic. Children will not only identify with Donald Duck because Donald's situation relates to their own life, but also because the way they read or the way they are exposed to it, imitates and prefigures the way Donald Duck lives out his own problems. Fiction reinforces, in a circular fashion, the manner in which the adult desires the comic be received and read.[25]

The 'adults' have become America, and adult-child relation is a mirror of the imperial relation. Their thesis is that the power of the comics lies in displacing the 'normal' emotional energies of family life and sexuality into domination. This is what I mean by calling their theory neo-Freudian. Hence the importance they attach to the absence of real parents in Disney; hence also the reference to the stories' timelessness. There is no progression between the stories, therefore they allow no progression in us. In reading them, we trap ourselves into their childishness.

Kunzle's strength is in showing the stories' contemporary references: not just in being set in places that are in the news, but also in relating to them in ways that reflect American attitudes. But he does not follow the logic of this, to see that there cannot then be fixed relationships between readers and comics, and comics and American political life. The term 'cultural imperialism' has swallowed all differences. We need to recover them in order to understand the comics. When Walt Disney (in films like *Saludos Amigos*) was literally preaching unity of the Americas and 'common interests', the comics were being xenophobic. When in the late 1940s other comics – the awful Korean War comics[26] – were indeed directly propagandising, the Disney comics were simply silent about Korea; there is not one story referring to the war. It is not that there is no relation between American imperialism abroad – it is that there are mediations, withdrawals, hesitations. And I have suggested that these are held in tension between the two poles of power and money.

Conclusion

I hope this incomplete discussion helps point up the difference my theorisation makes. Dorfman and Mattelart's work remains, despite my criticisms, one of the most subtle attempts I know to grasp the ideology of a group of comics. But (1) they lack a material production history which in this case requires a knowledge of the Disney empire, and of Disney's part in the internal tensions between American capital and the State; (2) their (neo-Freudian) conception of mechanism of influence can't grasp the shifting relations between stories and American power, and thus also between comics and readers. I postulate tentatively (because the research still remains to be done) that these shifts are between two typical poles of American middle-class ideology: a self-congratulatory but humorous desire for wealth; and an obsessive fear of power-politics; (3) because of their (linked) misunderstanding of these, they miss the complicated 'contract' that the comics established with their readers, including those in Latin America. This will surely have included elements of:

(a) playful surprise (it is interesting to see how many of Barks' fans speak of their delight in the unexpected elements in his stories);

(b) delight in the precise absence of the awful Disney 'innocence' of so much else coming out from the studios;

(c) the genuine confusions and uncertainties often displayed by Donald, and even Scrooge, in many situations. The characters become in many ways the pawns of the real situations into which they launch themselves;

(d) finally, of course, the use of recognisable if coded references to the world in which the readers were living. Some of the stories, no doubt, cross into propaganda. But it is eccentric propaganda, not one easily suiting the purposes of American capitalism.

These are no more than hints and gestures, designed to reopen a question which too many have thought Dorfman and Mattelart closed. The Disney comics are neither 'innocent' nor 'guilty'. They are too diverse and complicated for either. To say more than this would require a range of new kinds of research.

Which is a good way to end any argument.

Postscript

Cultural analysts should not prognosticate. Perhaps because we have to fracture the things we study for purposes of analysis, perhaps because we have to cut small pieces out of the living tissues of history and society in order to analyse them, perhaps for other reasons too, we tend to be terrible at prophecies. But forecasting and recommending seem to be almost inevitable parts of our frames of mind. I am no different. Though I have yet to be right about the future, I can't stay away from gazing. People's decisions and creativity continually defeat all my trials at predicting, only the past being neatly enough formed to be manageable. But still I can't keep my hands off the astrological tables. And though I recommend till I am blue in the face, the truth is that what people produce without my plans is always infinitely more interesting than I, the clever commentator, can envisage.

My publisher said: write a Postscript which gets away from all the detail and gives us your overall view. Tell us where you think things are going, and what you think should be done. What do you like, in the end? and what worries you? The trouble is, the moment I step back to consider the whole and my attitudes to it, I see another whole. I live in the Britain of the 1980s, where Capital has been revealed in all its mean-minded calculator mentality. The comics that I squabble about with my fellow analysts are often hanging on by the skin of their paper teeth. And yet they are, for many of my smaller fellow-humans, one of the few rat-holes they have to hide in when the Junkers from Downing Street and Fortress Wapping come dropping on them. Deciding now which are better, which worse, is like joining a bloody temperance movement again.

As I write this Postscript, two things have come to hand, together almost to the day. The one is a press report of a study by London librarians on which comics they feel can be recommended and which should be avoided.[1] Without yet having read it thoroughly, none the less there is a grim predictability about it all. 'Nothing positive to say' about the new *Eagle* (and with that total grasp of the history one expects by now, they are not at all sure if this is the same one started by Marcus Morris). *Dandy* and *Beano* are guilty of 'sexism by omission', but they get off lightly because they portray 'a world which never existed any-way'. (Dennis, what do you say to say to that? 'Aargh!') With baited breath (I have not misspelt that), I send for my copy. No doubt those librarians are good people, concerned people, who care for the 'state of the people'. But it has not stopped them casting the first stone.

One of the comics they damn as 'the worst example of the comic genre'

Battle is just re-running the powerful *Charley's War*, with its subtle anti-war narrative. What can I say? Who will take me seriously? These comics are for kids, and they may miss all my damned academic 'subtleties' – though of course they would never miss the damned condemnatory blatancies of sexism, racism, militarism, would they?? Yet as I write also, I have just put away in my collection the second issue of a new comic, *Crisis*. Greeted already as 'possibly the most important comic of the century' (why should the critics have all the good hyperboles?), it has torn to shreds the rule-book for comics in this country. In *Crisis* you will find (ex-*Action*) Pat Mills writing in *Third World War* about a world where the food corporations run Latin America like one vast Vietnamese 'secure village'; and newcomer John Smith telling a complicated tale of 'supermen and women' produced by biological experimentation, only to become intending führers. Ah, but this is not for 'children', is it? . . . and if it was?

In this book, I have worked hard at being the analyst. Assessing and weighing, investigating and evaluating. Not above a bit of anger when I find bad theory and empirical misrepresentation, but basically cool. Perhaps every now and then a bit of laughter or passion when something I really love comes up before my eyes, but most of the time outside it all. That is, of course, not true at all. I live in this damned country at this damned time and comics are part of my and my children's lives. And I now say passionately: let us have as many of the things as we possibly can. In the face of the capital-calculating machine called Thatcherism which uses morality like murderers use shotguns, all the little things like comics matter. Little by little, the cohorts of the 'competitive-minded' seek to shut down, enclose, militarise our imaginations. Comics prise open the bars just a little. Dreaming, eh? Give that chap a 'short, sharp shock'! I am quite willing to say passionately: all those in whom humanity remains prized above the 'laws of the market' have no business (you own none, you have none) helping to block the dreaming that people manage to do. Imagination, fantasy, call it what-you-will, is not some fixed drum which, filled with the wrong stuff, will then be unavailable for other purposes. For heaven's sake, let us have dreamers; or we will have hell. My defence of the comics is, to me, in the end a defence of the right to imagine.

Yes, understanding how these things I have been studying work does matter – but not as much as the living of them does. And those who would stop others living them take on themselves a share of the responsibility for all that is anti-human in Thatcherism. They will hate me for the analogy, but to me it is like anti-fascists in Germany in the 1930s wanting to argue over which books should be burned. That mentality is powerful. It has the power of institutions behind it, it has the power of a hundred-year old rhetoric behind it, it has the new and sinister power of the new Headmistress behind it.

Perhaps this is the best analysts should do. They shouldn't prognosticate. But maybe they can rage, and denounce. And celebrate where they can.

Notes and references

CHAPTER 1

1. See, for example, Stuart Hall & Martin Jacques, *The Politics of Thatcherism*, London: Lawrence & Wishart 1983. An extensive debate followed this, in the pages of *New Left Review*. See also my own *The New Racism: Conservatives and the ideology of the tribe*, London: Junction 1981.

2. Anne Beezer, and Jean Grimshaw, 'Methods for Cultural Studies Students', in David Punter (ed), *Introduction to Contemporary Cultural Studies*, London: Longman 1986, p. 95.

3. Colin Sumner, *Reading Ideologies*, London: Academic Press 1979, p. x.

4. H Eysenck & P Nias, *Sex, Violence and the Media*, London: Maurice Temple Smith 1976.

5. A recent BBC investigative programme, presented by Kate Adey, did in fact revisit a number of current claims of direct copycatting. In every case, it found that, on inspection, the evidence dissolved and became at the very least unreliable. See *Panorama*, 15 February 1988.

6. I am at the time of writing in process of putting together a volume of reprints of the *Best of Action*, which will make available a great deal of the material talked about in my chapters on it. This will hopefully include a large selection of the artwork which was 'lost' due to the withdrawal of the comic and the killing off of some stories. This book should be published by Titan Books (London) in the Autumn of 1989.

7. See, for example, Laurence Hogben, *From Cave Painting To Comic Strip*, London: Max Parrish 1949. On the very early history of the modern comic, see David Kunzle, *The Early Comic Strip*, Berkeley: University of California Press 1973.

8. The research is mentioned in Umberto Eco, 'A reading of Steve Canyon', *Twentieth Century Studies*, December 1976. His essay was reprinted recently in the Catalogue accompanying the ICA's exhibition *Comic Iconoclasm*, London 1987.

9. Jack Cox, *Take A Cold Bath Sir: The Story of the Boy's Own Paper*, Guildford: Lutterworth Press 1982, p. 30.

10. Obviously particular publishers would stamp something of their own character on their products. Morris was a determined Christian. In his original scheme, Dan Dare was to have been called 'Lex Christian'. He may not have kept the name, but he kept the squeaky clean character Morris wanted. But the requirements of holding a readership conditioned other things about his stories. The Mekon remains one of the great, attractive villains of all time. As with Milton's Satan, a far more interesting character than his opposite. I am happy to say that I never went for the *Eagle* as a child – it was always the *Lion* that grabbed me.

11. For a general, if rather flat, introduction to the characteristics of comic and cartoon conventions in Randall Harrison, *The Cartoon: Communication to the Quick*, Beverley Hill: Sage 1981. Of a quite different, but much more challenging kind, is Raymond Williams' introductory discussion of the idea of a 'convention' in his *Drama from Ibsen to Brecht*, Harmondsworth: Penguin 1952, pp. 3-8.

12. Compare Bob Hodge & David Tripp, *Children and Television: A Semiotic Approach*, Cambridge: Polity Press 1986. Hodge and Tripp are quoting a child talking about watching television cartoons: 'You sorta listen with your eyes.' (p. 41)

13. I have adapted this example from Randall Harrison, *The Cartoon*, p. 66.

14. There is actually a serious point to be made about calling such a strip 'harmless'. As I pointed out elsewhere, when George Pumphrey calmly divided all comics into two kinds, 'the harmless and the harmful', he was revealing a very great deal about his classification of the medium. (See my *A Haunt of Fears: the Strange History of the British Horror Comics Campaign*, London: Pluto Press 1984, p. 81.) Incapable of any positive virtues, and certainly not worthy of serious attention except when it becomes bad, the best that a comic can do for anyone is not harm them! That kind of classification has done untold damage to the history of comics in Britain, imposing all manner of constraints on what it is allowable to produce.

15. George Orwell, 'Boys' Weeklies', in *The Collected Essays, Journalism And Letters: Vol. 1, 1920-40*, Harmondsworth: Penguin 1970. Originally published 1940. The author of most of the stories, Frank Richards, did in fact reply to Orwell; and Penguin have conveniently included that with the essay in their volume (pp. 505-39).

16. For information on the American campaign, see in particular James Gilbert, *A Cycle Of Outrage*, New York: Oxford University Press 1987. A great deal of information and argument about this campaign is also to be found in ane of the general histories of American comics.

17. See my *A Haunt Of Fears*.

18. The following are the only further studies I have managed to locate. Relating to Australia, Augustine Brannigan, 'Crimes from comics: social and political determinants of reform of the Victoria obscenity law, 1938-54', *Australian & New Zealand Journal of Criminology*, Vol. 19, March 1986, pp. 23-42.

Vol. 19, March 1986, pp. 23-42. Relating to New Zealand, Roger Openshaw, '"Worthless and indecent literature": comics and moral panic in early post-war Australia', *History of Education Review* 1986, pp. 1-12. On Canada, Augustine Brannigan, 'Mystification of the innocents: delinquency in Canada, 1931-49', *Criminal Justice History* 1986. This is a pity. A cross-national comparison could provide fascinating insights into the ways in such campaigns work, and the political and cultural resources they draw on.

19. See, for example, Umberto Eco, 'The myth of Superman', in his *The Role Of The Reader*, London: Hutchinson 1979, pp. 107-24, a highly intelligent semiotic interpretation of the superhero story which I would nonetheless want to question. Discussions in later chapters of this book of time in narrative would be directly relevant to Eco. However, it is interesting that in recent years the superhero story has begun to change dramatically, through the reinterpretations of writers and artists like Frank Miller and Alan Moore (*The Dark Knight* series from D C Comics, rewriting Batman, was the formative case). Complaints are now being directed at these darkened re-visions of the stories, in which the naive good vs bad optimism of the old tales has been replaced with politically-aware doubt. See for example Charles Langley, 'Comics that are no laughing matter', *Weekend*, 16-22 March 1988, pp. 4-5.

20. For a general history of these, see Mark Estren, *A History of Underground Comix*, San Francisco: Straight Arrow Books 1974.

CHAPTER 2

1. Pat Mills (Originator of *Action*), *Interview*, 11 May 1985. I would like to record my thanks here to the very many people who helped me with my research on *Action*, either by allowing me to interview them, by answering letters, or by giving me access to important materials. In particular I owe a debt of real gratitude to Pat Mills, to John Sanders (both for a very frank interview with me, and for allowing me full access to IPC's art archive), to Colin Wyatt, and to Jack Adrian. But in not listing all other names, I am not discounting the very real help that others gave me.

2. Ibid.

3. Ibid.

4. Jack Adrian (Scriptwriter for *Hell's Highway* and *Kids Rule OK*), *Letter to author*, 18 February 1985.

5. 'Comic Strip Hooligans', *Daily Mail*, 17 September 1976, p. 27.

6. John Smith (Editor of *Action*, June-October 1976), *Interview*, 12 January 1987.

7. Bob Holbrow, 'Violence in comics – will it cease?', *Retail Newsagent*, 2 October l976, p. 7.

8. We should not overlook the general context of the mid-seventies. This was the time of the re-emergence of all kinds of 'concerned' bodies, look-ing with concern and censorious interest at the arts, the media, at education and so on. They ranged from the increasingly-influential National Viewers and Listeners Association, on the Right, to peculiar 'Left' versions of all this, as in the Delegation Opposing Violent Education which wrote via its 'negotiator' warning IPC that it might 'black' *Action*.

9. John Sanders (Managing Editor, I.P.C.), *Interview*, 26 July 1985.

10. George Spence (from John Menzies), *Telephone conversation*, 14 May 1985.

11. W E S Clarke (from W H Smith), *Interview*, 26 July 1985.

12. This fascinating insight was given to me by Colin Wyatt, then Art Assistant on *Action*, who was at this meeting. *Interview*, 29 September 1986.

13. J R Curtis, *Letter in Retail Newsagent*, 9 October 1976.

CHAPTER 3

1. At its end, *BlackJack* deteriorated drastically as a story, fell down the popularity ratings, and embarrassed its writer. Originally scripted by John Wagner, a boxing fan, it was handed on to Jack Adrian who loathed it. He had the task of turning world champ Barron into a singer after he went blind. With a sigh of relief from everyone, they discovered a miracle operation for his eyes, and ended the tale.

2. In this and *The Running Man*, the end arrives all of a sudden, suggesting that the energy of the story lay in its dilemma, not in the search for a solution to it.

3. Tom Tully (Writer of *Look out for Lefty*), *Interview*, 26 May 1987: '*Action* put two fingers up to authority.'

4. Barrie Mitchell (Artist on *Look out for Lefty*), *Interview*, 30 October 1986: '*Bullet* didn't have the punch of *Action*. Even though it was a new comic, D C Thomson was still restricted. Pat Mills was given a free hand, and *Action* was breaking new bounds.' Mitchell had a special insight since in the early days of its production, he worked as an artist in the *Action* office. This is highly unusual.

5. Steve McManus ('ActionMan'), *Interview*, 20 September 1986: 'You see, comics before *Action* had always treated what kids did outside of comics with disdain; whereas *Action* plunged actively into the world and said "We know what you're about".'

6. The Semantic Differential Test was developed by Osgood, as a tool for psychological investigations. See C Osgood, *The Measurement of Meaning*, Urbana: University of Illinois Press 1967. The use I have made of it derives much more from an interesting study reported by John Fiske (*Introduction to Communication Studies*, London: Methuen 1982, pp. 16-18).

7. See my comment on Cumberbatch et al, *Television and the Miners' Strike*, which appeared under that

that title in *Media Culture & Society*, Vol. 10, No. 1, 1988, pp. 107-112.

8. These figures exclude mentions of *2000 AD*. I discounted these for the simple reason that I had advertised for *Action* readers in that, and results including this comic were bound to be misleading.

9. The bracketed numbers are the computer references of the questionnaires. I have retained them here, to keep respondents' comments distinct.

10. Ien Ang, *Watching Dallas*, London: Methuen 1985.

11. See Donald Horton & R Richard Wohl, 'Mass communication and parasocial interaction', *Psychiatry*, Vol. 19, 1956, pp. 215-229.

CHAPTER 4

1. Bounds can be very strict. An episode where Sherlock Holmes spent an investigative night at the Inn ran into trouble – because IPC had house-rules against showing comic characters smoking. But the entire story depended on Holmes puffing himself out of the Inn. It made it, just.

2. Cliff Brown told me of his regret at the change. He felt sure that the new strip, for all its continuity of characters with the old, would not succeed. Maybe it was a victim of the 'policy' at IPC not to let strips run for more than one generation of readers – a policy to which there are many exceptions. Unfortunately, with *Scream Inn*, it is difficult to see how the other policy – of reprinting from the archives – could ever happen in this case.

3. *Scream Inn*'s characters may have died, but like all good (or bad) ghosts they did not pass away easily. On a visit to Swanage in the early 1980s, I came across a fairground. Its haunted house was entirely decorated with copies of the Innkeeper and his tribe.

4. Categorising was not always easy. When, for example, a reader asks that Uri Geller be allowed to challenge, and the artists then use a 'spoon bender', it is pretty obvious that these must be in the same category. This was not always quite so easy.

5. Vladimir Propp, *The Morphology of the Folktale*, Austin: University of Texas Press 1968.

6. Amabel Williams-Ellis, *Grimm's Fairy Tales*, Glasgow: Blackie 1959, pp. 40-1.

7. My alternative analysis of these kinds of strips here begins to have consequences. To several critics, Walter has cut a worrying figure: mocked for his 'softness', perhaps even set up as a gay fall-guy. See, for example, the bizarre account of Dennis and friends in Antony Easthope's *What A Man's Gotta Do*, London: Paladin 1986. My account points in a very different direction. Walter's 'crime' is his likeness to his father (compare how they are drawn to see this); he is an adult in child's clothing. He will not rebel, and therefore is an enemy of every true child in the game of absurd power.

CHAPTER 5

1. Clare Dellino, 'Comics that set a bad example', *Sunday Times*, 15 February 1981, p. 19.

2. See my 'Dennis rules OK! Gnashee!', *New Society*, 13 November 1980, pp. 332-3.

3. George Gale, 'Violent and Deformed – the prosecution case', *Times Education Supplement*, 5 February 1971.

4. Judith O'Connell, 'Sexist images in children's comics and television programmes', *University of Sheffield: Faculty of Educational Studies*, April 1982, abstracted in *Sheffield Educational Research: Current Highlights (SERCH)*, No. 4, April 1982. My thanks to Judith O'Connell for allowing me to read her original dissertation.

5. See 'Comic cuts call on naughty Lord Snooty', *Evening Tribune* (Wolverhampton) 7 September 1985, p. 1. I also have two short articles kindly sent to me by Pat Isiorho, but unfortunately unsourced. For an older, much-referenced article which effectively argues in an identical way, see Jennie Laishley, 'Can comics join the multi-racial society?', *Times Educational Supplement*, 24 November 1972.

6. Bob Dixon, *Catching Them Young*, Vol. 1 'Sex, Race and Class in Children's Fiction', Vol. 2, 'Political Ideas in Children's Fiction', London: Pluto Press 1977. This quote from Vol. 2, p. 9. The problem with Dixon's work is the fence on which he sits. He has the grace not to lose the sheer hilarity of these comics, but he can't escape the critics' language. There is in fact quite a large literature on comics which shares assumptions like these, whilst having to acknowledge that the evidence is rather more complicated. See, for example, Sara Zimet, *Print and Prejudice*, London: Hodder & Stoughton 1976.

7. Tim Walker, 'Chomp! Thatcher tucks into cowpie capers', *Observer*, 9 August 1987.

8. Mary Warnock, article on television and violence, *Woman & Home*, November 1983.

9. Mary Field, *Children and Film*, London: Methuen 1954.

10. Parliamentary Group Video Enquiry, *Video Enquiry, Video Violence and Children*, Part 1, 1983, para 11.4. See my *The Video Nasties*, London: Pluto Press 1984 for a full appraisal of this dreadful report, including its views on 'identification'.

11. David Lange, Robert Baker & Sandra Ball, *Mass Media and Violence*, Report to the National Commission on the Causes and Prevention of Violence, Vol XI, Washington: US Government Printing Office 1969, p. 368.

12. Donald Horton & R Richard Wohl, 'Mass media and parasocial interaction'.

13. Grant Noble, *Children In Front Of The Small Screen*, London: Constable 1975.

14. D Howitt & G Cumberbatch, 'Affective feeling for a film character and evaluation of an anti-social act', *British Journal of Clinical and Social Psychology*, 1972, pp. 102-8. Also see their essay 'Identification with aggressive television characters and children's moral judgements' in W W Hartup & J de Wit, *Determinants and Origins of Aggressive Behaviour*, The Hague: Mouton 1974.

15. Fredric Wertham, *Seduction Of The Innocent*, London: Museum Press 1954.

16. Martin Barker, *A Haunt Of Fears*, Ch. 5.

17. Owen D Edwards, 'Cow pie and all that', in *The D C Thomson Bumper Fun Book*, Paul Harris Publishing 1977.

18. Two very useful histories of the Penny Dreadfuls are Louis James, *Fiction For The Working Man*, Harmondsworth: Penguin 1974; and Michael Anglo, *Penny Dreadfuls*, London: Jupiter Books 1977. See also *Penny Dreadfuls and Comics*, Intro. Kevin Carpenter, Exhibition catalogue, Bethnal Green Museum of Childhood and Victoria and Albert Museum 1983.

19. 'The literature of the streets', *Edinburgh Review*, January 1887, pp. 40-65. This quote, p. 65.

20. The millenarian language so typical of the whole history of panics over the media is well captured in Geoffrey Pearson, 'Falling standards: a short, sharp history of moral decline', in Martin Barker (ed), *The Video Nasties*.

21. Edward Salmon, *Juvenile Literature As It Is*, London: Henry J Drane 1888, pp. 188-9.

22. Helen Bosanquet, 'Cheap Literature', *The Contemporary Review*, Vol. 79, May 1901, pp. 671-81.

23. Edward Salmon, *Juvenile Literature As It Is*, p. 198.

24. James Greenwood, *The Seven Curses Of London*, London: Stanley Reivers & Co 1869, p. 143.

25. Helen Bosanquet, 'Cheap literature', p. 678.

26. Mischievous literature', *The Bookseller*, 1 July 1868, pp. 445-9. This quote, p. 448. For comparison, see the same opposition at work during the 1950s campaign against the 'horror comics': 'The average American comic is skilfully and sometimes brilliantly drawn... This manifest proficiency makes the frequently violent content even more dangerous'; 'Nasty pictures nastily printed on nasty paper'. Both these are cited from my *A Haunt Of Fears*, footnote to Ch. 13.

27. Leo Lowenthal, 'The debate over art and popular culture', in his *Literature, Popular Culture and Society*, New York: Pacific Books 1961.

28. Samuel Johnson, 'Romances' (from *The Rambler* 1750-2), reprinted in *Selections* (ed. R W Chapman), Oxford: Oxford University Press 1955, pp. 81-5.

29. Geoffrey Pearson, *Hooligan: A History Of Respectable Fears*, London: MacMillan 1983.

30. Pat Rogers, *Literature and Popular Culture in Eighteenth Century England*, Brighton: The Harvester Press 1985, pp. 7-8.

31. Eleanor Maccoby & W Wilson, 'Identification and observational learning from films', *Journal of Abnormal and Social Psychology*, Vol. 55, 1957, pp. 76-87.

32. My interpretation also copes with a fact

pointed out in a response to the *Guardian*'s report on O'Connell's research. Leo Baxendale, originator of so many of the *Beano*'s characters, pointed out that this discrepancy in readership by girls and boys, if true, is relatively recent. His experience from fan mail in the 1950-60s was virtual equality of readership across genders – something borne out by surveys at the time. His comment is apt and sums up my argument: 'What seems to happen though is that girls grow out of the *Beano* reading age group and leave it behind as a part of their childhood' (Leo Baxendale, 'Minnie the Minx – more than a match for the boys', *Guardian*, 13 October 1982).

33. Tom Scott, Letter to *The Guardian*, 20 January 1984; see also 'Sirs give Dennis the Menace a hiding', *The Sun*, 7 December 1987.

34. Though see his *Catching Them Young*, Vol. 2, pp. 18-20, where he calls *Scream Inn* 'inventive and well-drawn', even 'performing a valuable therapeutic function' in allowing fears of the supernatural to be released in laughter. This kind of praise based on superficial understanding is no better than equivalent damnations. And I bet he hadn't seen that 'Witchdoctor' set . . .

CHAPTER 6

1. Vladimir Propp, *Morphology of the Folktale*.

2. Vladimir Propp, 'The Structural and Historical Study of the Wondertale', in *Theory and History of Folklore*, trans. Ariadna and Richard Martin, ed. Anatoly Liberman, Manchester: Manchester University Press 1984, pp. 69-70.

3. Version 1 is available in Amabel Williams-Ellis, *Grimm's Fairy Tales*.

4. Compare on this Victor Erlich's classic and first history of the Formalist movement, *Russian Formalism: History – Doctrine*, The Hague: Mouton 1955, with the much more critical Tony Bennett, *Formalism and Marxism*, London: Methuen 1979.

5. See, for an account of this debate, and examples of the arguments, Chris Pike (ed.), *The Futurists, The Formalists, and the Marxist Critique*, London: Ink Links 1979.

6. Lévi-Strauss's review, and Propp's reply, have been usefully included in the volume of Propp's later essays, *Theory and History of Folklore*.

7. Fredric Jameson, 'Magical narratives: romance as genre', *New Literary History*, Vol. 7, Part 1, 1975, pp. 135-163.

8. Robert Scholes, *Structuralism in Literature*, New Haven: Yale University Press 1974, pp. 68-74.

9. Roland Barthes. 'Introduction to the structural analysis of narrative', in his *Image, Music, Text*, trans. Stephen Heath, London: Fontana 1977.

10. In this distinction, Barthes is very close to Umberto Eco's, between 'open' and 'closed' texts. See Eco's *The Role of the Reader*. If there is a difference, it lies in Barthes' claiming that a liberatory text is one in which the narration is self-disclosing; whereas for Eco, an 'open' text is one in which the event-sequence is not closed, and time does not pass irrevocably.

11. Propp gives an interesting example of this. He is studying how different sorts of peasant society deal with the identical element in wondertales: the element of 'flight'. Variously, in his stories, Ivan the hero can be carried away by a flying horse, a bird, or a boat. 'But it happens that these forms represent bearers of the souls of the departed, with the horse predominating among agricultural and herding peoples, the eagle prevailing among hunters, and the boat predominant among inhabitants of the sea coast.' (pp. 106-7) The tales, then, draw on both the material social lives of these peoples, and also on their religious traditions. But the moment these motifs enter the tales, they become elements in the tales, no more, no less.

12. Jack Zipes, *Breaking the Magic Spell: Radical Theories of the Fairy Tale*, London: Heinemann 1979.

13. See Jack Zipes, *The Trials and Tribulations of Little Red Riding Hood*, London: Heinemann 1983.

14. Bryan Walker, *Interview*, 22 January 1982; Cliff Brown, *Interview*, 26 February 1982; Roy Davies, *Interview*, 15 April 1982.

CHAPTER 7

1. In fact all these endings are based on stories found in *Jackie*, from various points in its history. They are based on the following stories: (1) 'The girl with green eyes', No. 470, 6 January 1973; (2) 'Forever and ever', No. 681, 22 January 1977; (3) 'Throwaway love', No. 473, 27 January 1973; 'Take me in your arms', No. 158, 14 January 1967.

2. The following are all the main analyses I have managed to locate: Connie Alderson, *Magazines Teenagers Read*, London: Pergamom Press 1968; Jacqueline Sarsby, *Romantic Love and Society*, Harmondsworth: Penguin 1983, which was based on her 'Concepts of Love and Marriage Held by Adolescents: an investigation of relevant influences', Ph.D Thesis University of London 1974; Sue Sharpe, *Just Like A Girl: How girls learn to be women*, Harmondsworth: Penguin 1976; Angela McRobbie, 'Jackie: an ideology of adolescent femininity', Occasional Paper, Centre for Contemporary Cultural Studies, University of Birmingham 1978; 'Working class girls and the culture of femininity', in Centre for Contemporary Cultural Studies, *Women Take Issue*, London: Hutchinson 1978; and 'Just Like a Jackie Story', in Angela McRobbie and Trisha McCabe, *Feminism For Girls: an adventure story*, London: Routledge and Kegan Paul 1981; Julie Hollings, 'The portrayal of women in romance comic strips 1964-84', B.A. Dissertation University of Reading 1985; Sandra Hebron, 'Jackie and Woman's Own: ideological work and the social construction of gender identity', B.A. Dissertation, Communication Studies Department, Sheffield City Polytechnic, published as *Occasional Paper* May 1983; Judith O'Connell, 'Sexist Images in Children's Comics and Television', B.Ed Dissertation University of Sheffield 1982, abstracted in *Sheffield Education Research: Current Highlights* (SERCH) No. 4, August 1982; Gillian Murphy, 'Media Influence on the Socialisation of Teenage Girls', in James Curran, Anthony Smith and Pauline Wingate (eds), *Impacts and Influences: Essays on Media Power in the Twentieth Century*, London: Methuen 1987, pp. 202-17; Elizabeth Frazer, 'Teenage girls reading Jackie', *Media, Culture and Society*, Vol. 9, 1987, pp. 407-25. There was also a short, interesting article by Mary Talbot, 'Reading Jackie . . .' in the *Society of Strip Illustrators Newsletter*, 1986.

3. Julie Hollings, 'The portrayal of women in romance comic strips', p. 78.

4. Polly Toynbee, 'The magazines preach a stultifying message . . .', *Guardian*, 30 October 1978.

5. Connie Alderson, *Magazines Teenagers Read*.

6. 'Time to Say Goodbye' in fact ends as follows: realising that she is endangering his career as a successful accountant (he's spending too much time romancing with her, not studying for his exams), she takes the hint from his parents that she is doing him no good. And so she just goes away, miserably, to save him from himself. As I say, hardly a lack of morality, rather a self-sacrificial excess . . .

7. Sue Sharpe, *Just Like A Girl*, p. 66.

8. This is, of course, something which a number of critics within the women's movement have drawn attention to. They have shown that questionable ideas about 'independence' have developed within certain kinds of radical feminism. See, for example, Jean Grimshaw, '"Pure lust": the elemental feminist philosophy of Mary Daly', *Radical Philosophy* 49, 1988, pp. 24-30; and Pauline Johnson, 'Feminism and images of autonomy', *Radical Philosophy* 50, 1988, pp. 26-30.

9. Angela McRobbie has, as already listed, written several separate pieces about Jackie and its readers. For ease of reference in the main text, I have numbered these as follows: (1) 'Jackie: an ideology of adolescent femininity'; (2) 'Working Class Girls and the Culture of Femininity'; (3) 'Just Like A Jackie Story'. I'd like to record here my thanks to Angela for her friendly response to my criticisms of her work, and an apology if my criticisms seem harsh at times.

10. Brian Redhead, *Radio 4*, 8 pm, 12 October 1986.

11. Edward Salmon, 'What the working classes read', *The Nineteenth Century*, July 1886.

12. Jonathan Culler, *Saussure*, London: Fontana 1976.

13. A further significant example of this. McRobbie declares (1, p. 6) that thought-balloons in the strip stories represent something dubious, 'thinking being associated with a "higher" level of discourse, an "intellectual" pursuit'. We will see how questionable this is when we come to the stories.

CHAPTER 8

1. George Gerbner, 'The social role of the Confession Magazine' *Social Problems*, 6, 1957, pp. 29-40.

2. Angela McRobbie, 'Jackie: an ideology of adolescent femininity', pp. 22-3.

3. It is this, I think, that differentiates what I am saying from, for example, the proposals of Seymour Chatman (*Story And Discourse*, Ithaca: Cornell University Press 1978). Chatman suggests some apparently quite similar distinctions as the basis for analysing how narratives work. But he sees his distinctions applying equally to all narratives. Useful though they are, they do not seem to me to enable us to determine particular *kinds* of story.

4. Part of the problem with McRobbie's analysis is that she has confused different levels of motif. For example, we saw how she treated 'history' as a major organising principle, operating to distance us from social problems and thus render them anodyne. On my approach the historical placing of stories would be a piece of low-level 'setting'.

5. Julie Hollings, 'The portrayal of women in romance comics'. Hollings unfortunately does not indicate clearly which comics she sampled in gathering her statistics. Even so, the information is useful.

6. Sandra Hebron, 'Jackie and Woman's Own'. Hebron delivers a heavy-handed two-page analysis of the story, asserting among other things: "it could be argued that stories of this kind do provide the reader with a certain type of pleasure. They are framed and structured in such a way that the reader is encouraged to identify with the protagonist and engage with the problems in the text . . . and yet remain secure in the knowledge that everything will work out in the end". (pp. 41-2) Hmph. It is perhaps interesting that an analysis so heavily dependent on semiology, and on Stuart Hall's notion of "preferred reading" still feels the need to fall back as much as this on the concept of 'identification'.

8. Gordon Small, *Interview*, 18 February 1988.

9. Thomsons are themselves aware of the current low quality of the stories, and *Jackie* has recently been experimenting with a new form of drawn story: more contemporary, redolent of recent fashion and advertising art. To date, there is no information on readers' response to this. My fear is the publishers have only really focused on the look of the stories, not on their narrative form.

10. Elizabeth Frazer, 'Teenage girls reading Jackie'. The story she used was 'It's my nasty mind', from *Jackie*, 7 December 1985. It is curious to note that this is in fact a reworking of an old story, with the same title, from No. 366, 9 January 1971. There are some small but significant changes. If there is a pattern to them, it is to make the heroine less self-conscious.

11. Cynthia White noted this phenomenon in discussing women's and girls' magazines generally for the Royal Commission on the Press. See Cynthia White, 'The women's periodical press in Britain, 1946-76', *Royal Commission on the Press*, Working Paper No. 4, London: HMSO 1977, p. 43.

CHAPTER 9

1. Gillian Murphy, 'Media Influence on the Socialisation of Teenage Girls', p. 216.

2. Walter Lippmann, *Public Opinion*, London: George Allen & Unwin 1922. I must acknowledge a debt to an important essay by Kevin Robins, Frank Webster & Michael Pickering, 'Propaganda, information and social control', in Jeremy Hawthorn (ed), *Propaganda, Persuasion, Polemic*, London: Edward Arnold 1987, pp. 1-17. This first alerted me to the significance of Lippmann's ideas. In the end I disagree with the conclusions which the authors reach, that theorists like Lippmann offer a useful alternative to the behaviourists for understanding the power of propaganda. But their essay is particularly useful in addressing the theoretical and political context within which these authors wrote.

3. See Lippmann's series of articles beginning with 'The mental age of Americans', in *The New Republic*, 25 October 1922. There are now a number of fine histories and analyses of this period. Most notable, perhaps, are the following: Leon Kamin, *The Science and Politics of IQ*, New York: Wiley 1974; Allen Chase, *The Legacy of Malthus*, New York: Alfred Knopf 1977; Stephan Chorover, *From Genesis to Genocide*, Harvard: MIT Press 1979.

4. Franz Samelson, 'From "race psychology" to "studies in prejudice": some observations on the thematic reversal in social psychology', *Journal for the History of the Behavioural Sciences*, Vol. 14, 1978, pp. 265-78. I owe most of my understanding of this phase to Samelson's article. My thanks to Michael Billig for drawing this to my attention.

5. David Krech, Richard Crutchfield and Egerton Ballachey, *Individual in Society: A Textbook of Social Psychology*, New York: McGraw-Hill 1962, p. 67.

6. Roger Brown, *Social Psychology*, Glencoe: The Free Press 1965, pp. 176-7.

7. Gordon Allport, *The Nature of Prejudice*, Reading, Massachusetts: Addison-Wesley 1954, pp. 191-2, my emphasis.

8. Theodor Adorno et al., *The Authoritarian Personality*, New York: Harper 1950.

9. Michael Billig, *Fascists: A Social Psychological Study*, New York: Harcourt 1978. Billig shows, from a series of interviews with National Front members, that they have highly complex and differentiated ideas about race and immigration. These allow them, for example, to acknowledge differences among black people. Billig rightly argues that his research throws serious question over the whole approach to racism based on 'prejudice', 'attitudes' and 'stereotypes'. See also the useful discussion of the concept of

prejudice, specifically, in Frank Reeves, 'The concept of prejudice', Birmingham: S.S.R.C. *Research Unit on Ethnic Relations*, Working Paper No. 17, 1982.
10. Paul Secord & Carl Backman, *Social Psychology*, New York: McGraw-Hill 1974, pp. 20-1.
11. Nelson Cauthen, Ira Robinson & Herbert Krauss, 'Stereotypes – a review of the literature 1926-68', *Journal of Social Psychology*, Vol. 84, 1971, pp. 103-25.
12. See Richard LaPière, 'Attitudes versus actions', *Social Forces*, Vol. 13, 1934, pp. 230-37; Irwin Deutscher, 'Words and deeds', *Social Problems*, Vol. 13, No. 3, 1966, pp. 235-54; and Alan Wicker, 'Attitudes and actions', *Journal of Social Issues*, Vol. 25, No. 4, 1969, pp. 41-77.
13. Sara Zimet, *Print and Prejudice*.
14. See for example, the very useful Shearon Lowery & Melvin DeFleur, *Milestones in Mass Communication Research*, London: Longman 1983. For an illustration of the approach, easily displaying its problems, see Robert Merton, 'Studies in radio and film propaganda' (with Paul Lazarsfeld), in *Social Theory and Social Structure*, Glencoe: Free Press 1968, pp. 563-82.
15. Bernard Berelson and Patricia Salter, 'Majority and minority Americans: an analysis of magazine fiction', *Public Opinion Quarterly*, Vol. 10, 1946, pp. 168-90.
16. Nancy Larrick, 'The all-white world of children's books', *Saturday Review*, 11 September 1965.
17. Steve Neale, 'The same old story – stereotypes and difference', *Screen* 1980.
18. Compare, for example, the following both taken from Judith Stinton (ed), *Racism and Sexism in Children's Literature*, London: Writers and Readers 1979: 'These caricatures [of the Chinese] are part and parcel of the perception of Asians and their descendants as subhuman creatures, a perception which led members of the white community to persecute, ridicule, exploit and ostracise Chinese Americans.' (p. 81) 'For instance in Puerto Rican books, the minority child is repeatedly shown as living in a ghetto. The continual suggestion that this is the norm must surely help to make it so, when really these conditions are inherited rather than inherent.' (p. 4) In the first case, the stereotype (or caricatured perception) is seen as a distortion – and therefore powerful; in the second, the stereotype (or 'repeated showing') is seen as *too true* – and therefore powerful.
19. Richard Dyer, 'Stereotyping', in his (ed) *Gays in Film*, London: BFI 1977, pp. 27-39.
20. Ellen Seiter, 'Stereotypes and the media: a reevaluation', *Journal of Communication*, Spring 1986, pp. 14-26. See also T E Perkins, 'Rethinking stereotypes', in Michele Barrett et al (eds), *Ideology and Cultural Production*, London: Croom Helm 1979.
21. See R W Connell, 'Theorising gender', *Sociology*, Vol. 19, No. 2, 1985, pp. 260-72.

22. See David Bloor, *Knowledge and Social Imagery*, London: Routledge & Kegan Paul 1976, for a useful discussion of the problem of visual metaphors in thinking about ideology.
23. Polly Toynbee, *Guardian*, 30 October 1978.
24. It is indeed strange that Seiter, whose article is by far the most comprehensive critique of 'stereotyping' research I have come across, should end by positively recommending a return to Lippmann's formulations. In her article, Seiter in fact raises many of the objections which I have covered in this Chapter. Yet she ends by suggesting that the problems have arisen because theorists have moved too far from Lippmann. I cannot here review her arguments in detail, to show why I think she is mistaken.
25. See, for example, H H Hyman & P B Sheatsley, 'The authoritarian personality: a methodological critique', in R Christie & M Jahoda (eds), *Studies in the Scope and Method of the Authoritarian Personality*, Glencoe: Free Press 1954.
26. It does not, of course, follow from this that there cannot be miscategorisations. An example of such ideological miscategorisation would be the now the problem is transformed to the specific nature of the categories, from one in which it is the sheer tendency to categorise.
27. A recent article by Susan Condor expresses many of the same reservations as I have done about 'stereotype' research, though her target is specifically their use in 'race-research'. She goes so far as to suggest that the categories of such research can unwittingly assist the very racism it wants to study. See her ' "Race stereotypes" and racist discourse', in *Text*, Vol. 8, Nos. 1-2, pp. 69-90.

CHAPTER 10
1. Valerie Walkerdine, ' "Some day my Prince will come": young girls and the preparation for adolescent sexuality', in Angela McRobbie and Mica Nava (eds.), *Gender and Generation*, London: MacMillan 1984, pp. 162-84. There are clearly hazards in taking one essay as representative of a widespread movement of ideas, but I have little option. It is the only case I am personally aware of where post-structuralist ideas have been directly applied to comics; and my self-denying ordinance was to test approaches to ideology in that way.
2. See for example Wolfgang Iser, *The Act of Reading*, London: Routledge & Kegan Paul 1978 and *The Implied Reader*, Baltimore: Johns Hopkins University Press 1974; Susan Suleiman & Inge Crosman, *The Reader in the Text*, Princeton: Princeton University Press 1980. It should also be made clear, though, that some of the work on these notions had predated structuralism, in particular Wayne Booth's *The Rhetoric of Fiction*, Chicago: University of Chicago Press 1961.
3. See in particular Louis Althusser, *Lenin and Philo-*

sophy, and other essays, London: New Left Books 1971.

4. Julian Henriques, Wendy Hollway, Cathy Urwin, Couze Venn, and Valerie Walkerdine, *Changing The Subject: Psychology, Regulation and Subjectivity*, London: Methuen 1984.

5. Michel Foucault, *The History of Sexuality, Vol. 1: An Introduction*, Harmondsworth: Penguin 1981, pp. 31-2.

6. Once again, while giving her academic references properly, Walkerdine did not feel it necessary to state her sample. It is in fact either a one- or two-week period in August 1982. The stories to which she gives explicit reference are in *Bunty* and *Tracy*, 7 August 1982.

7. See, for example, Simon Clarke, *One-Dimensional Marxism*, London: Allison & Busby 1980; and Norman Geras, *Marx and Human Nature: Refutation of a Legend*, London: Verso 1983.

8. I owe my understanding of this point to my colleague Anne Beezer.

9. Cathy Urwin, 'Power relations and the emergence of language', in J Henriques et al., *Changing The Subject*, pp. 264-322.

10. There are other ways in which their theorisation leads to strange and unacceptable interpretations of empirical evidence. In a field in which I am more competent, Henriques makes some extraordinary claims about work on racism. Writing of the Scarman Report, he argues that this should be seen as a classic case of the operation of an individual/society opposition. He cites Scarman explaining away problems in the police as a function of 'the ill-considered, immature and racially-prejudiced actions of some officers' (cited, p. 61), while denying the existence of institutional racism. The problem was in the individual; social institutions were alright. But the Scarman Report revolves around problems of quite other kinds that cannot be made sense from Henriques' position. In an analysis of the Report's assumptions, Anne Beezer and I showed that fundamental to it is a view that the problems of racism are problems of culture. Scarman regards culture – remarkably like Henriques *et al.*, it has to be said – as productive of personality. This is the source of the problem, he implies. Thus, the reason black people didn't 'integrate' was because of their 'culture'. And the problem now is that black people are a 'people of the streets', which makes them proto-criminal. The reference to some individual police being racially prejudiced therefore had a different purpose. Scarman was in no position to deny that there had been racist behaviour from the police – the evidence was just too overwhelming. But his explanation took this form in order to exonerate the State. More than that, it made it possible for the State to disappear from his analysis, becoming instead 'rationality embodied' in the institution of the police as against 'cultures' which are by definition non-rational. Therefore the problem with those individual police was not that they were individuals but that they were too *enculturated*. The task for Scarman was to make us all accept the special position of the police, as the 'rational eye' of society. Henriques does not see any of this, because his approach leads to him just abstracting a few sentences without exploring the structure of Scarman's argument. For our full analysis, see Martin Barker & Anne Beezer, 'Scarman and the language of racism', *International Socialism* 2: 18, Winter 1983, pp. 108-25.

11. A lot of the preliminary work which led to my understanding this was done by a student of mine, Sandra Whilding, as part of her Humanities degree. See Sandra Whilding, 'A Question of Knowledge: Moral Values and Ideologies in *Bunty*,' B.A. Humanities Special Study, Bristol Polytechnic 1983. Her research was done earlier than Walkerdine's, using a sample of *Bunty* nos. 1292-1301, 1982.

12. Tania Modleski, *Loving With A Vengeance*, Archon 1982.

13. Ron Tiner, *Letter to author*, 3 March 1986. I am very grateful to Ron for the help he gave me towards understanding these points. He is another of a whole company of under-appreciated artists who work on the less glamorous comics.

14. I take the term and the idea from Tulloch and Alvarado's excellent *Dr Who: The Unfolding Text*, London: MacMillan 1983. They use the idea of a 'production history' in order to capture the intersection of the many influences which shape the character of a series such as Dr Who: the traditions of children's TV, the particular writers, producers, actors etc and how they interact, current policies at the BBC, audience responses and so on. They show how it is possible to examine the concrete interactions of these.

CHAPTER 11

1. George Pumphrey, *What Children Think Of Their Comics*, London: The Epworth Press 1956.

2. Ruth Strang, 'Why children read the comics', *Elementary School Journal*, 1943, pp. 336-42.

3. See for example, Robert L Thorndike, 'Words and the comics', *Journal of Experimental Education*, Vol. 10, No. 2, 1941, pp. 110-13; Florence Hesler, 'A comparison of comic book and non-comic book readers of the elementary school', *Journal of Educational Research*, Vol. 40, 1947, pp. 458-64; Scottish Council for Research in Education, *Studies in Reading: Vol. 1*, London: University of London Press 1948; C A Waite, 'The popularity of the comics: readers and non-readers', *Youth Libraries Group News*, October 1966, pp. 10-11, and 'The language of the infants' comic papers', *The School Librarian*, July 1968, pp. 140-5; J J Taylor, 'The reading of comics by secondary school pupils', *Uses of English*, Vol. 24, 1972, pp. 11-15; and finally, in a summation that preserved all the problems that had gone before, Frank Whitehead *et al.*, *Children's Reading Interests*, London: Evans/Methuen 1975, and *Children and the Books*, London: MacMillan 1977 (both on behalf of the Schools Council). There were, admittedly, voices raised even during this period who saw comics more positively – but still in relation to their possible uses in education. See, for example, Neil Rackham, 'Comics versus education', *New Education*, Vol. 4, August/Sept. 1968, pp. 9-10, and 'A Spoonful of sugar', *New Education*, Vol. 4, Nov. 1968, pp. 11-13; and Geoff Fenwick, 'Comics and education', *Bookmark*, No. 9, 1982, pp. 2-9.

4. Florence Hesler, 'Words and the comics', p. 464.

5. See, for example, the devastating reviews of this kind of research in Graham Murdock and Robin McCron, 'The television and delinquency debate', *Screen Education*, 30, 1978, pp. 57-68; and the more traditionally psychological but just as effective discussions in Dennis Howitt and Guy Cumberbatch, *Mass Media Violence and Society*, London: Paul Elek 1975. From an American perspective, the most powerful arguments have come in Willard Rowland, *The Politics of TV Violence*, London: Sage 1983, who like me sees the problem as being not simply one of inadequate data but of a disastrously narrowed agenda of questions.

6. The study was originally done for a doctoral dissertation: Lotte Bailyn, 'Mass media and children: a study of exposure habits and cognitive effects', *Doctoral dissertation*, Radcliffe College 1956. A much shortened version was published, under the same title, as *Psychological Monographs*, Vol. 73, No. 1, 1959. Unfortunately I have not been able to consult the original dissertation, which contains the detailed interview schedules for example.

7. It would be possible to make telling technical criticisms of many aspects of her study. But tempting though it is to damn her study in this way, I think there are more important and revealing problems with it.

8. My thanks to various friends in the comic world who helped me identify the comic she used. No title or date is given in the monograph; but it is, as closely as I have been able to determine, one of the four editions of *Strongman* (published by Magazine Enterprises, 1955). *Strongman* was a minor, short-lived comic. It is surely a worrying mark in itself that she should have taken as 'typical' such an out-of-the-way example.

9. Useful introductions to Uses and Gratifications research are Jay Blumler & Elihu Katz, *The Uses of Mass Communications: Current perspectives on gratification research*, Beverley Hills: Sage 1974, and Karl Rosengren, Lawrence Wenner & Philip Palmgreen, *Media Gratifications Research: Current perspectives*, Beverley Hills: Sage 1985.

10. Katherine M Wolfe & Marjorie Fiske, 'The children talk about the comics', *Communication Research*: 1948-9, New York: Harper & Bros 1949, pp. 3-50. This research was in fact part of a critical response to the early work of Fredric Wertham, who began his assault on crime comics in the late 1940s. For the context of this in America, see James Gilbert, *A Cycle of Outrage*, especially Chapter 7.

11 Perhaps the most important and innovative work has been done by David Morley. See his *The 'Nationwide' Audience*, London: BFI 1980; and also his more recent *Family Television: Cultural power and domestic leisure*, London: Comedia 1987. See also the sophisticated work of John Corner and Kay Richardson, in their *Documentary Television*, London: Edward Arnold 1986.

12. Angela McRobbie, 'Working class girls and the culture of femininity'.

13. Angela McRobbie, 'Just like a Jackie story'.

14. Jacqueline Sarsby, *Romantic Love and Society*, p. 104.

15. Jacqueline Sarsby, 'Concepts of love and marriage held by adolescents', p. 232.

16. Frank Coffield, Philip Robinson & Jacqueline Sarsby, *A Cycle of Deprivation? A case-study of four families*, London: Heinemann 1980.

17. Jacqueline Sarsby, *Romantic Love and Society*, p. 110.

18. Elizabeth Frazer, 'Teenage girls reading Jackie'. My thanks to Liz Frazer for discussing her work with me, and for giving me access to her interview-transcripts. Thanks also to Mary Talbot, on whose analysis of the strip the reader-research was built.

19. One of the best introductions to issues surrounding 'discourse' is Jonathan Potter & Margaret Wetherell, *Discourse and Social Psychology: Beyond attitudes and behaviour*, London: Sage 1987. It is they who point out that it is possible at the moment to have two books on discourse analysis which do not share any common topics, so scattered is the field.

20. The issue of 'non-ideology' was brought firmly back to my attention by Liz Frazer, to whom my thanks. She is right to stress its silent presence; and its very silence may be significant. Even in the work of Louis Althusser, who apparently denies that there can ever be an escape from the ideological, there is an opposite to ideology. Or rather, two. One can be spoken, the 'science of Marxism' which with one coupure was free; the other, known by its impossibility, would be to live unstructured by imaginary relations with the relations of production. But even in its impossibility, this alternative instructs that 'ideology' is still a limit or barrier which we cannot transcend, however much the eternal humanist in us might wish to.

21. An important discussion has been going on in feminist circles recently, over the Harlequin romances. See for example, Ann Snitow, 'Mass market romances: pornography for women is different', *Radical History Review*, 20, Spring/Summer 1979, pp. 141-61; Janice Radway, 'Women read the romance', *Feminist Studies*, Vol. 9, No. 1, 1983, pp. 53-78; Tania Modleski, *Loving With A Vengeance*; and Leslie Rabine, 'Romance in the age of electronics: Harlequin Enterprises', *Feminist Studies*, Vol. 11, No. 1, 1985, pp. 39-60. In that discussion, the issue I am raising here has also surfaced. In her study of a circle of romance-readers, Radway noted that the most avid readers are their most assiduous critics. They take care to distinguish those stories they do like, and find satisfying, from those they don't. Unfortunately Radway assumes from this that their critical attention to which they like and don't like somehow insulates them from influence. Why should that be?

22. This parallels, I think, the argument of Ien Ang, *Watching Dallas*. Ang shows, in her analysis of viewers' responses to *Dallas*, several different kinds of criticism. There are those who dismiss it, using the language of mass-culture critics. There are those who 'love its awfulness', taking pleasure in the very things the first group attacked. But there are also those who enjoy participating in it. The point is that they do not become uncritical. But they criticise it from the inside, in effect commenting on how well it lives up to its own criteria.

23. The book I have found most useful for getting to grips with this is an unfashionable one. Largely unnoticed by others in the field, Horst Ruthrof's *The Reader's Construction of Narrative*, London: Routledge & Kegan Paul 1981 is particularly useful to me for its first chapter. There he distinguishes two aspects of all texts, which he calls their 'presentational process' and 'presented world'. I have found this particularly useful as an analytic tool for exploring comics, perhaps especially because it throws up in a manageable form how we decide what will count as part of the narration within a picture-story.

24. Jonathan Culler, *On Deconstruction*, London: Routledge & Kegan Paul 1983, pp. 34-5.

25. George Gerbner, 'The social role of the Confession Magazine'.

CHAPTER 12

1. Valentin Volosinov, *Marxism and the Philosophy of Language*, trans. Ladislav Matejka & I R Titunik, New York: Seminar Press 1973. There is some controversy over the authorship of the book, some people saying that Volosinov never existed, and that the name is a pseudonym of Mikhail Bakhtin, another member of the group. Certainly, if Volosinov did exist, nothing is known of his fate in the 1930s. There is an excellent introduction to many of Volosinov's ideas in Tony Bennett's *Formalism and Marxism*, although Bennett is mainly interested in Volosinov for his contribution to a theory of 'the literary'.

2. See, for example, the reference to it in John Hartley's well-known book *Understanding News*, London: Methuen 1982. Hartley is discussing the language-reality relationship: 'The boo-value of "terrorist" is clearly not simply a linguistic value – it is at the same time an ideological one. But just as the people signified as terrorists in the news have no intrinsic properties which require the use of that sign to describe them, so there are no intrinsic properties in the sign "terrorist" which require it to be used with a boo-value. In Saussure's phrase, values "owe their existence solely to usage and general principle". In other words, every sign is in principle capable of signifying different values; even when "general acceptance" is established, signs still retain this capacity. There is, beyond the concept and sound-image of the sign, an evaluative accent which is exploited one way or the other in use. All signs have what Valentin Volosinov has called an "inner dialectical quality" which he terms their "multi-accentuality".' (p. 22)

This makes Volosinov look like a useful addition to Saussure, perhaps slightly correcting an imbalance in his account. One would never know that Volosinov spent two chapters delivering a comprehensive demolition of Saussure's theory of language, in preparation for stating his own.

3. 'Signs can arise only on *interindividual territory*. It is territory that cannot be called "natural" in the direct sense of the word. Signs do not arise between any two members of the species *Homo sapiens*. It is essential that the two individuals be *organised socially*, that they comprise a group (social unit); only then can the medium of signs take shape between them' (p. 12). Clearly 'social' means something much more specific for Volosinov than it does for Saussure.

4. Michael Stubbs, *Discourse Analysis*, Oxford: Blackwell 1983.

5. Indeed, Stubbs is positively heading away from a theory of power and ideology, towards ethnomethodology. In Chapter 3 of his book, Stubbs looks at classroom interaction, and discusses very interestingly the way teachers monitor children's language. But his account makes language-power only a *consequence* of already established power-relations. Language seems to play no independent part in their establishment.

6. There are interesting apparent exceptions. Certain feudal aristocracies cultivated an inability to talk to their serfs, by adopting a 'foreign' language – French being a favoured language in a number of countries (German, as I understand it, being preferred in France). Or again, the medieval church fought against having the Bible translated into English, so that it would remain a mystery, requiring a mediating interpreter. Such conscious refusals to communicate are no challenge to my argument.

7. I owe this example to my colleague Anne Beezer.

8. For a review of this area, see Teun A van Dijk, *Communicating Racism: Ethnic prejudice in thought and talk*, London: Sage 1987.

9. There are some obvious similarities with ideas developed by Jürgen Habermas, and other theorists of speech-acts, especially, perhaps, in their notions of *communicative competence*. Perhaps the crucial difference from Habermas is that there is no need to introduce an 'ideal speech situation', an image of pure rational discourse against which we can measure other situations for their deviation. See Jürgen Habermas, *Communication and the Evolution of Society*, London: Heinemann 1979.

10. Volosinov has a wonderful way of stating this: 'Orientation of the word toward the addressee has an extremely high significance. In point of fact, *word is a two-sided act*. It is determined equally by whose word it is and *for whom it is meant*. As a word, it is precisely *the product of the reciprocal relationship between speaker and listener, addresser and addressee*. Each and every word expresses the 'one' in relation to the 'other'. I give myself verbal shape from another's point of view, ultimately, from the point of view of the community to which I belong. A word is a bridge thrown between myself and another' (p. 86).

11. A set of essays by Mikhail Bakhtin on the 'novelistic tradition' was published a few years ago. In them, Bakhtin develops the bones of a view of this which seems to me to share a lot with what I have baldly outlined here. See Mikhail Bakhtin, *The Dialogical Imagination*, trans. Caryl Emerson & Michael Holmquist, Austin: University of Texas Press 1981.

12. Recently, a group of teachers in Hackney protested at what they saw as 'racist' tendencies in another such juvenile comic, *Beezer*, for its cover story *True Brit*. The story is built round an opposition between a boy Tommy Britain who has the power, when angry, to turn into True Brit, a kind of junior superhero; and the Silly Party who aim to cause disruption of daft kinds (like painting the white cliffs of Dover in rainbows, or turning the Royal Mint over to producing chocolate money). (See *Guardian*, 3 February 1988 for details of the dispute.) It provides an illuminating limit-case for my approach. The bald fact is that TB (in either guise) no longer represents childhood at all. He has become a miniature adult, but in a child's form. He does not act on his own behalf, but on behalf of an unspoken set of rules. In short, he is not really a character at all, but a cipher. I do not think it would be possible to understand the differences without first identifying the normal character of this genre. (I owe a lot of my understanding of this particular strip to a student of mine, Adrian Colston.)

CHAPTER 13

1. Ariel Dorfman & Armand Mattelart, *How To Read Donald Duck: Imperialist Ideology in the Disney Comic*, New York: International General 1976. There is a further discussion, in some ways better in my view, in Ariel Dorfman's *The Empire's Old Clothes*, London: Pluto Press 1985.

2. Dorfman and Mattelart's discussion connects with the discussion, beginning from Philippe Aries, *Centuries of Childhood*, London: Cape 1962 of the ways definitions of 'childhood' are caught up in capitalism's distinction between public and private life, its focus on the 'family' and its hardened gender-distinctions. The 'child' becomes the symbol simultaneously of 'naturalness' (unspoilt humanity) and 'danger' (therefore needing supervision).

3. Their book reproduces this frame (p. 78), but I have been unable to trace its source. In general, however, especially compared with other critics of comics, they are a model of propriety when it comes to giving references. The trouble is that they worked from Latin American editions, and their collection was destroyed when they were forced to leave Chile, after the military seizure of power.

4. Reinhold Reitberger & Wolfgang Fuchs, *Comics: The Anatomy of a Mass Medium*, Boston: Little, Brown 1972, p. 44.

5. Dave Wagner, 'Donald Duck: an interview', *Radical America*, Vol. 7, No. 1, 1973, pp. 1-19.

6. Mike Barrier, 'The Duck man', in Don Thompson & Dick Lupoff (eds), *The Comic-Book Book*, New York: Arlington 1973.

7. See, for example, the literature on racist jokes, including Edmund Leach, 'The official Irish joke-sters', *New Society*, 20, 7 December 1979; and Phil Cohen & Carl Gardner, *It Ain't Half Racist, Mum*, London: Comedia 1982.

8. See, for example, Mick Eaton, 'Comedy', *Screen*, Vol. 19, No. 4, 1978/9; and Terry Lovell, 'Situation comedy', in David Punter (ed), *Introduction to Contemporary Cultural Studies*; and Paul Attallah, 'The unworthy discourse: situation comedy in television', in Willard Rowland & Bruce Watkins (eds), *Interpreting Television: Current research perspectives*, London: Sage 1984.

9. See Sigmund Freud, *Jokes and their Relation to the Unconscious*, New York: Norton 1986; and Arthur Koestler, *The Act of Creation*, New York: MacMillan 1964. I have not had an opportunity to take account of the recent important-looking book by Michael Mulkay, *Humour*, Cambridge: Polity Press 1988.

10. Richard Schickel, *The Disney Version: The Life, Times, Art And Commerce Of Walt Disney*, New York: Simon & Schuster 1968.

11. Bob Thomas, *Walt Disney, A Biography*, London: W H Allen 1981. 'After Mickey Mouse began to capture the nation's affection, Walt assigned the prolific Ub Iwerks to devise a comic strip for newspapers. . . Ub's assistant, Win Smith, drew the Mickey Mouse comic for three months, then it was taken over by Floyd Gotfredson, who continued with the strip until 1975. Walt reviewed Gotfredson's work for the first year and a half, then lost interest.' (p. 100)

12. Richard Schickel, *The Disney Version*, p. 39.

13. Gilbert Seldes, 'No art, Mr Disney?', *Esquire* (USA), September 1937, pp. 91 & 171-2. Discussed in Richard Schickel, pp. 223-7.

14. Mike Barrier, 'The Duck man', in Don Thompson & Dick Lupoff, *The Comic-Book Book*. Mike Barrier has written a fuller biography of Barks, listing all his stories for Disney. Unfortunately this is now impossible to obtain; it is *Carl Barks and the Art of the Comic Book*, New York: Lilien 1981. Barks himself tells the story slightly differently: 'I had virtually no trouble with the editors because I was toothchatteringly *careful* about what I produced. Very seldom during the years did parts of a story come back for changes, which is fortunate, for I was of a sour puss temperament that blew my marbles in all directions at the first hint of having to do anything twice.' (Carl Barks, replies to fans edited by Geoffrey Blum, in *Donald Duck 248*, December 1986) Barks' own description is interesting for its greater sense of acknowledged rules and boundaries.

15. See, for example, Armand Mattelart, *Multinational Corporations and the Control of Culture: The ideological apparatus of imperialism*, Sussex: Harvester 1979; and Jeremy Tunstall, *The Media Are American*, London: Constable 1977.

16. Fred Fejes, 'Cultural imperialism: a reassessment', *Media, Culture & Society*, Vol. 3, No. 3, July 1981, pp. 281-89.

17. André Gunder Frank, *The Sociology of Development and the Underdevelopment of Sociology*, London Pluto Press 1971 (originally published in America in 1967); and *Capitalism and Underdevelopment in Latin America*, New York: Monthly Review Press 1967.

18. For a general discussion of Latin American theories of underdevelopment in this period, see Philip O'Brien, 'A critique of Latin American theories of dependency', in Ivar Oxaal et al., *Beyond the Sociology of Development: Economy and society in Latin America and Africa*, London: Routledge & Kegan Paul 1975, pp. 7-27.

19. Fred Fejes, *Imperialism, Media, and the Good Neighbour Policy*, New Jersey: Ablex Publishing 1986.

20. Richard Shale, *Donald Duck Joins Up; The Walt Disney Studio during World War II*, Ann Arbor: UMI Research Press 1982, p. 45. This is a useful, if somewhat unquestioning, book about Disney's involvement in politics. It details Disney's involvement in war work, from making training films for the Forces, to a film on why people should pay their taxes. The book also gives us some idea of the form of these films.

21. As Fejes puts it: 'An important theme was the common heritage of the Americas and their distinct identity as a whole, as opposed to Europe and Asia. Also stressed was the mutuality and harmony of interests and the interdependence among American states. The division of labour between the United States and Latin America, with the latter producing raw materials and the former producing manufactured goods, was depicted as natural and beneficial to all. Finally, it was assumed that all American states and peoples were bound by their commitment to liberal democracy and individual freedom, the two values which together represented the social idea for which all American states would strive and protect. Threats to these ideals and values always came from sources outside the hemisphere' (p. 77). Fejes gives very little information about the kinds of broadcasts, etc produced with these goals in mind. The little he does tell is suggestive. For example (p. 157) he tells of *Calvacade of America*, a radio series telling of the 'struggle for freedom' in the USA, *Fighting Youth*, built around interviews with men in the Army and martial music; earlier 'School of the Air' from CBS had run *Americans At Work*, praising American industrial development; and in the autumn of 1940 Republic Steel sponsored a series *Your Faithful Servant – Industry* which explored industry's role in the development of the Americas: 'on the other hand, any mention of Latin American industrial development was ignored' (p. 130).

22. David Kunzle, *Dispossessed By Ducks: The Imperialist Treasure Hunt In The Disney Comics*, Unpublished manuscript 1986. My grateful thanks to David for allowing me to see and use this – it is an outstanding piece of work, and deserves a publisher as soon as possible. I have not given page references since they can only confuse, when it is eventually published.

23. See Les Daniells. *Comix; A History of Comic Books in America*, New York: Outerbridge & Dienstfrey 1971, for a reproduction of this strip.

24. Interesting to see that Dorfman and Mattelart give a diametrically opposite reading of this story, seeing the ending as a self-justifying excuse for continued exploitation. Basically, 'we only got the gold, but you, you lucky people, got nature!' The thing that worries me, as I hope is becoming clear, is how we could ever decide between these interpretations. See *How To Read Donald Duck*, p. 52.

25. Ariel Dorfman & Armand Mattelart, *How To Read Donald Duck*, pp. 31-2.

26. See the final chapter of my *Haunt Of Fears* on these.

POSTSCRIPT

1. 'Librarians tear a strip off children's comics', *Times*, 29 September 1988. The Report is *Survey of Comics and Magazines for Children and Young People, 1988*, London: Camden Libraries and Arts, June 1988.

Questionnaire about published by I.P.C. in 1976/7

Thank you for agreeing to help me with my research.
The aim of this questionnaire is simply to find
out what some of its former readers remember about
the comic. So you will help me most if you just
answer what you feel you can. Don't worry if there
are some questions you can't answer.

I have asked you to put your name and address on
the questionnaire in case I might want to check
anything with you, or ask some further questions.
They would not be used for any other purposes.
But if you would rather not give these, just
leave these spaces blank.

When you have completed all you can of the
questionnaire, please return it to:

    Martin Barker
    Bristol Polytechnic
    Oldbury Court Road
    Bristol BS16 2JP.

... about yourself ...

Name   Present address

Age

In what area/town were you living in 1976?

What kind of reader of 'Action'
    do you think you were?

Casual	
Regular	
Committed	

What other comics were you reading around this time?

	Before Action	During Action	After Action	Regularly	Occasionally
Battle					
Bullet					
Valiant					
Vulcan					
Warlord					
Wizard					
2000AD					
Others (please say which)					

Which stories do you remember disliking? What did you dislike about them?

Was 'Action' different in any important ways from the other comics which were available then? Please circle the appropriate number on the scale:

Same as other comics	1	2	3	4	5	Different from other comics

If you can, please explain your answer to the above question.

What made you stop reading 'Action', as far as you can remember?

What age group do you feel 'Action' was aimed at? Tick more than one box if you want.

7-10	
11-13	
14-16	
17+	

What kind of person do you feel 'Action' was aimed at?

What do you remember about the complaints against 'Action'? For example, who were the people complaining? What were they worried about? What did you think about their complaints? What do you think now?

People can read a comic or anything else in many different ways. You might read it just by yourself. You might talk about it with friends. You might swap copies. It might be an important activity for a group. And so on.

Compared with other comics which you read, how much was reading 'Action' something private, or something shared? On the scale below, mark with a circle where you feel reading 'Action' came, and mark in with a square where you feel reading other comics came.

Private	1	2	3	4	5	Shared

Can you say anything else about how you felt about reading 'Action'? What part did it play in your life then?

... about 'Action' ...

What made you start reading 'Action', as far as you can remember?

List all the stories you can remember from the comic. (If you can't recall the title, a brief description will do as well.)

Which stories do you remember particularly enjoying? If you can, give an order of preference.

What did you enjoy about them?

The other main boys' comics at the time were: Battle, Valiant, Victor, Warlord.

If you read any of these, please circle the one you remember best. Then, in the table below, compare that comic with 'Action'. For 'Action', use a circle. For the comic you have chosen, use a square. (If you did not read any of them, you might still like to fill in the table for 'Action'.)

So, you might think that 'Action' and your other comic were both well-written, but the other comic was a bit better-drawn than 'Action'. You would then fill it in like this:

Well-written	①①	2	3	4	5	Badly-written
Well-drawn		②2	3	④	5	Badly-drawn

If you feel you can't decide or don't understand any of them, just mark 3.

The comic as a whole was:

Well-written	1	2	3	4	5	Badly-written
Well-drawn	1	2	3	4	5	Badly-drawn
Up-to-date	1	2	3	4	5	Out-of-date
Respectable	1	2	3	4	5	Unrespectable
Rightwing	1	2	3	4	5	Leftwing
Male	1	2	3	4	5	Female
Cynical	1	2	3	4	5	Not cynical
Patronising to readers	1	2	3	4	5	Not patronising to readers

The stories were:

Violent	1	2	3	4	5	Not violent
Fastmoving	1	2	3	4	5	Slowmoving
Predictable	1	2	3	4	5	Unpredictable
Believable	1	2	3	4	5	Unbelievable
Exciting	1	2	3	4	5	Boring
Optimistic	1	2	3	4	5	Pessimistic
Patriotic	1	2	3	4	5	Unpatriotic
Pro-authority	1	2	3	4	5	Anti-authority

Characters in the stories were:

Moral	1	2	3	4	5	Not moral
Vulnerable	1	2	3	4	5	Safe
Successful	1	2	3	4	5	Unsuccessful
Strong	1	2	3	4	5	Weak
Lonely	1	2	3	4	5	Not lonely
Handsome	1	2	3	4	5	Ugly
Trusted authority	1	2	3	4	5	Distrusted authority
Like me	1	2	3	4	5	Not like me
Like I wanted to be	1	2	3	4	5	Not like I wanted to be

If there are any other things you'd like to say about 'Action' (for example, particular memories you have) that you haven't been able to include within the questionnaire, would you write them on a separate sheet of paper? My sincere thanks again for your help.

Index

Tully, Tom 24
2000 AD 23

Underground Comix 14-5
Urwin, Cathy 223
uses and gratifications 244-8

Valentine 140
Valiant 18
violence 2-3, 29, 34, 35-45, 55-61, 95, 241-4, 276
Volosinov, Valentin 16, 120, 262-74

Wagner, Dave 285-6, 287
Wagner, John 17-18

Walker, Bryan 62, 68, 81, 112
Walker, Tim 95 (fn 304)
Walkerdine, Valerie 211-38
Warlord 17, 47-8
Warnock, Mary 95 (fn 304)
Weber, Max 1
Wertham, Fredric 14, 97
Whizzer & Chips 20
Whoopee! 62, 86
Wolfe, Katherine (& Fiske, Marjorie) 244-8

Zimet, Sara 205
Zipes, Jack 128-32